Social Psychology of Social Problems

Social Psychology of Social Problems

The Intergroup Context

Edited by

Agnieszka Golec de Zavala

and

Aleksandra Cichocka

palgrave
macmillan

First published 2013 by
PALGRAVE MACMILLAN

Palgrave Macmillan in the UK is an imprint of Macmillan Publishers Limited,
registered in England, company number 785998, of Houndmills, Basingstoke,
Hampshire RG21 6XS.

Palgrave Macmillan in the US is a division of St Martin's Press LLC,
175 Fifth Avenue, New York, NY 10010.

Palgrave Macmillan is the global academic imprint of the above companies
and has companies and representatives throughout the world.

Palgrave® and Macmillan® are registered trademarks in the United States,
the United Kingdom, Europe and other countries.

ISBN 978–0–230–28475–3

This book is printed on paper suitable for recycling and made from fully
managed and sustained forest sources. Logging, pulping and manufacturing
processes are expected to conform to the environmental regulations of the
country of origin.

A catalogue record for this book is available from the British Library.

A catalog record for this book is available from the Library of Congress.

10   9   8   7   6   5   4   3   2   1
22 21 20 19 18 17 16 15 14 13

Printed and bound in Great Britain by
CPI Antony Rowe, Chippenham and Eastbourne

Contents

Preface: Applied Social Psychology: How Psychology Helps Explain Pressing Social Problems

*Agnieszka Golec de Zavala and
Aleksandra Cichocka*

Social psychology of social problems: the intergroup context

On the day this book was being completed the world was commemorating the tenth anniversary of the September 11 terrorist attacks that took place in the first year of the new millennium. More attacks followed and a War of Terrorism was declared. The decade turned out to be marked with frequent outbursts of intergroup violence in its most extreme forms. At the end of the decade, following wars in Afghanistan and Iraq, Osama bin Laden – the mastermind behind these attacks, leader of Al-Qaeda and terrorist number one – was tracked down and killed.

The beginning of the decade also witnessed the new Intifada (the second or Al-Aqsa Intifada): the uprising of Palestinians against Israelis. The intensified violence in the Palestinian-Israeli conflict that has lasted over 60 years saw both sides using various forms of intergroup violence, including acts of terror. The last decade of the twentieth century left the Western world shaken by reports of atrocities, mass killings and massacres committed during the war in Balkans, while the first decade of twenty-first century suffered a new outburst of ethnic violence, mass-murder, forced displacement, starvation and multiple human rights violations in Darfur, Sudan. In 2011 the International Criminal Tribunal for the Former Yugoslavia judged the massacre in Srebrnica, where more than 8000 Bosnian Muslims were executed by Serb forces under the command of Ratko Mladić, to be an act of genocide (International Criminal Tribunal for the Former Yugoslavia, 2011). In 2010 the International Criminal Court in The Hague decided that there were grounds to hold the Sudanese President Omar al-Bashir with three counts of genocide, against the Fur, Masalit and Zaghawa ethnic groups. These counts included: 'genocide by killing, genocide by causing serious bodily or mental harm and genocide by deliberately inflicting on each target group conditions of life calculated to bring about the group's physical destruction' (International Criminal Court, 2010).

Intergroup violence not only affects the societies directly involved in conflicts. Forced displacement caused by wars and social unrest creates problems for both the displaced and for the hosting societies. However, asylum seekers are not the only migrating population. Another reason for mass migration from the poorer countries has been the search for better jobs and life conditions in the richer countries. The first decade of the twenty-first century saw also an unprecedented increase in a new type of migration, that of highly skilled workers. In the years 2004–2007 the European Union underwent its biggest enlargement so far. During those years 12 new states joined the Union, increasing the number of member states to 27. The single market reduced restriction of movement across European borders and so created a new inspiration for job-related immigration. Highly skilled immigrants contribute to the development of the global and knowledge-based economy. Current statistics indicate that there are more people living outside their country of birth than at any other point in history; immigration is therefore one of the defining features of the twenty-first century. Yet immigration creates a whole set of intergroup problems related to intergroup threats and social discrimination from host societies on one hand, and acculturation problems among immigrants, on the other.

The first decade of twenty-first century was also marked by increased democratization and improved conditions for historically disadvantaged social groups such as ethnic minorities and women. For example, there are currently 26 Hispanic Americans serving in the American Congress. The strongest presidential candidates in the United States in 2008 were a black man and a white woman. In 2008 the first black president of United States was elected. Moreover, today ten countries (including for example Brazil, India and Lithuania) have female presidents. The twenty-first century was also groundbreaking for sexual minorities. In 2001 the Netherlands was the first country to allow same-sex marriages. Ten years later, many New Yorkers celebrated the right to same-sex marriage in their state.

However, the growing openness of Western societies, free movement across formal borders, increased tolerance towards diversity and the empowerment of various social groups were accompanied by the formation and increased activity of ultra-conservative, isolationist and racist political movements. Various organizations were created to counteract the increasing tolerance towards and social advancement of formerly unprivileged social groups. In the United States the number of hate groups as counted by the Southern Poverty Law Center (Potok, 2011) topped 1000 in 2010 and has increased since 2000 by about 40 per cent.

Similarly, the economic growth of the European Union and increased immigration were accompanied by the strengthening of political groups characterized by extreme national or ethnic identification and hostility towards others. Probably the most striking recent example of such radicalization is the Norway terrorist attacks in 2011, in which eight people were killed as a consequence of a car bomb explosion in Oslo and 69 people were shot on the island of Utoya. These attacks were planned and executed by Anders Behring Breivik, a right-wing extremist driven by hostility to Islam, non-whites and left-wingers (*The Economist*, 2011).

The first decade of the new century saw significant social and political changes in the Arab world. On one hand, anti-Western attitudes radicalized, which led to terrorism and the escalation of conflict in Israel. Importantly, there were changes towards greater democratization and freedom. Several Arab nations revolted against their dictators and the years 2010 and 2011 were named the Arab Spring, a period when people in Tunisia, Libya and Egypt demonstrated against corruption, lack of political freedoms and worsening life conditions. After years of totalitarian rule the bases for more democratic societal organization were established. However, in Syria and Yemen, among others, similar social protests were violently crashed by the state.

The decade ended with a continuing worldwide economic crisis that sharpened existing social and economic divisions in the Western world. When our work on this book was coming to the end, rioting broke out in Great Britain (from 6 to 10 August 2011). Young people looted stores, fought the police and expressed their disappointment at the existing social system, which they feel unable to change. In the contrast to the Arab revolutions, the social unrest in London, Manchester, and Birmingham was an unorganized, violent outburst of frustration rather than organized social protest to bring about societal change. These riots left British society confounded and ashamed – they and the rest of the world could not understand what was happening, or why.

Social psychology of social problems

Political extremism, organized and unorganized violence, war, terrorism, genocide, discrimination, social divisions, intergroup threat and inequality – all the social problems in the intergroup context that shaped the beginning of the new millennium are interpreted and explained in this book through the use of social psychology. Relevant, classic and current social psychological knowledge and research are presented and reviewed in order to help explain and understand the problems at stake. Thus, we aim to ground what is often abstract, academic knowledge in real life. Importantly, the chapters show how this knowledge is of practical use and application – how it can be used to assist in solving the most pressing societal issues.

Each chapter demonstrates that social psychology is applied science with its many connections and cross-fertilizations in related domains such as political science, sociology, criminology and even epidemiology. The chapters show how to use the findings and theories of social psychology to deal with various societal problems and how to use the methodology of social psychology in order to study them. One of the forefathers of social psychology, Kurt Lewin, famously remarked that '[t]here is nothing as practical as a good theory'. The mission of social psychology has always been the understanding of human social behaviour. The domain experienced its most vigorous development after the Second World War when social psychological research and theory was used to understand and explain problems such as aggression, violence, pathological obedience. The aim in this was practical rather than purely theoretical. Social psychology as a science developed in response to real-life societal problems and its mission has always been to understand and explain in order to solve and prevent.

One of the goals of this book is to emphasize the applicability of social psychological knowledge and to present it as 'practical' knowledge to students of psychology and related social sciences. However, the book hopes to do even more. It is addressed to all those who actively work in the field, creating and participating in interventions in social problems in an intergroup context. It is written to provide guidance and assistance to practitioners.

The last chapter provides systematic guidance on how the theory can assist practical interventions to reduce and solve social problems. The authors argue for a multi-theory approach in defining and explaining real-life human behaviour and searching for solutions to real-life social problems. Gaining a full understanding of all the facets of the problem is an essential first step in applying social-psychological theories to solve practical problems. The particular organization of the present book by social problems rather than psychological theories can assist the multi-theoretical approach towards defining and understanding social problems that require intervention. In addition, many of the authors, though academics, are also experienced in the practical application of social psychological knowledge to assist solving real-life problems in intergroup settings.

Structure of the book

The book is divided into three sections. Part 1 focuses on problems of prejudice and discrimination: racism, sexism and social discrimination. Part 2 concentrates on problems related to social divisions, hierarchy and inequality: tyranny, pathological obedience, violent and non-violent social protest. Part 3 focuses on intergroup violence, extremism and terrorism. The chapters of each section are organized by societal problems rather than by offering a review of research related to a particular social psychological theory.

Each chapter begins by outlining the particular social problem discussed in the chapter and illustrates it with multiple examples. Next, it acquaints readers with classic works on the subject as well as the state-of-art social psychological research and theorizing that can facilitate our understanding of the issue(s) at stake. The chapters present various perspectives in social psychological science that help us understand the sources and the dynamics of the intergroup processes involved. Each chapter ends with a task for readers, referring them to a real-life example of a problem, and challenges them to find out more about its context and to use their social psychological knowledge to explain its causes and processes and to propose its solution. The last chapter provides guidance to assist readers who choose to meet the challenge.

Racism, sexism and social discrimination

The first four chapters discuss the negative societal consequences of group stereotypes and prejudice. In Chapter 1 Christopher Cohrs and Thomas Kessler focus on the sources and processes of stereotyping, prejudice and discrimination, discussing the social psychological theories of these basic intergroup phenomena studied by social psychologists since the domain was first defined. They present a comprehensive review of the current state of knowledge about sources, contexts, processes, moderators and the consequences of negative stereotyping, prejudice syndromes and discrimination. They discuss the societal and individual consequences of the ubiquity of prejudice and discrimination, pointing to the ethical, legal and psychological consequences of the conflict between prejudice and discrimination and liberal-democratic norms of fairness and equality. The authors also discuss the intra-, intergroup and individual level strategies used to reduce negative stereotypes, prejudice and discrimination.

The social psychological knowledge of processes of negative stereotypes, prejudice and discrimination presented in this first chapter lies at the core of our understanding of the societal problems in the context of intergroup relations. This knowledge is referred to again and again and is discussed throughout the book, although the remaining chapters in Part 1 make particular reference to it. Chapters 2 and 3 are devoted to two widely studied cases of social discrimination: racism and sexism.

In Chapter 2 Christopher M. Federico presents the current state of social psychological knowledge about racism. The author describes the differences between different manifestations of racism: 'blatant', 'classical', 'overt', 'old-fashioned' and 'new' racism: 'symbolic', 'modern', 'aversive' or 'ambivalent'. The chapter also discusses the sources and consequences of explicit and implicit racial attitudes and why and how people acquire racist attitudes and how social psychological knowledge has been used in order to fight racism. In Chapter 3 Janina Pietrzak analyses antecedents and various forms and manifestations of sex-based discrimination. She discusses the causes and consequences of sex-based stereotypes and legitimizing myths that maintain social and economic inequality between men and women, and affect legal systems, self-fulfilment and the optimal functioning of individuals. The chapter focuses in particular on the social psychological processes involved in maintaining lower economic and workplace achievements for women and discusses how social psychological knowledge can help solve the societal problems created by this aspect of sex-based stereotyping.

In the final chapter of Part 1, Leah K. Hamilton, Stelian Medianu and Victoria M. Esses discuss the issue of social discrimination in the context of one of the defining features of the twenty-first century: immigration. This chapter looks at the consequences of prejudice and discrimination for immigrants and discusses conditions of successful acculturation and the integration of immigrants into host societies. The authors discuss factors that influence the perception of immigrant groups such as the concept of national identity, intergroup threat and dehumanization. Some of these phenomena are relevant also to other aspects of intergroup relations discussed in more detail in Part 3, especially the chapter on destructive forms of social identification and the chapter on intergroup threat. Moreover, Chapter 4 offers the social psychological informed insight into the strategies that are used to optimize intergroup relations between immigrants and members of the societies in which they have chosen to settle.

Inequality, tyranny, violent and non-violent social protest

The following three chapters are devoted to the problem of unequal intergroup relations. They look at social inequality as a problem, analyse its sources and the factors that maintain social hierarchies and existing social inequalities. This section also deals with the conditions and societal consequences of systemic change that aims at democratization and reduction of social inequalities. Further, these chapters also look at another aspect of the social hierarchy: the mechanisms of tyranny and obedience.

In Chapter 5, Robbie M. Sutton, Aleksandra Cichocka and Jojanneke van der Toorn discuss why social inequality is an ethical, individual, interpersonal, intergroup and societal problem. This chapter focuses directly and exhaustively on the problem of social inequality, presenting theories that describe why social inequalities arise and why and how they are maintained. In particular, the chapter discusses how social ideologies and group stereotypes are used to justify, legitimize and maintain group-based hierarchies and social injustice. The authors explain how social psychological knowledge is used to inform bottom-up and top-down strategies to reduce the negative consequences of social inequalities.

In Chapter 6, Jacquelien van Stekelenburg and Bert Klandermans explore conditions of social change: factors that inspire the active opposition against social inequality and injustice. This chapter focuses on processes of social mobilization, sustained political participation (versus disengagement) and discusses the antecedent of social protest. It also deals with the understudied issue of the societal consequences of social protest. The authors discuss the processes through which social disengagement is turned into social protest and discuss conditions in which the protest is unorganized and violent. They also differentiate conditions in which social empowerment and politicization of social identity promote sustained participation for planned and organized social change. They discuss the role of group-based anger, social embeddedness and the development of politicized identity that create a platform and motivation for individual engagement in constructive social protest.

In Chapter 7, Stephen D. Reicher and S. Alexander Haslam look at the problem of unequal intergroup relations using a different perspective. The authors discuss and rediscover the depth and nuances of social psychological knowledge provided by the famous studies on obedience conducted in the 1960s by Stanley Milgram, inspired by the infamous figure of Adolf Eichmann. Next, Reicher and Haslam discuss insights and misunderstandings surrounding another famous study in social psychology, Zimbardo's Stanford prison experiment. The chapter sheds a new light on classic findings on obedience, power and tyranny, and is informed by the analysis based on social identity theory and the BBC prison study conducted and supervised by the authors of the chapter.

Intergroup violence, extremism and terrorism

Part 3 is devoted to the antecedents, ways, forms and consequences of intense intergroup conflicts. Chapters 8 and 9 discuss issues that frequently occur in the context of contentious intergroup relations: the role that the exaggerated 'ingroup love' and the perceived intergroup threat play in inspiring outgroup hostility and intergroup violence. These chapters concentrate on group-based extremism and analyse situations and consequences that breed intergroup threat.

Chapter 8 focuses on the negative consequences of intense, positive feelings for one's ingroup. It discusses various conceptualizations of exaggerated 'ingroup love' related to outgroup negativity and contentious approaches to intergroup relations. Agnieszka Golec de Zavala and Robert T. Schatz present classic and recent studies, theorizing differentiating constructive and destructive ingroup feelings in the context of national ingroups and beyond. The authors discuss the literature on ethnocentrism, ingroup favouritism and positive ingroup identification. They review political psychological studies findings on patriotism, nationalism and national identity. The chapter also describes recent work on collective narcissism, an extension of the concept of individual narcissism to the intergroup domain, and discusses the possibility that positive feelings for an ingroup can create a platform for the development of positive feelings towards outgroups.

In Chapter 9, Walter G. Stephan analyses the role that feelings of anxiety, fear and threat generate in intergroup relations. The author presents the intergroup threat theory that differentiates and describes four basic types of intergroup threat: realistic and symbolic threats, intergroup anxiety, and threat embedded in negative outgroup stereotypes. This theory has been applied to understand the antecedents of social problems related to immigration, racism, sexism, social inequality, prejudice against disabled people or victims of AIDS but also prolonged intergroup conflict and the radicalization of violence. The author discusses the psychological processes involved in intergroup threat reduction and presents various strategies to reduce intergroup threats that have been informed, among others, by the intergroup threat theory and related research reviewed in this chapter.

The next three chapters are related to three manifestations of intergroup violence. In Chapter 10, Daniel Bar-Tal, Eran Halperin, Roni Porat and Rafi Nets-Zehngut differentiate between intergroup conflicts that erupt over tangible versus non-tangible goals and discuss psychological processes that contribute to the continuation of intractable conflicts and impair chances of their peaceful resolution. Reviewing classical and contemporary literature and illustrating with multiple real-life examples, the authors define intergroup conflicts and describe characteristics that differentiate tractable from intractable conflicts. Perceived threats to important values, identity, basic human needs and societal beliefs that support conflict are analysed as major factors contributing to persistence of violent intergroup conflicts. The authors analyse the role of these factors, describing the mechanisms of conflict escalation and societal adaptation to protracted conflicts.

In Chapter 11, Michał Bilewicz and Johanna Ray Vollhardt continue the focus on intergroup violence and social psychological processes involved in its most extreme manifestations of mass killings and genocide. The authors review classic and current approaches in psychological and historical analysis of processes and conditions of genocide and mass killings. They discuss the processes through which ordinary human beings can become transformed into perpetrators of and passive bystanders at mass killings, and the processes that inhibit resistance among victims. The chapter focuses on the analysis of the transformation of stereotypes of victim groups in the early and later stages of genocide, moral transformations among perpetrators and bystanders and motivational transformations among victims, bystanders and perpetrators. The authors conclude with a discussion of how constructive social psychological processes can counteract these destructive transformations, which is important for the prevention of future genocides.

In Chapter 12 Keren Sharvit and Arie W. Kruglanski use a social psychological perspective to analyse the individual, group and organizational processes involved in radicalization and terrorism. They discuss various motivation theories to demonstrate how individuals can bring themselves to engage in terrorist actions. They point to theories of personal significance and terror management to define central personal motives associated with terrorism. The authors also show how group and societal processes can serve to support terrorist ideology and validate terrorist inclinations. Finally, they describe the variety of organizational structures used by terrorist groups and demonstrate how they contribute to planning terrorist acts and to recruitment and the maintenance of commitment.

The chapter ends with a discussion of the implications of these social psychological mechanisms for counter-terrorism.

Towards applying social psychology

In the final chapter, Robert A. C. Ruiter, Karlijn Massar, Mark van Vugt and Gerjo Kok propose a systematic method of the problem-driven application of social psychology, whose criteria of success are defined in terms of problem reduction. The chapter proposes a practical, step-wise procedure of application of social psychological knowledge called PATH (Problem, Analysis, Test, Help). This procedure aims at assisting our understanding of the nature of the problematic behaviour and identifying possible targets of intervention programmes by applying social psychological theory and research. In this procedure the target points of social intervention programmes are defined as tasks for implementation of a desired change. Those tasks have to be carefully outlined and planned using social psychological theory and empirical findings. Social psychological knowledge is used to help planning, implementing and evaluating interventions aimed at constructively solving an existing social problem or at changing a problematic aspect of human social behaviour.

All chapters in this book help to define the problem and analysis steps of PATH. They offer a multi-theoretical approach to understanding the sources and processes of social problems. In this way they help to better define, understand and explain the problem and better plan the interventions.

In summary, this book offers a methodology for using social psychological theory to inform the practice of solving societal problems. This methodology has already been used to plan interventions in such problems as stigmatization of people affected by AIDS described in detail in Chapter 13. The PATH approach can be further developed and used to inform constructive interventions in other social problems in the intergroup context, for example social inequality, discrimination, extremism, intergroup conflict and violence. The contributors have aimed to present the current state of social psychological (and related) knowledge to inform our understanding of these social problems. They have also challenged readers to use this knowledge to solve the particular cases they discuss. In such a way we hope to extend the 'applied' understanding of social psychology as social science. We believe that the way of using theory to serve practice as proposed in the final chapter can be successfully extended to social problems in intergroup domain. A principal aim of his book is to be a step in this process of learning. It is addressed to students because our hope is that future generations of social psychologists will carry on this mission. It is addressed to practitioners because we also hope to bridge the divide between those who study social problems and those political and social activists, politicians and practitioners who act in the field to solve them.

References

International Criminal Court (2010). *Pre-Trial Chamber I issues a second warrant of arrest against Omar Al Bashir for counts of genocide (ICC-CPI-20100712-PR557)*. Available at http://www.icccpi.int/menus/icc/press%20and%20media/press%20releases/press%20releases%20(2010)/pr557?lan= en-GB (accessed 31 March 2012).

International Criminal Tribunal for the Former Yugoslavia (2011). *The Former Yugoslavia – Conflicts*. Available at http://www.icty.org/sid/322 (accessed 31 March 2012).

Potok, M. (2011). The year in hate and extremism in 2010. *Intelligence Report*, 141. Available at http://www.splcenter.org/get-informed/intelligence-report/browse-all-issues/2011/spring/the-year-in-hate-extremism-2010 (accessed 4 April 2012).

The Economist (2011). Norway attacks. Manifesto of a murderer, 24 July. Available at http://www.economist.com/blogs/newsbook/2011/07/norway-attacks (accessed 31 March 2012).

Acknowledgements

● ●

The editors wish to thank Jenny Hindley, Paul Stevens and Cecily Wilson from Palgrave Macmillan and Elizabeth Stone from Bourchier for providing support for our work on the book. The inspiration for this book emerged from a discussion with Robbie Sutton and Jamie Joseph, to whom we are deeply indebted. We are also very grateful to all the authors for all their work on the chapters. Finally, we thank Luis de Matos for his help in the final stages of the book's preparation.

The publisher and authors would like to thank the organizations and people listed below for permission to reproduce material from their publications:

HarperCollins and Pinter and Martin Ltd for permission to reproduce the excerpts in chapter 7 and the appendix to chapter 7, taken from *Obedience to authority: an experimental view* by Stanley Milgram, first published 1974 by Harper and Row. Copyright 1974 by Stanley Milgram.

The Jewish Historical Institute in Warsaw, Poland for permission to reproduce figure 11.4.

Professor Randall Bytwerk for permission to reproduce 11.1 and for figure 11.2, both from the Calvin German Propaganda Archive.

Material is individually acknowledged throughout.

Every effort has been made to trace all copyright holders but, if any have been inadvertently overlooked, the publisher will be pleased to make the necessary arrangements at the first opportunity.

List of Figures

List of Tables

Notes on Contributors

Daniel Bar-Tal is Branco Weiss Professor of Research in Child Development and Education at the School of Education, Tel Aviv University, Israel.

Michał Bilewicz is an Assistant Professor at the Faculty of Psychology, University of Warsaw, Poland.

Aleksandra Cichocka is a doctoral candidate at the Centre for Research on Prejudice, Faculty of Psychology, University of Warsaw, Poland.

J. Christopher Cohrs is a Lecturer at School of Psychology, Queen's University, Belfast, UK.

Victoria M. Esses is Professor of Psychology and Director of the Centre for Research on Migration and Ethnic Relations at the University of Western Ontario, Canada.

Christopher M. Federico is Associate Professor of Psychology and Political Science at the University of Minnesota, Twin Cities.

Agnieszka Golec de Zavala is a Marie Curie Researcher at Institute of Social Research, Institute University of Lisbon, Portugal.

Eran Halperin is currently a Senior Lecturer at the Lauder School of Government, IDC Herzliya, Israel.

Leah K. Hamilton is a Postdoctoral Fellow at the Centre for Research on Migration and Ethnic Relations at the University of Western Ontario, Canada.

S. Alexander Haslam is a Professor at the School of Psychology, University of Exeter, UK.

Thomas Kessler is the Head of the Department of Social Psychology at Friedrich Schiller University Jena, Germany.

Bert Klandermans is a Professor at the Faculty of Social Sciences at the VU-University Amsterdam, the Netherlands.

Gerjo Kok holds the Chair of Applied Psychology at Maastricht University, the Netherlands.

Arie W. Kruglanski is a Distinguished Professor at the Department of Psychology and START Center, University of Maryland, USA.

Karlijn Massar is an Assistant Professor of Social Psychology at Maastricht University, the Netherlands.

Stelian Medianu is a doctoral candidate at the Department of Psychology and the Centre for Research on Migration and Ethnic Relations at the University of Western Ontario, Canada.

Rafi Nets-Zehngut is a Postdoctoral Fellow at the Leonard Davis Institute for International Relations at the Hebrew University, Israel.

Janina Pietrzak is an Assistant Professor at the Faculty of Psychology, University of Warsaw, Poland.

Roni Porat is a Student Lecturer at the Lauder School of Government, IDC Herzliya, Israel.

Stephen D. Reicher is a Professor at the School of Psychology, University of St Andrews, UK.

Robert A. C. Ruiter is an Associate Professor of Applied Psychology at Maastricht University, the Netherlands.

Robert T. Schatz is a Professor at the Department of Psychology, Metropolitan State College of Denver, Colorado, USA.

Keren Sharvit is a Lecturer at the Department of Psychology, University of Haifa, Israel.

Walter G. Stephan is Professor Emeritus at the Department of Psychology, New Mexico State Univeristy, Las Cruces, New Mexico, USA.

Robbie M. Sutton is a Reader in Psychology at University of Kent, Canterbury, UK.

Jojanneke van der Toorn is a Postdoctoral Associate at Yale University, New Haven, USA.

Jacquelien van Stekelenburg is an Associate Professor at the Sociology Department of the VU-University Amsterdam, the Netherlands.

Johanna Ray Vollhardt is an Assistant Professor at the Department of Psychology, Clark University, USA.

Mark van Vugt holds the Chair of Organisational Psychology at the Free University in Amsterdam, the Netherlands.

PART I

RACISM, SEXISM AND SOCIAL DISCRIMINATION

· ·

1

Negative Stereotypes, Prejudice and Discrimination

J. Christopher Cohrs and Thomas Kessler

● ●

In the fifth round of the World Values Survey, carried out between 2005 and 2008 with representative samples of respondents from 57 countries from around the world, 44 per cent of the respondents agreed or strongly agreed that 'men make better political leaders than women do'. Further, 53 per cent said they did not trust very much or did not trust at all (rather than trust a little or trust completely) 'people of another nationality' (http://www.worldvaluessurvey.org/). In the fourth round of the European Social Survey, carried out in 2008 and 2009 with representative samples of respondents from 17 European countries, 16 per cent of respondents disagreed or strongly disagreed that 'gay men and lesbians should be free to live their own life as they wish'. In addition, 48 per cent tended to agree that 'people over 70 are a burden on the country's health service these days' (http://ess.nsd.uib.no/). These survey results reflect negative stereotypes, prejudices and discrimination tendencies among substantial parts of the population towards particular categories of people: women, people of another nationality, gay men and lesbians and elderly people. Similar results have been published in a report on prejudice in eight European countries by Zick, Küpper and Hövermann (2011).

A series of field experiments carried out by Klink and Wagner (1999) in Germany documented various instances of actual behavioural discrimination, going beyond negative stereotypes and prejudice. For example, members of minority ethnic groups (e.g. Turkish, Polish, Middle Eastern) were less likely than Germans to get an appointment for viewing a house that was available for rent, less likely to receive an explanation as to how to find the way when lost, less likely to have a letter posted that they had allegedly lost, and less likely to get a reservation in a bar or high-end restaurant. In another field experiment conducted in Germany, job applicants with typical Turkish names were less likely to be invited for a job interview than similar applicants with a typical German name (Kaas & Manger, 2012). All these findings illustrate behavioural discrimination, based on distinctions made between different categories of people. Similar results have been found in other countries (e.g. about discrimination against Arab people in France: Kamiejski, De Oliveira & Guimond, in press).

In this chapter, we first discuss why negative stereotypics, prejudice and discrimination present serious social problems. Then, after examining how stereotypes, prejudice and discrimination can be defined, we introduce a group-based perspective on negative stereotypes, prejudice and discrimination and analyse in detail the causes of these phenomena: why groups develop norms about prejudice, why groups become more prejudiced in particular contexts, why some group members are more prejudiced than others, and finally under what conditions prejudice leads to actual discrimination. From this analysis we draw implications as to what can be done to reduce negative stereotypes, prejudice and discrimination. We close the chapter with a concrete task for the reader to explore in more depth the causes, consequences and possible interventions related to one particular kind of prejudice.

Why are negative stereotypes, prejudice and discrimination social problems?

Negative stereotypes, prejudice and discrimination present several problems for societies. First, social discrimination is inconsistent with liberal-democratic norms of fairness and equality and, in many countries, at least based on some criteria, is illegal. Article 14 of the European Convention on Human Rights, for example, states that 'the enjoyment of the rights and freedoms set forth in this Convention shall be secured without discrimination on any ground such as sex, race, colour, language, religion, political or other opinion, national or social origin, association with a national minority, property, birth or other status' (Council of Europe, 2010).

Second, negative stereotypes, prejudice and discrimination have negative effects on the mental and physical health of its targets. It has been documented, for example, that victims of discrimination experience higher levels of stress and depression and lower levels of well-being (Paradies, 2006). Even without its behavioural expression, the mere awareness that negative stereotypes and prejudice exist can constitute a threat to members of targeted groups that might impair their performance (Schmader, Johns & Forbes, 2008; Steele & Aronson, 1995). For example, girls who are aware of the stereotype that girls are less capable in maths than boys show reduced levels of performance in maths when the negative stereotype is salient in their minds. Similarly, women who are aware of the negative stereotype that they are less capable in the political domain tend to have less political knowledge and are less efficient in negotiations than men (Kray, Galinsky & Thompson, 2002; McGlone, Aronson & Kobrynowicz, 2006). This phenomenon is known as *stereotype threat* (see also Sutton, Cichocka & van der Toorn, this volume).

Third, being confronted with negative stereotypes and prejudice can lead members of targeted groups to feel more negatively about and to avoid future intergroup interactions (Tropp, 2003). It can also provoke behaviour that confirms the negative stereotypes. For example, Dutch Moroccan teenagers in the Netherlands reacted to perceiving negative stereotypes and prejudice against them with greater legitimization of criminality, aggression and religious extremism (Kamans et al., 2009). Such reactions can, in turn, render existing stereotypes and prejudice more intense and difficult to change, thereby further contributing to segregation and radicalization. Negative stereotypes, prejudice and discrimination also contribute to the justification of existing inequalities in societies, which have negative consequences for individuals, intergroup relations and societies in general (e.g. Wilkinson & Pickett, 2009; see also Sutton et al., this volume).

Finally, the negative consequences just mentioned (i.e. greater inequality and more conflictual intergroup relations) can also contribute to a reduced quality of life for those who practise prejudice and discrimination. For example, there may be costs due to increased anxiety to interact (Stephan & Stephan, 1985; see also Stephan, this volume) and, in turn, missed opportunities for cooperation as well as costs due to heightened feelings of insecurity, fear of crime and of being disrespected (e.g. Huo, Binning & Molina, 2010; J. Jackson & Stafford, 2009).

Before we proceed, we would like to note a particular focus of the chapter. The opening examples show that negative stereotypes, prejudice and discrimination can refer to many different target groups. Accordingly, this book includes chapters on racism, sexism, and attitudes and behaviour towards immigrants. In contrast to such group-specific approaches, in our chapter we focus on the generic social psychological processes involved and place less emphasis on differences between groups, assuming 'that there cannot be separate psychologies of prejudice in relation to this or that group, but that they are specific cases of the general picture of prejudice' (Sherif, 1948, p. 64).

What are stereotypes, prejudice and discrimination?

Stereotypes, prejudice and discrimination rest on the basic human tendency of social categorization. The human mind needs to simplify to be able to deal with the mass of information potentially available at any point in time. Categorization is a very efficient way of doing this (Macrae & Bodenhausen, 2000; Spears & Haslam, 1997). We tend to categorize individuals into social groups, and our reactions to them are then determined by their group membership. In other words, based on the human tendency to categorize people, individuals are *pre-judged because of* their group membership. This pre-judgement can have explicit, conscious and controlled aspects as well as implicit and automatic aspects which are unavailable to human consciousness (e.g. Devine & Sharp, 2009; see also Federico, this volume, for a discussion of implicit racial prejudice).

We categorize not only other people into groups but also ourselves as members of groups. Thus, we differentiate between *ingroups* and *outgroups*, seeing ourselves as similar to some people (those belonging to an ingroup) and different from others (those belonging to an outgroup; Sumner, 1906; Tajfel & Turner, 1979). The more important a particular group membership is to us, the more we tend to internalize ingroup norms as a basis for our experiences, judgements and actions. Based on such ingroup norms, we tend to perceive outgroup members in a stereotypical way, feel certain emotions towards them, evaluate them accordingly, and treat them differently from ingroup members.

Stereotypes, prejudice and discrimination – while closely interconnected – have been defined differently by different researchers. Setting these terminological issues aside for a moment, however, it seems that five aspects involved in these phenomena can be distinguished conceptually.

A *first, cognitive*, aspect refers to beliefs about the characteristics or traits of typical members of a social group. This may include positive and negative attributes related to particular domains. Such beliefs are not necessarily evaluative (although they often are) (e.g. someone might see members of one group as orderly and dutiful, and those of another group as impulsive and brisk). In general, these beliefs can be arranged along two dimensions: *warmth* and *competence* (Fiske et al., 2002). The warmth dimension comprises traits such as morality, sincerity and kindness, while the competence dimension includes traits such as efficacy, confidence and intelligence. Thus, on the negative side a typical member of some group may be seen (a) as cold and hostile, or (b) as incompetent and weak or (c) as both cold/hostile and incompetent/weak (e.g. homeless people). Analogous beliefs are possible on the positive side: A typical member of some other group may be seen as (a) warm and sincere, or (b) competent and efficacious or (c) both warm/sincere and competent/efficacious (e.g. child doctors). Finally, the characteristics or traits attributed to a particular group can also be *ambivalent* (e.g. rich people being competent but rather cold; the elderly being warm but rather incompetent; Fiske et al., 2002). The warmth dimension has been further differentiated into sociability (e.g. warm, nice, friendly) and morality (e.g. sincere, reliable, trustworthy), of which the latter sub-dimension is more important for evaluative beliefs about groups (Leach, Ellemers & Barreto, 2007).

A *second, emotional* aspect refers to feelings towards particular groups and their members. This includes positive and negative affect such as liking or disliking, but researchers have also examined specific emotional reactions to social groups (Cottrell & Neuberg, 2005; Smith, 1993). One example is intergroup anxiety (Stephan & Stephan, 1985). Others include anger, disgust, admiration, envy, contempt and pity towards groups and their members (Cottrell & Neuberg, 2005; Fiske et al., 2002).

A *third, evaluative* aspect refers to the evaluation of a particular group and their members along a continuum from negative to positive, or bad to good. This summary evaluation may be based on cognitive and affective components as well as on information about previous behaviour (e.g. L. A. Jackson et al., 1996; Stangor, Sullivan & Ford, 1991; Zanna, 1994).

A *fourth, conative* (from Latin *conatio* = an act of attempting) aspect refers to behavioural intentions or tendencies, and a *fifth, behavioural* aspect refers to actual behaviour displayed towards a group and its members. The difference between these two aspects is only that one is a behavioural tendency while the other is actual behaviour. In general, intergroup behavioural tendencies and behaviours can be categorized as active (approach) or passive (avoidance), and positive (facilitation) or negative (harm) (Cuddy, Fiske & Glick, 2007; Mummendey et al., 1992). Thus, one can differentiate between an ingroup and an outgroup by (a) actively showing more positive behaviour towards the ingroup, (b) passively withholding positive behaviour from the outgroup, (c) actively showing more negative behaviour towards the outgroup or (d) passively withholding negative behaviour from the ingroup. Examples of actively showing negative behaviour are harassment, physical violence and anti-locution (a mild form of hate speech). Examples of passively withholding positive behaviour include neglect, avoidance of intimacy, preserving social distance and unwillingness to cooperate. Behavioural tendencies can also be vicarious, in the sense of referring to support for political action rather than an individual's own behaviour. Such a desire or willingness to act negatively towards a group using public policy can consist in, for example, support for political persecution (e.g. Thomsen, Green & Sidanius, 2008), support for exclusion, expulsion and restriction of immigration (e.g. Canetti-Nisim & Pedahzur, 2003), or demands that immigrants assimilate rather than integrate (Zick et al., 2001; for more information on behavioural tendencies towards immigrants, see Hamilton, Medianu & Esses, this volume).

The examples used in the opening paragraph tap into the five aspects of cognition, emotion, evaluation, conation and behaviour. For example, the statement that men make better political leaders than women expresses a positive belief about men and a negative belief about women related to the domain of political leadership abilities and linked to the competence dimension. The statement that one does not trust people of another nationality expresses a negative evaluation of another group, possibly based on the belief that people of another nationality may be dishonest and emotional reactions of dislike, and implying a passive behavioural tendency of unwillingness to cooperate. The statement that gay men and lesbians should not be free to live their own life as they wish can be seen as an example of a vicarious behavioural tendency to restrict the freedom of gay men and lesbians.

Returning to terminological issues, how do the five aspects described above relate to the concepts of stereotypes, prejudice and discrimination? Whereas *stereotypes* are rather consensually seen as referring to cognitive aspects and *discrimination* in relation to behavioural aspects, *prejudice* can have multiple meanings. Whereas some researchers reserve the term for one particular aspect (e.g. emotion: Brewer & Kramer, 1985; evaluation: Zanna, 1994), other researchers see prejudice as a combination of several aspects (e.g. cognition and emotion: Levin & Levin, 1982; cognition, emotion and conation: Allport, 1954). In this chapter we largely adopt the definition proposed by Brown (2010): 'any attitude, emotion or behaviour towards members of a group, which directly or indirectly implies some negativity or antipathy towards that group' (p. 7). We focus on coherent *prejudice syndromes* which combine cognitive, emotional, evaluative and conative aspects. However, we distinguish prejudice as an internal concept from discrimination as the external expression of prejudice in actual behaviour.

Our view of prejudice syndromes is informed by the *BIAS map* (Behaviours from Intergroup Affect and Stereotypes; Cuddy, Fiske & Glick, 2007). This model assumes that particular cognitions are systematically related to particular emotional reactions (i.e. admiration, contempt, envy, pity) and particular active or passive behavioural tendencies. For example, the elderly, as a group seen as warm but rather incompetent, tend to elicit feelings of pity as well as behavioural tendencies of active facilitation (e.g. helping) and passive harm (e.g. neglect, ignoring). Conversely, rich people, as a group seen as competent but rather cold, tend to evoke feelings of envy as well as behavioural tendencies of passive facilitation (e.g. convenient cooperation) and active harm (e.g. sabotage). Other examples of prejudice syndromes that include various aspects are *blatant prejudice* and *subtle prejudice* (Pettigrew & Meertens, 1995; see also Federico, this volume, for a discussion of similar concepts). Blatant prejudice includes perceived threat, belief in inferiority of the target group, and opposition to intimate contact. Subtle prejudice includes perceived violations of cherished values, exaggeration of cultural differences, and absence of positive feelings towards the group. In the remainder of our chapter, we use the term *prejudice* in this more general sense, referring to the interrelated aspects of cognition, emotion, evaluation and behavioural tendencies towards a social group and its members, distinguished only from *discrimination* as actual behaviour.

Another terminological complication arises from the fact that the terms 'prejudice' and 'discrimination' are value-laden. In some cases, people seem to be hesitant to recognize a particular instance of intergroup differentiation as an instance of prejudice or discrimination. According to Mummendey and Otten (1998), negative reactions to social groups or their members are seen as a social problem (i.e. defined as prejudice and discrimination) only when such reactions are perceived as inconsistent with social norms and thus as inappropriate. In liberal-democratic societies, for example, many people see prejudice against foreigners as inappropriate and therefore socially problematic. The same people may see prejudice against fascists as less of a problem or may even perceive such prejudice as normative and recommendable. Thus, depending on which norms are prevalent in a particular social context, social differentiations and negative reactions are seen as legitimate and normative for some target groups, but socially problematic and unacceptable for others.

A group-based perspective on prejudice and discrimination

Social psychologists have examined prejudice and discrimination from two different perspectives. The classical perspective focuses on individuals as the entities that hold prejudices (see Federico, this volume). This individualistic view, albeit prominent, tends to underemphasize the role of group memberships and may be of limited use for the understanding of processes at the political and societal level. An alternative, group-based perspective follows *group norm theory* and *realistic group conflict theory* (Sherif & Sherif, 1953) as well as *social identity* and *self-categorization theory* (Haslam et al., 1997; Tajfel & Turner, 1979; Turner et al., 1987). It suggests that prejudice and discrimination are primarily *group-based* phenomena. They are concerned with how people *as group members* think about, feel and act towards other social groups and their members. 'As group members' means that prejudices towards certain social groups become inscribed in ingroup norms, and even ingroup structures and institutions. In other words, it is group members, rather than individuals, who hold socially shared prejudices about other groups. From this perspective, prejudices are the product of group processes and intergroup relations and as such are 'owned' by groups.

Several research findings support this perspective. In Crandall, Eshleman & O'Brien's (2002) first study, 150 undergraduate students were asked to assess whether it was definitely OK, maybe OK or definitely not OK to have negative feelings about 105 different social groups in the United States. Aggregating the ratings across all participants produced a prejudice acceptability score for each target group. Among the highest acceptability scores were those obtained for rapists, terrorists and racists, and among the lowest those for blind people, women who stay home to bring up children and mentally retarded people. Then another, independent, sample of 121 students rated how they personally felt towards each group, using a 'feeling thermometer' ranging from 0 (cold/not positive) to 50 (medium warm/average) to 100 (hot/very positive). Again aggregating the ratings across all participants produced a score indicating the mean level of prejudice for each target group. The correlation between the acceptability scores and the prejudice scores across the 105 groups was nearly perfect, $r = .96$. Thus, the levels of prejudice towards different groups closely corresponded to the social norms, the socially shared views of whether it was considered acceptable to be prejudiced.

That prejudice towards social groups depends on the social norms about prejudice shared within a group is also evident in research comparing levels of prejudice across different groups of people. Pettigrew's (1958, 1959) classic research about racial prejudice in different geographical regions and different cultural milieus is a case in point. Participants from the south of the United States were much more prejudiced than participants from the north, and English participants in South Africa were much less prejudiced towards black Africans than Afrikaners. This was the case even when socio-demographic characteristics and personality variables were statistically controlled for. These findings suggest that social norms about racial prejudice had developed differently in different geographical regions and different cultural milieus. Similarly, comparing larger cultures rather than regions or cultural milieus within nations, Bond (1988) found that cultures differed along a cultural value dimension ranging from cultural inwardness and superiority (i.e. high levels of prejudice) at one end to generalized tolerance for and harmony with others (i.e. low levels of prejudice) at the other. In some cultures, strong anti-prejudice norms have developed, in others not.

Social norms shared within groups develop in wider social contexts with particular intergroup relations. In other words, the consensuality and uniformity of prejudice within a particular social group depends on the relations of this group to other groups in a wider social context. This proposition can be illustrated by the occurrence of historical changes in social norms about particular groups. For example, in the United States since the Second World War the open expression of racial prejudice has continuously become less acceptable (e.g. Dovidio & Gaertner, 1986; Firebaugh & Davis, 1988). Even more dramatically, the views of British citizens about Germany and Germans during the Second World War became abruptly much more negative after 'the Blitz' against Britain in 1940 (Fox, 1997).

Although social norms produce relative consensus about prejudice within social groups, of course not all members of a particular group subscribe to its norms to the same extent. Accordingly, there are inter-individual differences in prejudice. Individuals who are prejudiced towards one social group are often also more likely to be prejudiced towards other groups (e.g. Allport, 1954; Zick et al., 2008), a phenomenon known as *generalized prejudice*.

What are the causes of prejudice and discrimination?

In the previous section, we have described that (a) prejudice is socially shared within groups, but (b) group norms are subject to influences of the broader intergroup context while (c) individuals differ in the degree to which their personal levels of prejudice are aligned with group norms. The specific causes related to these three propositions are examined in the sections below, followed by an analysis of the factors leading to the behavioural expression of prejudice (i.e. discrimination).

The role of group processes: why groups develop norms about prejudice

Human beings have always depended on social groups for their survival (Caporael & Brewer, 1991). Groups facilitate learning (social learning) and information sharing, support in the exploitation of opportunities (e.g. collective endeavours such as hunting) and provide protection from threats in the environment (Kurzban & Leary, 2001; Neuberg, Smith & Asher, 2000). Because of this ultimate importance of social groups, it needs to be ensured that they are well functioning. The level of functioning of a group may be reduced by free riders and cheaters within the group who impair group endeavours and reduce cohesion. As a way of dealing with such threats, several mechanisms have evolved that enhance cohesion, reduce competition within a social group and prevent its dissolution (Frank, 2003; Kessler & Cohrs, 2008). One such mechanism is group identification. Social identity theory (Tajfel & Turner, 1979) posits that humans tend to develop a subjective sense of identification with social categories to which they belong. Group identification promotes conformity to group norms (Jetten, Postmes & McAuliffe, 2002). Additional mechanisms reducing competition include social control (reward of norm conformity and punishment of deviation), social justice and group morality. These mechanisms are closely related to group identification. For instance, a sense of fairness within a social group is particularly important for highly identified individuals, and the use of just procedures ingroups enhances group identification (Huo et al., 1996; Tyler, Degoey & Smith, 1996).

Central to these mechanisms is the process of *normative differentiation* (Kreindler, 2005; Turner et al., 1987), which refers to differentiation among members within one's group according to the degree to which these conform to group norms (i.e. their prototypicality). This process leads to positive reactions towards highly prototypical group members, who embody the group norms best (Hogg & Hains, 1996), and negative reactions towards non-prototypical group members, who violate group norms (Marques et al., 1998; Marques, Abrams & Serôdio, 2001). The same is the case for highly prototypical groups and non-prototypical groups in a broader societal context (Mummendey & Wenzel, 1999; Wenzel, Mummendey & Waldzus, 2007). Prejudice towards immigrants, for example, can be understood in this way. Members of the 'host' society (e.g. Germans in Germany) may perceive immigrants as less prototypical for people in Germany than their ingroup, and thus develop prejudice (Kessler et al., 2010). Similarly, prejudice towards gay men and lesbians can be explained by so-called *symbolic beliefs* that the target group violates cherished values, customs and traditions of the ingroup (Esses, Haddock & Zanna, 1993). In short, groups that deviate from norms often become targets of prejudice. Deviance or norm violations can be seen as a *symbolic threat* that may undermine the validity of norms and thus group cohesion and functioning.

In addition to the threat implied by non-prototypicality, there are other sources of threat to group life that cause prejudice (Stephan & Renfro,

2002). Groups that are perceived as a *realistic threat* are also likely to become targets of prejudice. Such threats can take different forms, including threats to economic resources (e.g. immigrants, welfare recipients), physical safety (e.g. criminals, terrorists, people with HIV), and the cultural or social order (e.g. immigrants, 'dissident' groups; Duckitt & Sibley, 2007). There is ample empirical evidence that perceptions of various symbolic and realistic threats powerfully predict prejudice, as summarized in a meta-analysis by Riek, Mania & Gaertner (2006; see also Stephan, this volume).

The role of intergroup processes: why groups become more prejudiced in particular contexts

The formation of prejudice norms in social groups depends on the wider intergroup context. It is expressed in particular in the process of *category differentiation*, the tendency to defend or establish the superiority of one's own group over other groups (Kreindler, 2005; Tajfel & Turner, 1979). This tendency can be aroused by various conditions, including the presence of (1) salient ingroup–outgroup boundaries, (2) intergroup competition (conflict of interest) and (3) inequality in power or status (Duckitt, 2003).

Consider Sherif's (1966) classic research, the Robbers Cave study. Here, young boys participated in a summer camp. They were split into two groups on arrival, who stayed in different areas of the summer camp. In the first phase of the research, the groups engaged separately in several leisure activities. As a result, group norms emerged, group members devised a name and totem for their group, and the most likeable boys emerged as leaders. This is all in line with the normal group processes we have described in the previous section. However, in the next phase, an *intergroup* context was introduced. Various types of competition between the two groups were set up, for example softball or tug of war. As a result, the group norms changed. Tougher boys replaced the more likeable, conciliatory boys as group leaders, and negative behaviour towards the other group became acceptable and even desirable. In this study, the first condition of salient and pervasive ingroup–outgroup boundaries and the second condition of intergroup competition (conflict of interest) were clearly present. The boys were assigned to two different groups, with all the camp activities structured along group lines, and they were set up to engage in competition where one group's gains are the other group's losses. The result was the emergence of prejudice norms against the other group.

In real life, the salience of intergroup boundaries usually derives from the existence of convergent boundaries (i.e. the coincidence of distinctions based on multiple criteria) rather than from experimentally created distinctions based on a single criterion (which, as shown in research using the minimal group paradigm, can already lead to intergroup discrimination; Tajfel et al., 1971). For example, in so-called divided societies such as Northern Ireland or Cyprus, the main communities are often distinguished by religion, ethnicity, culture, language, political orientation and/or national identity – distinctions which together create a strong sense of separation between the groups.

Intergroup competition, also termed *negative interdependence*, usually occurs over resources such as jobs, benefits, land and so on. Intergroup competition also features as an important determinant of prejudice in realistic group conflict theory (Campbell, 1965). Later research has further distinguished between competition for 'symbolic' resources (e.g. prestige, value dominance) and competition for 'realistic' resources (e.g. material gains, jobs), for example in the context of anti-immigrant prejudice (Esses et al., 2005; see also Hamilton, Medianu & Esses, this volume). Such competition can be experienced either in terms of prevention (involving threat, the fear of loss and avoidance motivation) or in terms of promotion (involving hope of gain, the desire to win and approach motivation) (Duckitt, 2003). Group members tend to show social discrimination on negative resources (i.e. harming the outgroup) if competition is based on prevention, and social discrimination on positive resources (i.e. ingroup facilitation) if it is based on promotion (Sassenberg, Kessler & Mummendey, 2003).

Intergroup inequality in power or status is the third intergroup condition conducive to the formation of prejudice norms, in both dominant and subordinate groups. According to social dominance theory (Sidanius & Pratto, 1999), groups high in power or status develop ideologies that serve to justify and reinforce their dominant position (see Sutton, Cichocka & van der Toorn, this volume). Among these ideologies is prejudice against subordinate groups, which often includes negative beliefs, in particular on the competence dimension. An example would be African-Americans in the United States whom white Americans perceive as having lower status because of lower educational qualifications and skills (Devos & Banaji, 2005). A similar case in point could be people of Turkish origin in Germany who are less likely to get prestigious jobs than Germans because they are seen as less capable even if they have high qualifications (Kaas & Manger, 2012). Groups low in power or status, on the other hand, sometimes develop 'envious' or 'resentful' prejudice against dominant groups, which serves to challenge the existing situation and to mobilize resistance against their subordination. According to social identity theory (Tajfel & Turner, 1979), this is particularly likely when the intergroup boundaries are perceived to be relatively impermeable, but the status differences between the groups are perceived to be unstable and illegitimate (Bettencourt et al.,

2001). The resulting prejudice often includes negative beliefs, in particular on the warmth dimension (e.g. Poppe & Linssen, 1999). An example would be the 'barbarian image' (Alexander, Brewer & Herrmann, 1999) which refers to a very strong (e.g. highly competent) but cold and immoral outgroup.

The role of individual differences: why some group members are more prejudiced than others

Although prejudice is powerfully guided by social norms within groups, which in turn are partially dependent on the wider intergroup context, obviously not all group members subscribe to such prejudice norms to the same extent. The fact that there are individual differences in compliance with norms can again be explained by an evolutionary account (Kessler & Cohrs, 2008; Nettle, 2006). Although it has been argued above that groups have been important for individual survival and several mechanisms have evolved that make people prone to identify with groups and to comply with group norms, individualizing tendencies towards divergence from norms and openness to experiences can also be functional. This is because environmental conditions may change and individual responses can adapt faster to changing demands than social norms do. The result of these complementary functionalities of group identification and norm compliance versus divergence is a mix of both: the existence of individual differences.

Accordingly, individuals differ in how strongly they care about the social groups they belong to (for a discussion of consequences for prejudice, see also Golec de Zavala & Schatz, this volume). This general difference covers two aspects: firstly, individuals differ in how much they care about the social norms of their group, and secondly, individuals differ in how much they care about the positive differentiation of their group from other groups. Broadly speaking, the first aspect relates to the ideological attitude dimension of *right-wing authoritarianism* (RWA), which at its core is about preferences for normative differentiation and social conformity (Feldman, 2003); and the second to the dimension of *social dominance orientation* (SDO), which at its core is about category differentiation (Kreindler, 2005; see Federico, this volume; Sutton, Cichoka & van der Toorn, this volume). RWA is a construct that goes back to research on the 'authoritarian personality' by Adorno et al. (1950) as reintroduced by Altemeyer (1981). People with high levels of RWA tend to adhere to social norms and traditions that they perceive to be endorsed by society and its established authorities (conventionalism), to follow the authorities they perceive as established and legitimate (authoritarian submission), and to be aggressive against people and groups of people if they perceive that these targets deviate from established norms and that the aggression is legitimized by social conventions and authorities (authoritarian aggression). SDO represents a general preference for hierarchies between groups (Pratto et al., 1994) as well as 'general support for the domination of certain socially constructed groups over other socially constructed groups' (Sidanius & Pratto, 1999, p. 61). Both dimensions together have been shown to account for most of the inter-individual variance in prejudice (Altemeyer, 1998; McFarland, 2010). RWA is a particularly powerful predictor of prejudice based on normative differentiation and perceptions of threat, and SDO is a particularly powerful predictor of prejudice based on category differentiation and perceptions of competition and inequality (Cohrs & Asbrock, 2009; Dru, 2007; Duckitt & Sibley, 2010).

However, the answer to the question why some people are more prejudiced than others does not end with RWA and SDO. Individual differences in RWA and SDO are typically seen as ideological or attitudinal expressions of underlying personality and motivational dynamics (e.g. Jost et al., 2003; Sibley & Duckitt, 2008). A good deal of research has examined these personality or motivational sources of RWA and SDO. In this regard, the dual-process motivational model of ideology and prejudice is very prominent (Duckitt, 2001a; Duckitt & Sibley, 2010). It proposes, first, that RWA and SDO develop on the basis of two dimensions of worldviews: beliefs in a dangerous world in the case of RWA, and beliefs in a competitive-jungle world in the case of SDO. This proposition has been supported empirically, for example in the longitudinal study by Sibley, Wilson & Duckitt (2007). Secondly, the model proposes that these two dimensions of worldviews, in turn, develop on the basis of two personality domains (Asbrock, Sibley & Duckitt, 2010; Sibley & Duckitt, 2008). Individuals with low levels of openness to experience and high levels of conscientiousness tend to develop dangerous worldviews and in turn RWA, expressing their heightened concern for upholding ingroup norms. Related cognitive-motivational traits are personal needs for structure and cognitive closure (Jugert, Cohrs & Duckitt, 2009). In contrast, individuals with low levels of agreeableness tend to develop competitive-jungle worldviews and in turn SDO, expressing their heightened concern for ingroup superiority over other groups. A related cognitive-motivational trait is that of dispositional empathy (McFarland, 2010).

From prejudice to discrimination

Most of what we have covered so far is about prejudice as an internal phenomenon. According to several meta-analyses (Schütz & Six, 1996; Talaska, Fiske & Chaiken, 2008), the relationship between prejudice and discrimination is often only of moderate size. What factors facilitate (or impede) the expression of prejudice in actual behavioural discrimination, such as the refusal to invite job applicants with a Turkish background to a job interview or to offer help to a stranger with a Middle Eastern accent who got lost (Kaas & Manger, 2012; Klink & Wagner, 1999)?

Again, the role of social norms is important. Norms can make behavioural discrimination acceptable. In Crandall, Eshleman & O'Brien's (2002) research described above, a second study showed that the prejudice acceptability scores of different target groups (e.g. racists, drug users, ex-convicts, environmentalists, fat people, black Americans, Native Americans) were strongly correlated with judgements of how acceptable it would be to discriminate against a member of these groups in various domains (dating, housing, employment). If norms make behavioural discrimination more acceptable, individuals also become more likely to actually engage in behavioural discrimination. Individuals are more likely to 'put their money where their mouth is' when they perceive social support for their views (Terry, Hogg & McKimmie, 2000). This is reflected, for example, in findings that the level of violence against foreigners in Germany increased with increasing levels of prejudice in the general population, presumably because the violent perpetrators see themselves as carrying out what they believe the mainstream population thinks (Ohlemacher, 1994). Neumann and Frindte (2002), for example, found in interviews with young adults who had been convicted for acts of violence against foreigners that the interviewees believed that most peers would share their xenophobic prejudice. As a more subtle example, Sechrist and Stangor (2001) found that students in the United States who were prejudiced against blacks were more likely to show behavioural discrimination (measured as seating distance, that is, a passive form of discrimination) when they were made to believe that other students shared their prejudice than when they were made to believe that others did not share their views.

Such influences are counteracted by the existence of alternative norms, such as legal norms against discrimination, norms supporting diversity or egalitarian norms (Pettigrew, 1958). Everyday behaviour by others is also important. Blanchard et al. (1994) found in an experimental setting that when even one single person showed disagreement and expressed an antiracist opinion after hearing a racist remark, tolerance for racist acts was reduced.

Summary and integration: the causes of prejudice and discrimination

Summing up, prejudice depends heavily on group norms and thus may be considered primarily a group phenomenon. Because of the ultimate importance of social groups for human survival, groups tend to develop norms and mechanisms that ensure that members identify with the group and comply with its norms. Prejudice is more likely to be tolerated and accepted in intergroup contexts with salient and pervasive ingroup–outgroup boundaries and intergroup competition and inequality. These factors are often reflected in structural conditions, such as patterns of segregation and economic inequality in society. The extent to which group members subscribe to prejudicial group norms depends on their individual personality and cognitive-motivational dispositions to be concerned about social conformity (expressed in right-wing authoritarian ideological attitudes) and their dispositions to be concerned about the positive differentiation of their group from other groups (expressed in ideological attitudes of social dominance). Finally, whether prejudice translates into actual behavioural discrimination is again influenced by social norms.

Of course, real life is not as simple as this. An important question we have left out so far concerns the definition of ingroups and outgroups. It is important to consider the interrelations between *intra*group and *inter*group processes in more detail. Almost always, social categorizations into a common group (intragroup) and into different groups (intergroup) coexist. For example, white English people may perceive themselves and British Indians at the same time as members of the same category (e.g. British) and as members of different categories (e.g. white English versus Indian). Which of these levels of social categorization is more salient (i.e. psychologically influential) will determine which processes are more operative in driving prejudice. The more the common-group categorization is salient, the more prejudice will depend on perceptions of prototypicality and normative differentiation. The more the two-group categorization is salient, the more prejudice will depend on perceptions of competition and category differentiation. The level of social categorization is therefore subject to strategic negotiation itself. A dominant majority group may invoke a common-group categorization in order to gain legitimacy for their group's position by claiming that their group is more prototypical and thus more entitled to a larger share of resources than the other group (Weber, Mummendey & Waldzus, 2002). Conversely, a subordinate minority group that is less prototypical for society may instead insist on a two-group categorization in order to avoid becoming a target of normative differentiation. These phenomena can be seen in the differential acculturation preferences held by dominant majority groups and immigrant groups. Dominant groups typically tend to demand assimilation and acceptance of the mainstream national identity from immigrant groups, whereas immigrant groups tend to prefer integration and maintaining their own subgroup identity related to their culture of origin (Verkuyten, 2005).

What can be done to reduce prejudice and discrimination?

The multilayered nature of the causes of prejudice and discrimination implies that the search for strategies to reduce prejudice and discrimination has to address multiple levels (Duckitt, 2001b). Interventions can be aimed at *intragroup* processes, *inter*group processes and/or individual differences. Because, as we explained above, prejudice and discrimination are primarily a group phenomenon, targeting *groups* is likely to be more efficient than targeting individuals. Accordingly, Allport (1954) concluded after a review of studies on the reduction of prejudice that 'in certain studies whole communities, whole housing projects, whole factories, or whole school systems have been made the target of change ... New norms are created, and when this is accomplished, it is found that individual attitudes tend to conform to the new group norm' (p. 40; as cited in Crandall, Eshleman & O'Brien, 2002). However, because, as we have shown, group norms depend on intergroup relations and individual group members are not all alike, *intergroup* and *individual-level* strategies are also important.

Intragroup strategies

Intragroup strategies to reduce prejudice target the prejudice norms that have developed ingroups. As an illustrative example, Stangor, Sechrist & Jost (2001) gave undergraduate students feedback that their peers were less prejudiced towards African-Americans than they believed and found that this manipulation led to a reduction in prejudice which persisted one week later (see also the aforementioned study by Blanchard et al., 1994). An additional way to change ingroup norms builds on extended positive contact (Wright et al., 1997), the mere knowledge of ingroup members having positive relations to outgroup members. It conveys the idea that positive contact is actually established and with increasing numbers of observations positive relations to the outgroup become normative. Thus, prejudiced ingroup members may perceive themselves as deviants within their own group, which can be a potent way of reducing prejudice.

A more indirect intragroup strategy attempts to change the representation of the prototype of the group rather than specific prejudice norms. This strategy can potentially reduce prejudice towards various groups at the same time. Studies have shown that prejudice towards groups that are perceived as non-prototypical for an inclusive category will be reduced if the prototype of the inclusive category is represented as diverse (Waldzus et al., 2003). For example, if the category 'British' is perceived as a diverse category encompassing the English, Scottish, Welsh, British Indians and other minority ethnic groups, white English people are likely to show less prejudice towards minority ethnic groups in Britain. In this case the minority ethnic groups will not be perceived as deviant, and thus will not become a target of normative differentiation. Another instance of the same strategy is the promotion of multiculturalism as a diversity ideology. Various studies found that participants' levels of endorsement of multiculturalism were associated with less prejudice (e.g. Verkuyten, 2005). Experimentally increasing the salience of multiculturalism has also been shown to reduce prejudice (Richeson & Nussbaum, 2004; Verkuyten, 2005; Wolsko et al., 2000).

Intergroup strategies

Intergroup strategies to reduce prejudice include attempts to (1) reduce the salience and pervasiveness of group boundaries (e.g. through desegregation or individualizing contact); (2) transform competitive relationships into cooperative relationships by emphasizing common goals and a common identity; and (3) reduce inequality in status between groups. The first strategy is exemplified in the decategorization approach (Miller & Brewer, 1986). When group members refrain from perceiving themselves and others as members of particular groups, they tend to evaluate each other predominantly on individual merits. The second strategy refers to the *common ingroup identity model* (Gaertner & Dovidio, 2000). Cooperative relations between social groups have the strong potential that members of each group start to perceive all as belonging to a common ingroup. This transfers the original ingroup favouritism to all members, including both the former ingroup and the former outgroup. However, this strategy has two potential drawbacks. It may trigger intergroup conflict between the new common ingroup and a new outgroup at the higher level of categorization (e.g. re-categorizing East and West Germans as Germans may increase their prejudice against foreigners; Kessler & Mummendey, 2001). It can also lead to intragroup dynamics that produce prejudice towards non-prototypical (sub)groups (Wenzel, Mummendey & Waldzus, 2007).

Whereas the first two strategies have as a common feature that they tend to reduce the salience of the original boundaries between groups, the third strategy maintains the salience of the original groups, but enriches intergroup comparisons by adding various comparison dimensions. This has the potential that members of each group can perceive their ingroup as superior to the outgroup on some dimensions but as inferior on others. This can lead to positive relations between both groups and a generalization of positive contact experiences from individual group members to the outgroup as a whole because of the high salience of group memberships (Brown & Hewstone, 2005). Of course, a particularly effective way of producing evaluative equality would be to actually reduce objective inequalities between groups that are associated with status (e.g. access to public schools, professional careers).

Individual-level strategies

Strategies focusing on *individuals* include various programs based on direct or indirect approaches (Stephan & Stephan, 2001, 2005). The former type of programme addresses prejudice directly, for example in the form of multicultural education, diversity training, intercultural training or intergroup dialogues. The latter type of programme addresses prejudice indirectly, with the idea that prejudice can be reduced either 'as a by-product' (e.g. through cooperative learning groups or media entertainment) or through working on more general, underlying competences (e.g. conflict resolution techniques, moral and values education).

One question with which programmes focusing on individuals are faced with is that of individual-to-group generalization. If prejudice is essentially a group phenomenon, it is important to envisage possibilities where changing individuals may actually contribute to changing group norms (Sherif, 1970). One way how this can be facilitated is through selecting the right participants. Dissemination of any changes attained in the participants may become more likely in relation to the extent that the participants have some leadership roles or skills that allow them to influence others (e.g. Kelman, 1997). Another way of facilitating individual-to-group generalization is to actually focus directly on such skills in the intervention, in addition to addressing prejudice, norms or values. For example, programmes could try to achieve changes in behaviour such as social activism, neighbourhood choices, voting, donations – all behaviour that can potentially influence other people as well and change social norms.

Practical task for readers

Collect material documenting how elderly people are perceived in society (e.g. media portrayals, jokes) and interpret your findings: to what extent are there prejudice norms, i.e. socially shared beliefs about the elderly? What cognitive, emotional and conative reactions towards the elderly can you find? What could be the consequences for the target group (the elderly), as well as for society more generally?

Continued

What could be the causes of prejudice towards the elderly? Can you think of any causes at the intragroup, intergroup and individual-difference levels? Based on the causes identified, what could be useful interventions to reduce prejudice towards the elderly?

Suggested readings

Good sources on prejudice and discrimination against the elderly (also known as *ageism*) include the edited book by Nelson (2002), the special issue of the *Journal of Social Issues* edited by Nelson (2005) and the review article by Bugental & Hehman (2007).

References

Adorno, T., Frenkel-Brunswik, E., Levinson, D. & Sanford, N. (1950). *The Authoritarian Personality*. New York: Harper.

Alexander, M. G., Brewer, M. B. & Hermann, R. K. (1999). Images and affect: A functional analysis of out-group stereotypes. *Journal of Personality and Social Psychology, 77*, 78–93.

Allport, G. W. (1954). *The Nature of Prejudice*. Cambridge, MA: Addison-Wesley.

Altemeyer, B. (1981). *Right-wing Authoritarianism*. Winnipeg, Canada: University of Manitoba Press.

Altemeyer, B. (1998). The 'other' authoritarian personality. In M. P. Zanna (ed.), *Advances in Experimental Social Psychology* (vol. 30, pp. 47–91). San Diego, CA: Academic Press.

Asbrock, F., Sibley, C. G. & Duckitt, J. (2010). Right-wing authoritarianism and social dominance orientation and the dimensions of generalized prejudice: A longitudinal test. *European Journal of Personality, 24*, 324–340.

Bettencourt, B., Dorr, N., Charlton, K. & Hume, D. (2001). Status differences and in-group bias: A meta-analytic examination of the effects of status stability, status legitimacy, and group permeability. *Journal of Personality and Social Psychology, 127*, 520–542.

Blanchard, F. A., Crandall, C. S., Brigham, J. C. & Vaughn, L. A. (1994). Condemning and condoning racism: A social context approach to interracial settings. *Journal of Applied Psychology, 79*, 993–997.

Bond, M. (1988). Finding universal dimensions of individual variation in multicultural studies of values: The Rokeach and Chinese value surveys. *Journal of Personality and Social Psychology, 55*, 1009–1015.

Brewer, M. B. & Kramer, R. (1985). The psychology of intergroup attitudes and behavior. *Annual Review of Psychology, 36*, 219–243.

Brown, R. (2010). *Prejudice: Its Social Psychology*. Chichester: Wiley-Blackwell.

Brown, R. & Hewstone, M. (2005). An integrative theory of intergroup contact. *Advances in Experimental Social Psychology*, 37, 255–343.

Bugental, D. B. & Hehman, J. A. (2007). Ageism: A review of research and policy implications. *Social Issues and Policy Review*, 1, 173–216.

Campbell, D. T. (1965). Ethnocentric and other altruistic motives. In D. Levine (ed.), *Nebraska Symposium on Motivation* (vol. 13, pp. 283–311). Lincoln, NE: University of Nebraska.

Canetti-Nisim, D. & Pedahzur, A. (2003). Contributory factors to 'Political Xenophobia' in a multi-cultural society: The case of Israel. *International Journal of Intercultural Relations*, 27, 307–333.

Caporael, L. R. & Brewer, M. B. (1991). Reviving evolutionary psychology: Biology meets society. *Journal of Social Issues*, 47, 187–195.

Cohrs, J. C. & Asbrock, F. (2009). Right-wing authoritarianism, social dominance orientation, and prejudice against threatening and competitive ethnic groups. *European Journal of Social Psychology*, 39, 270–289.

Cottrell, C. A. & Neuberg, S. L. (2005). Different emotional reactions to different groups: A sociofunctional threat-based approach to 'prejudice'. *Journal of Personality and Social Psychology*, 88, 770–789.

Council of Europe (2010). *Convention for the Protection of Human Rights and Fundamental Freedoms, as amended by Protocols No. 11 and No. 14*. Available at http://conventions.coe.int/treaty/en/Treaties/Html/005.htm (accessed 14 February 2011).

Crandall, C. S., Eshleman, A. & O'Brien, L. (2002). Social norms and the expression and suppression of prejudice: The struggle for internalization. *Journal of Personality and Social Psychology*, 82, 359–378.

Cuddy, A. J. C., Fiske, S. T. & Glick, P. (2007). The BIAS map: Behaviors from intergroup affect and stereotypes. *Journal of Personality and Social Psychology*, 92, 631–648.

Devine, P. G. & Sharp, L. B. (2009). Automaticity and control in stereotyping and prejudice. In T. D. Nelson (ed.), *Handbook of Prejudice, Stereotyping, and Discrimination* (pp. 61–87). New York: Psychology Press.

Devos, T. & Banaji, M. R. (2005). American = white? *Journal of Personality and Social Psychology*, 88, 447–466.

Dovidio, J. F. & Gaertner, S. L. (1986). Prejudice, discrimination, and racism: Historical trends and contemporary approaches. In J. F. Dovidio & S. L. Gaertner (eds.), *Prejudice, Discrimination, and Racism* (pp. 1–34). New York: Academic Press.

Dru, V. (2007). Authoritarianism, social dominance orientation and prejudice: Effects of various self-categorization conditions. *Journal of Experimental Social Psychology*, 43, 877–883.

Duckitt, J. (2001a). A dual process cognitive-motivational theory of ideology and prejudice. In M. P. Zanna (ed.), *Advances in Experimental Social Psychology* (vol. 33, pp. 41–113). San Diego, CA: Academic Press.

Duckitt, J. (2001b). Reducing prejudice: An historical and multi-level approach. In M. Augoustinos & K. J. Reynolds (eds.), *Understanding Prejudice, Racism, and Social Conflict* (pp. 253–272). London: Sage.

Duckitt, J. (2003). Prejudice and intergroup hostility. In D. O. Sears, L. Huddy & R. Jervis (eds.), *Oxford Handbook of Political Psychology* (pp. 559–600). Oxford: Oxford University Press.

Duckitt, J. & Sibley, C. G. (2007). Right wing authoritarianism, social dominance orientation and the dimensions of generalized prejudice. *European Journal of Personality*, 21, 113–130.

Duckitt, J. & Sibley, C. G. (2010). Right-wing authoritarianism and social dominance orientation differentially moderate intergroup effects on prejudice. *European Journal of Personality*, 24, 583–601.

Esses, V. M., Haddock, G. & Zanna, M. P. (1993). Values, stereotypes, and emotions as determinants of intergroup attitudes. In D. M. Mackie & D. L. Hamilton (eds.), *Affect, Cognition, and Stereotyping: Interactive Processes in Group Perception* (pp. 137–166). San Diego, CA: Academic Press.

Esses, V. M., Jackson, L. M., Dovidio, J. F. & Hodson, G. (2005). Instrumental relations among groups: Group competition, conflict, and prejudice. In J. F. Dovidio, P. Glick & L. A. Rudman (eds.), *On the Nature of Prejudice: Fifty Years after Allport* (pp. 227–243). Malden, MA: Blackwell.

Feldman, S. (2003). Enforcing social conformity: A theory of authoritarianism. *Political Psychology*, 24, 41–74.

Firebaugh, G. & Davis, K. E. (1988). Trends in anti-Black prejudice, 1972–1984: Region and cohort effects. *American Journal of Sociology*, 94, 251–272.

Fiske, S. T., Cuddy, A. J. C., Glick, P. & Xu, J. (2002). A model of (often mixed) stereotype content: Competence and warmth respectively follow from perceived status and competition. *Journal of Personality and Social Psychology*, 82, 878–902.

Fox, J. (1997). *Film Propaganda in Britain and Nazi Germany: World War II Cinema*. Oxford: Berg.

Frank, S. A. (2003). Repression of competition and the evolution of cooperation. *Evolution*, 57, 693–705.

Gaertner, S. L. & Dovidio, J. F. (2000). *Reducing Intergroup Bias: The Common Ingroup Identity Model*. Philadelphia, PA: Psychology Press.

Haslam, S. A., Turner, J. C., Oakes, P. J., McGarty, C. & Reynolds, K. J. (1997). The group as a basis for emergent stereotype consensus. *European Review of Social Psychology*, 8, 203–239.

Hogg, M. A. & Hains, S. C. (1996). Intergroup relations and group solidarity: Effects of group identification and social beliefs on depersonalized attraction. *Journal of Personality and Social Psychology*, 70, 295–309.

Huo, Y. J., Binning, K. R. & Molina, L. E. (2010). Testing an integrative model of respect: Implications for social engagement and well-being. *Personality and Social Psychology Bulletin*, 36, 200–212.

Huo, Y. J., Smith, H. J., Tyler, T. R. & Lind, E. A. (1996). Superordinate identification, subgroup identification, and justice concerns: Is separatism the problem; is assimilation the answer? *Psychological Science*, 7, 40–45.

Jackson, J. & Stafford, M. (2009). Public health and fear of crime: A prospective cohort study. *British Journal of Criminology*, 49, 832–847.

Jackson, L. A., Hodge, C. N., Gerard, D. A., Ingram, J. M., Ervin, K. S. & Sheppard, L. A. (1996). Cognition, affect, and behavior in the prediction of group attitudes. *Personality and Social Psychology Bulletin*, 22, 306–316.

Jetten, J., Postmes, T. & McAuliffe, B. J. (2002). 'We're all individuals': Group norms of individualism and collectivism, levels of identification and identity threat. *European Journal of Social Psychology*, 32, 189–207.

Jost, J. T., Glaser, J., Kruglanski, A. W. & Sulloway, F. J. (2003). Political conservatism as motivated social cognition. *Psychological Bulletin*, 129, 339–375.

Jugert, P., Cohrs, J. C. & Duckitt, J. (2009). Inter- and intrapersonal processes underlying authoritarianism: The role of social conformity and personal need for structure. *European Journal of Personality*, 23, 607–621.

Kaas, L. & Manger, C. (2012). Ethnic discrimination in German's labour market: A field experiment. *German Economic Review*, 13, 1–20.

Kamans, E., Gordijn, E. H., Oldenhuis, H. & Otten, S. (2009). What I think you see is what you get: Influence of prejudice on assimilation to negative meta-stereotypes among Dutch Moroccan teenagers. *European Journal of Social Psychology*, 39, 842–851.

Kamiejski, R., De Oliveira, P. & Guimond, S. (in press). Ethnic and religious conflicts in France. In D. Landis & R. Albert (eds.), *Handbook of Ethnocultural Conflict*. New York: Springer.

Kelman, H. C. (1997). Group processes in the resolution of international conflicts: Experiences from the Israeli-Palestinian case. *American Psychologist*, 52, 212–220.

Kessler, T. & Cohrs, J. C. (2008). The evolution of authoritarian processes: Fostering cooperation in large-scale groups. *Group Dynamics: Theory, Research, and Practice*, 12, 73–84.

Kessler, T. & Mummendey, A. (2001). Is there any scapegoat around? Determinants of intergroup conflicts at different categorization levels. *Journal of Personality and Social Psychology*, 81, 1090–1102.

Kessler, T., Mummendey, A., Funke, F., Brown, R., Binder, J., Zagefka, H., et al. (2010). We all live in Germany but... Ingroup projection, group-based emotions and prejudice against immigrants. *European Journal of Social Psychology*, 40, 985–997.

Klink, A. & Wagner, U. (1999). Discrimination against ethnic minorities in Germany: Going back to the field. *Journal of Applied Social Psychology*, 29, 402–423.

Kray, L. J., Galinsky, A. D. & Thompson, L. (2002). Reversing the gender gap in negotiations: An exploration of stereotype regeneration. *Organizational Behavior and Human Decision Processes*, 87, 386–410.

Kreindler, S. A. (2005). A dual group process model of individual differences in prejudice. *Personality and Social Psychology Review*, 9, 90–107.

Kurzban, R. & Leary, M. R. (2001). Evolutionary origins of stigmatization: The functions of social exclusion. *Psychological Bulletin*, 127, 187–208.

Leach, C. W., Ellemers, N. & Barreto, M. (2007). Group virtue: The importance of morality (vs. competence and sociability) in the positive evaluation of in-groups. *Journal of Personality and Social Psychology*, 93, 234–249.

Levin, J. & Levin, W. C. (1982). *The Functions of Prejudice and Discrimination*. New York: Harper & Row.

Macrae, C. N. & Bodenhausen, G. V. (2000). Social cognition: Thinking categorically about others. *Annual Review of Psychology*, 51, 93–120.

Marques, J. M., Abrams, D. & Serôdio, R. G. (2001). Being better by being right: Subjective group dynamics and derogation of in-group deviants when generic norms are undermined. *Journal of Personality and Social Psychology*, 81, 436–447.

Marques, J. M., Abrams, D., Pàez, D. & Martinez-Taboada, C. (1998). The role of categorization and in-group norms in judgments of groups and their members. *Journal of Personality and Social Psychology, 75,* 976–988.

McFarland, S. (2010). Authoritarianism, social dominance, and other roots of generalized prejudice. *Political Psychology,* 31, 453–477.

McGlone, M. S., Aronson, J. & Kobrynowicz, D. (2006). Stereotype threat and the gender gap in political knowledge. *Psychology of Women Quarterly,* 30, 392–398.

Miller, N. & Brewer, M. B. (1986). Categorization effects on ingroup and outgroup perception. In J. F. Dovidio & S. L. Gaertner (eds.), *Prejudice, Discrimination, and Racism* (pp. 209–230). San Diego, CA: Academic Press.

Mummendey, A. & Otten, S. (1998). Positive-negative asymmetry in social discrimination. *European Review of Social Psychology, 9,* 107–143.

Mummendey, A. & Wenzel, M. (1999). Social discrimination and tolerance in intergroup relations: Reactions to intergroup difference. *Personality and Social Psychology Review,* 3, 158–174.

Mummendey, A., Simon, S., Dietze, C., Grünert, M., Haeger, G., Kessler, S., et al. (1992). Categorization is not enough: Intergroup discrimination in negative outcome allocation. *Journal of Experimental Social Psychology,* 28, 125–144.

Nelson, T. D. (ed.) (2002). *Ageism: Stereotyping and Prejudice Against Older Persons.* Cambridge, MA: Massachusetts Institute of Technology.

Nelson, T. D. (ed.) (2005). Ageism: Prejudice against our feared future self [special issue]. *Journal of Social Issues,* 61.

Nettle, D. (2006). The evolution of personality variation in humans and other animals. *American Psychologist,* 61, 622–631.

Neuberg, S. L., Smith, D. M. & Asher, T. (2000). Why people stigmatize: Towards a biocultural framework. In T. F. Heatherton, R. E. Kleck, M. R. Hebl & J. G. Hull (eds.), *The Psychology of Stigma* (pp. 31–61). New York: Guilford Press.

Neumann, J. & Frindte, W. (2002). Der biografische Verlauf als Wechselspiel von Ressourcenerweiterung und -einengung. In W. Frindte & J. Neumann (eds.), *Fremdenfeindliche Gewalttäter* (pp. 111–151). Wiesbaden: Westdeutscher Verlag.

Ohlemacher, T. (1994). Public opinion and violence against foreigners in the reunified Germany. *Zeitschrift für Soziologie,* 23, 222–236.

Paradies, Y. (2006). Ethnicity and health: A systematic review of empirical research on self-reported racism and health. *International Journal of Epidemiology,* 35, 888–901.

Pettigrew, T. F. (1958). Personality and sociocultural factors in intergroup attitudes: A cross-national comparison. *Journal of Conflict Resolution,* 2, 29–42.

Pettigrew, T. F. (1959). Regional differences in anti-Negro prejudice. *Journal of Abnormal and Social Psychology,* 59, 28–36.

Pettigrew, T. F. & Meertens, R. W. (1995). Subtle and blatant prejudice in Western Europe. *European Journal of Social Psychology,* 25, 57–75.

Poppe, E. & Linssen, H. (1999). In-group favouritism and the reflection of realistic dimensions of difference between national states in Central and

Eastern European nationality stereotypes. *British Journal of Social Psychology,* 38, 85–102.

Pratto, F., Sidanius, J., Stallworth, L. M. & Malle, B. F. (1994). Social dominance orientation: A personality variable predicting social and political attitudes. *Journal of Personality and Social Psychology,* 67, 741–763.

Richeson, J. A. & Nussbaum, R. J. (2004). The impact of multiculturalism versus color-blindness on racial bias. *Journal of Experimental Social Psychology,* 40, 417–423.

Riek, B., Mania, E. & Gaertner, S. (2006). Intergroup threat and outgroup attitudes: A meta-analytic review. *Personality and Social Psychology Review,* 10, 336–353.

Sassenberg, K., Kessler, T. & Mummendey, A. (2003). Less negative = more positive? Social discrimination as avoidance or approach. *Journal of Experimental Social Psychology,* 39, 48–58.

Schmader, T., Johns, M. & Forbes, C. (2008). An integrated process model of stereotype threat effects on performance. *Psychological Review,* 115, 336–356.

Schütz, H. & Six, B. (1996). How strong is the relationship between prejudice and discrimination? A meta-analytic answer. *International Journal of Intercultural Relations,* 20, 441–462.

Sechrist, G. & Stangor, C. (2001). Perceived consensus influences intergroup behavior and stereotype accessibility. *Journal of Personality and Social Psychology,* 80, 645–654.

Sherif, M. (1948). The necessity of considering current issues as part and parcel of persistent major problems: Illustrated by the problem of prejudice. *International Journal of Opinion and Attitude Research,* 2, 63–68.

Sherif, M. (1966). *In Common Predicament: Social Psychology of Intergroup Conflict and Cooperation.* Boston: Houghton & Mifflin.

Sherif, M. (1970). On the relevance of social psychology. *American Psychologist,* 25, 144–156.

Sherif, M. & Sherif, C. W. (1953). *Groups in Harmony and Tension.* New York: Harper.

Sibley, C. G. & Duckitt, J. (2008). Personality and prejudice: A meta-analysis and theoretical review. *Personality and Social Psychology Review,* 12, 248–279.

Sibley, C. G., Wilson, M. S. & Duckitt, J. (2007). Effects of dangerous and competitive worldviews on right-wing authoritarianism and social dominance orientation over a five-month period. *Political Psychology,* 28, 357–371.

Sidanius, J. & Pratto, F. (1999). *Social Dominance: An Intergroup Theory of Social Hierarchy and Oppression.* Cambridge: Cambridge University Press.

Smith, E. R. (1993). Social identity and social emotions: Toward new conceptualizations of prejudice. In D. M. Mackie & D. L. Hamilton (eds.), *Affect, Cognition, and Stereotyping: Interactive Processes in Group Perception* (pp. 297–315). San Diego, CA: Academic Press.

Spears, R. & Haslam, S. A. (1997). Stereotyping and the burden of cognitive load. In R. Spears, P. J. Oakes, N. Ellemers & S. A. Haslam (eds.), *The Social Psychology of Stereotyping and Group Life* (pp. 171–207). Oxford: Blackwell.

Stangor, C., Sechrist, G. & Jost, J. T. (2001). Changing racial beliefs by providing consensus information. *Personality and Social Psychology Bulletin,* 27, 486–496.

Stangor, C., Sullivan, L. A. & Ford, T. E. (1991). Affective and cognitive determinants of prejudice. *Social Cognition,* 9, 359–380.

Steele C. M. & Aronson, J. (1995). Stereotype threat and the intellectual test performance of African-Americans. *Journal of Personality and Social Psychology*, 69, 797–811.

Stephan, W. G. & Renfro, C. L. (2002). The role of threat in intergroup relations. In D. M. Mackie & E. R. Smith (eds.), *From Prejudice to Intergroup Emotions: Differentiated Reactions to Social Groups* (pp. 191–207). New York: Psychology Press.

Stephan, W. G. & Stephan, C. W. (1985). Intergroup anxiety. *Journal of Social Issues*, 41, 157–175.

Stephan, W. G. & Stephan, C. W. (2001). *Improving Intergroup Relations*. Thousand Oaks, CA: Sage.

Stephan, W. G. & Stephan, C. W. (2005). Intergroup relations program evaluation. In J. F. Dovidio, P. Glick & L. A. Rudman (eds.), *On the Nature of Prejudice: Fifty Years After Allport* (pp. 431–446). Malden, MA: Blackwell.

Sumner, W. G. (1906). *Folkways: A Study of the Sociological Importance of Usages, Manners, Customs, Mores, and Morals.* New York: Dover.

Tajfel, H. & Turner, J. C. (1979). An integrative theory of intergroup conflict. In W. G. Austin & S. Worchel (eds.), *The Social Psychology of Intergroup Relations* (pp. 33–47). Monterey, CA: Brooks/Cole.

Tajfel, H., Billig, M. G., Bundy, R. P. & Flament, C. (1971). Social categorization and intergroup behaviour. *European Journal of Social Psychology*, 1, 149–178.

Talaska, C. A., Fiske, S. T. & Chaiken, S. (2008). Legitimating racial discrimination: Emotions, not beliefs, best predict discrimination in a meta-analysis. *Social Justice Research*, 21, 263–296.

Terry, D. J., Hogg, M. A. & McKimmie, B. M. (2000). Attitude–behaviour relations: The role of in-group norms and mode of behavioural decision-making. *British Journal of Social Psychology*, 39, 337–361.

Thomsen, L., Green, E. G. T. & Sidanius, J. (2008). We will hunt them down: How social dominance orientation and right-wing authoritarianism fuel ethnic persecution of immigrants in fundamentally different ways. *Journal of Experimental Social Psychology*, 44, 1455–1464.

Tropp, L. R. (2003). The psychological impact of prejudice: Implications for intergroup contact. *Group Processes and Intergroup Relations*, 6, 131–149.

Turner, J. C., Hogg, M. A., Oakes, P. J., Reicher, S. D. & Wetherell, M. S. (1987). *Rediscovering the Social Group: A Self-Categorization Theory.* Oxford: Blackwell.

Tyler, T., Degoey, P. & Smith, H. (1996). Understanding why the justice of group procedures matters: A test of the psychological dynamics of the group-value model. *Journal of Personality and Social Psychology*, 70, 913–930.

Verkuyten, M. (2005). Ethnic group identification and group evaluation among minority and majority groups: Testing the multiculturalism hypothesis. *Journal of Personality and Social Psychology*, 88, 121–138.

Waldzus, S., Mummendey, A., Wenzel, M. & Weber, U. (2003). Towards tolerance: Representations of superordinate categories and perceived in-group prototypicality. *Journal of Experimental Social Psychology*, 39, 31–47.

Weber, U., Mummendey, A. & Waldzus, S. (2002). Perceived legitimacy of intergroup status differences: Its prediction by relative ingroup prototypicality. *European Journal of Social Psychology*, 32, 449–470.

Wenzel, M., Mummendey, A. & Waldzus, S. (2007). Superordinate identities and intergroup conflict: The ingroup projection model. *European Review of Social Psychology*, 18, 331–372.

Wilkinson, R. G. & Pickett, K. E. (2009). Income inequality and social dysfunction. *Annual Review of Sociology*, 35, 493–511.

Wolsko, C., Park, B., Judd, C. M. & Wittenbrink, B. (2000). Framing interethnic ideology: Effects of multicultural and color-blind perspectives on judgments of groups and individuals. *Journal of Personality and Social Psychology*, 78, 635–654.

Wright, S. C., Aron, A., McLaughlin-Volpe, T. & Ropp, S. A. (1997). The extended contact effect: Knowledge of cross-group friendships and prejudice. *Journal of Personality and Social Psychology*, 73, 73–90.

Zanna, M. P. (1994). On the nature of prejudice. *Canadian Psychology*, 35, 11–23.

Zick, A., Küpper, B. & Hövermann, A. (2011). *Intolerance, Prejudice and Discrimination: A European Report*. Berlin: Friedich-Ebert-Stiftung.

Zick, A., Wagner, U., van Dick, R. & Petzel, T. (2001). Acculturation and prejudice in Germany: Majority and minority perspectives. *Journal of Social Issues*, 57, 541–557.

Zick, A., Wolf, C., Küpper, B., Davidov, E., Schmidt, P. & Heitmeyer, W. (2008). The syndrome of group-focused enmity: The interrelation of prejudices tested with multiple cross-sectional and panel data. *Journal of Social Issues*, 64, 363–383.

2

The Social Context of Racism

Christopher M. Federico

● ●

On 4 November 2008, Barack Obama defeated John McCain to become the 44th president of the United States of America and the first African-American elected to that post. This historic event led many to ask whether the United States had finally overcome a long legacy of racial inequality and become a 'post-racial' society. However, the virulence of the opposition to the new president and his policies in some quarters since then has raised numerous questions about whether racism continues to influence Americans' attitudes. In particular, both popular commentators and scholars have noted that the worst vitriol directed at the president – such as the persistent allegations that he was born outside the United States and that he is actually a Muslim – tends to depict him as an 'alien' who is outside the American mainstream (Tesler & Sears, 2010). But how can we be sure that this hostility really stems from racism, as opposed to mere partisan or ideological discord? Are there 'subtle' forms of racism that still lurk beneath the surface of an ostensibly tolerant culture?

Questions like these have received a great deal of attention from social psychologists interested in the problem of racism throughout the history of the field. In this regard, social psychologists have attempted not only to uncover the psychological bases of racial antagonism and chart the extent of its influence on other attitudes and behaviour, but also to use their findings to develop interventions capable of stemming the tide of racism. In this chapter, I review social psychologists' continuing efforts to understand and ameliorate racism. In particular, I take a closer look at how social psychologists have defined and classified various manifestations of racism, the major explanations they have offered for racism, and research on the factors that may lessen the prevalence and impact of racism.

Racism in its 'overt' guise

Like other terms in the social and behavioural sciences, 'racism' often takes on a bewildering variety of meanings. In both everyday language and the writings of psychologists, the term has often been used interchangeably with other terms or as a mere synonym for *racial prejudice* – that is, the affective component of racial hostility (Dovidio & Gaertner, 2010; Sears, 1988). Nevertheless, 'racism' is often defined so as to refer specifically to an ideology that posits the superiority of some groups and the inferiority of others, while justifying unequal, discriminatory treatment for those regarded as racial subordinates (Duckitt, 1992). This definition is particularly common among social scientists who focus on racism as a phenomenon of unequal power relations between different groups, and it has been adopted by psychologists interested in racism as a device for legitimizing group hierarchy (Bobo, 1999; Sidanius & Pratto, 1999; see also Jost, Banaji & Nosek, 2004).

According to this definition, the set of attitudes that qualifies most readily as racism has been referred to as 'old-fashioned' racism (Sears & Henry, 2005), 'classical' racism (Sidanius, Pratto & Bobo, 1996), 'blatant' racism (Pettigrew & Meertens, 1995), and 'overt' racism (Huddy & Feldman, 2009). This form of racism centres on the perceived biological (or otherwise inherent) inferiority of subordinate groups and support for openly discriminatory practices and institutions (Sears, 1988). However, research convincingly suggests that this ideal-type form of racism has waned in the contemporary era. This shift has been studied most thoroughly in the American context, where a wealth of public-opinion data indicates that whites have largely discarded the key attitudes associated with overt racism (Bobo, 2001). Overt racism now exerts a smaller influence on racial-policy attitudes and candidate preferences (Kinder & Sears, 1981; Sears, 1988). As but one example of this, consider several decades' worth of data on white Americans' attitudes towards school integration compiled by Bobo (2001). While roughly 68 per cent of whites surveyed in the early 1940s felt that black and white children should attend separate schools, only 4 per cent of whites surveyed in 1995 expressed this opinion (Bobo, 2001, pp. 269–270). Trends in white attitudes are similar for other trappings of overt racism, such as support for the segregation of public transportation, blatant job discrimination, and beliefs about the inherent inferiority of non-whites. These changes extend to the political realm as well, to return to the example cited at the outset of this chapter. For example, while majorities of whites rejected the notion of voting for a black president in the late 1950, the percentage of whites who hold this opinion has dropped precipitously since then. By the eve of the 2008 election, the percentage of whites who refused to vote for a black candidate had dropped below 10 per cent. So, in one seemingly clear piece of evidence for a 'post-racial' shift, whites had become more open to the idea of a black president even before Barack Obama's electoral victory (Bobo & Dawson, 2009).

Despite this liberalization in white opinion, other observations suggest that contemporary societies – including American society – are far from being post-racial. Above all, a mountain of data suggests that enormous racial disparities in income, wealth and overall social well-being continue to exist (e.g. Bobo & Dawson, 2009) and that discrimination is far from being a thing of the past (for a review, see Sidanius & Pratto, 1999). Moreover, public opinion continues to be characterized by a profound 'racial divide' (Kinder & Winter, 2001). Compared with members of subordinate racial groups, members of dominant groups are less likely to believe discrimination is a serious problem (Bobo, 2001), more likely to attribute racial inequality to characteristics of low-status group members (e.g. lack of effort) as opposed to structural problems (e.g. discrimination; see Huddy & Feldman, 2009; Hunt, 2007), and more likely to believe society has made progress towards racial equality (Eibach & Ehrlinger, 2006). Finally, changes in dominant racial groups' attitudes towards the *principle* of racial equality have not been accompanied by increased support for specific government policies aimed at reducing racial inequality in various social domains (Bobo, 2001; Sears, 1988). As such, the decline of overt forms of racism has not brought us to the point where race is a non-issue.

The 'new' racisms

The fact that race continues to matter in these respects has presented social psychologists with a puzzling question: if overt racism has indeed waned, then what accounts for dominant racial group members' tendency to downplay the existence of racism and discrimination and their apparent lack of enthusiasm for efforts to increase racial equality? Researchers have suggested a number of explanations. One argument suggests that perceived 'realistic' competition between racial groups – a theme I return to below – may account for the disparity. That is, while support for the principle of racial equality may not be immediately threatening to dominants' perceived group interests, aggressive efforts to fight discrimination and inequality may seem more realistically threatening. In turn, this may lead to a denial of discrimination and hostility towards policies designed to help racial minorities (Bobo, 1999). A second argument suggests that the disparity may stem from politics rather than race. Specifically, dominants' reliance on individualistic explanations for racial disadvantage and their lack of support for policies such as affirmative action may stem instead from a race-neutral conservative ideological orientation that emphasizes self-reliance, minimal government and meritocracy (Sniderman & Piazza, 1993).

However, perhaps the most influential arguments about the contradictory nature of contemporary racial attitudes come from the various 'new racism' theories offered in recent decades (Sears & Henry, 2005). These approaches suggest that new forms of racial antagonism became influential after the decline of overt racism. Importantly, most of these 'new' racisms lack two key features of racism in the strict, overt sense: they eschew claims about the inherent inferiority of subordinates and reject overt racial discrimination (Huddy & Feldman, 2009; Pearson, Dovidio & Gaertner, 2009). Nevertheless, they reflect forms of racial animus that account for contemporary political hostility towards subordinate racial groups and policies designed to help them. Below, several of these 'new racisms' are discussed.

Symbolic racism and its cousins

The first and most influential of the 'new' racisms – *symbolic racism* – was identified by David Sears and his colleagues in the 1970s. Symbolic racism consists of a 'blend' of negative affect towards African-Americans and concern for traditional individualistic values (self-reliance, hard work, etc.; see Sears, 1988). Symbolic racism usually takes the form of an antipathy towards blacks rooted in the perception that they fail to live up to said values (Sears & Henry, 2003). More specifically, symbolic racism consists of four beliefs: 'that Blacks no longer face much prejudice or discrimination, that their failure to progress results from their unwillingness to work hard enough, that they are demanding too much too fast, and that they have gotten more than they deserve' (Sears & Henry, 2005, p. 100). These beliefs are thought to arise over the course of pre-adult socialization, beginning with the early acquisition of negative feelings towards blacks (Sears & Henry, 2003, 2005).

The measurement of symbolic racism has varied considerably over time. However, most of the questionnaire items that have been used to measure it broadly converge on the themes highlighted above, and successive revisions of the scale have resulted in a set of key items. Examples of items that are used to measure the concept include the following (Sears & Henry, 2005): 'Over the past few years, blacks have gotten more than they deserve', 'Irish, Italians, Jews and many other minorities overcame prejudice and worked their way up. Blacks should do the same without any special favors', '[i]t's really a matter of some people not trying hard enough; if blacks would only try harder they could be just as well off as whites', '[g]enerations of slavery and discrimination have created conditions that make it difficult for blacks to work their way out of the lower class'. Agreement with the first three of these items and disagreement with the fourth indicates a higher level of symbolic racism.

The original theory of symbolic racism has also spawned lines of research on other related forms of new racism, including 'modern racism' (McConahay, 1986) and 'racial resentment' (Kinder & Sanders, 1996; Tesler & Sears, 2010). Both these concepts are similar in content to symbolic racism, and they are measured using similar items. Nevertheless, each construct tends to emphasize some themes more than others. For example, modern racism combines subtle racial animus with a sense of conscious opposition to old-fashioned forms of racial hostility. In comparison, racial resentment focuses primarily on antagonism stemming from the perception that blacks are getting 'undeserved' favours (Huddy & Feldman, 2009).

In any case, symbolic racism and its cousins are potent predictors of race-related political preferences. Several decades of research consistently indicate that it is a strong predictor of attitudes towards racial policies, such as affirmative action, busing and economic assistance to minorities; and hostility towards black political candidates, such as Jesse Jackson and – more recently – Barack Obama (Kinder & Sears, 1981; Sears et al., 1997; Tesler & Sears, 2010). These effects hold up even in the presence of controls for other relevant variables, such as party identification, ideology, overt racism and personal self-interest. In fact, the predictive power of symbolic racism often outstrips that of these other variables. Moreover, research suggests that symbolic racism is also a strong predictor of attitudes towards policies that are not explicitly racial but which have become implicitly linked to African-Americans in political discourse, such as welfare spending (Gilens, 1999; Mendelberg, 2001).

Research on symbolic racism has also generated considerable controversy (Huddy & Feldman, 2009). Besides noting numerous inconsistencies in the conceptualization and measurement of the construct across studies, many critics have noted that research on symbolic racism may confuse race-based opposition to policies such as affirmative action with opposition based on race-neutral political values (Sniderman & Tetlock, 1986). In this vein, some have argued that the traditional individualistic content of symbolic racism items may make it difficult for political conservatives to disagree with them, regardless of their actual feelings about blacks (Sniderman & Piazza, 1993). For example, when faced with a question like 'the Irish, Italians, Jews and many other minorities overcame prejudice and worked their way up – Blacks should do the same without any special favors', conservatives – who should prefer that *all* people 'work their way up' and reject 'special favours' for members of *all races* – may be unable to express their individualism without giving the 'racist' response. Studies have also suggested that symbolic racism may have different meanings to liberals and conservatives, reflecting racial prejudice among the former and a strong preference for self-reliance and minimal government among the latter (Feldman & Huddy, 2005). Thus, despite their explanatory utility, symbolic racism and its relations are susceptible to questions about whether they tap into racism in the strict sense or some other mix of social attitudes.

Aversive racism

While the symbolic racism approach focuses on how newer forms of racial antagonism may have displaced overt racism, other new racism models focus on the *conflicted* nature of contemporary of racial attitudes. The best example of this approach is Pearson, Dovidio & Gaertner's *aversive racism* model (Pearson, Dovidio & Gaertner, 2009). On the one hand, aversive racists – a category which includes many whites – are consciously egalitarian. They genuinely accept the notion of racial equality and do not think of themselves as 'racists'. This is, of course, consistent with the general observation that most whites have abandoned overt racism. On the other hand, they also have residual and typically unconscious negative feelings about blacks based on feelings of discomfort, fear and anxiety. Taken together with their desire to be egalitarian, this anxiety causes aversive racists to worry about acting inappropriately or seeming prejudiced in encounters with African-Americans. They deal with this conflict and worry by avoiding interracial contact, or by engaging in contact only in tightly regulated situations.

Unlike symbolic racism, which is clearly associated with hostility towards efforts to help blacks, aversive racism is associated with *behavioural instability* (Pearson, Dovidio & Gaertner, 2009). Typically, aversive racists avoid outright displays of bias (e.g. blatant discrimination against members of racial minority groups), due to their consciously egalitarian beliefs. However, since these beliefs coexist uneasily with underlying feelings of discomfort towards African-Americans, aversive racism may lead to bias under certain conditions. In particular, aversive racists tend to display racial biases (1) when the latter can be rationalized away as having nothing to do with race; (2) when the biases are not easily detected by oneself or others; and (3) when situational norms governing behaviour are unclear (see Pearson, Dovidio & Gaertner, 2009).

For example, in a classic study, Gaertner and Dovidio (1977) showed that white participants did not discriminate against black victims when offering help in emergencies if they were the only witnesses present. However, when participants believed that other bystanders were present and that a failure to offer help could be attributed to a non-racial factor – the perception that the other bystanders might offer help – they were less likely to help black victims. Other studies have produced similar results, revealing that whites are more likely to show bias against black versus white job applicants when both have ambiguous qualifications (Dovidio & Gaertner, 2000) and more likely recommend the death penalty for black versus white defendants when they were led to believe that a black juror had also recommended death (thereby discounting the possibility of racial bias; Dovidi et al., 1997). Finally, public opinion research has revealed parallel results. For example, 'race-coded' issues like welfare and capital punishment are more likely to be evaluated in terms of racial attitudes when political leaders offer appeals that are covertly racial rather than blatantly racial (e.g. merely showing blacks in a campaign advertisement that mentions welfare-dependency versus a voiceover that explicitly accuses blacks of being excessively dependent on welfare; see Mendelberg, 2001).

Racial ambivalence

Like the aversive racism model, the theory of racial ambivalence focuses on the conflicted nature of contemporary racial attitudes in the United States (Katz & Hass, 1988). Specifically, this approach notes that whites may simultaneously have negative and positive feelings towards blacks, producing a state of emotional ambivalence. The model starts from the assumption that pro-black and anti-black sentiments have different antecedents. Positive attitudes stem from a combination of egalitarianism and humanitarianism. Negative attitudes stem from individualism. While egalitarian concern for the condition of African-Americans should lead to positive emotion in the form of sympathy, individualistic concerns about self-reliance should lead to negative emotion in the form of disapproval. Since American political culture values both egalitarianism and individualism – with political elites typically invoking both considerations in debates about race (Sniderman & Piazza, 1993) – many whites should experience value conflict when considering racial matters. As a result, their feelings about African-Americans should be accordingly ambivalent.

Consistent with these arguments, research suggests that humanitarian and egalitarian values are most strongly associated with pro-black attitudes, while individualistic values are most strongly associated with anti-black attitudes. Priming humanitarianism and egalitarianism increases pro-black sentiment but not anti-black sentiment, whereas priming individualism increases anti-black but not pro-black sentiment (Katz & Hass, 1988). Individuals also differ in the extent to which they experience the racial ambivalence associated with holding pro-black and anti-black attitudes at the same time (Hass et al., 1992; see also Federico, 2006). Finally, studies also suggest that higher levels of ambivalence are associated with emotional discomfort, at least when race is salient (Hass et al., 1992). Thus, for many whites, the wholly negative thrust of overt racism has given way to conflicted – and somewhat troubling – feelings about blacks.

Explicit and implicit racial attitudes

As we have seen, the most common psychological explanations for continued resistance to the acknowledgement of racism and policies aimed at increasing racial equality among members of dominant racial groups invoke some notion of a 'new' racism. A related but somewhat distinct approach focuses on the distinction between explicit and implicit racial attitudes (Dovidio et al., 2009; Greenwald et al., 2002). *Explicit* attitudes are evaluations that are conscious, controlled, and deliberative in nature. They are typically measured using self-report questionnaire items. Most conventional social-psychological measures of racism assess explicit evaluations of subordinate racial groups. In contrast, *implicit* attitudes are evaluative responses that are relatively unconscious, difficult to control and quickly and automatically activated when an attitude object is brought to mind. They are essentially evaluative associations between an object (e.g. African-Americans) and negative or positive affect (see also Cohrs & Kessler, this volume). Importantly, in the domain of race, the relationship between explicit attitudes and implicit attitudes is often weak and variable. Many individuals who express positive racial attitudes at an explicit level nevertheless show a pattern of negative evaluative associations at an implicit level (Dovidio & Gaertner, 2010; Nosek, Banaji & Greenwald, 2002; see also Devine, 1989).[1] This raises the possibility that unconscious negative evaluations may contribute to whites' low level of enthusiasm for policies designed to help minorities, even in the absence of explicit racial hostility.

Psychologists have developed several methods for the measurement of implicit racial attitudes. One of the oldest uses *affective priming* (e.g. Fazio et al., 1995). In a common version of this paradigm, participants are subliminally primed with black or white category exemplars (e.g. photos) and then asked to indicate whether each of a series of affectively charged words refers to something good or bad. Bias is indicated by quicker responses to 'good' words following white primes and to 'bad' words following black primes. This pattern indicates a stronger associative link between the category 'white' and positive affect and the category 'black' and negative affect. A second technique is the well-known *Implicit Association Test* (IAT; Greenwald, McGhee & Schwartz, 1998). In the 'race' version of the IAT, participants begin by classifying category exemplars (e.g. black and white faces) according to race by pressing one of two assigned buttons. In a second stage, participants perform a similar task in which they classify positive or negative stimuli according to valence. In the final two phases, participants classify both pairs of stimuli simultaneously. In the 'compatible' phase, participants are asked to use one button to identify either white exemplars or positive stimuli and another to identify either black exemplars or negative stimuli. In the 'incompatible' phase, the pairings are reversed (e.g. black-positive, white-negative). Bias – and an overall negative implicit attitude towards blacks – is indicated by faster responding to the compatible pairings than the incompatible pairings. Finally, a newer measure is the *affect misattribution procedure* (AMP; Payne et al., 2005). In the AMP, participants are quickly (but not subliminally) shown a picture of a black or white face. They are then shown a picture of an unfamiliar Chinese character and asked to indicate whether the character is pleasant or unpleasant. A negative attitude towards a particular racial group is indicated by the proportion of 'unpleasant' responses to characters presented after pictures of individuals from that group. The AMP has a number of benefits, including high reliability, large effect sizes, and resistance to censoring on the part of participants, potentially making it an attractive option for future work on implicit racial attitudes.

Measured in these ways, implicit attitudes have numerous consequences for race-related judgements and behaviours (Dovidio et al., 2009; Huddy & Feldman, 2009). In particular, implicit attitudes strongly predict judgements and behaviours that are relatively spontaneous in nature, such as nonverbal behaviours in interracial interactions (e.g. eye contact). Explicit racial attitudes more strongly predict deliberate expressions of racial hostility (Blanton & Jaccard, 2008; Dovidio & Gaertner, 2010; Dovidio et al., 2009). Moreover, implicit racial attitudes predict hostility towards political candidates from subordinate racial groups (Payne et al., 2010; Schmidt & Nosek, 2010) and social-policy attitudes (Craemer, 2008; Knowles, Lowery & Schaumberg, 2010).

While the study of implicit racial attitudes has had an enormous impact, there is controversy about precisely what a biased response on an implicit measure means. In particular, psychologists have raised questions about whether implicit measures – like the 'new racism' measures discussed above – actually measure racism in the strict sense (Huddy & Feldman, 2009). For example, some have questioned whether mere evaluative associations qualify as 'racism' when unaccompanied by conscious acceptance of the proposition that certain groups are inherently inferior or otherwise 'bad' (Arkes & Tetlock, 2004). Others have pointed out the arbitrary nature of the measurement scales produced by implicit measures and have cautioned against using them to draw conclusions about individuals' attitudes (Blanton & Jaccard, 2008). However, even among researchers who accept that implicit measures tap into some form of racial animus, there is disagreement about the nature of the attitude involved (see Dovidio & Gaertner, 2010, for a review). While early treatments sometimes conceptualized implicit measures as a 'bona fide pipeline' capable of getting past social-desirability biases to 'real' attitudes (e.g. Fazio et al., 1995), most researchers now shy away from this view. More recent approaches have suggested that implicit racial attitudes are overlearned associations reflecting culture rather than personal evaluations (e.g. Craemer, 2008; Karpinski & Hilton, 2001). Other approaches suggest that they are older, more accustomed responses that have been subsequently been written over by conscious explicit evaluations (Wilson, Lindsey & Schooler, 2000). Finally, another argument suggests that implicit attitudes reflect the operation of an automatic 'associative' system of evaluation distinct from the 'propositional' or true–false system of judgement connected with explicit attitudes (Gawronski & Bodenhausen, 2006). Thus, while implicit measures have extended the study of racial attitudes in new directions and revealed consequential patterns, researchers need to remain cautious in offering assessments of their meaning.

Psychological factors underlying racism

Besides defining and classifying manifestations of racism, social psychologists have also devoted considerable attention to why and how people acquire racist attitudes. Almost a century of work on this topic has produced a variety of approaches. The dominant approaches of different eras tended to focus on some themes more than others as a function of broader trends in the discipline and in society as a whole (Duckitt, 1992). The themes themselves have varied enormously, ranging from a focus on personality to a focus on the structure of relations between groups in society as a whole. In this section, I review several key perspectives on the foundations and origins of racism (see also chapter on prejudice by Cohrs and Kessler, this volume).

Dispositional influences: Personality and racism

One of the oldest psychological literatures on racism focuses on the origins of the latter in personality (Sibley & Duckitt, 2008). By far, the dispositional characteristics most heavily emphasized in this literature are those connected with cognitive rigidity, closemindedness, and intolerance of ambiguity. Specifically, decades of research have suggested that rigid individuals with a dislike of cognitive uncertainty and nuance tend to be attracted to racist ideas and ethnocentric thinking. Thus, early work on this relationship focused on the relationship between racism and traits like intolerance of ambiguity and generalized cognitive rigidity (see Allport, 1954; Frenkel-Brunswik, 1948).

However, the most influential early work of this sort was the landmark volume *The Authoritarian Personality* (Adorno et al., 1950). Drawing on classic psychoanalytic ideas, Adorno and his colleagues argued that a general syndrome of conventionalism and submissiveness to authority – a stable 'authoritarian personality' – may account for individual differences in attraction to racist or ethnocentric ideas and movements. Specifically, authoritarianism was thought to be rooted in harsh childrearing, resulting in a rigid, defensive style of thinking characterized by the repression of hostile impulses and their projection onto outgroups. While this model became enormously influential in the years following the publication of *The Authoritarian Personality*, theoretical and methodological criticisms of the approach eventually piled up (Hyman & Sheatsley, 1954) and interest in personality and racism faded for several decades.

However, interest in the topic has picked back up in recent decades, often driven by improvements in the measurement of personality constructs long associated with intergroup hostility. For example, individual differences in a variable related to cognitive rigidity, the *need for cognitive closure*, has been generally implicated in racism and other forms of intergroup bias (Kruglanski, 2004). Individuals who are dispositionally high in the need for closure crave certainty and 'seize' on information in order to attain it as quickly as possible; once they have reached a state of subjective certainty, they firmly 'freeze' on their conclusions in order to maintain closure (Webster & Kruglanski, 1994). Fleshing out older arguments, Kruglanski and his colleagues (2006) argue that high levels of ingroup identification, bias in favour of the ingroup, and bias against outgroups is attractive to those high in the need for closure, given the certainty provided by closing ranks around a valued social identity. Not surprisingly, this logic commonly plays itself in the context of race, with numerous studies suggesting that individuals with a high need for closure tend to be more prone to racial stereotyping and racist beliefs (Jost et al., 2003; Kruglanski et al.,

2006). Research on authoritarianism has also been revitalized in recent decades by Altemeyer's (1996) work on *right-wing authoritarianism* (RWA). Altemeyer replaces *The Authoritarian Personality*'s psychodynamic framework with a social learning account and defines the construct in terms of submission to ingroup authorities, aggression towards outgroups, and conventionalism. Confirming earlier findings on authoritarianism, a large body of research indicates that high RWAs are more likely to exhibit racism and ethnocentrism more generally (Altemeyer, 1996).[2]

Another individual-difference predictor of racism that has received a great deal of attention in recent years is social dominance orientation (SDO), a crucial element of social dominance theory (SDT; Pratto et al., 1994; Sidanius & Pratto, 1999). SDT is a general model of the factors that promote intergroup hierarchy in human societies. In the context of this model, SDO is an individual difference corresponding to one's general orientation towards group hierarchy; those high in SDO are accepting of group inequality and the domination of some groups by others. It predicts a variety of beliefs that legitimize group inequality and provide support for institutions and policies that further inequality. Importantly, these beliefs include both overt racism and 'new' forms of racism like symbolic racism. All of the latter are highly correlated with SDO, especially among members of dominant racial groups (Sidanius & Pratto, 1999).

Importantly, both RWA and SDO have traditionally been conceptualized as stable personality variables. However, in light of research suggesting that RWA and SDO are less situationally stable than originally believed (e.g. Schmitt, Branscombe & Kappen, 2003), recent scholarship has reconceptualized the two variables as ideological dimensions (Duckitt & Sibley, 2009). According to this model, deeper personality dimensions predispose people to different *worldviews,* which are differentially associated with RWA and SDO. Finally, RWA and SDO ultimately produce support for racism – the first through processes that encourage an aversion to social difference and the second as a result of processes that emphasize the subjugation of other groups. In other words, while RWA and SDO may indeed predict racism, they are best understood as ideological variables that intervene between personality dimensions and racism, as opposed to personality variables in and of themselves (Sibley & Duckitt, 2008; see also Cohrs & Kessler, this volume).

Social influences on the acquisition of racist attitudes

Perhaps the most durable assumption about the acquisition of racist attitudes is that they are socially learned or moulded in the context of relationships, typically with parents or peers (Allport, 1954; Sears &

Levy, 2003). To cite but one key example, Sears and his colleagues argue that symbolic racism is learned from parents and others during pre-adult socialization, with the transmission of negative affect towards minorities occurring early on and the absorption of individualistic values and the widespread cultural belief that blacks violate those values taking place somewhat later (e.g. Sears, 1988). Nevertheless, research has not subjected this argument to detailed empirical scrutiny (Sears & Henry, 2005).

More generally, evidence racist attitudes are learned from parents is mixed (Duckitt, 1992; Sears & Levy, 2003). Estimated correlations between parents' and children's racial attitudes are quite variable and often weak (Aboud & Doyle, 1996). Nevertheless, some patterns do emerge. In particular, the transmission of racial attitudes from parents to children appears to be stronger in majority racial groups, and parents' attitudes typically have a stronger impact on younger children's attitudes than on older children's attitudes (Carlson & Iovini, 1985; see also Duckitt, 1992). The effect of age finds an echo in other lines of research. In this vein, Doyle and Aboud (1995) note that racism and other hostile intergroup attitudes emerge as a default by preschool, but then decline starts around age seven as a result of key milestones in cognitive development. These developmental changes include an enhanced ability to understand that individuals belong to multiple groups, greater skill in attending to counter-stereotypic information, and an improved ability to realize that not all outgroup members are identical. Nevertheless, recent work suggests that these developmental changes may be more pronounced with respect to explicit racial attitudes than implicit racial attitudes. On this score, Baron and Banaji (2006) examined the implicit and explicit racial attitudes of American six-year-olds, ten-year-olds and adults. Their results indicated a clear decline in explicit racial hostility with age, as the older children and adults showed considerably less explicit racial bias than the younger children. However, implicit racial attitudes – as indexed by the IAT – were remarkably similar across all three age groups, showing a pro-white/anti-black bias at all ages.

Other perspectives have focused on how racism may be rooted in norms associated with particular social networks. This suggestion follows from a general line of research indicating that peers, social networks and 'reference groups' have large effects on individuals' attitudes (Alwin, Cohen & Newcomb, 1991; Crandall, Eshleman & O'Brien, 2002; for a more detailed review, see Cohrs & Kessler, this volume). Along these lines, a variety of studies have reported correlations between individuals' racial attitudes and those of their peers (e.g. Bagley & Verma, 1979) or significant others (Silverman, 1974). Other studies have pointed towards large subcultural differences in racial attitudes that cannot be explained by other factors. For example, Pettigrew (1959) famously observed that whites from the American South had far more negative attitudes towards blacks than whites from elsewhere in America, despite having similar levels of authoritarianism. This suggested the operation of regional social norms regarding 'appropriate' racial attitudes – an argument bolstered by the additional finding that anti-black prejudice was strongly related to a measure of conformity among Southern whites.

Thus, evidence suggests that racism may be embedded in the views characteristic of one's social network. Nevertheless, like findings regarding the influence of parents, the utility of these results are limited in certain respects (Duckitt, 1992; Sears & Levy, 2003). Above all, the data they rely on are largely correlational, making it difficult to determine whether the correlations are due to a causal influence of social networks on racial attitudes rather than self-selection into 'agreeable' social networks on the basis of prior attitudes. Moreover, they do not allow researchers to distinguish between effects due to social learning – in which racial attitudes are learned from peers and internalized – and effects due to mere conformity. As such, much work remains to be done with respect to this question (see Sears & Henry, 2005, for further discussion; but see also Cohrs & Kessler, this volume). That said, it is worth noting that experimental manipulations of perceived norms about intergroup attitudes in one's social network can influence the extent to which people actually express racial hostility in the form of discrimination (Blanchard et al., 1994; Sechrist & Stangor, 2001).

Moving beyond the context of concrete relationships, a variety of analyses have looked how racial attitudes may be shaped by a more impersonal socialization agent: the mass media. Analyses of this sort have often focused on the role of mass entertainment – especially entertainment aimed at children – in conveying the racial attitudes that are ostensibly normative for society as a whole (Milner, 1983). Unfortunately, much of this work focuses more on documenting biases in the media than on the effects of these biases on individuals' attitudes (Duckitt, 1992). However, recent studies have filled this gap somewhat by looking at how racially biased attitudes – and the stereotypical beliefs that go along with them – may be reinforced by news-media coverage of certain social and political issues, particularly crime and poverty. For example, a number of studies have shown that news coverage that represents the criminal population and the persistently poor as overly black may reinforce racial resentment and increase its impact on policy judgments (Gilens, 1999; Gilliam & Iyengar, 2000; Mendelberg, 2001).

Intergroup relations and social identity

Other perspectives focus on the general psychology of intergroup relations, as opposed to the dispositions and learned attitudes of individuals (Bobo, 1988; Hogg, 2003). A key premise of these approaches is that racism is not merely an attitudinal characteristic of individuals; rather, it is situated in and derives from the context of identification with racial groups and structural relationships between racial groups. While many of the theoretical models that fall into this category were developed in part to shed light on racism, most of them are general in nature and attempt to make sense of intergroup relations in a variety of contexts.

One of the earliest of these models, *realistic conflict theory*, focuses specifically on the consequences of material competition between groups. According to this approach, hostility between groups will arise when they are in real or perceived zero-sum competition for valued resources or positions of power (LeVine & Campbell, 1972; Sherif et al., 1961; see also Cohrs & Kessler, this volume) This effect should be especially pronounced when individuals believe that their own outcomes are connected with how well their group as a whole fares. Conversely, when this state of negative interdependence is removed and groups must cooperate to achieve some mutually valued goal, hostility will subside. The logic of realistic conflict theory has been fruitfully applied to the study of racial attitudes. For example, Bobo (1988, 1999) has developed survey measures of perceived zero-sum resource competition between racial groups (e.g. over jobs, etc.). Consistent with the theory, whites who perceive zero-sum competition between blacks and whites are more likely to express negative feelings about blacks and oppose policies aimed at dealing with racial inequality (e.g. affirmative action). Recent studies have refined this conclusion somewhat, indicating that perceptions of harm to the dominant ingroup – apart from corresponding consequences for subordinate outgroups – are sufficient to produce hostility towards policies aimed helping subordinates (Lowery et al., 2006).

Other lines of research reveal similar patterns. For example, research suggests that *fraternal relative deprivation* – a perception that one's group is losing out relative to other groups (Runciman, 1966) – among American whites is strongly related to negative attitudes towards blacks (Vanneman & Pettigrew, 1972). Moreover, studies on the *sense of group position* suggests that racism is likely to be strongest among dominant-group members who feel that subordinates are attempting to 'usurp' a position of social superiority that only the ingroup's characteristics entitle it to (Blumer, 1958; Bobo, 1999). Similarly, social dominance theory argues that racism should be strongest among dominant-group members with high levels of social dominance orientation, who should be more strongly motivated than others to pursue their groups' interests (Sidanius & Pratto, 1999).

Material competition between groups may thus play a key role in explaining racial hostility. However, other theories suggest that psychological identification with a group may be sufficient to cause intergroup biases even in the absence of conflict over actual resources. This was most famously demonstrated in the 'minimal group studies' conducted by Henri Tajfel and his colleagues (Tajfel & Turner, 1986, for a review; see also Cohrs & Kessler, this volume). In these studies, participants were divided into completely arbitrary groups – or *minimal groups* – on the basis of trivial procedures. Tajfel's studies demonstrated that individuals allocated more resources to members of their own group than members of other groups. In an effort to explain this 'ingroup favoritism,' Tajfel and Turner (1986) introduced *social identity theory* (SIT). Like other perspectives, SIT assumes that individuals want to enhance their self-esteem. However, in doing so, the theory notes that self-esteem can derive from both personal identity, or parts of the self which relate to unique individual characteristics; and social identity, or parts of the self that stem from group memberships. As such, the desire for self-esteem implies that individuals will want their groups to compare favourably to other groups when social identity is salient, leading to ingroup favouritism.

While some researchers have minimized the potential role of social identity concerns in the real world of racial attitudes (e.g. Sears & Henry, 2005), reviews of the literature suggest that ingroup favouritism plays itself out frequently in the context of race. For example, ingroup favouritism in allocations of resources and in feelings about ingroups versus outgroups is rampant not just in minimal groups but in real-world groups as well, including racial groups (Mullen, Brown & Smith, 1992; see also Hogg, 2003; Kinder & Kam, 2009). Moreover, among members of dominant racial groups, higher levels of ingroup identification are reliably associated with a variety of racist attitudes (Levin et al., 1998; Sidanius & Pratto, 1999). Finally, other studies suggest that the denial of racial inequality among members of dominant racial groups may result from a need to defend one's social identity against the implications of a belief that it benefits from unjust privileges. Along these lines, Lowery, Knowles and Unzueta (2007) find that white Americans are more likely to deny the existence of white privilege when threatened with negative feedback. Thus, in a variety of respects, social identity may account for variation in racial attitudes.

Psychological approaches to fighting racism

As noted above, social psychologists have not merely tried to understand racism. They have also actively considered strategies for combating it. Many of these strategies have been developed not only with an eye to confronting racism, but with a focus on reducing intergroup conflict more generally. In this section, I review factors that may reduce racial hostility.

Education

One of the variables most frequently cited as an antidote to racial hostility is education. In fact, its solvent effect in the domain of racial attitudes is celebrated not just in social psychology but throughout the social and behavioural sciences (Duckitt, 1992). Indeed, a vast empirical literature indicates that higher levels of educational attainment are associated with more positive attitudes towards racial minorities and greater tolerance more generally (Greeley & Sheatsley, 1971; Lipset, 1960; McClosky & Zaller, 1984; Sniderman & Piazza, 1993). This effect is usually attributed to several changes associated with education. These include: (1) improved learning of democratic norms, especially the norm of tolerance; (2) improved cognitive skills, which makes it easier for people to realize the logical implications of the norm of tolerance; and (3) greater exposure to and comfort with diverse perspectives and ways of life.

Despite these positive findings, other studies indicate that the effects of education on racial attitudes may be more complex than this traditional view suggests. Specifically, numerous analyses demonstrate that education has two distinct effects. On one hand, it does reduce absolute levels of racial hostility, as noted above. On the other hand, education also appears to strengthen the impact of racism on policy judgements (Federico, 2004; Federico & Holmes, 2005; Federico & Sidanius, 2002; Sidanius, Pratto & Bobo, 1996). For example, while white Americans who have completed a college degree show lower levels of symbolic racism than those with less education, the relationship between symbolic racism and attitudes towards welfare are actually *stronger* among college-educated whites. So, while education may very well reduce overall levels of racism, it also boosts the political impact of whatever racism 'survives' the educational process.

Intergroup contact

Of course, variables like education – however helpful – are difficult to actively manipulate and use as practical tools for reducing racism. Social psychologists have considered a number of other approaches that might be more useful as direct interventions. Perhaps the most storied approach of this sort is intergroup contact theory (Pettigrew & Tropp, 2005). The earliest formulations of contact theory suggested that contact with disliked racial outgroups might be sufficient to reduce racism via simple learning. Subsequent developments of the theory concluded that contact may need to occur under certain conditions in order to be effective. In this spirit, Gordon Allport (1954) famously described four conditions needed for the successful reduction of intergroup hostility via contact: (1) equal status within the contact setting; (2) cooperative interaction between members of different groups; (3) superordinate goals; and (4) support from legitimate authorities. Later iterations of the approach have also emphasized other important conditions, such as the formation of intergroup friendships (Pettigrew, 1998).

A wealth of data has provided support for contact theory across a variety of intergroup contexts. For example, a recent meta-analysis by Pettigrew and Tropp (2006) indicated that intergroup contact does generally reduce hostility between groups – an effect which is stronger when more of Allport's original four conditions are met. Importantly, 51 per cent of the datasets reviewed by Pettigrew and Tropp focused on racial or ethnic contact, and independent analysis of these studies indicated effects that were as strong as those observed in non-racial/non-ethnic contexts. However, quality of contact – as indexed by Allport's four conditions – was particularly important in improving racial attitudes via contact.

Changes in categorization

Other strategies for reducing racism – among other forms of intergroup hostility – have focused specifically on variables related to categorization. The shared premise of these approaches is that racial hostility can be reduced by minimizing the extent to which individuals think in terms of relevant racial categories. For example, the *decategorization* approach does this by encouraging members of different groups to think of themselves primarily as distinct individuals rather than members of various social categories and to form personalized impressions of outgroup members (Brewer & Miller, 1984; Miller, 2002). Other strategies that fall into this category focus on emphasizing the fact that individuals often belong to multiple groups that result in different, non-overlapping ingroup/outgroup distinctions (Crisp et al., 2003). Studies provide supportive evidence for the efficacy of both of these decategorization strategies (see Dovidio & Gaertner, 2010).

On the other hand, the *recategorization* approach focuses on promoting the formation of a *common ingroup identity* that encompasses both the ingroup and outgroup (Gaertner & Dovidio, 2005). The aim of this strategy is to turn former outgroup members into new members of an expanded ingroup without forcing them to forsake their original (subgroup) identities. While this strategy has been applied successfully in numerous intergroup contexts, evidence specifically suggests that it is effective in reducing racial hostility (Gaertner et al., 1996; Nier et al., 2001; Sidanius et al., 2008). For example, in a large field study conducted at a multi-racial high school, Gaertner and his colleagues (1996) found lower levels of hostility towards racial outgroups among students who perceived themselves to be 'on the same team' or part of a unified student body. Despite these benefits, studies suggest limits to the recategorization strategy. For example, individuals may project the standards of their own subgroup onto the common ingroup, leading other subgroups to be seen as substandard members of the superordinate group (Mummendey & Wenzel, 1999). Similarly, superordinate identities may become 'owned' by high-status racial groups, leading to a situation in which low-status racial groups perceive a tradeoff between their subgroup and superordinate group identities and disidentify with the common ingroup (Sidanius et al., 1997).

Conclusion

In this chapter, I have attempted to provide a broad overview of social psychology's contributions to our understanding of racism. Importantly, social psychologists' efforts in this area provide some of the best examples of how basic scientific work and a practical interest in confronting major social problems can work in tandem with one another. As noted near the beginning of this chapter, the persistence of racial inequality – despite positive changes like those discussed at the beginning of this chapter, such as the election of America's first black president – has been a spur to action for social psychologists for much of the field's history. Some of social psychology's most important steps in understanding racism have been driven by a practical desire to find remedies for racial conflict. For example, the pressing need to identify variables that might reduce racial hostility has repeatedly led to basic advances in our understanding of the factors that contribute to more or less negative intergroup attitudes. One can clearly see this dynamic at work in the development of contact theory, where successive refinements of the original contact hypothesis were often driven by practical experience with less-than-successful efforts to bring racial groups together (Pettigrew & Tropp, 2005). As such, the area is definitely one where Kurt Lewin's suggestion that 'there is nothing so practical as a good theory' would appear to ring true.

Moreover, efforts to make sense of and confront the problem of racism have also spurred important developments in our understanding of the psychology of intergroup conflict more generally. For example, two perspectives that were originally advanced in large part to explain racism and racial prejudice – realistic conflict theory and social identity theory – have in turn made basic contributions to our understanding of intergroup dynamics and the psychology of collective identity in many other domains, including work on international relations, partisan and ideological conflict in the domestic political realm, and conflict between religious groups (Bobo, 1988; Hogg, 2003).

Looking to the future, a critical challenge for social psychologists interested in racism is one of theoretical and empirical integration. Research in this area has pointed not just to a wide range of explanations for racism, but also to many different *types* of racism. As such, research in this area would benefit from efforts to simplify and consolidate the far-ranging body of work that has emerged over the decades. Recent work has already taken important steps in this direction, such as social dominance theory's efforts to integrate individual-difference and intergroup analyses of intergroup attitudes (Sidanius & Pratto, 1999) and ongoing efforts to clarify the relationship between implicit and explicit racial attitudes (e.g. Gawronski & Bodenhausen, 2006; Wilson, Lindsey & Schooler, 2000). If history is any guide, integrative work of this sort should open new avenues for the field's joint mission of understanding and combating the problem of racial hostility.

Practical task for readers

President Barack Obama's popularity fell noticeably over the course of his first two years in office, from highs in the 70 per cent range in January 2009 to levels in the 40 per cent range in January 2011. This chapter has been largely about what social psychologists have discovered regarding contemporary racism and its influence on other attitudes and behaviour. What findings from this body of work suggest that we might be able attribute the decline in President Obama's approval ratings – at least in part – to racial hostility on the part of American whites? Based on what we know from the social-psychological literature on racism, do you think a white president with a similar political agenda – facing similar economic conditions – would enjoy higher approval ratings? Why or why not?

Suggested readings

For up to date additional readings on the social psychology of racial antagonism, please see the chapter in the handbook of social psychology by

Dovidio and Gaertner (2010) and the annual review article by Huddy and Feldman (2009).

References

Aboud, F. E. & Doyle, A. B. (1996). Parental and peer influences on children's racial attitudes. *International Journal of Intercultural Relations*, 20, 371–383.

Adorno, T. W., Frenkel-Brunswik, E., Levinson, D. & Sanford, R. N. (1950). *The Authoritarian Personality*. New York: Harper.

Allport, G. W. (1954). *The Nature of Prejudice*. Reading, MA: Addison-Wesley.

Altemeyer, B. (1996). *The Authoritarian Specter*. Cambridge, MA: Harvard University Press.

Alwin, D. F., Cohen, R. L. & Newcomb, T. (1991). *Political Attitudes over the Life Span*. Madison: University of Wisconsin Press.

Arkes, H. & Tetlock, P. E. (2004). Attributions of implicit prejudice, or 'Would Jesse Jackson "fail" the implicit Association Test'? *Psychological Inquiry*, 15, 257–278.

Bagley, C. & Verma, G. (1979). *Racial Prejudice, the Individual and Society*. Westmead, UK: Saxon House.

Baron, A. S. & Banaji, M. R. (2006). The development of implicit attitudes: Evidence of race evaluations from ages 6, 10 & adulthood. *Psychological Science*, 17, 53–58.

Blanchard, F. A., Crandall, C. S., Brigham, J. C. & Vaughn, L. A. (1994). Condemning and condoning racism: A social context approach to interracial settings. *Journal of Applied Psychology*, 79, 993–997.

Blanton, H. & Jaccard, J. (2008). Unconscious racism: A concept in pursuit of a measure. *Annual Review of Sociology*, 34, 277–297.

Blumer, H. (1958). Race prejudice as a sense of group position. *Pacific Sociological Review*, 1, 3–7.

Bobo, L. (1988). Group conflict, prejudice, and the paradox of contemporary racial attitudes. In P. A. Katz & D. M. Taylor (eds.), *Eliminating Racism: Profiles in Controversy*. New York: Plenum.

Bobo, L. (1999). Prejudice as group position: Micro-foundations of a sociological approach to racism and race relations. *Journal of Social Issues*, 55, 445–472.

Bobo, L. (2001). Racial attitudes and relations at the close of the twentieth century. In N. Smelser, W. J. Wilson & F. Mitchell (eds.), *America Becoming: Racial Trends and Their Consequences* (pp. 262–299). Washington, DC: National Academy Press.

Bobo, L. & Dawson, M. C. (2009). A change has come: Race, politics, and the path to the Obama presidency. *Du Bois Review*, 6, 1–14.

Brewer, M. B. & Miller, N. (1984). Beyond the contact hypothesis: Theoretical perspectives on desegregation. In N. Miller & M. B. Brewer (eds.), *Groups in Contact: The Psychology of Desegregation* (pp. 281–302). Orlando, FL: Academic Press.

Carlson, J. M. & Iovini, J. (1985). The transmission of racial attitudes from fathers to sons: A study of blacks and whites. *Adolescence*, 20, 233–237.

Craemer, T. (2008). Nonconscious feelings of closeness toward African Americans and support for pro-Black policies. *Political Psychology*, 29(3), 407–436.

Crandall, C. S., Eshleman, A. & O'Brien, L. (2002). Social norms and the expression and suppression of prejudice: The struggle for internalization. *Journal of Personality and Social Psychology*, 82, 359–378.

Crisp, R. J., Ensari, N., Hewstone, M. & Miller, N. (2003). A dual-route model of crossed categorization effects. In W. Stroebe & M. Hewstone (eds.), *European Review of Social Psychology* (vol. 13, pp. 35–74). Hove, UK & Philadelphia: PA: Psychology Press.

Cunningham, W. A., Preacher, K. J. & Banaji, M. R. (2001). Implicit attitude measures: Consistency, stability, and convergent validity. *Psychological Science*, 12, 163–170.

Devine, P. G. (1989). Stereotypes and prejudice: Their automatic and controlled components. *Journal of Personality and Social Psychology*, 56, 5–18.

Dovidio, J. F. & Gaertner, S. L. (2000). Aversive racism and selection decisions: 1989 and 1999. *Psychological Science*, 11, 319–323.

Dovidio, J. F. & Gaertner, S. L. (2010). Intergroup bias. In S. T. Fiske, D. Gilbert & G. Lindzey (eds.), *Handbook of Social Psychology* (pp. 1084–1121). New York: Wiley.

Dovidio, J. F., Kawakami, K., Smoak, N. & Gaertner, S. L. (2009). The roles of implicit and explicit processes in contemporary prejudice. In R. E. Petty, R. H. Fazio & P. Brinol (eds.), *Attitudes: Insights from the New Implicit Measures* (pp. 165–192). New York: Psychology Press.

Dovidio, J. F., Smith, J. K., Donnella, A. G. & Gaertner, S. L. (1997). Racial attitudes and the death penalty. *Journal of Applied Social Psychology*, 27, 1468–1487.

Doyle, A. B. & Aboud, F. E. (1995). A longitudinal study of white children's racial prejudice as a social-cognitive development. *Merrill-Palmer Quarterly*, 41, 209–228.

Duckitt, J. (1992). *The Social Psychology of Prejudice*. Westport, CT: Praeger.

Duckitt, J. & Sibley, C. G. (2009). A dual-process motivational model of ideological attitudes and system justification. In J. T. Jost, A. C. Kay & H. Thorisdottir (eds.), *Social and Psychological Bases of Ideology and System Justification* (pp. 292–313). New York: Oxford University Press.

Eibach, R.P. & Ehrlinger, J. (2006). 'Keep your eyes on the prize': Reference points and group differences in assessing progress towards equality. *Personality and Social Psychology Bulletin*, 32, 66–77.

Fazio, R. H., Jackson, J. R., Dunton, B. C., and Williams, C. J. (1995). Variability in automatic activation as an unobtrusive measure of racial attitudes: A bona fide pipeline? *Journal of Personality & Social Psychology*, 69, 1013–1027.

Federico, C. M. (2004). When do welfare attitudes become racialized? The paradoxical effects of education. *American Journal of Political Science*, 48, 374–391.

Federico, C. M. (2006). Ideology and the affective structure of whites' racial perceptions. *Public Opinion Quarterly*, 70, 327–353.

Federico, C. M. & Holmes, J. W. (2005). Education and the interface between racial attitudes and criminal-justice attitudes. *Political Psychology*, 26, 47–76.

Federico, C. M. & Sidanius, J. (2002). Racism, ideology, and affirmative action, revisited: The antecedents and consequences of 'principled objections' to affirmative action. *Journal of Personality and Social Psychology*, 82, 488–502.

Feldman, S. & Huddy, L. (2005). Racial resentment and white opposition to race-conscious programs: Principles or prejudice? *American Journal of Political Science*, 49, 168–183.

Frenkel-Brunswik, E. (1948). Tolerance of ambiguity as an emotional and perceptual personality variable. *Journal of Personality*, 18, 108–143.

Gaertner, S. L. & Dovidio, J. F. (1977). The subtlety of white racism, arousal, and helping behavior. *Journal of Personality and Social Psychology*, 35, 691–707.

Gaertner, S. L. & Dovidio, J. F. (2005). Categorization, recategorization, and intergroup bias. In J. F. Dovidio, P. G. Glick & L. Rudman (eds.), *On the Nature of Prejudice: Fifty Years After Allport* (pp. 71–88). Malden, MA: Blackwell.

Gaertner, S. L., Rust, M. C., Dovidio, J. F., Bachman, B. A. & Anastasio, P. A. (1996). The contact hypothesis: The role of a common ingroup identity on reducing intergroup bias among majority and minority group members. In J. L. Nye & A. M. Brower (eds.), *What's Social About Social Cognition: Research on Socially Shared Cognition in Small Groups* (pp. 230–260). Newbury Park, CA: Sage.

Gawronski, B. & Bodenhausen, G. V. (2006). Associative and propositional processes in evaluation: An integrative review of implicit and explicit attitude change. *Psychological Bulletin*, 132, 692–731.

Gilens, M. (1999). *Why Americans Hate Welfare: Race, Media, and the Politics of Antipoverty Policy*. Chicago: University of Chicago Press.

Gilliam, F. D. & Iyengar, S. (2000). Prime suspects: The influence of local television news on the viewing public. *American Journal of Political Science*, 44, 560–573.

Greeley, A. & Sheatsley, P. (1971). Attitudes toward racial integration. *Scientific American*, 225, 13–19.

Greenwald, A. G., McGhee, D. E. & Schwartz, J. K. L. (1998). Measuring individual differences in implicit cognition: The Implicit Association Test. *Journal of Personality and Social Psychology*, 74, 1464–1480.

Greenwald, A. G., Banaji, M. R., Rudman, L. A., Farnham, S. D., Nosek, B. A. & Mellot, D. S. (2002). A unified theory of implicit attitudes, beliefs, self-esteem and self-concept. *Psychological Review*, 109, 3–25.

Hass, R. G., Katz, I., Rizzo, N., Biley, J. & Moore, L. (1992). When racial ambivalence evokes negative affect, using a disguised measure of mood. *Personality and Social Psychology Bulletin*, 18, 786–97.

Hetherington, M. & Weiler, J. D. (2009). *Authoritarianism and Polarization in American Politics*. Cambridge: Cambridge University Press.

Hogg, M. A. (2003). Intergroup relations. In J. Delamater (ed.), *Handbook of Social Psychology* (pp. 479–501). New York: Kluwer Academic/Plenum.

Huddy, L. & Feldman, S. (2009). On assessing the political effects of racial prejudice. *Annual Review of Political Science*, 12, 423–444.

Hunt, M. O. (2007). African American, Hispanic, and White beliefs about Black/White inequality, 1977–2004. *American Sociological Review*, 72, 390–415.

Hyman H. H. & Sheatsley P. B. (1954). The authoritarian personality: A methodological critique. In R. Christie & M. Jahoda (eds.), *Studies in the Scope and Method of 'the Authoritarian Personality'* (pp. 50–122). Glencoe, IL: Free Press.

Jost, J. T., Banaji, M. R. & Nosek, B. A. (2004). A decade of system justification theory: Accumulated evidence of conscious and unconscious bolstering of the status quo. *Political Psychology, 25,* 881–919.

Jost, J. T., Glaser, J., Kruglanski, A. W. & Sulloway, F. (2003). Political conservatism as motivated social cognition. *Psychological Bulletin, 129,* 339–375.

Karpinski, A. & Hilton, J. L. (2001). Attitudes and the Implicit Association Test. *Journal of Personality and Social Psychology, 81,* 774–778.

Katz, I. & Hass, R. G. (1988). Racial ambivalence and American value conflict: Correlational and priming studies of dual cognitive structures. *Journal of Personality and Social Psychology, 55,* 893–905.

Kinder, D. R. & Kam, C. D. (2009). *Us against Them: Ethnocentric Foundations of American Opinion.* Chicago: University of Chicago Press.

Kinder, D. R. & Sanders, L. M. (1996). *Divided by Color: Racial Politics and Democratic Ideals.* Chicago: University of Chicago Press.

Kinder, D. & Sears, D. (1981). Prejudice and politics: Symbolic racism versus racial threats to the good life. *Journal of Personality and Social Psychology, 40,* 414–431.

Kinder, D. R. & Winter, N. (2001). Exploring the racial divide: Whites, blacks, and opinion on national policy. *American Journal of Political Science, 45,* 439–456.

Knowles, E. D., Lowery, B. S. & Schaumberg, R. L. (2010). Racial prejudice predicts opposition to Obama and his health care reform plan. *Journal of Experimental Social Psychology, 46,* 420–423.

Kruglanski, A. W. (2004). *The Psychology of Closed-Mindedness.* New York: Psychology Press.

Kruglanski, A.W., Pierro, A., Mannetti, L. & DeGrada, E. (2006). Groups as epistemic providers: Need for closure and the unfolding of group centrism. *Psychological Review, 113,* 84–100.

Levin, S., Sidanius, J., Rabinowitz, J. L. & Federico, C. M. (1998). Ethnic identity, legitimizing ideologies and social status: A matter of ideological asymmetry. *Political Psychology, 19,* 373–404.

LeVine, R. A. & Campbell, D. T. (1972). *Ethnocentrism: Theories of Conflict, Ethnic Attitudes, and Group Behavior.* New York: Wiley.

Lipset, S. M. (1960). *Political Man.* New York: Doubleday.

Lowery, B. S., Knowles, E. D. & Unzueta, M. M. (2007). Framing inequity safely: The motivated denial of White privilege. *Personality and Social Psychology Bulletin, 33,* 1237–1250.

Lowery, B. S., Unzueta, M. M., Knowles, E. D. & Goff, P. A. (2006). Concern for the ingroup and opposition to affirmative action. *Journal of Personality and Social Psychology, 90,* 961–974.

McClosky, H. & Zaller, J. (1984). *The American Ethos.* Cambridge, MA: Harvard University Press.

McConahay, J. B. (1986). Modern racism, ambivalence, and the modern racism scale. In J. F. Dovidio & S. L. Gaertner (eds.), *Prejudice, Discrimination and Racism* (pp. 91–126). New York: Academic.

Mendelberg, T. (2001). *The Race Card*. Princeton, NJ: Princeton University Press.

Miller, N. (2002). Personalization and the promise of contact theory. *Journal of Social Issues*, 58, 387–410.

Milner, D. (1983). *Children and Race: Ten Years On*. London: Ward Lock Educational.

Mullen, B., Brown, R. & Smith, C. (1992). Ingroup bias as a function of salience, relevance, and status: An integration. *European Journal of Social Psychology*, 22, 103–122.

Mummendey, A. & Wenzel, M. (1999). Social discrimination and tolerance in intergroup relations: Reactions to intergroup difference. *Personality and Social Psychology Review*, 3, 158–174.

Nier, J. A., Gaertner, S. L., Dovidio, J. F., Banker, B. S. & Ward, C. M. (2001). Changing interracial evaluations and behavior: The effects of a common group identity. *Group Processes and Intergroup Relations*, 4, 299–316.

Nosek, B. A., Banaji, M. R. & Greenwald, A. G. (2002). Harvesting implicit group attitudes and beliefs from a demonstration website. *Group Dynamics*, 6, 101–115.

Payne, B. K., Cheng, C. M., Govorun, O. & Stewart, B. (2005). An inkblot for attitudes: Affect misattribution as implicit measurement. *Journal of Personality and Social Psychology*, 89, 277–293.

Payne, B. K., Krosnick, J. A., Pasek, J. Lelkes, Y., Akhtar, O. & Tompson, T. (2010). Implicit and explicit prejudice in the 2008 American presidential election. *Journal of Experimental Social Psychology*, 46, 367–374.

Pearson, A. R., Dovidio, J. F. & Gaertner, S. L. (2009). The nature of contemporary prejudice: Insights from aversive racism. *Social and Personality Psychology Compass*, 3, 314–338.

Pettigrew, T. F. (1959). Regional differences in anti-Negro prejudice. *Journal of Abnormal and Social Psychology*, 59, 28–36.

Pettigrew, T. F. (1998). Intergroup contact theory. *Annual Review of Psychology*, 49, 65–85.

Pettigrew, T. F. & Merteens, R. W. (1995). Subtle and blatant prejudice in Western Europe. *European Journal of Social Psychology*, 25, 57–75.

Pettigrew, T. F. & Tropp, L. R. (2005). Allport's intergroup contact hypothesis: Its history and influence. In J. F. Dovidio, P. G. Glick & L. Rudman (eds.), *On the Nature of Prejudice: Fifty Years After Allport* (pp. 262–277). Malden, MA: Blackwell.

Pettigrew, T. F. & Tropp, L. R. (2006). A meta-analytic test of intergroup contact theory. *Journal of Personality and Social Psychology*, 90, 750–783.

Pratto, F., Sidanius, J., Stallworth, L. M. & Malle, B. F. (1994). Social dominance orientation: A personality variable predicting social and political attitudes. *Journal of Personality and Social Psychology*, 67, 741–763.

Runciman, W.G. (1966) *Relative Deprivation and Social Justice*. London: Routledge & Kegan Paul.

Schmidt, K. & Nosek, B. A. (2010). Implicit (and explicit) racial attitudes barely changed during Barack Obama's presidential campaign and early presidency. *Journal of Experimental Social Psychology*, 46, 308–314.

Schmitt, M. T., Branscombe, N. R. & Kappen, D. M. (2003). Attitudes toward group-based inequality: Social dominance or social identity? *British Journal of Social Psychology*, 42, 161–186.

Sears, D. O. (1988). Symbolic racism. In P. A. Katz & D. A. Taylor (eds.), *Eliminating Racism: Profiles in Controversy* (pp. 53–84). New York: Plenum.

Sears, D. O. & Henry, P. J. (2003). The origins of symbolic racism. *Journal of Personality and Social Psychology, 85,* 259–275.

Sears, D. O. & Henry, P. J. (2005). Over thirty years later: A contemporary look at symbolic racism. In M. P. Zanna (ed.), *Advances in Experimental Social Psychology* (vol. 37, pp. 95–150). San Diego, CA: Elsevier Academic Press.

Sears, D. O. & Levy, S. (2003). Childhood and adult political development. In D. O. Sears, L. Huddy & R. Jervis (eds.), *Oxford Handbook of Political Psychology* (pp. 60–109). New York: Oxford University Press.

Sears, D. O., van Laar, C., Carrillo, M. & Kosterman, R. (1997). Is it really racism? The origins of white Americans' opposition to race-targeted policies. *Public Opinion Quarterly, 61,* 16–53.

Sechrist, G. & Stangor, C. (2001). Perceived consensus influences intergroup behavior and stereotype accessibility. *Journal of Personality and Social Psychology, 80,* 645–654.

Sherif, M., Harvey, O. J., White, B. J., Hood, W. R. & Sherif, C. (1961). *Intergroup Conflict and Cooperation: The Robbers Cave Experiment.* Norman, OK: Institute of Group Relations, University of Oklahoma.

Sibley, C. G. & Duckitt, J. (2008). Personality and prejudice: A meta-analysis and theoretical review. *Personality and Social Psychology Review, 12,* 248–279.

Sidanius, J. & Pratto, F. (1999). *Social dominance: An Intergroup Theory of Social Hierarchy and Oppression.* New York: Cambridge University Press.

Sidanius, J., Pratto, F. & Bobo, L. (1996). Racism, conservatism, affirmative action and intellectual sophistication: A matter of principled conservatism or group dominance? *Journal of Personality and Social Psychology, 70,* 476–490.

Sidanius, J., Feshbach, S., Levin, S. & Pratto, F. (1997). The interface between ethnic and national attachment: Ethnic pluralism or ethnic dominance? *Public Opinion Quarterly, 61,* 103–133.

Sidanius, J., Levin, S., van Laar, C. & Sears, D. O. (2008). *The Diversity Challenge: Social Identity and Intergroup Relations on the College Campus.* New York: Russell Sage.

Silverman, B. I. (1974). Consequences, discrimination, and the principle of belief congruence. *Journal of Personality and Social Psychology, 29,* 497–508.

Sniderman, P. & Piazza, T. (1993). *The Scar of Race.* Cambridge, MA: Harvard University Press.

Sniderman, P. & Tetlock, P. (1986). Symbolic racism: Problems of motive attribution in political analysis. *Journal of Social Issues, 42,* 129–150.

Stenner, K. (2005). *The Authoritarian Dynamic.* Cambridge: Cambridge University Press.

Tajfel, H. & Turner, J. C. (1986). The social identity theory of intergroup behavior. In S. Worchel & W. Austin (eds.), *Psychology of Intergroup Relations.* Chicago: Nelson-Hall.

Tesler, M. & Sears, D. O. (2010). *Obama's Race.* Chicago: University of Chicago Press.

Vanneman, R. & Pettigrew, T. (1972). Race and relative deprivation in the urban United States. *Race, 13,* 461–486.

Webster, D. M. & Kruglanski, A. W. (1994). Individual differences in need for cognitive closure. *Journal of Personality and Social Psychology*, 67, 1049–1062.

Wilson, T. D., Lindsey, S. & Schooler, T. (2000). A model of dual attitudes. *Psychological Review*, 107, 101–126.

Notes

1. Some researchers have suggested that the weakness of the estimated correlation between implicit and explicit racial attitudes may be due to measurement error (see Huddy & Feldman, 2009). Common implicit measures – such as those based on affective priming – contain considerable measurement error. Studies which have used latent-variable modelling to correct for this error have found stronger positive relationships between implicit and explicit attitudes (Cunningham, Preacher & Banaji, 2001). Moreover, implicit measures that are known to be more reliable show larger, more stable relationships with explicit measures (e.g. Payne et al., 2005).

2. Other recent approaches have attempted to measure authoritarianism using childrearing values as a proxy for respondents' orientation towards authority and convention (e.g. Stenner, 2005). These measures have proven to be reliable, valid, and less conflated with political beliefs than other measures (especially the RWA scale), and they too are strong predictors of racial hostility (e.g. racial resentment; see Hetherington & Weiler, 2009; Stenner, 2005).

3

Antecedents and Manifestations of Sexism

Janina Pietrzak

● ●

On 20 June 2011 the Supreme Court of the United States of America issued a decision concerning a class action lawsuit brought against Wal-Mart by 1.5 million female current and past employees. The women were suing Wal-Mart for what they alleged was unlawful discrimination in employment, pay and promotions.

Wal-Mart is the largest private employer in the United States. At the time the lawsuit was brought, women constituted 62 per cent of the total workforce, but only 36 per cent of assistant managers, 14 per cent of managers and 10 per cent of district managers (Drogin, 2003); the higher-paying the job, the fewer women there were performing it. The lowest-paying jobs were staffed almost entirely by women. The proportion of female managers at Wal-Mart was almost half of what it was at competing stores in the years 1975–99 (Bendick, 2003). Women were paid between 58 and 92 per cent of what men were paid as an hourly rate for the same job (Drogin, 2003).

The Supreme Court decided that these women did not have grounds to sue Wal-Mart as a group; that there was no proof that they experienced a common fate that would make these 1.5 million individuals a 'class' – beyond being women and working at Wal-Mart. The decision leaves much to debate. If the basis for discrimination is gender, why is gender not sufficient as a categorization criterion? Aren't the aforementioned statistics evidence of discrimination? Should we allow corporations to discriminate against women because gender discrimination is a cultural, rather than just a corporate, norm?

In this chapter, I outline some of the possible explanations for this inequality. Although it is possible that managers at Wal-Mart were engaging in conscious discrimination – knowingly not promoting women – it is more likely that such widespread discrepancies between men's and women's career paths were the result of unconscious discrimination. Such discrimination is founded on shared beliefs concerning the inherent traits, values, preferences and abilities of women versus men (Bem & Bem, 1970; Jackman, 1994). Because these beliefs are acquired through common cultural upbringing, there is no need for an explicit conspiracy or conscious individual decision to treat men and women differently – discrepancies in treatment come as a natural result of rational (or rationalized) reasoning concerning who will be better at a given job. As we will see, there is little real evidence to support this reasoning, because the assumptions it is based on are largely false.

It is worth keeping in mind that the issues raised here result from a society that devalues women. This difference in value is near-universal, though it is expressed in various ways. The problems women face in many societies are far graver than those described here. Sexual exploitation in times of war, human trafficking and prostitution, bride-burning, denial of property rights, genital mutilation – these are examples of suffering endured primarily or entirely by women (Morgan, 1996; United Nations, 2010). In first world nations, its consequences are much more subtle – less physical, less tragic. However, we believe that the mechanisms behind social ills rooted in sexist beliefs are the same. The difficulty in studying sexism in its more extreme forms will have to be overcome if social psychology is to be relevant in solving the world's more grievous problems.

Differences between men and women

Sex is one of the basic characteristics according to which we build expectations about behaviour, personality, preferences (e.g. Stangor et al., 1992). An exit point for considerations of sex-based discrimination must be an examination of actual differences that exist between the sexes. Putting aside physical distinctions, decades of studies have sought to pinpoint differences in the cognitive abilities of men and women. These studies have shown small but reliable differences (summarized in Helgeson, 2005). For example, women perform better than men in tasks that require rapid mathematical calculations, memory for spatial positions of objects, verbal fluency, short-term memory; men outperform women on tasks requiring mental rotation, aim, spatial perception, spatial visualization, mechanical skill and mathematical reasoning.

There are also beliefs about men and women that are not fixed in fact. Sex-based stereotypes are stable and widespread, designating men as more emotionally stable, open, extraverted, and conscientious, while women are seen as more friendly and agreeable (Williams, Satterwhite & Best, 1999). Already at birth, daughters are described as more delicate, finer featured, weaker and more feminine than sons (Karraker, Vogel & Lake, 1995). Boys are rated as stronger, louder, faster, meaner and hardier than girls, and so are encouraged to be more active (Stern & Karraker, 1989). By the time they have been at school for a few years, attributions for successes and failures follow sex-typed lines: boys are assumed to fail due to lack of effort; girls fail due to lack of natural talent. These differential beliefs about men and women are relatively stable throughout life.

Since it is implausible to think that such differences already exist in newborns, our interpretations must come from unconscious expectations about what boys and girls are like. Where do we get these expectations? One theory, common among non-scientists, is essentialism. According to essentialists, each gender contains an evolutionarily determined biological core, or 'essence', that makes it distinct from the other (e.g. Silverman, Choi & Peters, 2007). Differences between the sexes are seen as the direct or indirect result of this biological inheritance, and thus invariant and inevitable (Keller, 2005). This theory, though popular, is difficult to prove empirically.

Social role theory, meanwhile, proposes that the biological underpinnings of differences we observe are minimal in comparison to the impact of culture.

Social role theory

The unequal status of men and women, near ubiquitous in human history, is often explained through the unequal division of labour, determined by a woman's childbearing and childrearing responsibilities (Eagly, 1987). Women, both during pregnancy and later during a child's infancy, are anchored to the home. Duties related to maintaining the home therefore naturally fall to them. Men, meanwhile, are able to engage in activities outside the home, thus building connections and influence in the community. This division of labour, itself not based on any psychological or cognitive limitation, is generalized to form the basis of assumptions about women's and men's mental attributes. This leap of logic is the basis for the sex-based stereotypes and discrimination that women, and men, face daily.

Our shared cultural beliefs about appropriate roles for women and men to play in society are called gender roles. These beliefs are not only *descriptive*, based on our observations of what women and men typically do, prefer and value. They are also *prescriptive*, indicating what women and men *should* do, prefer and value (Eagly, 1987; Eagly & Karau, 2002; Heilman, 2001). For example, in most cultures women stay at home with an infant after giving birth. This observation gives rise to a descriptive belief about women, but also to a normative sense that staying at home is the appropriate thing for a woman to do. Women who promptly return to work, then, are seen as violating their gender role. As we will see below, gender-role violations are costly.

These two kinds of beliefs are positively, though not strongly, correlated (Burgess & Borgida, 1999). We assume that what people typically do is what they are inherently suited to. This makes sense: I would not spend my time writing scientific texts if they turned out to be incomprehensible; I do not often skateboard, because it puts me at risk of injury. What is problematic about this process is that we infer traits and predispositions from behaviours that are determined by external factors (Hoffman & Hurst, 1990). If a woman stays at home to take care of an infant, we infer that she is a good carer. We do not consider that she might prefer to return to work but cannot afford childcare. External factors (such as access to education, opportunities for development, freedom from family responsibilities) can create 'typical' behaviours that have nothing to do with underlying traits and values. The fact that men more often work, and so follow a more linear career path, while women more often veer away from a career when children are born, is partly determined biologically, but it can lead to assumptions about predispositions to pursue a career versus homemake.

The gender roles we are assigned therefore translate into characteristics we, as men and women, should have.[1] The stereotype content model (Fiske et al., 2002, 1999; see also Bilewicz & Vollhardt, this volume; Cohrs & Kessler, this volume) suggests that men and women are perceived at opposing poles of two dimensions: competence and warmth (alternately called communality and agency, Eagly, 1987, or instrumentality and expressiveness, Lewin, 1984). The warmth dimension includes attributes such as kindness, nurturing and empathy, while competence involves self-confidence, dominance and independence. In general, women are perceived as warmer than men but less competent. Of course, 'men' and 'women' are not homogenous categories. Subgroups of each gender can be rated very differently: housewives are perceived as high in warmth and low in competence, while a 'career woman' is defined by her high competence but low warmth (Fiske et al., 1999). How a group is judged on these two dimensions determines the affect directed at group members

(Fiske et al., 2002). High-competence, high-warmth groups inspire admiration, while low-competence, low-warmth groups are targets of contempt. Mixed combinations are likely to inspire mixed emotions. Groups that are judged as high in warmth and low in competence, for example, need not evoke hostility – they are essentially harmless, pitiable. On the other hand, groups that are high in competence and low in warmth can evoke fear and envy. These mixed emotions, when directed towards different subgroups of women, provide the framework for ambivalent sexism.

Ambivalent sexism

In recent years, researchers have moved away from definitions of sexism that focus exclusively on hostile or negative perceptions of women (for a discussion of an analogous progression in racism, see Federico, this volume). The latter half of the twentieth century saw much change in views concerning men and women, and their roles in society (Bolzendahl & Myers, 2004; Diekman & Eagly, 2000; Diekman & Goodfriend, 2006). As women entered the workforce and gained economic and political power, overt expressions of prejudice towards them have gradually decreased (Loo & Thorpe, 1998; Spence & Hahn, 1997). This is not to say that sexism has waned. These once blatant prejudices are now manifested more subtly. Janet Swim and colleagues (Swim et al., 1995) called this new, covert hostility 'modern sexism'. In contrast to 'old-fashioned sexism', modern sexism is displayed as more politically grounded, as resentment towards policies that 'favour' one group over another, paired with denial of continuing discrimination, and antagonism towards the demands women 'unfairly' make. A related perspective on these new manifestations of sexism was proposed by Tougas et al. (1995). These authors propose that 'neosexism' develops in individuals who believe that changes brought about by women's liberation unfairly disadvantage men. These new measures of prejudice are less vulnerable to social desirability concerns, because they are easily rationalized as an embrace of egalitarian values.

Ambivalent sexism theory (Glick & Fiske, 1996, 1997; Glick et al., 2000) characterizes sexism as having two components, which, though intuitively opposed, are in fact rooted in the same assumptions. Hostile sexism is antagonistic: hostile sexists respond with animosity to women whom they see as power-hungry and manipulative. Benevolent sexism, on the other hand, is one of the most subtle 'new' forms of prejudice, and can be perceived both by the sexist and by the target as favourable (Barreto & Ellemers, 2005). This seemingly benign set of beliefs is composed of three separate subdimensions originating in three basic assumptions. *Protective paternalism* is the belief that, because women are the weaker sex, they should be protected and cherished by men. *Complementary gender differentiation* is the belief that men and women are essentially different in ways that are complementary – women have a specific set of skills and traits that are valuable, and that men do not possess (e.g. moral purity) and vice versa. Finally, *heterosexual intimacy* is the belief that men and women are interdependent and necessary to each other as romantic partners. These three dimensions together – protective paternalism, complementary gender differentiation and heterosexual intimacy – though subjectively positive, justify the power and role imbalance between men and women by rewarding women who stay in their prescribed roles (Glick & Fiske, 2001). Neither sex is better; they are simply specialized to excel at certain aspects of social life. Such a 'fair' balance in skills and capabilities restores faith in the status quo (Jost & Kay, 2005; see Sutton, Cichocka & van der Toorn, this volume, for a discussion of other inequality-perpetrating mechanisms).

A study including 15,000 participants in 19 nations (Glick et al. 2000) showed the cross-cultural validity of this approach to studying sexism. In general, men show greater support for hostile sexism than do women. However, levels of benevolent sexism among women seem to depend on gender equality and on levels of hostile sexism among men – greater hostility among men is accompanied by higher levels of benevolent sexism among women. This relationship has been interpreted as indicating that women embrace benevolent sexism as a defence against the hostility they might encounter if they behaved 'inappropriately' for their gender (Fischer, 2006).

Benevolent sexism has indeed been linked to positive responses to women adhering to traditional roles and negative responses towards women who break out of traditional roles. Crimes committed by traditional women are seen as less serious, and are punished more leniently, by benevolent sexists than crimes committed by men or non-traditional women (Herzog & Oreg, 2008). In a series of studies concerning perceptions of rape victims and perpetrators, Viki and colleagues (Abrams et al., 2003; Viki & Abrams, 2002; Viki, Abrams & Masser, 2004) showed that benevolent sexists were *more* likely to ascribe blame to women who were victims of acquaintance rape and *less* likely to ascribe blame to perpetrators if the women behaved 'inappropriately'. While a prototypical rape scenario involves a stranger as perpetrator, statistics show that most rape perpetrators are known to the victim (e.g. Rand & Robinson, 2011). As such, people seek to explain and justify acquaintance rape, often citing the victim's behaviour as provocative and minimizing the seriousness of the event. For example, if a woman meets a man at a party, invites him back to her apartment and is then raped, benevolent sexists might see her as responsible (Abrams et al. 2003). Hostile sexists, meanwhile, minimize the seriousness of rape and are more likely to excuse the behaviour of rapists due to excessive sex drive, lack of ability to stop the incident, lack of understanding of the victim's refusal, and so on (Yamawaki, 2007). These ascriptions have legal implications: when less blame is attributed to the perpetrator, shorter jail sentences are recommended as punishment (Viki et al., 2004).

Benevolent sexism can have adverse cognitive effects on its targets as well. Exposure to benevolent sexism increases self-doubt, which affects performance on cognitive tasks (Dardenne, Dumont & Bollier, 2007) and prompts self-surveillance and body shame, leading to a focus on appearance management (Calogero & Jost, 2011). Mothers' benevolent sexism negatively affects daughters' academic goals and achievement (Montañés et al., 2012). In essence, being the recipients of subjectively positive but stereotypical messages funnels women's attention to gender-normed activities and topics, which undermines their performance in traditionally male realms and cements the gender status quo.

How does this translate to women's place in society?

How does sexism lead to employment discrepancies such as those observed at Wal-Mart? Women, formerly relegated to the home, now comprise 46 per cent of the workforce in the United States (Catalyst, 2011), 45 per cent of workers and 60 per cent of university graduates in the European Union (European Commission, 2011), and a not inconsequential percentage of politicians and business leaders: 19 per cent of the world's parliamentary seats (Inter-Parliamentary Union, 2010) and 18 per cent of corporate officer positions in *Financial Post 500* companies (Catalyst, 2011). However, only 6 per cent of top-earner positions in the global top 500 companies are held by women, and more than 30 per cent of companies have no female senior officers (Mulligan-Ferry et al., 2010). A typical board of ten members in top-listed companies in Europe has just one female member (European Commission, 2011).

Leadership positions seem to elude even highly qualified women. While their dominant place in the home is unchallenged, women attempting to attain high status positions still face seemingly irrational barriers. For example, in the United States, of the eight top-rated traits important in a leader, women outscore men on five (honesty, intelligence, compassion, creativity and extraversion), and match or are outscored by men on three (hard work, ambition and decisiveness; Taylor et al., 2008). Despite the high match between a woman's perceived qualities and leadership requirements, women are chosen by only 6 per cent of respondents when asked about who makes a better leader.

There seems to be a basic 'lack of fit' (Heilman, 1983) between what women are deemed capable of and what leadership requires. These findings inspired Eagly and Karau to formulate role incongruity theory (2002), the idea that the role of a leader is incongruous with the female gender role. This is why women are less likely to be chosen for roles of leadership, and are more negatively evaluated when they fill those roles. For example, successful female managers were rated as more hostile and less rational than identically described male managers (Heilman, Block & Martell, 1995). Women who exhibit a communication style that is typically task-oriented – i.e. a rapid, firm way of speaking, few hesitations, upright posture – are rated as less influential, likable, and hirable than similar men, especially by men (Carli, LaFleur & Loeber, 1995; Rudman, 1998). At the same time, women – but not men – who behave with greater friendliness are judged as less competent (Carli, Lafleur & Loeber, 1995). A parallel difference in perception occurs when women and men are compared ingroup discussion: identical discussion input is received more negatively when it is made by a female leader than when it is made by a male leader; these women are also perceived as more bossy and domineering (Butler & Geis, 1990).

Violating gender norms itself can contribute to more extreme evaluations of particular behaviours. Because women are not expected to be dominant, the same assertive behaviour is perceived as more extreme when a woman performs it than when a man performs it, thus earning her an 'aggressive' label (Eagly & Karau, 2002). Negative behaviour, if performed by a woman, is perceived by men as more negative, and is more likely to be seen as intentional (Hewstone, 1990). Positive outcomes, when their author is a woman, are evaluated more cautiously because they are unexpected (Steinpreis, Anders & Ritzke, 1999).

Such violations affect men as well. Men who behave in gender-incongruent ways – such as exhibiting modesty – face negative responses (Moss-Racusin, Phelan & Rudman, 2010), and those who fulfil stereotype-incongruent roles are accorded less status than men in congruent roles (Brescoll, Dawson & Uhlmann, 2010). Even working for a woman can be a blow to a man's status (Brescoll et al., 2012).

A key aspect of role incongruity theory is that women and men 'fit' different types of jobs. Women are not condemned to spend their time unemployed; they are selected over men for jobs that line up with societal expectations for women: nurses, teachers, caretakers, secretaries. This 'sex-typing' of jobs can be based on assumptions about the skills or attributes necessary to perform it well (nurturance vs strength, for example), traditional division of labour, or it can be based on the relative proportions of men and women already performing the job (Heilman, 1983). Sex-typing is so common that it occurs as jobs are being created – descriptions of non-existent positions contain gendered assumptions, which may affect individual decisions about whether or not to apply. Such differences are common across countries (e.g. Anker, 1998) and cannot be explained by self-selection due to job preference or education.

The mismatch between women's inferred natural talents and the requirements of leadership are likely to be greatest at the highest levels of leadership, where human relationships play a lesser role, and more abstract, long-range thinking is required (Eagly & Karau, 2002), and criteria for performance are less quantifiable (Heilman, 2001). This unbreachable, invisible barrier to advancement has been termed the 'glass ceiling' (Cotter et al., 2001). A converse effect is observed for men entering a feminine domain. Men considered for a receptionist job, for example, were rated as less likely to be interviewed than women, and, in particular, feminine women (Glick, Zion & Nelson, 1988). If men are hired in such domains, they are likely to be promoted or 'tracked' into more masculinized positions – regardless of their own preferences (Williams, 1992). This 'glass escalator' takes them away from low-status roles that seem inappropriate for a man.

Thus, although today women are more likely to be managers than they were even a few decades ago, leadership stereotypes are still masculine (Powell, Butterfield & Parent, 2002) and still affect how working women are perceived. In the following sections, I describe how sexism affects women at various stages of the employment process: hiring, workplace environment and work-home balance. These mechanisms demonstrate how the gender status quo is maintained, wherein women, even if they work, are held in low-status positions while men attain power, such as at Wal-Mart.

Hiring

Stereotypical assumptions about attributes

In the wake of the women's liberation movement in the United States, the 1970s saw a number of studies conducted to demonstrate discrimination in hiring practices. In a typical study, participants are given identical information about candidates applying for a single job. These candidates differ only in terms of their sex – their qualifications are identical or comparable, only the name at the top of the CV differs (e.g. Jane versus John). A meta-analysis of 49 studies using experimental manipulations of CVs in selection (Davison & Burke, 2000) showed that men, in general, are selected over women with identical qualifications. This general finding was qualified, however, by the type of job in question. For jobs that were male sex-typed, such as used-car salesman, men were preferentially selected. Women were reliably preferentially selected for jobs that were female sex-typed, such as director of a day-care centre. Because leadership positions are closely associated with stereotypically male attributes (Eagly & Karau, 2002), people are more likely to choose a male than a female for a high-status position.

Heilman's (1983) 'lack of fit' model describes how stereotypes might play into selection processes: candidates' inferred attributes are compared with job requirements, and a mismatch leads to a lower likelihood of hiring. These attributes need not be actual (a woman candidate might be seen as warmer than a man, but she is not necessarily so); nor are the job requirements necessarily objective (an employer may think that dominance is important, but a cooperative approach may in fact be more effective). A meta-analysis assessing the relative strength of sex and qualifications on hiring recommendations showed that the former criterion accounted for only 4 per cent, while the latter 35 per cent of variance (Olian, Schwab & Haberfeld, 1988). It is both obvious and reassuring that qualifications are taken into consideration when making hiring decisions. However, the practical impact of the 4 per cent should not be dismissed. Even if sex discrimination accounts for only 1 per cent of the variance in employee promotion, this can lead to grave disproportions of men and women at top levels of management, even if their original qualifications were equal, and an equal number of candidates of each sex apply at each stage for promotion (Martell, Lane & Emrich, 1996).

Physical appearance

Interviews are often the first moment at which appearance can be taken into consideration by potential employers. In Western cultures, a woman's value is determined in large part by her appearance (Fredrickson & Roberts, 1997). Due to this emphasis on externality, women feel more body shame, and are more likely to self-objectify and worry about how they look to other people than men do (e.g. Calogero & Jost, 2011). Even the way individuals are presented in the media reflects assumptions about the different predispositions of men and women: photos of men are more likely to be focused on the face, emphasizing thought, while women are more often depicted in full figure (Archer et al., 1983).

Attractiveness does not affect perceptions of men in job contexts, while for women it has real implications (Heilman & Stopeck, 1985). Attractive women are perceived more gender stereotypically – warmer, but less competent – than women who are less attractive (Eagly & Karau, 2002;

Lippa, 1998). They are therefore disadvantaged in interviews for managerial level positions, but advantaged when applying for lower-level positions (Heilman & Stopeck, 1985). Feminine women applying for high-status positions are rated as significantly less competent (Glick et al., 2005), and less socially competent (Wookey, Graves & Butler, 2009) than less feminine women.

What defines a woman in an interviewer's mind comes in part from the media. Priming male interviewers with 'women as sex objects' has a clear effect on how women are later interviewed and evaluated. Rudman and Borgida (1995) showed participants a series of television advertisements that 'portrayed women as interchangeable, decorative objects whose sole function is to please' (p. 495). Men shown these particular ads – as compared with men who watched neutral ads – asked more sexist questions during the interview, remembered more about the candidate's physical appearance and less about her qualifications, and rated the candidate as significantly less competent. Such media messages affect women too: female college students who were shown advertisements of stereotypical women showed decreased leadership aspirations than women who did not see such advertisements (Davies, Spencer & Steele, 2005).

Paradoxically, perceiving women only as physical objects, rather than individuals, not only leads to judging them to be less competent, but also as less warm and moral (Heflick, Goldenberg, Cooper & Puvia, 2011). This finding, wherein women are seen as *less* stereotypical when their appearance is emphasized than when it is not, can be explained by objectification theory (Fredrickson & Roberts, 1997). Treating women as 'things' rather than people denies them humanity, which has negative consequences for their mental health and cognitive performance (Fredrickson & Roberts, 1997). Sexualized women are more liable to be likened to animals (Vaes, Paladino & Puvia, 2011), but a simple focus on appearance leads to a 'mechanistic' perception of women (Heflick et al., 2011). Both of these perceptions are dehumanizing, with all the consequences it entails (Haslam, 2006; see also Bilewicz & Vollhardt, this volume; Hamilton, Medianu & Esses, this volume).

The workplace environment

Biased performance evaluations

Sexism can play into performance evaluation in a few ways. First, a self-fulfilling prophecy might be observed, wherein evaluators with certain expectations about women's performance are more likely to observe behaviours that match those (low) expectations. The internalization of culturally fostered beliefs about their own (lack of) capabilities can affect women's perceptions of the likelihood of success and can lead them to avoid greater responsibilities and hamper their ambitions (Lips, 2000). Even if internalization does not occur, stereotype threat processes (Davies, Spencer & Steele, 2005; Spencer, Steele & Quinn, 1999; see also Cohrs & Kessler, this volume) can prove detrimental to performance in stereotyped domains.

Second, different expectations about women's and men's capabilities affect interpretations of the outcomes they achieve. When completing male sex-typed tasks, women's successes are more likely to be attributed to luck, or other unstable causes, while men's successes are more likely to be attributed to skill, a cause that is stable (Swim & Sanna, 1996). These effects are more extreme when responsibility is ambiguous, such as ingroup tasks, and are attenuated when a woman's competence has been clearly demonstrated (Heilman, 2001).

Finally, women who violate gender norms are punished for behaviours that are valued among men. Cases of women suing for sex discrimination in the past have often focused on women in managerial positions who are not promoted due to lack of adherence to a traditional gender role (Fiske et al., 1991). In one case, Ann Hopkins claimed she was denied partnership at Price Waterhouse because of her agentic managerial style, although her competence was never in question. Ms Hopkins was judged based on irrelevant criteria – e.g. her style of dress – because those were the criteria that her sex evoked. This case prompted research into what is called the backlash effect: women who take on a 'masculine' leadership style (directive, task-oriented) are evaluated more negatively than their male counterparts (Rudman & Glick, 1999). An analogous effect can be observed for men: men who violate gender norms by appearing weak or uncertain also suffer a backlash, which is thought to be provoked by a hostile response to a man threatening the established status hierarchy (Moss-Racusin, Phelan & Rudman, 2010; Rudman & Fairchild, 2004). In a series of interviews with men in feminized professions, Williams (1992) found that choosing a nurturing, care-taking role was perceived as deviant for a man and was often met with suspicion or discomfort.

Attributional ambiguity

One of the paradoxes of sexism is that women as individuals deny that they are victims of it, while acknowledging that sexism exists and affects women in general (Crosby, 1984). While external, objective examination might show that a woman is making 70 per cent of a man's wage for equal work, she is unlikely to feel less satisfied or more aggrieved. To understand this apparent contradiction, it is worth looking at the explanations given for personal outcomes. In any work outcome – Did I get hired? Did I get the pay increase I wanted? – there are a great number of contributing factors to which we can attribute success or failure. Crocker and Major (1989) call this uncertainty about the causes for outcomes – where one of the possible explanations is discrimination – attributional ambiguity. Women are much more likely to blame themselves for failure than they are to ascribe causality to external factors such as discrimination (Crosby, 1984). In part, this is due to our need to exist in a controllable and pre-dictable universe – if my outcomes are due to internal factors, I have more control over them than if they are due to external factors. Moreover, indi-viduals who attribute negative outcomes to discrimination elicit negative responses from their social surroundings: they are perceived as irritat-ing complainers who refuse to take responsibility for their own mistakes (Kaiser, Dyrenforth & Hagiwara, 2006; Kaiser & Miller, 2001).

Women are also less likely to make accurate attributions because of how evaluation is communicated to them. In one study of lawyers, women were given more favourable direct comments concerning their work than men, while being rated more harshly on objective criteria that mattered for promotion (Biernat, Tocci & Williams, 2011). Additionally, ratings of interpersonal warmth affected women's overall evaluation more than men's. The authors suggest that positive narrative feedback is given to demonstrate a conscious lack of prejudice, while the numerical rat-ings reflect actual assessments. Such 'shifting standards' (Biernat, 2003; Biernat & Kobrynowicz, 1997; Foschi, 1996) – thanks to which women are praised more but paid less, assigned less important tasks and given fewer promotions – creates uncertainty for women about how to achieve their career goals.

Harassment

Any 'unwelcome sexual advances, requests for sexual favours, and other verbal or physical harassment of a sexual nature' constitute sexual harass-ment (EEOC, nd). Many, if not most, female employees experience sexually harassing behaviours in the workplace (e.g. Cortina et al., 2001). Men, when describing behaviours that women label as harassment, tend to use terms such as 'teasing' or 'having some fun with' (Hoffman, 2006). Sexual harassment is likely to stem from the prescriptive component of gender roles (Burgess & Borgida, 1999). One aspect of gender stereotypes is that men should initiate sexual contact, and women respond. When women are perceived in a stereotypical way, as submissive or passive, this can evoke complementary stereotypical behaviours from men, i.e. sexual advances. Men, therefore, believe that they are creating a warm and welcoming atmosphere by indicating sexual interest. This kind of treatment, in fact, leads women to avoid situations in which they could be gaining opportunities for training or networking.

Sexual harassment can have an impact beyond its direct victims. An atmosphere that is hostile towards women affects occupational and physical well-being. This hostility need not be physical or overt; more subtle, indirect forms of hostility can be equally harmful. One subtle way that an atmosphere of hostility towards women is propagated is through sexist humour. Hearing sexist jokes can make women angry, disgusted and uncomfortable (LaFrance & Woodzicka, 1998). Though seemingly innocuous, finding sexist jokes amusing is linked with acceptance of interpersonal violence and beliefs about the inherently antagonistic nature of cross-sex relations (Ryan & Kanjorski, 1998). Hearing such jokes creates the perception that sexism is tolerated, and leads to actual discrimination (Ford et al., 2008; Ford, Wentzel & Lorion, 2001).

The work-home balance

Most people in Western countries declare that a more satisfying marriage is one in which both husband and wife have jobs (compared with one in which the husband is the sole provider; Pew Research Center, 2010). However, as more women enter the workforce and contribute to household earnings, there is no parallel contribution made by men towards housework. This 'second shift' (Hochschild & Machung, 1989) means that women return home, often from a full day at work, and face the responsibility of managing the household, while men return home and 'help out' when necessary. Even when household chores are split, women are much more likely to be responsible for daily routine tasks (cooking, childcare) that impose a rigid schedule, whereas men are more likely to take on jobs that are more flexible in timing (cleaning out gutters, changing the oil). The difference in workload has been calculated at about five hours more per week for parents with young children (Milkie, Raley & Bianchi, 2009).

An undoubted influence on women's achievement in working life is their parental status. Structural barriers to progress, such as lack of job-protected maternity leave and adequate childcare facilities, can have lasting and harmful effects on a woman's career. Indirect evidence of this can be found by comparing pay ratios, and probabilities of returning to the same employer after childbirth, in countries with varied policies (Waldfogel, 1998). More optimistic evidence comes from the changing relationship between education and childbearing in nations that facilitate continued work and study for women with children (Kravdal & Rindfuss, 2008).

Biased perceptions of mothers

Mothers in the workforce suffer additional discrimination. Describing a worker as having a two-year-old child leads people to perceive her as less competent than if she is described without this phrase (Cuddy, Fiske & Glick, 2004). Visibly pregnant women are devalued on dimensions relevant to work, especially by men (Halpert, Wilson & Hickman, 1993). Wages follow as might be expected: while the gender gap in hourly wages has been narrowing, the gap between mothers and childless women has been widening (Waldfogel, 1998). Most of this gap (up to 5 per cent) can be explained by labour-market experience, occupation, full-time versus part-time work schedules, education. The remainder of this gap has been explained by the assumption employers have about women putting less effort into their work once they have children. One female executive stated, 'once I had my child, my boss didn't think I was working as hard. In his eyes, my rating went from "superb" when I first started, to "terrible" after the baby arrived' (Halpert, Wilson & Hickman, 1993). No direct evidence exists for this assumed productivity lapse (Anderson, Binder & Krause, 2003).

This 'motherhood penalty' (Ridgeway & Correll, 2004) is said to surface because the motherhood role conflicts with the 'ideal worker' role (Correll, Benard & Paik, 2007). Cultural expectations that a mother will prioritize children above all else lead to an assumption that her commitment to her career will falter (Fuegen et al., 2004; Ridgeway & Correll, 2004; Russo, 1979). It is not surprising that women perceived in this way are not valued in the workplace, are less likely to be hired or promoted, and less likely to receive a high salary.

The same is not true for fathers. Men seem to benefit from a 'fatherhood bonus' in which they are held to a lower standard (Fuegen et al., 2004) and are seen as more committed and more likely to be promoted than are childless males (Correll, Benard & Paik, 2007). Indeed, Wal-Mart managers, when justifying systematically higher wages given to men than to women, claimed that male employees earned more because they 'had families to support' (McLamb, 2003).

Solutions

While intergroup contact is touted as a *sine qua non* to reducing prejudice in many contexts, it makes little difference in reducing sexism. However, creating more equal status between men and women can bring about change (see also Sutton et al., this volume). As more women achieve higher power positions, they meet and overcome prejudicial attitudes about their capabilities, and become the evaluators rather than the evaluated (Eagly,

2007). A meta-analysis of leadership in context showed that women are judged as more effective as leaders when their subordinates are women, or when effectiveness is judged by more women (Eagly, Karau & Makhijani, 1995). Making sex less salient – by increasing the number of women candidates, eliminating information about sex, or increasing personalized information (Davison & Burke, 2000; Tosi & Einbender, 1985) – can make sex less influential in decisions concerning employment (Heilman, 1983).

A number of initiatives have been introduced by governments in order to reduce sexism and increase participation of women in business (European Commission, 2011). Soft measures include governance codes that encourage and promote gender equality through peer pressure. Hard measures include gender quotas, set by legislation. A 2003 law in Norway set a quota of 40 per cent of each sex to be on the boards of all public limited companies. Similar quotas have been introduced in Spain (in 2007), Iceland (in 2010) and France (in 2011). Although it appears that the proportion of women in high positions is rising in these countries, it is still too early to evaluate the effects of these laws fully (European Commission, 2011). Norway and Denmark have also banned the use of sexist advertising (Holmes, 2008).

Diversity and equality programmes are becoming common in many non-governmental organizations as well (EC, 2011). Specific goals are being set for increasing and maintaining a diverse workplace; family-friendly policies are being introduced to allow all employees to engage more comfortably with their families while not sacrificing productivity; networks of mentors and coaches for women, currently uncommon, are being introduced by businesses to provide support in career development.

Such policies, be they legislated or recommended, can be a very effective way of equalizing chances and including minorities into the workplace. However, they can also be a factor that undermine minority members by creating ambiguity about their actual merits. Women who are aware that they are selected based on their sex devalue their positions (Major, Feinstein & Crocker, 1994). Thus, care must be taken to ensure that all employees understand the policies and how qualifications versus other criteria are weighted.

One of the unusual aspects of the Wal-Mart case described at the beginning of this chapter is that so many women came together to identify their gender as a common characteristic that led to differential treatment. Why is collective action among women so unlikely? It requires that individuals who share a group identity become aware of a shared fate and shared interests (see Van Stekelenburg & Klandermans, this volume). Women, making up half of the human population, can overlook the similarities in their experience when confronted with all the differences between them. Heightening women's sensitivity to the existence of everyday, minor incidents of sexism, such as hearing negative comments about gender equality, or hearing sexist language, can decrease their own sexism. Encouraging men to empathize with the targets of sexism will decrease hostile, though not benevolent, sexism (Becker & Swim, 2011).

Individual attempts to reduce sexism seem least effective and most costly. Confronting people who make sexist remarks can be very difficult. Even when women find such remarks offensive, social pressures to maintain social harmony or fear of retaliation can create conflict about an appropriate response (Swim & Hyers, 1999). When the remark is a 'joke' then there is the risk of being termed 'humourless', thus less likable, which affects evaluation (Dodd et al., 2001; Kaiser & Miller, 2001).

Conclusion

In some ways, our society has become more inclusive: we provide subtitles for those who cannot hear; multiracial identities can be declared in the census; we acknowledge that a couple can live together before marriage; in some cases, we acknowledge that two people of the same sex can be married to each other. It may seem that our old prejudices have been left by the wayside, replaced by a new, open-hearted acceptance of our motley humanity.

Yet from another perspective, our society remains as prejudiced as it ever was – only the manifestations of our prejudices are altered. Sexism, like other forms of prejudice (see Cohrs & Kessler, this volume), has changed as industrialization and globalization introduced new opportunities for and new necessities of intergroup contact. Women are asked to walk a fine line, being both feminine and just masculine enough. Adhering to traditional gender roles means lack of power, earnings and independence; violating those roles is met with hostility, obstruction and, sometimes, expulsion from the workplace. Solving this problem will require effective, as yet undiscovered, research-based interventions.

Practical task for readers

This chapter revolves around sexism towards women. This is due to women's relative lower outcomes on a variety of employment-related measures. However, men are also discriminated against based on gender (e.g. Funk & Werhun, 2011; Moss-Racusin, Phelan & Rudman, 2010; Rudman & Fairchild, 2004; Sargent, 2005). Think of a job in which a man might have difficulty succeeding. How would the

---

Continued

mechanisms described in this chapter affect his hiring, evaluation and promotion? Which effects will be symmetrical? Which will not? How might other group identities (race, sexual orientation) play into these processes?

Suggested readings

For more information see the book by Eagly and Carli (2007) and the articles by Glick and Fiske (2001) and Vandello et al. (2008).

References

Abrams, D., Viki, G. T., Masser, B. & Bohner, G. (2003). Perceptions of stranger and acquaintance rape: The role of benevolent and hostile sexism in victim blame and rape proclivity. *Journal of Personality and Social Psychology*, 84, 111–125.

Anderson, D. J., Binder, M. & Krause, K. (2003). The motherhood wage penalty revisited: Experience, heterogeneity, work effort and work-schedule flexibility. *Industrial and Labor Relations Review*, 56, 273–294.

Anker, R. (1998). *Gender and Jobs: Sex Segregation of Occupations in the World*. Geneva, Switzerland: International Labour Organization.

Archer, D., Iritani, B., Kimes, D. D. & Barrios, M. (1983). Face-ism: Five studies of sex difference in facial prominence. *Journal of Personality and Social Psychology*, 45, 725–735.

Barreto, M. & Ellemers, N. (2005). The burden of benevolent sexism: How it contributes to the maintenance of gender inequalities. *European Journal of Social Psychology*, 35, 633–642.

Becker, J. C. & Swim, J. K. (2011). Seeing the unseen: Attention to daily encounters with sexism as way to reduce sexist beliefs. *Psychology of Women Quarterly*, 35(2), 227–242.

Bem, S. L. & Bem, D. J. (1970). Case study of a nonconscious ideology: Training the woman to know her place. In D. J. Bem (ed.), *Beliefs, Attitudes, and Human Affairs*. Belmont, CA: Brooks/Cole.

Bendick, Jr., M. (2003). *The Representation of Women in Store Management at Wal-Mart Stores, Inc.* Washington DC: Bendick and Egan Economic Consultants, Inc. Available at http://www.walmartclass.com/staticdata/reports/r1.2.html (accessed 26 April 2012).

Biernat, M. (2003). Toward a broader view of social stereotyping. *American Psychologist*, 58, 1019–1027.

Biernat, M. & Kobrynowicz, D. D. (1997). Gender and race-based standards of competence: lower minimum standards but higher ability standards for devalued groups. *Journal of Personality and Social Psychology*, 72, 544–557.

Biernat, M., Tocci, M. J. & Williams, J. C. (2011). The language of performance evaluations: Gender-based shifts in content and consistency of judgment. *Social Psychological and Personality Science*. doi: 10.1177/1948550611415693

Bolzendahl, C. I. & Myers, D. J. (2004). Feminist attitudes and support for gender equality: Opinion change in women and men, 1974-1998. *Social Forces*, 83, 759–789.

Brescoll, V. L., Dawson, E. & Uhlmann, E. L. (2010). Hard-won and easily lost: The fragile status of leaders in gender-stereotype-incongruent occupations. *Psychological Science*, 21, 1620–1642.

Brescoll, V. L., Uhlmann, E. L., Moss-Racusin, C. & Sarnell, L. (2012). Masculinity, status, and subordination: Why working for a gender stereotype violator causes men to lose status. *Journal of Experimental Social Psychology*, 48, 354–357.

Burgess, D. & Borgida, E. (1999). Who women are, who women should be: Descriptive and prescriptive gender stereotyping in sex discrimination. *Psychology, Public Policy, and Law*, 5, 665–692.

Butler, D. & Geis, F. L. (1990). Nonverbal affect responses to male and female leaders: Implications for leadership evaluations. *Journal of Personality and Social Psychology*, 58, 48–59.

Calogero, R. & Jost, J. T. (2011). Self-subjugation among women: Stereotype exposure, self-objectification, and the protective function of the need to avoid closure. *Journal of Personality and Social Psychology*, 100, 211–228.

Carli, L. L., LaFleur, S. J. & Loeber, C. C. (1995). Nonverbal behavior, gender, and influence. *Journal of Personality and Social Psychology*, 68, 1030–1041.

Catalyst (2011). *Statistical Overview of Women in the Workplace*. Available at http://www.catalyst.org/file/541/qt_statistical_overview_of_women_in_the_workplace.pdf (accessed 26 April 2012).

Correll, S.J., Benard, S. & Paik, I. (2007). Getting a job: is there a motherhood penalty? *American Journal of Sociology*, 112, 1297–1338.

Cortina, L. M., Magley, V. J., Williams, J. H. & Langhout, R. D. (2001). Incivility in the workplace: Incidence and impact. *Journal of Occupational Health Psychology*, 6, 64–80.

Cotter, D. A., Hermsen, J. M., Ovadia, S. & Vanneman, R. (2001). The glass ceiling effect. *Social Forces*, 80, 655–681.

Crocker, J. & Major, B. (1989). Social stigma and self-esteem: The self-protective properties of stigma. *Psychological Review*, 96, 608–630.

Crosby, F. (1984). The denial of personal discrimination. *American Behavioral Scientist*, 27, 371–386.

Cuddy, A. J. C., Fiske, S. T. & Glick, P. (2004). When professionals become mothers, warmth doesn't cut the ice. *Journal of Social Issues*, 60, 701–718.

Dardenne, B., Dumont, M. & Bollier, T. (2007). Insidious dangers of benevolent sexism: Consequences for women's performance. *Journal of Personality and Social Psychology*, 93, 764–779.

Davies, P. G., Spencer, S. J. & Steele, C. M. (2005). Clearing the air: Identity safety moderates the effects of stereotype threat on woemn's leadership aspirations. *Journal of Personality and Social Psychology*, 88, 276–287.

Davison, H. K. & Burke, M. J. (2000). Sex discrimination in simulated employment contexts: A meta-analytic investigation. *Journal of Vocational Behavior*, 56, 225–248.

Diekman, A. B. & Eagly, A. H. (2000). Stereotypes as dynamic constructs: Women and men of the past, present, and future. *Personality and Social Psychology Bulletin, 26*, 1171– 1181.

Diekman, A.B. & Goodfriend, W. (2006). Rolling with the changes: A role congruity perspective on gender norms. *Psychology of Women Quarterly, 30*, 369–383.

Dodd, E. H., Giuliano, T. A., Boutell, J. M. & Moran, B. E. (2001). Respected or rejected: Perceptions of women who confront sexist remarks. *Sex Roles, 45*, 567–577.

Drogin, R. (2003). *Statistical Analysis of Gender Patterns in Wal-Mart Workforce*. Expert report submitted in *Dukes v. Wal-Mart Stores* (Case no. C-01-2252 MJJ). United States District Court, Northern District of California.

Eagly, A.H. (1987). *Sex Differences in Social Behavior: A Social-Role Interpretation*. Hillsdale, NJ: Erlbaum.

Eagly, A. H. (2007). Female leadership advantage and disadvantage: resolving the contradictions. *Psychology of Women Quarterly, 31*, 1–12.

Eagly, A. H. & Carli, L. L. (2007). *Through the Labyrinth: The Truth About How Women Become Leaders*. Boston, MA: Harvard Business School Press.

Eagly, A. H. & Karau, S. J. (2002). Role Congruity Theory of prejudice toward female leaders. *Psychological Review, 109*, 573–598.

Eagly, A. H., Karau, S. J. & Makhijani, M. G. (1995). Gender and the effectiveness of leaders: A meta-analysis. *Psychological Bulletin, 117*, 125–145.

European Commission. (2011). *The Gender Balance in Business Leadership*, Commission Staff Working Paper SEC (2011 246 final). Brussels, Belgium: European Commission.

Fischer, A. R. (2006). Women's benevolent sexism as reaction to hostility. *Psychology of Women Quarterly, 30*, 410–416.

Fiske, S. T., Bersoff, D. N., Borgida, E., Deaux, K. & Heilman, M. E. (1991). Social science research on trial: Use of sex stereotyping research in Price Waterhouse v. Hopkins. *American Psychologist, 46*, 1049–1060.

Fiske, S. T., Cuddy, A. J. C., Glick, P. & Xu., J. (2002). A model of (often mixed) stereotype content: competence and warmth respectively follow from perceived status and competition. *Journal of Personality and Social Psychology, 82*, 878–902.

Fiske, S. T., Xu, J., Cuddy, A. J. C. & Glick, P. (1999). (Dis)respecting versus (dis)liking: Status and interdependence predict ambivalent stereotypes of competence and warmth. *Journal of Social Issues, 55*(3), 473–489.

Ford, T. E., Boxer, C. F., Armstrong, J. & Edel, J. R. (2008). More than 'just a joke': the prejudice-releasing function of sexist humor. *Personality and Social Psychology Bulletin, 34*, 159–170.

Ford, T. E., Wentzel, E. R. & Lorion, J. (2001). Effects of exposure to sexist humor on perceptions of normative tolerance of sexism. *European Journal of Social Psychology, 31*, 677–691.

Foschi, M. (1996). Double standards in the evaluation of men and women. *Social Psychological Quarterly, 59*, 237–254.

Fredrickson, B. & Roberts, T.A. (1997). Objectification theory: Toward understanding women's lived experiences and mental health risks. *Psychology of Women Quarterly*, 21, 173–206.

Fuegen, K., Biernat, M., Haines, E. & Deaux, K. (2004). Mothers and fathers in the workplace: How gender and parental status influence judgments of job-related competence. *Journal of Social Issues*, 60, 737–754.

Funk, L. C. & Werhun, C.D. (2011). 'You're such a girl!' The psychological drain of the gender-role harassment of men. *Sex Roles*, 65, 13–22.

Gerber, G. L. (2009). Status and the gender stereotyped personality traits: Toward an integration. *Sex Roles*, 61, 297–316.

Glick, P. & Fiske, S. T. (1996). The ambivalent sexism inventory: Differentiating hostile and benevolent sexism. *Journal of Personality and Social Psychology*, 70, 491–512.

Glick, P. & Fiske, S. T. (1997). Hostile and benevolent sexism: Measuring ambivalent sexist attitudes toward women. *Psychology of Women Quarterly*, 21, 119–135.

Glick, P. & Fiske, S. T. (2001). An ambivalent alliance: Hostile and benevolent sexism as complementary justification for gender inequality. *American Psychologist*, 56, 109–118.

Glick, P., Fiske, S. T., Mladinic, A., Saiz, J. L., Abrams, D., Masser, B., et al. (2000). Beyond prejudice as simple antipathy: Hostile and benevolent sexism across cultures. *Journal of Personality and Social Psychology*, 79, 763–775.

Glick, P., Larsen, S., Johnson, C. & Branstiter, H. (2005). Evaluations of sexy women in low- and high-status jobs. *Psychology of Women* Quarterly, 29, 389–395.

Glick, P., Zion, C. & Nelson, C. (1988). What mediates sex discrimination in hiring decisions? *Journal of Personality and Social Psychology*, 55, 178–186.

Halpert, J.A., Wilson, M.L. & Hickman, J. (1993). Pregnancy as a source of bias in performance appraisals. *Journal of Organizational Behavior*, 14, 649–63.

Haslam, N. (2006). Dehumanization: An integrative review. *Personality and Social Psychology Review*, 10, 252–264.

Heflick, N. A., Goldenberg, J. L., Cooper, D. P. & Puvia, E. (2011). From women to objects: Appearance focus, target gender, and perceptions of warmth, morality and competence. *Journal of Experimental Social Psychology*, 47, 572–581.

Heilman, M. E. (1983). Sex bias in work settings: The Lack of Fit model. *Research in Organizational Behavior*, 5, 269–298.

Heilman, M. E. (2001). Description and prescription: How gender stereotypes prevent women's ascent up the organizational ladder. *Journal of Social Issues*, 57, 657–674.

Heilman, M. E., Block, C. J. & Martell, R. F. (1995). Sex stereotypes: Do they influence perceptions of managers? *Journal of Social Behavior and Personality*, 10, 237–252.

Heilman, M. E. & Stopeck, M. H. (1985). Being attractive, advantage or disadvantage? Performance-based evaluations and recommended personnel actions as a function of appearance, sex, and job type. *Organizational Behavior and Human Decision Processes*, 35, 202–215.

Helgeson, V. S. (2005). *The Psychology of Gender* (2nd edn). Upper Saddle River, NJ: Pearson Education.

Herzog, S. & Oreg, S. (2008). Chivalry and the moderating effect of ambivalent sexism: Individual differences in crime seriousness judgments. *Law and Society Review*, 42, 45–74.

Hewstone, M. (1990). The 'ultimate attribution error'? A review of the literature on intergroup causal attribution. *European Journal of Social Psychology*, 20(4), 311–335

Hochschild, A. & Machung, A. (1989). *The Second Shift: Working Parents and the Revolution at Home*. New York: Viking.

Hoffman, C. & Hurst, N. (1990). Gender stereotypes: Perception or rationalization? *Journal of Personality and Social Psychology*, 58, 197–208.

Hoffman, E. (2006). On-the-job sexual harassment: How labels enable men to discriminate through sexual harassment and exclusion. In B. Fleury-Steiner & L.B. Neilsen (eds.), *The New Civil Rights Research: A Constitutive Approach* (pp. 119–156). Farnham, UK: Ashgate.

Holmes, S. (2008). Scandinavian split of sexist ads. *BBC News*. Available at http://news.bbc.co.uk/2/hi/europe/7365722.stm (accessed 26 April 2012).

Inter-Parliamentary Union (2011). *Women in Parliament in 2010: The Year in Perspective*. Geneva, Switzerland: Inter-Parliamentary Union. Available at http://www.ipu.org/pdf/publications/wmnpersp10-e.pdf (accessed 26 April 2012).

Jackman, M. (1994). *The Velvet Glove: Paternalism and Conflict in Gender, Class, and Race Relations*. Berkeley: University of California Press.

Jost, J. T. & Kay, A. C. (2005). Exposure to benevolent sexism and complementary gender stereotypes: Consequences for specific and diffuse forms of system justification. *Journal of Personality and Social Psychology*, 88, 498–509.

Kaiser, C. R., Dyrenforth, P. S. & Hagiwara, N. (2006). Why are attributions to discrimination interpersonally costly? A test of system- and group-justifying motivations. *Personality and Social Psychology Bulletin*, 32(11), 1523–1536.

Kaiser, C. R. & Miller, C. T. (2001). Stop complaining! The social costs of making attributions to discrimination. *Personality and Social Psychology Bulletin*, 27, 254–263.

Karraker, K. H., Vogel, D. A. & Lake, M. A. (1995). Parents' gender-stereotyped perceptions of newborns: The eye of the beholder revisited. *Sex Roles*, 33, 687–701.

Keller, J. (2005). In genes we trust: The biological component of psychological essentialism and its relationship to mechanisms of motivated social cognition. *Journal of Personality and Social Psychology*, 88, 686–702.

Kravdal, Ø. & Rindfuss R. R. (2008). Changing relationships between education and fertility: A study of women and men born 1940 to 1964. *American Sociological Review*, 73, 854–873.

LaFrance, M. & Woodzicka, J. W. (1998). No laughing matter: Women's verbal and nonverbal reactions to sexist humor. In J. K. Swim & C. Stangor (eds.), *Prejudice: The Target's Perspective* (pp. 61–80). San Diego, CA: Academic Press.

Lewin, M. (1984). Psychology measures femininity and masculinity: 2. From '13 gay men' to the instrumental-expressive distinction. In Lewin (ed.), *In the Shadow of the Past: Psychology Portrays the Sexes* (pp. 179–204). New York: Columbia University Press.

Lippa, R. (1998). The nonverbal judgment and display of extraversion, masculinity, femininity, and gender diagnosticity: A lens model analysis. *Journal of Research in Personality*, 32, 80–107.

Lips, H. M. (2000). College students' visions of power and possibility as moderated by gender. *Psychology of Women Quarterly*, 24, 39–43.

Loo, R. & Thorpe, K. (1998). Attitudes toward women's roles in society: A replication after 20 years. *Sex Roles*, 39, 903–912.

McLamb, K. (2003). *Declaration of Kim LcLamb in support of plaintiffs' motion for class certification* (Case no. C-01-2252 MJJ). United States District Court, Northern District of California. Available at http://www.walmartclass.com/staticdata/walmartclass/declarations/McLamb_Kim.htm (accessed 26 April 2012).

Major, B., Feinstein, J. & Crocker, J. (1994). Attributional ambiguity of affirmative action. *Basic and Applied Social Psychology*, 15, 113–141.

Martell, R. F., Lane, D. M. & Emrich, C. (1996). Male–female differences: A computer simulation. *American Psychologist*, 51, 157–158.

Milkie, M. A., Raley, S. B. & Bianchi, S. M. (2009). Taking on the second shift: Time allocations and time pressures of U.S. parents with preschoolers. *Social Forces, 88*, 487–518.

Montañés, P., de Lemus, S., Bohner, G., Megías, J. L., Moya, M. & Garcia-Retamero, R. (2012). Intergenerational transmission of benevolent sexism from mothers to daughters and its relation to daughters' academic performance and goals. *Sex Roles*. doi 10.1007/s11199-011-0116-0

Morgan, R. (1996). *Sisterhood is Global: The Interational Women's Movement Anthology*. New York: The Feminist Press at CUNY.

Moss-Racusin, C. A., Phelan, J. E. & Rudman, L.A. (2010). When men break the gender rules: Status incongruity and backlash against modest men. *Psychology of Men & Masculinity*, 11, 140–151.

Mulligan-Ferry, L., Soares, R., Combopiano, J., Cullen, J. & Riker, L. (2011). *2010 Catalyst Census: Financial Post 500 women senior officers and top earners.* New York: Catalyst. Available at http://www.catalyst.org/publication/467/2010-catalyst-census-financial-post-500-women-senior-officers-and-top-earners (accessed 26 April 2012).

Olian, J. D., Schwab, D. P. & Haberfeld, Y. (1988). The impact of applicant gender compared to qualifications on hiring recommendations: A meta-analysis of experimental studies. *Organizational Behavior and Human Decision Processes,* 41, 180–195.

Pew Research Center (2010). *Men's lives often seen as better. Gender equality universally embraced, but inequalities acknowledged.* Available at http://www.pewglobal.org/2010/07/01/gender-equality/ (accessed 26 April 2012).

Powell, G. N., Butterfield, D. A. & Parent, J. D. (2002). Gender and managerial stereotypes: have the times changed? *Journal of Management*, 28, 177–193.

Rand, M. R. & Robinson, J. E. (2011). *Criminal Victimization in the United States, 2008 – Statistical Tables* (Report NCJ 231173). United States Bureau of Justice Statistics. Available at http://www.bjs.gov/index.cfm?ty=pbdetail&iid=2218 (accessed 26 April 2012).

Ridgeway, C. & Correll, S. (2004). Motherhood as a status characteristic. *The Journal of Social Issues*, 60, 683–700.

Rudman, L. A. (1998). Self-promotion as a risk factor for women: The costs and benefits of counterstereotypical impression management. *Journal of Personality and Social Psychology*, 74, 629–645.

Rudman, L. A. & Borgida, E. (1995). The afterglow of construct accessibility: The behavioral consequences of priming men to view women as sexual objects. *Journal of Experimental Social Psychology*, 31, 493–517.

Rudman, L. A. & Fairchild, K. (2004). Reactions to counterstereotypic behavior: The role of backlash in cultural stereotype maintenance. *Journal of Personality and Social Psychology*, 87, 157–176.

Rudman, L. A. & Glick, P. (1999). Feminized management and backlash toward agentic women: The hidden costs to women of a kinder, gentler image of middle managers. *Journal of Personality and Social Psychology*, 77, 1004–1010.

Russo, N. F. (1979). Overview: Sex roles, fertility, and the motherhood mandate. *Psychology of Women Quarterly*, 4, 7–15.

Ryan, K. M. & Kanjorski, J. (1998). The enjoyment of sexist humor, rape attitudes, and relationship aggression in college students. *Sex Roles*, 38, 743–756.

Sargent, P. (2005). The gendering of men in early childhood education. *Sex Roles*, 52, 251–259.

Silverman, I., Choi, J. & Peters, M. (2007). The hunter-gatherer theory of sex differences in spatial abilities: Data from 40 countries. *Archives of Sexual Behavior*, 36, 261–268.

Spence, J. T. & Hahn, E. D. (1997). The Attitudes Toward Women Scale and attitude change in college students. *Psychology of Women Quarterly*, 21, 17–34.

Spencer, S. J., Steele, C. M. & Quinn, D. M. (1999). Stereotype threat and women's math performance. *Journal of Experimental Social Psychology*, 35, 4–28.

Stangor, C., Lynch, L., Duan, C. & Glass, B. (1992). Categorization of individuals on the basis of multiple social features. *Journal of Personality and Social Psychology*, 62, 207–218.

Steinpreis, R. E., Anders, K. A. & Ritzke, D. (1999). The impact of gender on the review of the curriculum vitae of job applicants and tenure candidates: A national empirical study. *Sex Roles*, 41, 509–528.

Stern, M. & Karraker, M. H. (1989). Sex stereotyping of infants: A review of gender labeling studies. *Sex Roles*, 20, 501–522.

Swim, J. K., Aikin, K. J., Hall, W. S. & Hunter, B. A. (1995). Sexism and racism: Old-fashioned and modern prejudices. *Journal of Personality and Social Psychology*, 68(2), 199–214.

Swim, J. K. & Sanna, L. J. (1996). He's skilled, she's lucky: A meta-analysis of observers' attributions for women's and men's successes and failures. *Personality and Social Psychology Bulletin*, 22, 507–519.

Taylor, P., Morin, R., Cohn, D., Clark, A. & Wang, W. (2008). *A Paradox in Public Attitudes. Men or Women: Who's the Better Leader?* Pew Research Center Social & Demographic Trends Report. Washington DC; Pew Research Center. Available at http://pewsocialtrends.org/files/2010/10/gender-leadership.pdf (accessed 26 April 2012).

Tosi, H. L. & Einbender, S. W. (1985). The effects of the type and amount of information in sex discrimination research: A meta-analysis. *Academy of Management Journal*, 28, 712–723.

Tougas, F., Brown, R., Beaton, A.M. & Joly, S. (1995). Neosexism: Plus ça change, plus c'est pareil. *Personality and Social Psychology Bulletin*, 21, 842–849.

United Nations. (2010). *The World's Women 2010: Trends and Statistics.* New York: United Nations Department of Economic and Social Affairs. Available at: http://unstats.un.org/unsd/demographic/products/Worldswomen/WW_full%20report_BW.pdf (accessed 26 April 2012).

Vaes, J., Paladino, M. & Puvia, E. (2011). Are sexualized women complete human beings? Why men and women dehumanize sexually objectified women. *European Journal of Social Psychology.* doi: 10.1002/ejsp.824.

Vandello, J. A., Bosson, J. K., Cohen, D., Burnaford, R. M. & Weaver, J. R. (2008). Precarious manhood. *Journal of Personality and Social Psychology*, 95, 1325–1339.

Viki, G. T. & Abrams, D. (2002). But she was unfaithful: Benevolent sexism and reactions to rape victims who violate transitional offender role expectations. *Sex Roles*, 47, 289–293.

Viki, G. T., Abrams, D. & Masser, B. (2004). Evaluating stranger and acquaintance rape: The role of benevolent sexism in perpetrator blame and recommended sentence length. *Law and Human Behavior*, 28, 295–303.

Waldfogel, J. (1998). Understanding the 'family gap' in pay for women with children. *Journal of Economic Perspectives*, 12(1), 137–156.

Williams, C. L. (1992). The glass escalator: Hidden advantages for men in the 'female' professions. *Social Problems*, 39(3), 253–267.

Williams, J. E., Satterwhite, R. C. & Best, D. L. (1999). Pancultural gender stereotypes revisited: The Five Factor Model. *Sex Roles*, 40, 513–525.

Wookey, M. L., Graves, N. A. & Butler, J. C. (2009). Effects of a sexy appearance on perceived competence of women. *The Journal of Social Psychology*, 149, 116–118.

Yamawaki, N. (2007). Rape perception and the function of ambivalent sexism and gender-role traditionality. *Journal of Interpersonal Violence*, 22, 1–18.

Note

1. In fact, status, more than gender, provokes inferences about personality traits that are stereotypically linked to the genders. Women of high status are described and describe themselves as more instrumental, less submissive and less expressive than women of low status; the reverse is true for men (Gerber, 2009).

4

Towards an Understanding of Immigration as a Defining Feature of the Twenty-first Century

Leah K. Hamilton, Stelian Medianu and Victoria M. Esses[1]

● ●

Migration is considered a defining feature of the twenty-first century. Evidence suggests that there are more people living outside of their country of birth than at any other point in history, and the number of international migrants is increasing at an annual rate of approximately 3 per cent (International Organization for Migration, 2011; United Nations, Department of Economic and Social Affairs, Population Division, 2009).

Increased mobility is the result of many global trends. International migration has been fuelled by growing disparities in employment rates, levels of income and social well-being, both within and between countries. In addition, demographic trends in developed countries, such as low fertility rates coupled with ageing populations, have led to an increased reliance on immigrants to meet current and future labour force needs. Immigration is also affected by environmental catastrophes and civil unrest (Castles, 2000; International Organization for Migration, 2011; United Nations High Commissioner for Refugees, 2011a). The scope of immigration is expected to increase throughout the twenty-first century (Castles, 2000), resulting in an estimated 230 million people living outside their country of birth by 2050 (United Nations, Department of Economic and Social Affairs, Population Division, 2009).

In addition to changing in scope, worldwide migration has changed as a result of evolving goals, policies and integration strategies of destination countries. For instance, countries that once had policies restricting 'non-white' immigration (e.g. Australia's Immigration Restriction Act, Canada's Chinese Head Tax) now receive a large proportion of their immigrants from the very countries they once tried to restrict (e.g. China). As such, immigrants to Western countries represent diverse ethnicities, cultures, languages and religions.

A second major area of policy change has been in the desired character-istics of potential immigrants. Historically, developed countries benefited from the immigration of low-skilled workers who helped to create new infrastructure (Martinez-Herrera, 2008). Over the past few decades, how-ever, immigration policies in advanced economies have shifted toward attracting 'the best and the brightest'. These highly skilled workers are expected to contribute to national economies by filling labour and skills shortages, ultimately helping nations position themselves in an economy that has become increasingly global and knowledge-based.

At the same time as Western nations seek to increase immigration by skilled workers, many attempt to reduce immigration by individu-als who are 'undocumented' or 'unauthorized'. The perceived problem of undocumented immigration has led host nations to develop a variety of procedures aimed at tightening border controls and preventing undocu-mented immigrants from remaining in the country (Buschschluter, 2009; Homeland Security, 2006). In Arizona, a controversial state immigration bill (Senate Bill 1070) was passed in April 2010. It authorizes police officers to detain an individual when they have 'reasonable suspicion' that the person is 'unlawfully present in the United States' (State of Arizona, 2010). This law has generated intense debate between pro-ponents who argue that such measures are needed to combat illegal immigration, and opponents who believe that it infringes on civil liberties and will result in racial profiling (Pew Research Center Publications, 2010b).

In addition to attempting to control 'undocumented' migration, many nations struggle to control the inflow of refugees and asylum seekers. According to the United Nations High Commissioner for Refugees (2011b), there are currently more than ten million refugees worldwide, with many seeking resettlement opportunities. The international community has for-malized its commitment to helping refugees by signing the 1951 Geneva

Refugee Convention or its 1967 Protocol (United Nations High Commissioner for Refugees, 2008). Although many Western nations have committed to protecting refugees, in reality refugee claimants are often viewed with hostility. Evidence suggests that beliefs that refugee claimants are fraudulent are widespread (Esses et al., 2008). Moreover, refugees are often dehumanized, which can lead members of host societies to feel contempt towards them, rather than the compassion one might otherwise expect (Esses et al., 2008).

In addition to challenges associated with attempting to 'control' immigration, many countries have experienced challenges associated with integrating even desirable immigrants into the political, economic and cultural fabrics of their society. In particular, despite being selected for immigration via policies designed to attract skilled workers, many highly skilled immigrants find themselves unemployed or underemployed, working in jobs that do not fully utilize their skills (Gilmore, 2009; Martinez-Herrera, 2008). Immigrants have also encountered challenges with additional components of integration, such as obtaining citizenship. In Germany, a major immigrant-receiving country, official German policies have not fostered the integration of immigrants (Zick et al., 2001). For instance, although Germany recently changed its citizenship laws to make citizenship acquisition somewhat easier, it is still the case that fewer than 25 per cent of eligible immigrants from Turkey and the former Yugoslavia – sizeable immigrant groups that are not part of the European Union – have become German citizens (Constant, Gataullina & Zimmerman, 2007). Cross-national examinations of orientations towards immigration and acculturation have demonstrated that, compared with host country members in other nations, the majority of Germans do not support the integration of immigrants (Berry, 1998). Ultimately, Germany has been considered a country in which acculturation processes occur in a nonsupportive social context (Zick et al., 2001).

Germany is not the only country in which immigrants are not always viewed favourably by members of the host society. In fact, evidence suggests that immigration is often met with resistance, while immigrants themselves face hostility and discrimination. Recently, Gallup International Polls demonstrated that the majority of American and British residents (58 per cent and 60 per cent respectively) indicated they would like to see immigration levels to their country decrease (Newport, 2006). Similarly, a recent public opinion poll in the United States indicated that 50 per cent of Americans view immigrants as a burden because they take jobs, housing, and require health care (Pew Research Center Publications, 2010a).

Not surprisingly, the consequences of experiencing prejudice or discrimination are extremely negative for immigrants. For example, perceiving oneself as a target of prejudice or discrimination is a major stressor

(Dion, 2002) and is associated with lower psychological well-being (Jasinskaja-Lahti, Liebkind & Solheim, 2009) and acculturative stress symptoms (Jasinskaja-Lahti, Liebkind & Perhoniemi, 2006). In addition, prejudice and discrimination can result in poor labour-market outcomes for immigrants (Esses, Dietz & Bhardwaj, 2006), and difficulty in securing affordable and suitable housing (Dion, 2001).

While attitudes towards immigrants are important, so too are immigrants' attitudes towards members of the host society. For instance, immigrants who perceive their host country favourably are likely to have positive expectations regarding the warmth of the welcome they will receive from the host society. Together, both groups' attitudes will affect a nation's social climate, the extent to which immigrants are effectively integrated and can contribute to society, and the collective vision of national identity (Esses, Dovidio & Hodson, 2002). Consequently, managing migration effectively involves balancing the needs of both immigrants and members of the host country.

Psychological contributions to understanding challenges associated with immigrants and immigration

Psychological theories and research findings have much to contribute to our understanding of the complex opportunities and challenges associated with immigration. Two areas of research in psychology – acculturation and intergroup relations (Berry, 1990, 2001) – represent the discipline's largest contributions to the study of immigrants and immigration.

Acculturation

According to Redfield, Linton and Herskovits (1936, pp. 149), acculturation refers to 'those phenomena which result when groups of individuals having different cultures come into continuous first-hand contact, with subsequent changes in the original culture patterns of either or both groups'. Acculturation can involve changes at both the group level and individual level. As Berry (1990) explains, at the group level, acculturation can involve changes in the economic, social and/or political structure of the groups. At the individual level, acculturation can involve changes in terms of the identity, values, attitudes and behaviours of the individual. Thus, to understand acculturation and its societal implications, one needs to investigate changes at both group and individual levels (Sam, 2006).

According to Berry's (2003) framework, acculturation at the group level depends on the specific features of the society of origin of immigrants (e.g. political situation, economic conditions, demographic factors) as well as on the specific features of the society of settlement (e.g. immigration history, immigration policy, attitudes towards immigration, social support). At the individual level, acculturation depends on factors such as the demographic (e.g. age, gender), cultural (e.g. language, religion), economic (e.g. status), personal (e.g. health, prior knowledge), migration motivation (e.g. push versus pull) and expectations (e.g. excessive versus realistic) of immigrants. At the individual level, acculturation also depends on the strategies that immigrants choose. Berry suggests that there are two main issues that underlie this choice. The first is the extent to which individuals want to maintain their heritage identity and culture, and the second is the extent to which individuals desire to have contact with individuals who do not share their heritage identity and culture (that is, members of the host society). Individuals' preferences regarding these issues result in four acculturation strategies: assimilation, integration, separation and marginalization (Berry, 1997).

When immigrants do not seek relationships with their own cultural group but seek relationships with the host society, the acculturation strategy adopted is one of *assimilation.* On the other hand, when immigrants seek relationships with their own cultural group but do not seek relationships with the host society, the acculturation strategy adopted is one of *separation.* When immigrants are interested in maintaining relationships with both their own cultural group and the host society, the acculturation strategy adopted is one of *integration.* Finally, when immigrants are not interested in or able to maintain relationships with either their own cultural group or the host society, the acculturation strategy adopted is one of *marginalization* (Sam, 2006).

It is important to note that the above strategies assume that immigrants are free to choose how they relate to the host society and to their own cultural group. However, this is not always the case. To illustrate, consider what conditions must exist for immigrants to be able to adopt the *integration* strategy. First, immigrants must be willing to adopt the values of the host society. Second, the host society must be willing to organize its institutions so that they meet the needs of various immigrant groups. For this to occur, the host society needs to build a climate promoting cultural diversity, low levels of prejudice, and a sense of attachment to the larger society from all cultural groups (Sam, 2006).

Numerous studies have been conducted to investigate immigrants' relative preference for the four acculturation strategies. These studies have been conducted in a variety of countries and have examined relative preferences among many different acculturating groups, including Portuguese, Hungarians and Koreans in Canada (Berry et al., 1989) and Asian Indian immigrants in the United States (Berry & Krishnan, 1992). Results have revealed that, generally speaking, integration is the most preferred mode of acculturation, and marginalization is the least preferred. Importantly, evidence from multiple studies suggests that the acculturation strategy adopted by individuals is predictive of their adaptation. Of note, integration is associated with the lowest levels of acculturative stress (Berry et al., 1987) and with positive psychological and sociocultural adaptation (Liebkind, 2001); marginalization is associated with the highest level of acculturative stress (Berry et al., 1987) and is least adaptive.

As an extension of Berry's model of acculturation, Bourhis et al. (1997) incorporate in their interactive acculturation model (IAM) not only the acculturation orientation of the immigrant group, but also the acculturation orientation of the host society. According to Bourhis and colleagues, the two main questions facing host community members are the following: 1) Do you find it acceptable that immigrants maintain their cultural heritage? and 2) Do you accept that immigrants adopt the culture of your host community? If host community members answer affirmative to both these questions, the acculturation orientation adopted by host community members is one of *integration*. The integration orientation suggests that members of the host society endorse cultural pluralism that supports a multicultural society. If host community members do not want immigrants to adopt the host culture, but they do want them to maintain their heritage culture, the acculturation orientation adopted by host community members is one of *segregation*. The segregation orientation suggests that members of the host society do not want contact with immigrants. Rather, they may favour separate ethnic enclaves and question the rightful status of immigrants in the host society. If host community members want immigrants to adopt the host culture and do not want immigrants to maintain their heritage culture, the acculturation orientation adopted by host community members is one of *assimilation*. The assimilation orientation suggests that members of the host society will be more likely to consider fully assimilated immigrants as rightful members of the host society, compared with immigrants who are not fully assimilated. If host community members do not want immigrants to adopt the host culture, and they do not want them to maintain their heritage culture, the acculturation orientation adopted by host community members is either one of *exclusion* or *individualism*. The exclusionist orientation reflects the belief that immigration and immigrants are dangerous to the nation and that immigration should be prevented; the individualism orientation reflects the belief that immigrants are individuals and should be treated on an individual basis, based on their personal characteristics (Bourhis et al., 1997). Host community members who endorse individualism define themselves and others as individuals, rather than through their group membership (e.g. as immigrants or members of the host community).

According to Bourhis et al. (1997), the acculturation orientations of immigrant groups must be considered in conjunction with the acculturation orientations of host community members. When the acculturation orientation of an immigrant group matches the orientation of the host community, the groups are considered to be concordant. In contrast, when the acculturation orientation of an immigrant group does not match (or only partially matches) the orientation of the host community, the groups are considered to be discordant. Bourhis et al. (1997) argue that discordant orientations result in problematic or conflictual relational outcomes, including communication breakdowns, discriminatory behaviours, and acculturative stress among members of the immigrant group.

While research suggests that the majority of host community members endorse the more welcoming integrationism and individualism orientations towards immigrants (Bourhis, Barrette, El-Geledi & Schmidt, 2009; Bourhis, Montaruli, El-Geledi, Harvey & Barrette, 2010), variation in acculturation orientations exist not only among host community members but also within host community members (Bourhis & Dayan, 2004; Montreuil & Bourhis, 2004). That is, evidence suggests that members of host communities may endorse different acculturation orientations towards different immigrant groups within their community (e.g. valued versus devalued immigrants; Bourhis et al., 2010; Montreuil & Bourhis, 2004).

What accounts for individual differences in host members' acculturation preferences? We turn now to an examination of research that helps us to understand the factors that shape host community members' perceptions of immigrants and immigration.

Perceptions of immigrants by members of the host society

Although many nations are committed to supporting the full integration of immigrants in society, public attitudes towards immigrants and immigration are not uniformly positive either between or within nations. In fact, many major immigrant-receiving nations are home to groups devoted to anti-immigration activism (e.g. National Front Australia, Immigration Watch Canada). Most anti-immigration groups espouse the view that immigrants (particularly non-white immigrants) are responsible for many of society's woes, from poverty and crime to environmental degradation (Southern Poverty Law Center, 2011).

Although anti-immigration groups often have extreme views, research suggests that negative attitudes towards immigrants are not limited to anti-immigration organizations (Esses, Hodson & Dovidio, 2003). In fact, negative sentiments and such arguments against immigration are often evident in public discourse on immigration, and colour many media depictions of immigrants (Chavez, 2001), though often in less extreme forms.

The role of national identity

How we construe national identity and national attachment plays an important role in determining attitudes towards immigrants and immigration. In terms of construal, evidence suggests that people's beliefs differ about the basis of national identity. As also discussed by Golec de Zavala and Schatz (Chapter 8, this volume), some individuals hold nativist perceptions of national identity, believing that national identity stems from being born in a particular country (or having lived there for an extended period of time) and from practising the dominant religion in that country (Jones, 1997). Nativist identity is closely aligned with ethnic identity, which involves defining the national group in terms of ethnicity (Smith, 2001). In contrast, others hold civic/cultural perceptions of national identity, believing that national identity is based on a personal commitment to a country's laws and institutions, as well as feeling part of that country's national group.

The distinction between nativist/ethnic and civic/cultural beliefs about national identity is important because, by definition, the nativist/ethnic construal of national identity excludes most immigrants groups, while this is not the case for the civic/cultural construal. In addition, research has demonstrated that, compared with individuals who hold civic/cultural perceptions of national identity, those who hold nativist perceptions of national identity have less favourable attitudes towards immigrants and are more likely to support reduced levels of immigration (Jones, 1997). Similarly, among individuals who endorse an ethnic construal of national identity, national identity is significantly associated with negative feelings towards asylum seekers (Pehrson & Green, 2010; Study 1a).

In addition to construal of national identity, forms of attachment to one's nation also influence immigration attitudes. In particular, individuals who are higher in nationalism – believing that their nation is superior to all others – hold more negative attitudes towards immigrants and immigration. In contrast, individuals who are higher in patriotism – expressing pride and love for their nation – do not hold such attitudes (Esses et al., 2005a; see also Golec de Zavala & Schatz, Chapter 8, this volume).

Recently, research has shown that perceived outgroup threat may play an important role in the relation between national identification –

defined as the importance attached to one's national group membership – and attitudes towards immigrants. Verkuyten (2009) found that stronger national identification predicted reduced support for multiculturalism, more negative attitudes towards Muslims, and less support for equal rights for immigrants and ethnic minority groups. All of these effects were mediated by perceived threat from these groups. Thus, the extent to which host community members are attached to their national group membership may influence perceptions of outgroup threat, which in turn may affect how they respond to immigrants and immigration.

Perceptions of intergroup threat and competition

Most immigration policies are designed to promote the successful integration of immigrants into society. By emphasizing financial resources and familial support, many immigration policies are designed to ensure the economic success of immigrants while benefiting the larger society. Despite these efforts to maximize the economic success of both immigrants and their host society, evidence suggests that negative attitudes towards immigrants and immigration at times stem from the belief that immigrants compete with non-immigrants for important resources such as jobs (e.g. see Esses et al., 2005b; Stephan & Stephan, 2000). Importantly, evidence suggests that these competition beliefs may not be justified. Murray, Batalove & Fix from the Migration Policy Institute (2006) reviewed the divergent findings regarding the 'competition question' in the United States, describing how the impact of immigration on native workers' employment outcomes is contested. Some researchers (e.g. Borjas, 2003) argue that immigrants depress native workers' wages, while others (e.g. Peri, 2006) find that immigrants actually raise wages for native workers. According to Murray and colleagues, the mixed findings regarding the 'competition question' are the result of different methodological approaches used to answer different research questions. Ultimately, regardless of whether they are grounded in reality, competition beliefs are important because they are at the root of prejudice towards immigrants. Stephan and Stephan (2000), in their integrated threat theory of prejudice, propose that four types of intergroup threat form the bases of prejudice: realistic threats (e.g. threats to one's economic/political power), symbolic threats (e.g. perceived differences in values), negative stereotypes (e.g. believing that outgroup members are lazy), and intergroup anxiety (e.g. feeling personally threatened by intergroup interactions (for a detailed discussion see Stephan, this volume). In several studies, Stephan and colleagues have found that these four types of threat can lead to prejudice against a variety of immigrant groups (Stephan et al., 2005).

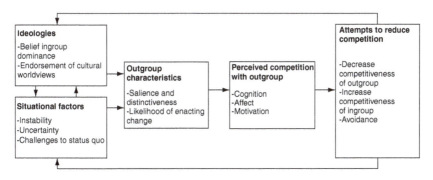

Figure 4.1   Unified instrumental model of group conflict.
Source: Esses et al., 2005b.

Relatedly, Esses and colleagues have proposed and tested the Unified Instrumental Model of Group Conflict (Esses et al., 2005b). This model provides a useful framework for understanding a variety of intergroup relations, including relations between immigrants and members of host countries.

As shown in Figure 4.1, the presence of certain ideologies and situational factors may predispose individuals to perceive intergroup competition with immigrants. Both belief systems that foster group dominance and those that foster cultural worldviews that provide meaning to people's lives may lead to chronic perceptions of group competition. However, the resources seen to be at risk may differ. Belief systems that foster group dominance may lead to perceived competition over relatively tangible resources such as access to jobs and political power.

Dominant group members are likely to be high in social dominance orientation (SDO), an ideology characterized by a belief ingroup inequality and support for the dominant groups' privileged position in society (Sidanius & Pratto, 1999; see also Cohrs & Kessler, this volume; Federico, this volume). Individuals who are higher in SDO are likely to believe that immigration decreases the number of jobs available for non-immigrants, suggesting that they perceive competition with immigrants over jobs (Esses, Hodson & Dovidio, 2003). Interestingly, individuals who are higher in SDO also perceive zero-sum competition for value dominance (Esses, Hodson & Dovidio, 2003). In other words, they tend to view immigrants' values as incompatible with their own, and as a threat to the moral fabric of society.

It is likely that the foundation of zero-sum beliefs about symbolic factors rests on cultural worldviews that provide meaning to people's lives. Because these worldviews are often absolute in nature, they may be threatened by other worldviews seen as competing for obtaining 'truth'. Individuals who are higher in right-wing authoritarianism and religious fundamentalism (Altemeyer, 1996; Altemeyer & Hunsberger, 1992) have a tendency to strongly endorse their cultural worldviews and to perceive outgroups as threatening their values. Hence, they are likely to express prejudice and discrimination towards these outgroups, including immigrants (Altemeyer & Hunsberger, 1992; Jackson & Esses, 1997).

While a variety of ideologies make certain people more likely to harbour chronic perceptions of group competition, situational factors also play a role in promoting perceived competition and threat. Social instability and perceived challenges to the status quo are two situational factors that heighten perceived competition between groups. For instance, events such as an economic recession or demands by immigrants for equal rights may increase perceptions of competition with immigrants for both tangible resources (e.g. jobs) and more symbolic factors such as values. Early support for this proposition was found in a laboratory experiment by Esses and colleagues (1998). In this study, participants read an editorial that either emphasized immigrants' success in a difficult job market or discussed immigrants in general without mentioning this issue. As predicted by the Unified Instrumental Model of Group Conflict, participants who read the editorial highlighting immigrants' success in a difficult job market subsequently expressed less favourable attitudes towards new immigrants, were more likely to endorse restrictive immigration policies, and were less likely to support assistance that would empower immigrants (Esses, Jackson & Armstrong, 1998; Jackson & Esses, 2000).

Ideologies and situational factors that foster perceived group competition may be mutually reinforcing (see Figure 4.1). Individuals who have a tendency to see the world in zero-sum terms (e.g. those higher in SDO) may be particularly sensitive to situational factors that promote perceptions of group competition (e.g. a difficult job market), and these situations may reinforce people's existing ideologies.

While ideologies and situational factors may be mutually reinforcing in initiating the process of perceiving group competition and conflict, in order for perceptions of group competition to arise, a relevant outgroup must be available. Groups with certain characteristics are at an increased risk of being perceived as a source of competition. For instance, groups that are large (or growing), and are distinct from the ingroup in appearance (e.g. Muslims, particularly those who appear visibly distinct) or behaviour are likely to be seen as competitors. Importantly, however, outgroups – in order to be seen as true competitiors – must be seen as threatening the status quo and, thus, the dominant group's position in society.

In the Unified Instrumental Model of Group Conflict, the tendency to perceive group competition due to ideologies and situational factors,

combined with the ready availability of a relevant outgroup, result in perceived competition with that outgroup. This perceived competition leads
people to attempt to reduce group competition. These actions take many
forms that reflect *prejudice* and *discrimination*. For instance, outgroup derogation and discrimination serve to reduce the outgroup's competitiveness
via various negative attitudes and attributions about outgroup members that ultimately establish the outgroup's lack of worth. Such efforts
may involve increased endorsement of stereotypes about the outgroup, or
more extreme measures, including overt discrimination against the outgroup, and opposition to policies that may alter the status quo (Jackson &
Esses, 2000; Pratto & Lemieux, 2001). For example, Jackson and Esses
(2000) found that perceptions of economic competition with immigrants
led to reduced support for policies that empower immigrants. *Ingroup*
favouritism may operate in conjunction with, or instead of, such forms
of outgroup derogation. This favouritism may involve expressing attitudes that enhance the status of the ingroup and justify its entitlement to
both the tangible and symbolic resources at stake (Jost, Burgess & Mosso,
2001). The third strategy that groups may use to reduce group competition
involves *avoidance*. In extreme cases, the outgroup may be denied access to
the ingroup's territory. For instance, Esses and colleagues (2003) found that
perceptions of competition with immigrants for both tangible and symbolic
resources resulted in greater support for restrictive immigration policies.

Finally, as depicted by the outer arrows in Figure 4.1, the Unified Instrumental Model of Group Conflict is cyclical. The attempts to reduce group
competition may feed back to the ideologies and situational factors that
initially fostered the competition. For instance, derogating immigrants in
order to confirm their lack of worth may strengthen ideologies such as SDO,
further perpetuating perceptions of competition. In contrast, changes to
situational factors (e.g. as a result of successful attempts to reduce competition) may reduce uncertainty and challenges to the status quo, thereby
reducing the situational factors that initially promoted group competition.

While the majority of research on perceptions of immigrants has been
examined from the perspective of majority group members in a host society, there is some evidence to suggest that the perceptions of non-majority
group members do not differ from those of majority group members.
In laboratory experiments conducted by Esses and colleagues (e.g. Esses
et al., 2008), findings do not change when non-majority group members
are included in the analyses. Likewise, findings from field studies suggest
that non-majority group members perceive intergroup competition with
other non-majority groups. Bobo and Hutchings (1996) conducted a field
study using a heterogeneous sample of whites, African-Americans, Asian-
Americans and Latinos in Los Angeles. In their examination of perceptions

of zero-sum competition for scarce resources, Bobo and Hutchings found that 'significant numbers of people of all racial backgrounds see group relations in zero-sum terms' (Bobo & Hutchings, 1996, p. 958).

As described in the Unified Instrumental Model of Group Conflict, immigrant groups that are perceived as highly distinct from the ingroup are at an increased likelihood of being viewed as sources of competition and threat. One such group is refugees, who are at times portrayed as a source of disease, as competitors for scarce resources such as health care and social assistance, and as threats to traditional values. This may result in dehumanization, which has been described as 'the worst kind of prejudice' (Harris & Fiske, 2006, p. 848).

Dehumanization

Despite Western nations' stated commitment to the protection of refugees, individuals seeking entry into Western countries as asylum seekers are often viewed with hostility and contempt, and are perceived as not deserving of assistance (Human Rights Watch, 2001). In recent years, the dominant discourse surrounding refugee claimants has become increasingly dehumanizing, with the media and political elites often promoting such perceptions (El Refaie, 2001; Leach, 2003). For example, refugees are often portrayed in metaphorical terms, described as 'waves of refugees' who threaten to flood Western countries in an attempt to 'sponge off the welfare system' (Ferguson, 1999; as cited in Lee, 2000, p. 55). Refugees are often portrayed as groups of criminals, lacking in morals, and as 'cockroaches' or 'parasites'. In this discourse, the refugee danger is imminent and of dramatic proportions. According to this discourse, Western countries need to arm themselves with more stringent refugee legislation to keep the refugee hordes from invading.

By understanding the psychological concept of *dehumanization*, we may gain insight into determinants of resistance to policies designed to assist refugees. Dehumanization involves the denial of full humanness to others, and their exclusion from the human species (for example, Bar-Tal, 2000; Haslam, 2006). In an integrative review of dehumanization, Haslam (2006) suggests that an important way in which others may be denied full humanness is in an animalistic sense in which they are seen as not having risen above their animal origins; that is, as less than human. Further, Haslam suggests that this dehumanization is characterized by a perception that the dehumanized lack such characteristics as refinement, morality, self-control and cognitive sophistication.

Attempts to assess dehumanization have focused on several of these specific dimensions. Leyens and colleagues (Delgado et al., 2009; Leyens et al., 2000) suggest that one way of dehumanizing (in their terms, infrahumanizing) outgroups is to deny that they experience complex, secondary emotions. That is, the dehumanized may experience primary emotions (e.g. pleasure, fear), just as animals may, but not the secondary emotions generally attributed only to humans (e.g. hope, remorse). This infrahumanization predicts rejection of Muslim immigrants in Europe (Leyens et al., 2007).

According to Schwartz and Struch (1989), people infer a group's humanity by looking at the extent to which their values reflect that they have 'transcended their basic animal nature and developed their human sensitivities and moral sensibilities' (Schwartz & Struch, 1989, p. 155). 'Prosocial' values (e.g. equality, helpfulness, forgiveness) are such an example, because they 'reflect a conscious desire to promote the welfare of others' (Schwartz & Struch, 1989, p. 155). If people perceive that a group lacks prosocial values, then they will judge that group to be less human and thus less worthy of humane treatment. Consequently, to assess dehumanization, Schwartz and his colleagues have utilized measures of the perceived values of a group (Schwartz, Struch & Bilsky, 1990; Struch & Schwartz, 1989).

Esses and colleagues recently examined the dehumanization of refugees along this moral dimension (Esses et al., 2008). In addition to assessing dehumanization using the value attributions suggested by Schwartz and colleagues (1990), they included an assessment of the *barbarian/enemy image* (Alexander, Brewer & Herrmann, 1999), which centrally includes perceptions of a group as immoral. They also developed a new measure to assess the extent to which refugees are seen as violating procedures and cheating the system, which is a view that is prevalent in the media (e.g. Francis, 2001; see also Louis et al., 2007). The three measures were highly intercorrelated, and predicted emotions towards refugees and support for exclusion of refugees. Importantly, dehumanization was demonstrated to be distinct from overall negative attitudes towards refugees (Esses et al., 2008).

In a recent study, Esses, Medianu, and Lawson (2010) further examined the animalistic component of dehumanization. Using a sequential priming task, their study revealed that participants implicitly dehumanized refugees by associating them with animals more than with humans. These results suggest that the media's use of animalistic metaphors to refer to refugees may be harmful, finding their way into our system of cognitive beliefs, emotions and perhaps even behavioural propensities.

An important issue in theorizing on dehumanization is understanding why some individuals dehumanize members of other groups, particularly low-status, seemingly victimized groups, such as refugees. One possibility may be that people dehumanize other groups because they want to protect their privileged positions and keep other groups, such as refugees, in their place. By perceiving refugees as not completely part of the human ingroup, individuals may justify the status quo, believing that refugees deserve their negative outcomes (Opotow, 1995; Schwartz & Struch, 1989). As a result, existing systems and the status quo are maintained and perpetuated (Jost & Hunyady 2002). Based on this reasoning, we would expect that social dominance orientation (SDO) would be a strong predictor of the dehumanization of refugees. Initial research on the dehumanization of refugees on moral dimensions has demonstrated that higher SDO individuals are indeed especially likely to dehumanize refugees (Esses et al., 2008; see also Louis et al., 2007).

The dehumanization of refugees may lead to specific negative emotional reactions to members of the group. In particular, as summarized by Haslam (2006), dehumanization may lead to contempt and lack of admiration for a group. Similarly, research on the *stereotype content model* indicates that groups that are dehumanized through perceptions that they are low in competence and warmth elicit feelings of contempt, as well as some pity (Fiske et al., 2002; Harris & Fiske, 2006). We would expect, then, that to the extent that refugees are dehumanized, they will elicit feelings of contempt and lack of admiration. Empirical findings are consistent with this prediction (Esses et al., 2008; see also Verkuyten, 2004).

One central goal of dehumanization research is to determine why the needs and rights of refugees are often denied, and why individuals often want to exclude refugees from their nation. Evidence suggests that there has been growing hostility and intolerance towards refugees in countries of refuge (Office for Democratic Institutions and Human Rights, 2009). Dehumanization may be a key determinant in the legitimization of further victimization (e.g., Bar-Tal, 2000; Haslam, 2006; Opotow, 1995).

The role of the media

The media play a large role in framing public policies and discourse about immigrants and immigration. Yet in addition to disseminating policy messages, the media also construct and promote their own positions on these issues. Thus, the media are not only a reflection of public opinion; they also *shape* public opinion (Chavez, 2001). To illustrate, consider how immigration has been portrayed in two popular American magazines. As Chavez (2001) explains, in July 1976, *Time* magazine celebrated the United States' bicentennial birthday. The cover of the magazine displayed the text: 'The Promised Land', in bold letters, printed in red, white and blue. This text 'formed a protective semicircle above the text "America's

New Immigrants"' (Chavez, 2001, p. 1). The magazine itself contained images of immigrants from various periods in US history and from different countries. Thus, *Time*'s July 1976 issue portrayed immigration in a positive light, as a central part of American identity and history (Chavez, 2001).

In contrast, in October 1994, *The Nation* magazine portrayed immigration in a very different light. As described by Chavez (2001), the cover of the magazine displayed the following text: 'The Immigration Wars'. The central image showed a multitude of people moving along the western border of the United States, clearly signifying the mass movement of immigrants or refugees. The image also showed the Statue of Liberty and, right above it, a leashed dog barking aggressively as if protecting the United States from the immigrant invasion. The content of the magazine further reinforced these negative portrayals of immigration, with a sense of alarm regarding the potentially negative effects of immigration on the United States (Chavez, 2001).

To date, the strongest evidence supporting the causal link between media exposure and prejudice against immigrants comes from studies using experimental designs. In one such study, Esses et al. (2008) examined the role of the media in promoting the dehumanization of refugees. Specifically, they examined whether or not media depictions of refugees as immoral individuals who attempt to cheat the system cause negative emotional reactions to refugees (e.g. contempt) and unfavourable evaluations of refugees and current refugee policy. In this study, participants were randomly assigned to one of two conditions. In the experimental condition, participants read a real editorial that had appeared in a Canadian newspaper: it described Canada's refugee programme as being very costly, and dehumanized refugees by portraying them as immoral cheaters who do not follow fair procedures (either because they are smuggled in to Canada or because they jump the queue). In the control condition, the editorial was adapted so that it described Canada's refugee programme as very costly but it did not dehumanize refugees. Compared with participants who read the control condition editorial, those who read the dehumanizing editorial expressed more contempt and less admiration for refugees. In addition, participants who read the dehumanizing editorial expressed more negative attitudes towards refugees and towards Canada's refugee policy. Mediational analyses suggested that contempt and lack of admiration mediated the effect of the dehumanizing editorial on attitudes towards refugees and refugee policy. Thus, results demonstrated that, by dehumanizing refugees, the media can influence the public's attitudes towards the group, as well as their support for relevant policies.

Evidence supporting the link between the media and prejudice and discrimination against immigrants has also been found outside of the laboratory. As Zick and colleagues (2001) outline, when violence against immigrants erupted in Germany in the early 1990s, nearly all of the violent outbursts were reported in the media (e.g. in Hoyerswerda in September 1991, Rockstock in August 1992, Solingen in May 1993). Each media report was followed by higher rates of registered crimes against immigrants in the subsequent month (Zick et al., 2001). Thus, it appears that the media not only shape public attitudes, but also have the power to shape behaviour.

How exactly do the media influence public attitudes and behaviour? One possibility may be that prejudice and stereotyping are shaped by social influence mechanisms. That is, people change their attitudes and stereotypes based on what they think the consensus is about those attitudes and stereotypes (Stangor, Sechrist & Jost, 2001). Pedersen and colleagues (2008), in their study on beliefs about consensus as they relate to attitudes towards indigenous Australians and asylum seekers, found that individuals greatly overestimated community support for their views on both groups. Furthermore, as individuals' attitudes towards these groups became increasingly negative, their estimates of consensus regarding this position became progressively higher. For instance, while individuals who held very positive attitudes towards asylum seekers overestimated community support for their position by 33.7 per cent, those with very negative attitudes overestimated community support for their position by 80.7 per cent (Pedersen, Griffiths & Watt, 2008).

Pedersen and colleagues (2008) posit that the tendency for prejudiced people to exaggerate perceptions of consensus may stem from contact with the media. As Watt and Larkin (2010) explain, the media constantly bombard us with other people's opinions, thus adding to normative information about public attitudes. For instance, if the media convey that public attitudes towards immigrants are negative, people who see these messages may come to believe that the majority of host country members are prejudiced against immigrants. For individuals who are already prejudiced, such representations would lead to the belief that the majority of host country members also hold prejudiced attitudes. In contrast, individuals who are nonprejudiced would feel that their more positive attitudes towards immigrants are not shared by the majority.

The *false consensus effect* has important practical implications for immigrants. As Watt and Larkin (2010) outline, if individuals who hold negative attitudes towards immigrants and immigration believe that their attitudes are shared by the majority of host community members, this illusion of consensus could make them more willing to express their opinions, less likely to compromise, and ultimately more willing to act on their beliefs.

How can we foster more positive relations between immigrants and members of host societies?

As we have illustrated, the extent to which immigrants are viewed favourably by members of host societies, and ultimately integrate effectively into society, depends on the interplay between a number of complex psychological processes. In addition to informing our understanding of these processes, the psychological literature also provides insight into strategies we can use to optimize intergroup relations between immigrants and members of the societies in which they have chosen to settle.

Optimizing acculturation

It has been noted that Bourhis' interactive acculturation model (IAM) has contributed to our understanding of acculturation in large part due to its emphasis on the intergroup nature of the acculturation process (Liebkind, 2001). In particular, Bourhis and colleagues have illustrated the importance of host community members' acculturation orientations in determining whether or not social relations between immigrants and members of the host community are harmonious.

In several studies, Bourhis and colleagues have demonstrated that endorsement of the integrationist and individualist acculturation orientations is associated with the most harmonious intergroup relations between immigrants and host community members. Consider the results of one study conducted among college students in Montreal, Quebec. As Montreuil and Bourhis (2004) explain, immigrants in Montreal can acculturate to the Francophone majority host community, and/or to the Anglophone minority community. When examining the acculturation orientations of members of the host society, Bourhis found that the endorsement of acculturation orientations was similar among both Francophones and Anglophones; both groups strongly endorsed the integrationist and individualist acculturation orientations. However, Anglophones endorsed these orientations more strongly than did Francophones. The acculturation orientations endorsed by Francophone and Anglophone host community members affected the extent to which immigrants felt welcomed in their host community. Immigrants who were attending English language colleges and acculturating into the Anglophone community felt much more welcome than did those who were attending French language colleges and acculturating into the Francophone community. Likewise, immigrants desired closer relations with Anglophones than with Francophones. Given the impact that host community members' acculturation orientations have on acculturation processes, policy makers would do well to promote integrationist and individualist acculturation orientations among host community members, perhaps via public discourse on multiculturalism and cultural diversity, as discussed below.

Improving perceptions of immigrants by members of the host society

Psychologists have a fairly good understanding of the bases of negative attitudes towards immigrants and immigration. Given that we are aware of many of the determinants of these attitudes, what can we do to foster more favourable attitudes towards immigrants and immigration?

The role of national identity

As several researchers (Esses et al., 2005a; Jones, 1997; Pehrson & Green, 2010) have illustrated, individuals' construal of national identity and national attachment are important determinants of their attitudes towards immigrants and immigration. Hence, it stands to reason that, if we can change the way in which national identity is perceived, we may be able to increase the favourability of individuals' attitudes towards immigrants and immigration. To test this assertion, Esses and colleagues examined the effects of persuasive communications that manipulated the way in which national identity was portrayed.

This approach was informed by Gaertner and Dovidio's common ingroup identity model (Gaertner & Dovidio, 2000, 2008; Gaertner, Dovidio & Houlette, 2010). Specifically, Gaertner, Dovidio and their colleagues have demonstrated that intergroup biases can be reduced by altering how individuals categorize ingroup and outgroup members (e.g. Dovidio, Gaertner & Saguy, 2007; Gaertner et al., 2008). If members of different groups are prompted to broaden group boundaries in such a way that the ingroup is more broadly defined to include certain outgroups, attitudes and behaviours towards members of these former outgroups become more positive through processes involving ingroup favouritism. Of importance, it has also been demonstrated that the promotion of a common ingroup identity reduces bias to some extent by reducing perceived threats from former outgroups (Riek et al., 2010). Recategorization can be promoted by emphasizing an existing common group membership such as national identity (Gaertner & Dovidio, 2005).

In a laboratory experiment, Esses and colleagues (2005a) tested whether or not persuasive communications can be used to promote a common national identity, and the effects of such a construal on attitudes towards immigrants and immigration. In this study, they presented participants with one of four editorials about immigrants and immigration: neutral; emphasizing common ethnic roots; emphasizing a common national identity; or emphasizing common ethnic roots *and* a common national identity. Results demonstrated that, compared with the neutral editorial, the three editorials designed to promote a common ingroup identity resulted in more favourable attitudes towards immigrants. Importantly, this effect varied depending on participants' level of social dominance orientation (SDO). Among individuals lower in SDO, there was a tendency to respond more favourably to immigrants when a common identity was promoted, but individual comparisons of the three common ingroup identity conditions to the neutral condition were not significant. In contrast, among individuals higher in SDO, those who read either the editorial that emphasized a common national identity, or both common ethnic roots and a common national identity, responded significantly more favourably to immigrants, compared with individuals who read the neutral editorial. Hence, for individuals higher in SDO (who often hold particularly unfavourable attitudes towards immigrants), promoting a common national identity that includes immigrants leads to more positive attitudes towards immigrants.

These findings are consistent with the basic tenets of the common ingroup identity model – emphasizing membership in a common national identity fosters more favourable attitudes towards immigrants. Esses and colleagues (2008) further suggest that these results may inform interventions designed to create more humanizing perceptions of refugees. For example, emphasizing that 'we are all part of the human race' may foster a more inclusive, common ingroup identity and reduce dehumanization.

Importantly, the development of a common ingroup identity does not come at the cost of completely abandoning one's former (and less inclusive) identity (Gaertner & Dovidio, 2005). In fact, it is possible for individuals to conceive of two groups (e.g. native-born individuals and non-native-born individuals) as distinct groups existing within a superordinate identity (e.g. Australians). This form of *recategorization* has implications for acculturation because it does not result in people relinquishing their initial identity (e.g. assimilation). Consequently, immigrants who identify with their host society can maintain their heritage identity and thus experience the positive effects associated with the integrationist acculturation orientation.

Although recategorization of ingroup and outgroup members into a superordinate group typically has beneficial effects, consideration should be given to moderating conditions that influence whether or not recategorization will result in decreased bias as intended. For instance, evidence suggests that recategorization can lead to an increase in intergroup bias among individuals who are highly committed to their ingroup (Crisp, 2006; Crisp, Stone & Hall, 2006). Moreover, research by Mummendey and colleagues (e.g. Wenzel, Mummendey & Waldzus, 2007) indicates that when superordinate identity *and* subgroup identities are salient, bias towards the other subgroup (that is, the former outgroup) may result. Members of one or both subgroups may perceive their subgroup's characteristics as more prototypical of the common, recategorized group. Consequently, they believe that their subgroup is more representative of the recategorized group and therefore superior to the other subgroup.

The role of public policy and discourse on immigration

The potential utility of the common ingroup identity model as a tool for promoting positive attitudes towards immigrants and immigration is inextricably linked with public policy and discourse on immigration. In Canada – a country that was recently named a global leader when it comes to immigration policies (United Nations Development Programme, 2009) – an inclusive national identity has played a prominent role in public discourse on immigration. A country with one of the highest rates of permanent immigration (per capita) in the world (Citizenship and Immigration Canada, 2008a), roughly 20 per cent of Canada's population is foreign-born (Statistics Canada, 2010). Forty years ago, Canada became the first country to adopt multiculturalism as an official national policy (Citizenship and Immigration Canada, 2008b). This policy promotes mutual intergroup cooperation and 'ensures that all citizens can keep their identities, can take pride in their ancestry and have a sense of belonging' (Citizenship and Immigration Canada, 2008b, para. 2).

The Canadian Government has also been very vocal about the fact that Canada relies on immigrants to meet its labour-force needs, and that immigrants have contributed to Canada's cultural fabric. Indeed, the government describes Canada as a country 'built on immigration and diversity' (Government of Canada, 2011, 'Canada's Immigration Programs', para. 1). In other words, Canadian policies and public discourse have fostered the development of a common national identity that includes individuals born in Canada as well as those who are foreign-born. At the same time, given the strong focus on multiculturalism, immigrants in Canada are not expected to give up their pre-migration identities.

Consistent with the tenets of the common ingroup identity model, Canada's inclusive national identity comes hand-in-hand with favourable public attitudes towards immigrants and immigration, as compared with most other immigrant-receiving nations (Jedwab, 2008). For example,

Gallup International Polls conducted in 2005 and 2006 demonstrated that, compared with Americans and Britons, Canadians are much more positive about immigration. While the majority of United States and British residents (58 per cent and 60 per cent respectively) indicated they would like to see the level of immigration to their country decreased, only a minority of Canadians (about 20 per cent) felt this way (Newport, 2006). In fact, roughly 80 per cent of Canadians either said they would like to see immigration levels increase (22 per cent of respondents) or stay the same (58 per cent of respondents; Newport, 2006).

Conclusion

As worldwide migration trends continue to evolve, nations are confronted with new challenges in effectively integrating immigrants into all aspects of society. Researchers in the field of psychology have contributed significantly to our understanding of the complex dynamics between immigrants and host community members, identifying both barriers to, and facilitators of, positive intergroup relations. In this chapter we described research from two broad areas of psychology that have made substantial contributions to the study of immigrants and immigration: acculturation and intergroup relations. Our review included a discussion of strategies that can be used to optimize intergroup relations between immigrants and members of the host society. These strategies include promoting a common ingroup identity that includes both immigrants and members of the host society through both public policy and discourse.

While psychologists continue to conduct research that furthers our understanding of important issues surrounding migration, important gains may be made by establishing links with policymakers who develop and modify policies and practices used in the management of migration (Wills, 2010). Ultimately, psychological theories and research findings can help to facilitate the effective management of migration as it becomes an increasingly important issue in the twenty-first century.

Practical task for readers

Find an article on immigration and the integration of immigrants that appeared in your local or national newspaper within the past year. Write a psychologically informed 'letter to the editor' of the newspaper in which the article appeared. Indicate whether you believe the article promotes positive attitudes towards immigrants

> **Continued**
>
> and encourages successful acculturation (or not). Using the literature reviewed in this chapter, discuss why such promotion is beneficial to society. Discuss the social-psychological mechanisms that would lie behind the possible (positive or negative) effects of the article on prospects of successful acculturation.

Suggested readings

To read more about psychological perspectives on immigration, see two issues of the *Journal of Social Issues*: the 2010 issue edited by Deaux, Esses, Lalonde & Brown; and the 2001 issue edited by Esses, Dovidio & Dion.

References

Alexander, M. G., Brewer, M. B. & Herrmann, R. K. (1999). Images and affect: A functional analysis of out-group stereotypes. *Journal of Personality and Social Psychology, 77*, 78–93.

Altemeyer, B. (1996). *The Authoritarian Specter.* Cambridge, MA: Harvard University Press.

Altemeyer, B. & Hunsberger, B. (1992). Authoritarianism, religious fundamentalism, quest, and prejudice. *The International Journal for the Psychology of Religion, 2*, 113–133.

Bar-Tal, D. (2000). *Shared Beliefs in a Society.* Thousand Oaks, CA: Sage.

Berry, J. W. (1990). Psychology of acculturation. In J. J. Berman (ed.), *Nebraska Symposium on Motivation, 1989: Cross-cultural Perspectives* (pp. 201–234). Lincoln: University of Nebraska Press.

Berry, J. W. (1997). Immigration, acculturation and adaptation. *Applied Psychology: An International Review, 41*, 5–68.

Berry, J. W. (1998). Acculturative stress. In P. Balls Organista, K. M. Chun & G. Marin (eds.), *Readings in Ethnic Psychology* (pp. 117–122). New York: Routledge.

Berry, J. W. (2001). A psychology of immigration. *Journal of Social Issues, 57*, 615–631.

Berry, J. W. (2003). Conceptual approaches to acculturation. In K. Chun, P. Balls-Organista & G. Marin (eds.), *Acculturation: Advances in Theory, Measurement and Applied Research* (pp. 17–37). Washington: APA Books.

Berry, J. W., Kim, U., Minde, T. & Mok, D. (1987). Comparative studies of acculturative stress. *International Migration Review, 21*, 491–511.

Berry, J. W., Kim, U., Power, S., Young, M. & Bujaki, M. (1989). Acculturation attitudes in plural societies. *Applied Psychology: An International Review*, 38, 185–206.

Berry, J. W. & Krishnan, A. (1992). Acculturative stress and acculturation attitudes among Indian immigrants to the United States. *Psychology and Developing Societies*, 4, 187–212.

Bobo, L. & Hutchings, V. L. (1996). Perceptions of racial group composition: Extending Blumer's theory of group position to a multiracial social context. *American Sociological Review*, 61, 951–972.

Borjas, G. (2003). The labor demand curve is downward sloping: Reexamining the impact of immigration on the labor market. *The Quarterly Journal of Economics*, 118, 1335–1374.

Bourhis, R. Y., Barrette, G., El-Geledi, S. & Schmidt, R. S. (2009). Acculturation orientations and social relations between immigrant and host community members in California. *Journal of Cross-Cultural Psychology*, 40, 443–467.

Bourhis, R. Y. & Dayan, J. (2004). Acculturation orientations towards Israeli Arabs and Jewish immigrants in Israel. *International Journal of Psychology*, 39, 118–131.

Bourhis, R. Y., Moïse, L. C., Perreault, S. & Senécal, S. (1997). Towards an interactive acculturation model: A social psychological approach. *International Journal of Psychology*, 32, 369–386.

Bourhis, R.Y., Barrette, G., El-Geledi, S., & Schmidt, R. (2009). Acculturation orientations and social relations between immigrants and host community members in California. *Journal of Cross-Cultural Psychology*, 40, 443–467.

Bourhis, R. Y., Montaruli, E., El-Geledi, S., Harvey, S.-P. & Barrette, G. (2010). Acculturation in multiple host community settings. *Journal of Social Issues*, 66, 780–802.

Buschschluter, V. (2009). Satellite Helps Fight Illegal Immigration. BBC News. Available at http://news.bbc.co.uk/2/hi/europe/7818478.stm (accessed 20 February 2010).

Castles, S. (2000). International migration at the beginning of the twenty-first century: Global trends and issues. *International Social Science Journal*, 52, 269–281.

Chavez, L. R. (2001). *Covering Immigration: Popular Images and the Politics of a Nation*. Berkley: University of California Press.

Citizenship and Immigration Canada (2008a). Annual report to Parliament on immigration: 2008. Available at http://www.cic.gc.ca/english/resources/publications/annual-report2008/section1.asp (accessed 20 January 2011).

Citizenship and Immigration Canada (2008b). Canadian multiculturalism: An inclusive citizenship. Available at http://www.cic.gc.ca/english/multiculturalism/citizenship.asp (accessed 22 January 2011).

Constant, A. F., Gataullina, L. & Zimmerman, K. F. (2007). Naturalization proclivities, ethnicity and integration. The Institute for the Study of Labor. Discussion Paper No. 3260. Available at http://www.econstor.eu/bitstream/10419/35155/1/559866496.pdf (accessed 10 February 2011).

Crisp, R. J. (2006). Commitment and categorization in common ingroup contexts. In R. J. Crisp & M. Hewstone (eds.), *Multiple Social Categorization: Processes, Models and Applications* (pp. 90–111). Hove, UK: Psychology Press/Taylor & Francis.

Crisp, R. J., Stone, C. H. & Hall, N. R. (2006). Recategorization and subgroup identification: Predicting and preventing threats from common ingroups. *Personality and Social Psychology Bulletin*, 32, 230–243.

Delgado, N., Rodríguez-Pérez, A., Vaes, J., Leyens, J-P. & Betancor, V. (2009). Priming effects of violence on infrahumanization. *Group Processes & Intergroup Relations*, 12, 699–714.

Deaux, K., Esses, V., Lalonde, R., & Brown, R. (eds.) (2010). Immigrants and hosts: Perceptions, interactions, and transformations [special issue]. *Journal of Social Issues*, 66.

Dion, K. L. (2001). Immigrants' perceptions of housing discrimination in Toronto: The Housing New Canadians project. *Journal of Social Issues*, 57, 523–539.

Dion, K. L. (2002). The social psychology of perceived prejudice and discrimination. *Canadian Psychology*, 43, 1–10.

Dovidio, J. F., Gaertner, S. L. & Saguy, T. (2007). Another view of 'we': Majority and minority group perspectives on a common ingroup identity. *European Review of Social Psychology*, 18, 296–330.

El Refaie, E. (2001). Metaphors we discriminate by: Naturalized themes in Austrian newspaper articles about asylum seekers. *Journal of Sociolinguistics*, 5, 352–371.

Esses, V. M., Jackson, L. M. & Armstrong, T. L. (1998). Intergroup competition and attitudes toward immigrants and immigration: An instrumental model of group conflict. *Journal of Social Issues*, 54, 699–724.

Esses, V. M., Dovidio, J. F. & Dion, K. L. (2001). Immigrants and immigration [special issue]. *Journal of Social Issues*, 57.

Esses, V. M., Dovidio, J. F. & Hodson, G. (2002). Public attitudes toward immigration in the United States and Canada in response to the September 11, 2001 'Attack on America'. *Analyses of Social Issues and Public Policy*, 2, 69–85.

Esses, V. M., Hodson, G. & Dovidio, J. F. (2003). Public attitudes toward immigrants and immigration: Determinants and policy implications. In C. M. Beach, A. G. Green & J. G. Reitz (eds.), *Canadian Immigration Policy for the 21st Century* (pp. 507–535). Montreal, Canada: McGill-Queen's University Press.

Esses, V. M., Dovidio, J. F., Semenya, A. H. & Jackson, L. M. (2005a). Attitudes toward immigrants and immigration: The role of national and international identities. In D. Abrams, J. M. Marques & M. A. Hogg (eds.), *The Social Psychology of Inclusion and Exclusion* (pp. 317–337). Philadelphia, PA: Psychology Press.

Esses, V. M., Jackson, L. M., Dovidio, J. F. & Hodson, G. (2005b). Instrumental relations among groups: Group competition, conflict, and prejudice. In J. F. Dovidio, P. Glick & L. A. Rudman (eds.), *On the Nature of Prejudice: Fifty Years After Allport* (pp. 227–243). Malden, MA: Blackwell Publishing.

Esses, V. M., Dietz, J. & Bhardwaj, A. (2006). The role of prejudice in the discounting of immigrant skills. In R. Mahalingam (ed.), *Cultural Psychology of Immigrants* (pp. 113–130). Mahwah, NJ: Lawrence Erlbaum.

Esses, V. M., Veenvliet, S., Hodson, G. & Mihic, L. (2008). Justice, morality, and the dehumanization of refugees. *Social Justice Research*, 21, 4–25.

Esses, V. M., Medianu, S. & Lawson, A. (2010). *The Dehumanization of Immigrants and Refugees*. Paper presented at the 22nd Annual Convention of the American Psychological Society, Boston, MA.

Fiske, S. T., Cuddy, A. J. C., Glick, P. & Xu, J. (2002). A model of (often mixed) stereotype content: Competence and warmth respectively follow from perceived status and competition. *Journal of Personality and Social Psychology*, 82, 878–902.

Francis, D. (2001). Cities fight for fair refugee policies. *National Post*. Available at www.dianefrancis.com (accessed 1 November 2005).

Gaertner, S. L. & Dovidio, J. F. (2000). *Reducing Intergroup Bias: The Common Ingroup Identity Model*. Philadelphia: Psychology Press.

Gaertner, S. L. & Dovidio, J. F. (2005). Categorization, recategorization, and intergroup bias. In J. F. Dovidio, P. Glick & L. A. Rudman (eds.), *On the Nature of Prejudice: Fifty Years After Allport* (pp. 71–88). Malden, MA: Blackwell Publishing.

Gaertner, S. L. & Dovidio, J. F. (2008). Addressing contemporary racism: The common ingroup identity model. In C. Willis-Esqueda (ed.), *Motivational Aspects of Prejudice and Racism. Nebraska Symposium on Motivation* (pp. 111–133). New York, NY: Springer Science.

Gaertner, S. L., Dovidio, J. F., Guerra, R., Rebelo, M., Monteiro, M. B., Riek, B. M., & Houlette, M.A. (2008). The common ingroup identity model: Applications to children and adults. In S. R. Levy & M. Killen (eds.), *Intergroup Relations* (pp. 204–219). New York: Oxford University Press.

Gaertner, S. L., Dovidio, J. F. & Houlette, M. A. (2010). Social categorization. In J. F. Dovidio, M. Hewstone, P. Glick & V. M. Esses (eds.). *The SAGE Handbook of Prejudice, Stereotyping, and Discrimination*. London: Sage Publications Inc.

Gilmore, J. (2009). The 2008 Canadian immigrant labour market: Analysis of quality of employment. Statistics Canada Catalogue no. 71-606-X. Ottawa. Labour Statistics Division. No. 5. Available at http://www.statcan.gc.ca/pub/71-606-x/71-606-x2009001-eng.pdf (accessed 31 March 2010).

Government of Canada (2011). Connect2Canada: Canada's immigration programs. Available at http://www.connect2canada.com/facts-faits/immigration/ (accessed 22 January 2011).

Harris, L. T. & Fiske, S. T. (2006). Dehumanizing the lowest of the low: Neuroimaging responses to extreme outgroups. *Psychological Science*, 17, 847–853.

Haslam, N. (2006). Dehumanization: An integrative review. *Personality and Social Psychology Review*, 10, 252–264.

Homeland Security (2006). Department of Homeland Security unveils comprehensive immigration enforcement strategy for the nation's interior. Available at http://www.dhs.gov/xnews/releases/press_release_0890.shtm (accessed 20 February 2010).

Human Rights Watch (2001). 50 years on: What future for refugee protection? Available at http://www.hrw.org/en/reports/2000/12/12/50-years-what-future-refugee-protection (accessed 16 February 2011).

International Organization for Migration (2011). About migration. Available at http://www.iom.int/jahia/Jahia/about-migration/lang/en (accessed 15 January 2011).

Jackson, L. M. & Esses, V. M. (1997). Of scripture and ascription: The relation between religious fundamentalism and intergroup helping. *Personality and Social Psychology Bulletin*, 23, 893–906.

Jackson, L. M. & Esses, V. M. (2000). The effect of economic competition on people's willingness to help empower immigrants. *Group Processes and Intergroup Relations*, 3, 419–435.

Jasinskaja-Lahti, I., Liebkind, K. & Perhoniemi, R. (2006). Perceived discrimination and well-being: A victim study of different immigrant groups. *Journal of Community and Applied Social Psychology*, 16, 267–284.

Jasinskaja-Lahti, I., Liebkind, K. & Solheim, E. (2009). To identify or not to identify? National disidentification as an alternative reaction to perceived ethnic discrimination. *Applied Psychology: An International Review*, 58, 105–128.

Jedwab, J. (2008). Receiving and giving: How does the Canadian public feel about immigration and integration? In J. Biles, M. Burstein & J. Frideres (eds.), *Immigration and Integration in Canada: In the Twenty First Century* (pp. 211–230). Kingston, Ontario, Canada: School of Policy Studies Queen's University.

Jones, F. L. (1997). Ethnic diversity and national identity. *Australian and New Zealand Journal of Sociology*, 33, 285–305.

Jost, J. T., Burgess, D. & Mosso, C. O. (2001). Conflicts of legitimation among self, group, and system: The integrative potential of system justification theory. In J. T. Jost & B. Major (eds.), *The Psychology of Legitimacy: Emerging Perspectives on Ideology, Justice, and Intergroup Relations* (pp. 363–388). New York, NY: Cambridge University Press.

Jost, J. T. & Hunyady, O. (2002). The psychology of system justification and the palliative function of ideology. In W. Stroebe & M. Hewstone (eds.), *European Review of Social Psychology* (vol. 13, pp. 111–153). Hove, UK: Psychology Press.

Leach, M. (2003). 'Disturbing practices': Dehumanizing asylum seekers in the refugee 'Crisis' in Australia, 2001–2002, *Refuge*, 21, 25–33.

Lee, R. (2000). Post-communism Romani migration to Canada. *Cambridge Review of International Affairs*, 13, 51–70.

Leyens, J.-P., Demoulin, S., Vaes, J., Gaunt, R. & Paladino, M. P. (2007). Infra-humanization: The wall of group differences. *Social Issues and Policy Review*, 1, 139–172.

Leyens, J.-P., Paladino, P. M., Rodriguez-Torres, R., Vaes, J., Demoulin, S., Rodriguez-Perez, A. & Gaunt, R. (2000). The emotional side of prejudice: The attribution of secondary emotions to ingroups and outgroups. *Personality and Social Psychology Review*, 4, 186–197.

Liebkind, K. (2001). Acculturation. In R. Brown & S. Gaertner (eds.), *Blackwell Handbook of Social Psychology* (vol. 4, pp. 386–406). Oxford: Blackwell.

Louis, W. R., Duck, J., Terry, D. J., Schuller, R. & Lalonde, R. (2007). Why do citizens want to keep refugees out? Threats, fairness, and hostile norms in the treatment of asylum seekers. *European Journal of Social Psychology*, 37, 53–73.

Martinez-Herrera, M. (2008). Attractive immigration policies: 'A worldwide fight for the skilled workers.' Available at http://www.upf.edu/iuslabor/012008/EEUUManuelMartinez.pdf (accessed 16 January 2011).

Montreuil, A. & Bourhis, R. Y. (2004). Acculturation orientations of competing host communities toward valued and devalued immigrants. *International Journal of Intercultural Relations*, 28, 507–532.

Murray, J., Batalova, J. & Fix, M. (2006). The impact of immigration on native workers: A fresh look at the evidence. *Migration Policy Institute – Insight*, 18, 1–16.

Newport, F. (2006). Canadians more positive about immigration than Americans or Britons. *Gallup News Service*. Available at http://www.gallup.com/poll/21592/Canadians-More-Positive-About-Immigration-Than-Americans-Britons.aspx (accessed 20 January 2011).

Office for Democratic Institutions and Human Rights (2009). Hate crimes in the OSCE region – incidents and responses. Annual report for 2008. Available at http://www.osce.org/odihr/40203 (accessed 23 February 2011).

Opotow, S. (1995). Drawing the line: Social categorization, moral exclusion, and the scope of justice. In B. B. Bunker & J. Z. Rubin (eds.), *Conflict, Cooperation, and Justice: Essays Inspired by the Work of Morton Deutsch* (pp. 347–379). San Francisco: Jossey-Bass.

Pedersen, A., Griffiths, B. & Watt, S. E. (2008). Attitudes toward out-groups and the perception of consensus: All feet do *not* wear one shoe. *Journal of Community and Applied Social Psychology*, 18, 543–557.

Pehrson, S. & Green, E. G. T. (2010). Who we are and who can join us: National identity content and entry criteria for new immigrants. *Journal of Social Issues*, 66, 695–716.

Peri, G. (2006). Immigrants, skills, and wages: Measuring the economic gains from immigration. *Immigration Policy Center - In Focus*, 5, 1–8.

Pew Research Center Publications (2010a). Growing opposition to increased offshore drilling: Obama's ratings little affected by recent turmoil. Available at http://people-press.org/reports/pdf/627.pdf (accessed 8 February 2011).

Pew Research Center Publications (2010b). Hispanics and Arizona's new immigration law. Available at http://pewresearch.org/pubs/1579/arizona-immigration-law-fact-sheet-hispanic-population-opinion-discrimination (accessed 23 January 2011).

Pratto, F. & Lemieux, A. F. (2001). The psychological ambiguity of immigration and its implications for promoting immigration policy. *Journal of Social Issues*, 57, 413–430.

Redfield, R., Linton, R. & Herskovits, M. J. (1936). Memorandum for the study of acculturation. *American Anthropologist*, 38, 149–152.

Riek, B. M., Mania, E. W., Gaertner, S. L., McDonald, S. A. & Lamoreaux, M. J. (2010). Does a common ingroup identity reduce intergroup threat? *Group Processes and Intergroup Relations*, 13, 403–423.

Sam, D. L. (2006). Acculturation: Conceptual background and core components. In D. L. Sam & J. W. Berry (eds.), *The Cambridge Handbook of Social Psychology* (pp. 11–26). Cambridge: Cambridge University Press.

Schwartz, S. H. & Struch, N. (1989). Values, stereotypes, and intergroup antagonism. In D. Bar-Tal, C. G. Grauman, A. W. Kruglanski & W. Stroebe (eds.), *Stereotypes and Prejudice: Changing Conceptions* (pp. 151–167). New York: Springer-Verlag.

Schwartz, S. H., Struch, N. & Bilsky, W. (1990). Values and intergroup motives: A study of Israeli and German students. *Social Psychology Quarterly*, 53, 185–198.

Sidanius, J. & Pratto, F. (1999). *Social Dominance: An Intergroup Theory of Social Hierarchy and Oppression*. New York: Cambridge University Press.

Smith, A. D. (2001). *Nationalism: Theory, Ideology, History*. Cambridge: Polity Press.

Southern Poverty Law Center (2011). Active anti-immigrant groups. Available at http://www.splcenter.org/get-informed/intelligence-files/ideology/anti-immigrant/active_hate_groups (accessed 15 February 2011).

Stangor, C., Sechrist, G. B. & Jost, J. T. (2001). Changing racial beliefs by providing consensus information. *Personality and Social Psychology Bulletin*, 27, 486–496.

State of Arizona (2010). Senate Bill 1070. Available at http://www.azleg.gov/legtext/49leg/2R/bills/SB1070S.pdf (accessed 23 January 2011).

Statistics Canada (2010). Study: Projections of the diversity of the Canadian population. Available at http://www.statcan.gc.ca/daily-quotidien/100309/dq100309a-eng.htm (accessed 20 January 2011).

Stephan, W. G., Renfro, C. L., Esses, V. M., Stephan, C. W. & Martin, T. (2005). The effects of feeling threatened on attitudes toward immigrants. *International Journal of Intercultural Relations*, 29, 1–19.

Stephan, W. G. & Stephan, C. W. (2000). An integrated threat theory of prejudice. In S. Oskamp (ed.), *Claremont Symposium on Applied Social Psychology* (pp. 23–46). Hillsdale, NJ: Lawrence Erlbaum.

Struch, N. & Schwartz, S. H. (1989). Intergroup aggression: Its predictors and distinctness from in-group bias. *Journal of Personality and Social Psychology*, 56, 364–373.

United Nations, Department of Economic and Social Affairs, Population Division (2009). International migration report 2006: A global assessment. Available at http://www.un.org/esa/population/publications/2006_MigrationRep/report.htm (accessed 24 January 2011).

United Nations Development Programme (2009). *Human Development Report 2009: Overcoming Barriers: Human Mobility and Development*. New York: Palgrave Macmillan.

United Nations High Commissioner for Refugees (2008). 2008 global trends. Available at http://www.unhcr.org/4a375c426.html (accessed 19 August 2009).

United Nations High Commissioner for Refugees (2011a). All in the same boat: The challenges of mixed migration. Available at http://www.unhcr.org/pages/4a1d406060.html (accessed 22 January 2011).

United Nations High Commissioner for Refugees (2011b). Refugee figures. Available at http://www.unhcr.org/pages/49c3646c1d.html (accessed 22 January 2011).

Verkuyten, M. (2004). Emotional reactions to and support for immigrant policies: Attributed responsibilities to categories of asylum seekers. *Social Justice Research*, 17, 293–314.

Verkuyten, M. (2009). Support for multiculturalism and minority rights: The role of national identification and out-group threat. *Social Justice Research*, 22, 31–52.

Watt, S. E. & Larkin, C. (2010). Prejudiced people perceive more community support for their views: The role of own, media, and peer attitudes in perceived consensus. *Journal of Applied Social Psychology*, 40, 710–731.

Wenzel, M., Mummendey, A. & Waldzus, S. (2007). Superordinate identities and intergroup conflict: The ingroup projection model. *European Review of Social Psychology*, 18, 331–372.

Wills, M. (2010). Psychological research and immigration policy. *Journal of Social Issues*, 66, 825–836.

Zick, A., Wagner, U., van Dick, R. & Petzel, R. (2001). Acculturation and prejudice in Germany: Majority and minority preferences. *Journal of Social Issues*, 57, 541–557.

Note

1. Preparation of this article was supported by a Social Sciences and Humanities Research Council of Canada grant to the third author.

PART II

INEQUALITY, TYRANNY, VIOLENT AND NON-VIOLENT SOCIAL PROTEST

5

The Corrupting Power of Social Inequality: Social-Psychological Consequences, Causes and Solutions

Robbie M. Sutton, Aleksandra Cichocka and Jojanneke van der Toorn[1]

In September 2008, the global financial crisis that had been brewing for a year went critical. A cascade of bad debts meant that the value of financial assets evaporated, and normal lending between banks ceased. It was widely thought within government and banking circles that within days, if not hours, automatic teller machines would be unable to dispense money (Brown, 2011). Thanks to the actions of world governments, this looming cataclysm was avoided. But in averting disaster, governments suspended principles such as justice and equality. Instead, the governments took on the bad debts of investment banks. In this way banks' debts were transferred to taxpayers, who were also to be affected by the resulting cuts in public services. To illustrate, after the Irish Government agreed to bail out its banks, the average Irish person owed something in the order of US$500,000 to international lenders (CNBC, 2011). This belt-tightening was not experienced to the same degree by the investment bankers whose decisions had largely caused the crisis. Indeed, extraordinarily high bonuses paid to bankers were largely preserved. This is despite the role that such bonuses may have played in the crisis (by rewarding risky investments), and despite government pressure to curb them (Aldrick, 2011).

This episode illustrates one of our key themes in this chapter: just as violence begets violence, inequality tends to breed still more inequality. Here, our focus is on the inequalities of wealth and income that exist within societies, such as nation states, rather than inequalities between states. The recent financial crisis was in part precipitated by this type of wealth inequality. It occurred (like the crash that triggered the Great Depression in 1929) at a time when wealth inequality was already exceptionally high, and has served to widen it further (Reich, 2010). In this chapter, we first outline theory and research on the social-psychological consequences of inequality. We then review theory on the social-psychological processes that underpin inequality. Finally, we conclude the chapter by considering the prospect that wide inequalities may be reduced by changing people's psychological responses to inequality.

Why inequality is a problem

Negative consequences of inequality

A wealth of research linking inequality to negative outcomes was summarized by Wilkinson and Pickett (2010). They found remarkably consistent evidence that differences in income inequality between 25 of the world's richest nations are associated with a range of negative outcomes as documented by official statistics, including mental illness ($r = .73$), lower levels of trust ($r = .66$), shorter life expectancy ($r = .44$), infant mortality ($r = .42$), obesity ($r = .57$), poor children's educational performance ($r = .45$), teenage births ($r = .73$), homicides ($r = .47$), and imprisonment rates ($r = .75$). Analyses of such outcomes as a function of different levels of inequality across the American states produced similar findings.

For seasoned social psychologists, these correlation coefficients (r values) are impressive. Squaring them suggests that anything between 20 per cent and 50 per cent of the differences between countries in these different measures of well-being are explained by differences in social inequality. Wilkinson and Pickett (2010) also effectively ruled out alternative explanations of their findings. For example, the relationship between inequality and reduced well-being holds even when poverty levels in societies are controlled for. Thus, the increasing levels of poverty that are associated with inequality do not account for their results. Wilkinson and Pickett (2010) suggest that inequality is indeed a social problem, and that reducing it would help solve many of the other social problems afflicting rich nations. But their studies are correlational, meaning that cause-and-effect cannot be conclusively demonstrated. Further, to interpret their correlations we need to have a theoretical understanding of *how* inequality might adversely affect well-being. To this end, we now consider lines of research that illustrate how inequality can produce negative outcomes.

Value violation

Albeit to varying degrees, people across cultures value equality (Deutsch, 1985; Schwarz, 1992). It is strongly associated in people's minds with fairness and justice (Chen, 1999), a crucial concept in the field of human rights (Conte, Davidson & Burchill, 2004), and is a simple and popular rule for allocating resources (Samuelson & Allison, 1994). In experimental games involving decisions about the allocation of money, people will pay money out of their own accounts in order to ensure that allocations are reasonably equal (Camerer, 2003). Also, a recent survey showed that Americans underestimated the extent of wealth inequality in their country and wanted it to be still more equal (Norton & Ariely, 2011).

In keeping with a line from Shakespeare's Hamlet (Act II, Scene II) that 'there is nothing good or bad, but thinking makes it so', many negative outcomes arise because of the fact that, in general, people do not like inequality. Violations of the equality principle elicit a range of negative emotions, including anger, irritation and disappointment. Adverse reactions to inequality occur even among people who are not disadvantaged, and among people who value equality as a practical, easy-to-agree way of distributing wealth, rather than as a principle of justice (Stouten, de Cremer & van Dijk, 2005). The springing up of street protests against bankers' spectacularly large bonuses, notably in the United States and United Kingdom, are a good indication of the gut-level emotions that people feel when confronted with clear evidence of inequality.

There is a good chance that you have experienced inequality in your life. Have you ever been troubled by receiving lower grades, or lower pay, than someone else? How about when you received better outcomes than others? Not surprisingly, people usually express stronger negative reactions, or do so more quickly and effortlessly, when they receive less than others (Ham & van den Bos, 2008). Low-status people also have more reasons to be angry about inequality – out of envy and painful feelings of inferiority, as well as a sense of injustice (Leach, 2008). However, a number of studies have shown that people evaluate inequality negatively even when they are its beneficiaries (e.g. van den Bos & Lind, 2001). These studies show that the emotional price paid by those at the bottom of inequality hierarchies is not mirrored by an emotional benefit to those at the top. The net emotional effect of inequality averaged across the entire population is therefore negative (see also Napier & Jost, 2008).

Relative deprivation

Increasing levels of inequality mean that more individuals in a society are deprived of resources enjoyed by richer members of society (Yitzhaki, 1979). The sense that one lacks what others have is called *relative deprivation* (Crosby, 1976; Smith & Kim, 2007). Relative deprivation has a number of negative effects. It breeds discontent (Olsen et al., 1995), a competitive approach to relations with outgroups (Halevy et al., 2010), and violence at both interpersonal and intergroup levels (Moghaddam, 2005). It also motivates attempts to overcome deprivation by means that are illegitimate (e.g. theft: Hennigan et al., 1982) or self-defeating (e.g. gambling: Callan et al., 2008). Relative deprivation is most marked, and most harmful, when individuals perceive that they are *entitled* to the things that they lack (Kessler & Mummendey, 2002). It is also marked when the deprivation is salient. For example, it has been shown that it is harmful to one's health to have friends and neighbours who are much richer than oneself (Pham-Kanter, 2009). This circumstance likely triggers the kinds of social comparisons that lead to a sense of relative deprivation. As we shall see, however, a shared sense of relative deprivation on behalf of one's group can motivate people to challenge inequality (Major, 1994). To some extent, then, a problem shared can be a problem solved (see also van Stekelenburg & Klandermans, this volume).

Disengagement from education

In highly stratified societies, those who are lower in status tend to disengage from education (Teachman, 1987). Disengagement does not just mean reduced motivation, but also that one's sense of self-worth becomes detached from one's educational achievements (Lesko & Corpus, 2006). Consistent with relative deprivation theory, this tendency is strongest when the inequality in educational outcomes is seen as unjust – an outcome of discrimination and disadvantage. It is also worse when the inequality is perceived as a product of the disadvantages confronting the ingroup, rather than the advantages that aid the outgroup.

Hypocrisy

Inequality does not only have adverse effects on lower-status groups. Lammers, Stapel and Galinsky (2010) experimentally manipulated power by using pairs of particpants and assigning one of each pair to a manager role and the other to a subordinate role. They found that power increased hypocrisy – those who were in the more powerful positions acted less morally but evaluated their own morality more highly. Those in lower-status positions, however, were at once more moral, in relative terms, but also more inclined to evaluate their own morality more harshly. Thus, the privileges enjoyed by elites can cause them to pursue their own interests with more abandon, while convincing themselves that they are especially moral. The disadvantages experienced by people with lower status can cause them to be more self-critical and self-sacrificing. This and other findings suggest that, indeed, power generally corrupts (Gruenfeld et al., 2008; Kipnis, 1972).

This social psychological dynamic clearly has the potential to perpetuate and even aggravate inequality over time. Real-world data seem to mirror this pattern: in the US, people in the lowest one-fifth of income earners donate proportionally more of their income (4.3 per cent) to charity than the highest one-fifth (2.1 per cent) (Greve, 2009; see also Piff et al., 2010). Interestingly, however, Lammers and colleagues found that when the power hierarchy seemed to be legitimate, powerful people were no longer more inclined to be hypocritical. Hypocrisy seems therefore to be part of an attempt to defend oneself from the perception that one's privileges are undeserved.

Selfishness

According to some theorists (e.g. Putnam, 2000), inequality erodes trust and regard for others, and so reduces people's willingness to sacrifice their own interests in order to help others, or to promote the interest of their society as a whole. This prediction has been supported by a study in which inequality was experimentally manipulated. Anderson, Mellor and Milyo (2008) set up an economic game in which they either gave each player equal payments at the beginning, or gave them highly unequal payments. This was a public goods game, in which the more each player donated, the more the group earned as a whole. Results showed that players who started with the same amount of money later donated more money. Groups in which the initial payments were unequal fared less well because their members were less inclined to donate to further the common cause. The effect of declining social cohesion may therefore damage the group's material welfare.

Is inequality really so bad?

We have seen that there are several grounds to believe that inequality is harmful. The findings we have reviewed seem to show that, all else being equal, people prefer – and generally thrive in – relatively egalitarian social arrangements. Inequality triggers negative emotional and cognitive responses such as relative deprivation, degrades group processes and intergroup relations, and undermines lower-status groups' engagement in legitimate and constructive means of advancement. Because inequality tends to more adversely affect lower- than higher-status groups, it can be seen to be self-perpetuating (see also Van der Toorn, Tyler & Jost, 2011, and the stereotype threat phenomenon reviewed in Cohrs and Kessler, this volume). More controlled experiments are required in which participants are experimentally assigned to either equal or unequal social arrangements. These will help determine precisely if when and how inequality is harmful.

Thus far, research suggests that many of the apparent harms done by inequality depend on how people construe it. If lower-status groups focus on their disadvantages, as opposed to the advantages enjoyed by others, more negative consequences may follow – as we have already seen in the case of education. Leach and Spears (2008) also found that this focus can result in lower-status groups deriving more malicious enjoyment from misfortunes befalling higher-status groups. Also, inequality seems to breed more psychological problems when it is perceived as illegitimate. Recognizing illegitimacy not only makes people less happy generally (Napier & Jost, 2008) but under some circumstances may erode motivation and foster harmful resentment among lower-status groups.

One factor that influences the perceived legitimacy of inequality is its supposed economic impact. For many people, one of the main justifications of income inequality is that it helps create wealth, for example by providing an incentive to be entrepreneurial, innovative and hard-working (Rawls, 1971). However, there are reasons to think that inequality may be antagonistic to wealth creation. As we have seen, inequality can impede wealth creation by undermining the cooperative pooling of resources (Anderson, Mellor & Milyo, 2008). Wilkinson and Pickett (2010) analyze World Intellectual Property Organization data and show that there is an inverse correlation between social inequality and the number of patents taken out in a country. This suggests that social inequality may be detrimental to industrial creativity. Inequality has this effect, perhaps, by preventing people from being sufficiently educated, aspirational, confident and economically supported to realize their creative potential.

Research on the relation between inequality and economic growth is necessarily correlational, and its results mixed. Some studies suggest that inequality hampers growth (Aghion, Caroli & Garcia-Penalosa, 1999; Bénabou, 1996), others that it encourages growth (Forbes, 2000), and still others that the economic effects of inequality depend on other factors such as whether left- or right-wing parties are in government (Bjørnskov, 2008). Some findings also suggest that the effect of inequality on overall wealth is an inverted U-shape: very low, and very high, levels of inequality are inimical to economic growth (Banerjee & Duflo, 2003). Certainly, it is clear that we cannot take it for granted that high levels of inequality promote economic growth, and might therefore be justified.

A problem confronting this debate, though, is that the realistic policy choice is not between complete equality and some inequality. At least, this conclusion is suggested by the experience of some countries that have tried to impose equality forcefully (e.g. communist Russia). Corruption and black economies undermine these efforts, and authoritarian government produces its own problems. The scientific evidence that we review in the next section also suggests that inequality is unlikely ever to disappear completely, because it is underpinned by a host of social-psychological processes. Realistically, therefore, policymakers need to decide how much inequality there should be. In this regard, the research we have seen thus far generally supports Wilkinson and Pickett's (2010) position that social problems, at least in many of the world's richest nations, would be alleviated if inequality were reduced from current levels.

The social psychological underpinnings of inequality

In the following section we will discuss three major theories that seek to explain when and why people support social inequality, even though doing so sometimes conflicts with their self-interest. These three theories are among the most influential in social psychology: social identity theory, social dominance theory, and system justification theory.

Social identity theory

This theory was the first systematic attempt to explain how individuals relate to their groups and how groups relate to each other. It posits that people derive their self-esteem, at least in part, from their belongingness in social groups. They strive to maintain their positive social identities based on favourable comparisons with other groups (Tajfel & Turner, 1986; see also Cohrs & Kessler, this volume; Federico, this volume). Therefore, people think positively about groups they belong to and are more likely to distribute valuable resources in favour of the group. If lower- and higher-status groups are equally prone to ingroup-favouring distribution of resources, then inequality will be aggravated, because the rich are in command of more resources to begin with.

Social identity theory also suggests other means by which inequality may be self-perpetuating. Inequality threatens groups' positive identity, by presenting lower-status groups with palpable evidence of their inferiority, and higher-status groups with evidence that they may be selfish and oppressive. As a result, groups may be motivated to bolster their self-esteem in ways that degrade intergroup relations and interfere with prospects for greater equality. This is illustrated in a study by Moscatelli, Albarello and Rubini (2008), who assigned groups either to equal or unequal status relations. The authors found that in unequal social setups, both low- and high-status groups used biased language, describing actions by ingroup members more favourably than outgroup members' actions. When groups shared the same level of status, they did not show this ingroup-favouring bias.

Social identity theory also identifies conditions under which members of disadvantaged groups may respond to their position in ways that tend to perpetuate inequality. As we shall see later in this chapter, when leaving their low-status group is impossible (i.e. group boundaries are impermeable), and when relations between groups are seen as legitimate and stable, then people try to preserve a positive collective identity through processes known as *social creativity* (Tajfel & Turner, 1976). These strategies involve finding a positive way to define and stereotype the group. So, lower-status groups often embrace stereotypes that allow them to find something positive and distinctive about themselves (e.g. we are friendly), but tend to perpetuate inequality by justifying their collective disadvantage (and by demotivating them from individual achievements, e.g. we are not hard-working). When group boundaries are permeable, individuals from low-status groups may attempt to leave the group (i.e. engage in *individual mobility*). As we shall see later in this chapter, individual mobility strategies can result in the success of individuals from minority backgrounds, but do not advance the cause of the group as a whole. However, as we shall also see, when relations between groups are seen as illegitimate, low-status group members might take collective action to improve their position in society, in other words by engaging in *social competition* with the high-status group. This strategy can result in the equalization of relations between groups. One of the enduring legacies of social identity theory is to specify the social conditions that determine how people respond to inequality: it has informed and inspired much of the research that we review in this chapter.

Social dominance theory and inequality-legitimizing myths

Societies seek to maintain fairly peaceful relations between social groups and minimize group conflicts. Social dominance theory proposes that in the course of evolution this has been achieved by the development of ideologies that support stable dominance of some groups over others. Because these ideologies help in legitimizing social inequality and discrimination they are called hierarchy-enhancing legitimizing myths (Pratto et al., 1994). Legitimizing myths are widely accepted by members of society. They give people cues as to how to behave and how resources should be distributed in society. They also offer explanations of why societies are organized the way they are. Some examples of hierarchy-enhancing legitimizing myths include sexism, racism and nationalism, but also meritocratic ideologies (Pratto et al., 1994). German Nazism can serve as a case of hierarchy-enhancing ideology. It was characterized by a strong belief in the supremacy of the Aryan race, which was to be represented by the German nation. It also prescribed how one should treat those who were not members of the 'master race' – such as Jews, Gypsies, slaves and the disabled. Hierarchy-enhancing myths are balanced by attempts to attenuate social inequalities through ideologies that promote more inclusive and egalitarian social systems. Examples include human rights movements, some religious movements and socialist ideology.

While it is true that most societies are organized hierarchically, individuals differ in their support for certain groups dominating others. Social dominance orientation (SDO) is an individual difference variable corresponding to a 'general desire for unequal relations among social groups' (Sidanius et al., 2001; p. 312). People high in SDO tend to agree with statements such as 'some groups of people are simply inferior to other groups' but disagree with statements like 'we should do what we can to equalize conditions for different groups' (Pratto et al., 1994).

Because members of dominant groups have a privileged position within the social hierarchy, they tend to have a stronger SDO than members of subordinate groups (as is the case for men, compared with women, Pratto et al., 1994). This is true even when a group's dominance has not been long-standing. Experiments and field studies have shown that individuals' SDO increases when their group achieves, or is given, a higher status position (Liu & Huang, 2008; Schmitt, Branscombe & Kappen, 2003).

People's SDO also depends on other factors besides group membership, such as their personality and upbringing. For example, SDO has been associated with unaffectionate socialization, tough-mindedness, low empathy (Duckitt, 2001) and low agreeableness (Sibley & Duckitt, 2008). All of these factors predispose individuals to see the world as a competitive jungle in which people have to fight for their place in society. Hence, SDO is a robust predictor of intergroup prejudice (see also Cohrs & Kessler, this volume). Specifically, people high in SDO tend to dislike people who challenge existing social inequality (e.g. protestors, feminists). They also tend to derogate those who belong to socially subordinate groups (e.g. the unemployed, handicapped people, immigrants). In this way, social dominators justify their privileged position (Duckitt & Sibley, 2007).

Justification of unequal social systems

System justification theory (Jost & Banaji, 1994; Jost & Van der Toorn, 2012) states that as much as people have the need to perceive themselves and the groups to which they belong in a positive light, they are also motivated to defend, justify and bolster the systems in which they live. Justification of social systems satisfies three basic human motives (Jost & Hunyady, 2005). First, it reduces feelings of uncertainty and, thus, satisfies epistemic motives. People support existing systems because they are familiar and predictable. Second, system justification satisfies existential motives by helping people cope with threat and making them believe they live in an environment that will meet their material needs. Finally, it satisfies relational motives by coordinating interpersonal relations and providing people with a sense of shared reality with those around them (Jost, Ledgerwood & Hardin, 2007). Because inequality is a pervasive feature of most current social arrangements, the system-justification motive currently impels people to justify inequality.

Ideologies that justify inequality

People justify the social system in various ways. They may endorse system-justifying ideologies that serve to strengthen the status quo. Examples of these ideologies include meritocracy (the belief that individuals' status is based on merit, i.e. talent and motivation, rather than luck or preferential treatment); the American dream (the belief that everyone has a fair chance for success and prosperity: Mandisodza, Jost & Unzueta, 2006); the protestant work-ethic (the belief that hard work is virtuous and, thus, is rewarded); the belief in a just world (that people get what they deserve: Lerner, 1980); or political conservatism (support for traditional societal institutions; opposition to societal change and tolerance of social inequality: Jost et al., 2003).

There is much evidence that endorsement of system-justifying ideologies is related to support for inequality. For example, whites who are reminded of the protestant work ethic are more likely to show anti-black attitudes

(Biernat, Vescio & Theno, 1996; Katz & Hass, 1988). Also, the belief that the world is generally a just place in which people get what they deserve leads people to blame the disadvantaged for their fate. For example, it is associated with derogation of the poor, AIDS and cancer patients, and accident and rape victims (see Sutton et al., 2008, for a review).

System justification among the disadvantaged

Importantly, not only members of advantaged social groups engage in justification of unequal social relations. The disadvantaged also contribute to the perpetuation of inequality by justifying the status quo. Indeed, because the social system does not so clearly satisfy their epistemic, existential and relational needs, members of low-status groups may experience cognitive dissonance – an uncomfortable clash between system-justifying myths and the realities that they experience. For this reason, the disadvantaged are found to sometimes endorse system-justifying ideologies even more than members of advantaged groups (Jost et al., 2003).

There is substantial evidence that members of low-status groups internalize extant inequality. As a consequence, they think and act in ways that reinforce their low status. For example, women are systematically paid less than men for similar work and face other disadvantages in the workplace (Catalyst, 2010; Eurostat, 2008). Although some women are engaged in efforts to redress these disadvantages, studies suggest that, in general, women themselves tend to think they deserve less compensation than men for work of equal quality. This phenomenon is known as 'depressed entitlement' (Hogue & Yoder, 2003; Jost, 1997). Further, overweight individuals who believe in the protestant work-ethic are more willing to think that people have control over how much they weigh and that being overweight is a personal failure (Quinn & Crocker, 1999). Also, members of disadvantaged groups who believe in meritocracy (Major et al., 2002) or are primed with meritocracy (McCoy & Major, 2007) are less likely to recognize instances of discrimination.

Complementary stereotyping

Theories of social dominance orientation (SDO) and social identity imply that unequal social relations are related to negative reciprocal stereotyping between social groups. According to these theories, the primary function of stereotypes is to positively differentiate the ingroup from the outgroup (Tajfel, 1981). System justification theory assumes that supporting and legitimizing inequality is not only achieved through intergroup negativity but also by so-called complementary stereotypes (Jost & Banaji, 1994). This view is inspired by Allport's (1958) claim that the 'rationalizing and justifying function of a stereotype exceeds its function as a reflector of group attributes' (p. 192). In complementary stereotypes 'advantaged and disadvantaged group members are seen as possessing distinctive, offsetting strengths and weaknesses' (Kay & Jost, 2003, p. 825). Examples are popular beliefs that money cannot buy love and that the poor are more likely to be happy while the rich are often miserable. In the wake of the global financial crisis, individuals are likely to engage in complementary stereotyping of bankers – seeing them as competitive and high in status, but also as selfish and even malevolent. These complementary stereotypes are accompanied by Schadenfreude when misfortunes befall bankers (Cikara & Fiske, 2012).

Such complementary stereotypes suggest that everyone receives at least some share of positive and negative outcomes. However, the positive characteristics that are afforded the disadvantaged are not necessarily associated with support for changing their position in society. Paternalistic stereotypes are an example of such attitudes in that they portray groups as deserving of compassion and pity but not respect (Cuddy, Fiske & Glick, 2007). One of the most common cases of paternalistic stereotyping is benevolent sexism – the protection and idealization of traditional women (Glick & Fiske, 1996). Women are often seen as warmer and more communal than men but, at the same time, as less competent and more dependent (see also Pietrzak, Chapter 3, this volume). As a consequence, benevolent sexism reinforces gender inequality by justifying divisions of labour and making women more tolerant of gender discrimination (Sutton, Douglas & McClellan, 2011). Cross-national research confirms that levels of gender inequality are higher in nations with greater endorsement of benevolent sexism (Glick et al., 2004).

How can inequality be reduced?

Even if some degree of inequality is inevitable, various strategies can be employed to reduce it. One strategy some governments employ to diminish income inequality is taxation by which the rich are taxed proportionally more than the poor. Another is the minimum wage standard aimed at ensuring that the poorer segments of society do not live beneath the poverty line. In this section, we discuss some strategies that have been investigated in depth by social psychologists. These strategies work, or are intended to work, by altering social-psychological processes. They can be roughly distinguished by whether they are executed from the bottom up (i.e. through changing individual psychologies, for example by reducing prejudice or removing psychological barriers to engage in protest) or from the top down (i.e. through changing the structural environment, for example by implementing government mandated affirmative action policies).

Bottom-up strategies

Consciousness raising

The system-justifying tendencies we learned about in the previous section often occur unconsciously and, as such, are hard to tackle. Deutsch, in his seminal work on distributive justice (Deutsch, 1985) addresses the problem of raising consciousness about inequality, outlining the conditions that awaken and intensify both victims' and victimizers' sensitivity to injustice. For both parties, these cognitive and motivational factors include the falsification and delegitimization of ideologies and myths that justify injustice, as well as exposure to new ideologies, models and reference groups. In addition, people need to have a sense that any actions they would undertake to redress the injustice will be effective and without harmful consequences to their group or themselves.

Collective versus individual action

Though rarer than one would expect based on self-interest theories, people sometimes challenge inequality. Collective action is a strategy aimed at improving the group's position or treatment from the bottom-up, by mobilizing individuals (usually disadvantaged group members) to band together and act in concert against injustice. The likelihood of collective action is increased when people are aggrieved, feel a sense of collective efficacy, and are identified with the disadvantaged group (see Van Stekelenburg & Klandermans, this volume).

Collective action may ensue especially when injustice is experienced at the group level (i.e. fraternalistic relative deprivation), such as the American Civil Rights Movement against racial discrimination (Major, 1994). Violent street protests have taken place in countries such as the United Kingdom and Greece over a sense of collective injustice whereby privileged groups have emerged relatively unscathed from the financial crisis while middle- and low-income earners are hit by increased taxes and reduced public services. When injustice is framed at the individual level (i.e. egoistic relative deprivation), people may instead revert to individual strategies (Dube & Guimond, 1986), such as actions designed to raise their own status and improve their personal identity (Tajfel, 1974,

1978), as well as attempts to move out of the low-status group (Wright, Taylor & Moghaddam, 1990). Individual action tends to enhance one's personal position but is unlikely to contribute to the reduction of intergroup inequality (e.g. Branscombe & Ellemers, 1998).

In fact, the social mobility of a few individuals has been shown to demotivate other members of lower status groups who have not managed to move up (Martin et al., 1987). In addition, their success actually undermines others' interest in collective action by focusing attention on personal rather than collective injustice, and by encouraging them to see the lower status of their group as more legitimate and stable (Wright, 2001). Finally, Ellemers, Wilke, and van Knippenberg (1993) suggest that seeing a few ingroup members succeed may elicit intragroup rather than intergroup comparisons. As such, the ability of some group members to advance up the status hierarchy is, ironically, conducive to the legitimization and perpetuation of an unequal status quo.

Prejudice reduction

As we have seen, inequality is often underpinned by negative stereotypes and prejudice towards lower-status groups. One strategy to reduce inequality is therefore to reduce prejudice held by higher-status groups towards those less fortunate. Prejudice reduction techniques are reviewed in depth by Cohrs and Kessler (Chapter 1, this volume), so we do not dwell on them here. However, we do pause to consider a potential downside of some prejudice reduction techniques, which itself illustrates the dilemmas and ironies that afflict efforts to reduce inequality in society. Specifically, prejudice reduction typically entails a focus away from group categories, with less identification, differentiation between groups, and/or ingroup favouritism. This focus away from the group is antagonistic to collective action by lower-status groups to improve their circumstances (Wright & Lubensky, 2008). Thus, prejudice reduction techniques may succeed in fostering social harmony at the same time as they perpetuate social inequality.

Take, for example, the extensive literature on the benefits of intergroup contact, which is the most studied method of prejudice reduction. Intergroup contact theory (Allport, 1954; Brown & Hewstone, 2005; Pettigrew & Tropp, 2006) proposes that interpersonal contact is one of the most effective ways to reduce prejudice between majority and minority group members. As people learn more about the other group through increased communication, prejudice should diminish, resulting in improved intergroup relations. When this contact is positive and meets other conditions specified by contact theory, intergroup contact is indeed an effective way to reduce prejudice. But it may have negative effects on support for social change. Saguy et al. (2009) found that members of disadvantaged minority groups expected fairer and more equal treatment from the majority group following positive contact. These expectations turned out not only likely to be unrealistic but also to dampen the motivation to agitate for social change.

Top-down strategies

Social psychological research focusing on intervention strategies that aim to reduce inequality from the top down has largely concerned affirmative action and quota policies. The rationale behind these tactics is that once we change the structure, attitudes do not lag far behind. This approach fits well with the research on system justification that we discussed earlier in this chapter. If people are motivated to justify the way things are, then they should start justifying a new status quo quite rapidly. Kay and colleagues (2009) have called this phenomenon *injunctification,* that is, the motivated tendency to see 'what is' as 'the way it should be'. For example, female participants who were motivated to justify the system thought women *should* be actively represented in the political realm when they were informed that there *are* many (versus few) women in politics.

This research highlights the importance of changing people's *perceptions* of the status quo and suggests that efforts to reduce inequality may be enhanced by marketing campaigns that suggest the status quo is relatively equal (Kay et al., 2009). The implication is that system justification can, when the system is perceived as supportive of equality, help rather than hinder the drive towards greater equality. Further, research even suggests that people justify an anticipated status quo (Kay, Jimenez & Jost, 2002), and social changes that are framed as being supportive of the ideological status quo (e.g. reductions in carbon emissions to protect the American way of life: Feygina, Goldsmith, & Jost, 2010). So, system justification may lead people to support increases in equality – as long as those changes seem inevitable or necessary to protect the broader status quo.

Affirmative action

This is the broad term denoting policies aimed at increasing the representation of underrepresented groups (e.g. based on race, ethnicity, colour, disability, religion, gender) in areas such as employment and education. Affirmative action aims to actively (rather than passively, see Crosby, 1994) reach the goal of equal opportunity. It addresses members of groups that were historically disadvantaged in employment and education based on their group membership, by now giving them privileged access in these domains. For example, affirmative action in education may mean expanding recruitment efforts to encourage minority applications (e.g. by promoting the university at a variety of high schools, including those with large numbers of minorities) or revising the selection process to get rid of potential bias (i.e. by making the admission process blind so that a reviewer is not aware of the demographic background of the applicant; Crosby, 2004).

Quota usage is a type of affirmative action that places the emphasis on category membership over merit. For example, the Northern Irish Police Service in the UK adheres to a 50:50 recruitment quota for Catholics and non-Catholics (Brown, 2011). Points systems have also been used, for example by some US universities who awarded extra admission 'points' on the basis of racial background, which was later deemed unconstitutional by the Supreme Court (Brown, 2011). Many nations (e.g. Norway, France and Spain) impose gender quotas on top-level jobs to equalize the number of men and women in top positions (Bagues & Esteve-Volart, 2007). Quotas have also been used to reduce inequality based on race or disability, as in Poland, which requires enterprises to pay a levy unless 6 per cent of their staff is disabled (Metts, 2000).

Affirmative action policies are predicated on the idea that minorities who make it up the hierarchy will not only serve as role models for other minorities, but that they will be likely to create conditions that are conducive to minorities. However, there is no clear evidence for this. As we have seen, the success of a small number of minority group members may actually demotivate others. Those who have risen up the hierarchy are angered by the collective injustice confronting their group but are unlikely to support collective efforts to address it (Wright & Taylor, 1999). According to Ellemers (2001), individuals who have overcome discrimination are likely to perceive themselves as non-prototypical group members, and to apply negative stereotypes to other group members. A consequence of this dissociation of the self from the group may be that their success does not do anything to help the group's situation (see also Weber & Crocker, 1983).

Another problem for affirmative action policies is that they lead to negative reactions among both majority and minority group members. Majority members are concerned that affirmative action policies give minority members undeserved advantages at the expense of the majority group (e.g. Tougas & Beaton, 1993) and that their rights and treatment are not sufficiently considered (e.g. Newman, 1989). Beneficiaries of affirmative action programmes are marked by a stigma of incompetence (Heilman, Block & Lucas, 1992). Heilman, Simon and Repper (1987) showed that sex-based (versus merit-based) preferential selection had adverse consequences for how women viewed themselves and their performance. Being selected based on one's category membership conveys the message that one did not deserve the job, even if the category membership is a tie-breaker used to separate two candidates judged as equal in competence.

Affirmative action policies remain controversial with arguments being made on both sides (see Crosby et al., 2003). The social psychological evidence discussed in this section suggests, at best, that affirmative action policies should be pursued only with a cautious eye on unintended negative consequences.

Educational initiatives

Another politically controversial top-down approach to reducing inequality is to intervene on the education system. The Head Start and Sure Start programmes in the United States and United Kingdom are prominent examples. In these interventions, disadvantaged youngsters from urban neighbourhoods are given access to enhanced pre-school education. These initiatives are accompanied by support given to the parents of such children, on issues as diverse as behaviour management and nutrition. These programmes yield clear benefits in the short-term, with IQ scores, educational performance and conduct all improving significantly. However, longer-term effects are not as clear. Although there is some evidence that white children, at least, benefit from the programme – in that they are more likely to attend college having participated in such programmes – studies generally show that there is little or no improvement on the test scores of participants in later years. One problem is that the benefits of such early-years interventions may only be maintained if they are coordinated with careful attention to the participants in later years (see Bierman et al., 2008, for a review).

In sum, the literature on reducing inequality with top-down interventions does not give great cause for optimism. Such interventions generally focus on those at the disadvantaged end of the social spectrum, but select only a few for special treatment. Even the few who are fortunate to receive special attention are unlikely to benefit, given the wider ideological and material obstacles to their advancement. Further, some interventions may unintentionally undermine these individuals' motivation and self-esteem. In response to these and other difficulties, Wilkinson and Pickett (2010) argue that reducing inequality directly – by addressing the distribution of wealth – may be far more effective than well-intentioned but disparate, expensive and often minimally effective interventions on those at the wrong end of inequality. To paraphrase a cliché, better to remove the cliff than to station a bunch of ambulances beneath it. However, changing the structure of society and the distribution of wealth is beyond the powers of social psychologists. What we can do is to identify the social-psychological processes that contribute to inequality, those that might aid progress towards a more egalitarian society, and, in the meantime, those that minimize the harms that inequality does to society and to individuals.

Conclusion

We have seen that inequality is associated with a range of social ills such as crime, mortality, educational failure and obesity. Further, we have reviewed theories and research findings that suggest how inequality brings about some of these harms (while noting that not enough of this research is experimental). Specifically, high levels of inequality cause distress by violating widely shared values such as justice and social cohesion. They elicit destructive feelings of relative deprivation, foster selfishness and prejudice, cause higher-status groups to be hypocritical, and lower-status groups to disengage from education while pursuing self-defeating and sometimes anti-social means of advancement. Many of the ill effects of inequality appear to aggravate inequality further – meaning that, if left unchecked, inequality has a self-perpetuating power.

Efforts to reduce inequality, and the harms that it appears to cause, face severe challenges. Leaving aside political and economic barriers, we have touched upon some specifically psychological obstacles to egalitarian reform. The essential dilemma facing individuals is a choice between *coping* with inequality and *combating* inequality. The psychological mechanisms that support one tend to be at odds with those that support the other. For example, people can come to terms with the status quo by adopting ideological positions that legitimize inequality. If they belong to a disadvantaged group, they may dissociate themselves from it. These processes of denial, disidentification and acceptance may suppress open conflict between higher- and lower-status groups; promote happiness; and help lower-status people to feel less embittered, excluded and bewildered, and to make choices that promote their personal interest. However, these same processes cause lower-status people to be disinclined to acknowledge the reality of inequality, still less to take steps to overturn it. Conversely, when people perceive existing inequalities as illegitimate, they may be more inclined to support social change, but are also likely to pay a psychological toll for their view of the society in which they live. Thus, mechanisms that allow people to cope with inequality, and even allow some to escape its clutches, tend, ironically, to perpetuate inequality.

It is possible that this dilemma stems from a fundamental and intractable property of human psychology. It is reminiscent of the choice between problem-focused and emotion-focused coping: in other words, to devote one's energies to the solution of problems, versus leaving those problems unsolved in favour of managing one's psychological response to them (Folkman & Lazarus, 1980). The clear evidence that people value equality, and related values such as justice, gives more ground for optimism. Inequality is likely to arouse at least an uncomfortable state of dissonance, which provides a motivational spur for thought and action. Some of the research we have encountered suggests that people may actively strive to bring about greater equality if they believe that it is inevitable, achievable, being realized, or a goal that is widely shared by others. Further research and theory is likely to uncover more ways in which the dilemma between coping with and combating inequality can be resolved.

Practical task for readers

In 2009 a group of women sued a Swedish university for gender discrimination after they were denied admission into the psychology programme because of their gender. At the time of their application, the university was using gender quotas in some of its programmes aimed at promoting gender equality in professions that are over-represented by women. As a consequence, men received preferential treatment for admission into the psychology programme. Imagine you are a social psychologist serving as a consultant on this case. Please choose a side (i.e. the university or the students who filed the complaint) and use the social-psychological theories that were discussed in this chapter to prepare your defence or prosecution.

Suggested readings

To learn more about psychology of inequality, consider reading Jost & Hunyady (2005), Pratto et al. (1994), Tajfel & Turner (1986), Wilkinson & Pickett (2010), Wright & Lubensky (2008).

References

Aghion, P., Caroli, E. & García-Peñalosa, C. (1999). Inequality and economic growth: The perspective of the New Growth Theories. *Journal of Economic Literature*, 37, 1615–1660.

Aldrick, P. (2011). Bank bosses resist investor demands for bonus reforms. *Daily Telegraph*, 10 May. Available at http://www.telegraph.co.uk/finance/newsbysector/banksandfinance/8505370/Bank-bosses-resist-investor-demands-for-bonus-reforms.html (accessed 13 June 2011).

Allport, G. W. (1958). *The Nature of Prejudice.* Garden City, NY: Doubleday Anchor Books.

Anderson, L. R., Mellor, J. M. & Milyo, J. (2008). Inequality and public good provision: An experimental analysis. *The Journal of Socio-Economics, 37,* 1010–1028.

Bagues, M. F. & Esteve-Volart, B. (2007). Can gender parity break the glass ceiling? Evidence from a repeated randomized experiment. *FEDEA Working Paper,* 2007–2015.

Banerjee, A. V. & Duflo, E. (2003). Inequality and growth: What can the data say? *Journal of Economic Growth, 8,* 267–299.

Benabou, R. (1996). Inequality and growth. *NBER Macroeconomics Journal, 11,* 11–74.

Bierman, K. L., Domitrovich, C. E., Nix, R. L., Gest, S. D., Welsh, J. A., Greenberg, M. T., Blair, C., Nelson, K. E. & Gill, S. (2008). Promoting academic and social-emotional school readiness: The Head Start REDI program. *Child Development, 79,* 1802–1817.

Biernat, M., Vescio, T. K. & Theno, S. A. (1996). Violating American values: a 'value congruence' approach to understanding outgroup attitudes. *Journal of Experimental Social Psychology, 32,* 387–410.

Bjørnskov, C. (2008). The growth-inequality association: Government ideology matters. *Journal of Development Economics, 87.* 300–308.

Branscombe, N. R. & Ellemers, N. (1998). Coping with group-based discrimination: Individualistic versus group-level strategies. In J. K. Swim and C. Stangor (eds.), *Prejudice: The Target's Perspective* (pp. 243–266). San Diego, CA: Academic Press.

Brown, G. (2011). Brief 8: Combating horizontal inequalities through affirmative action. *Crise.* Oxford: University of Oxford. Available at http://www.crise.ox.ac.uk/policywork.shtml (accessed 16 May 2011).

Brown, G. (2011). Take back the future. *Newsweek.* Available at http://www.newsweek.com/2011/05/15/take-back-the-future.html (accessed 13 June 2011).

Brown, R. & Hewstone, M. (2005). An integrative theory of intergroup contact In: M. Zanna (ed.), *Advances in Experimental Social Psychology* (vol. 37 pp. 255–343). San Diego: Academic Press.

Callan, M. J., Ellard, J. H., Shead, N. W. & Hodgins, D. C. (2008). Gambling as a search for justice: Examining the role of personal relative deprivation in gambling urges and behavior. *Personality and Social Psychology Bulletin, 34,* 1514–1529.

Camerer, C. F. (2003). *Behavioral Game Theory: Experiments in Strategic Interaction.* Princeton: Princeton University Press.

Catalyst. (2010). Catalyst census: Fortune 500 women board directors. Available at www.catalyst.org/publication/460/2010-catalyst-census-fortune-500-women-board-directors (accessed 16 May 2011).

Chen, X. P. (1999). Work team cooperation: The effects of structural and motivational changes. In M. Foddy & M. Smithson (eds.), *Resolving Social Dilemmas: Dynamic, Structural, and Intergroup Aspects* (pp. 181–192). Philadephia, PA: Psychology Press.

Cikara, M. & Fiske, S. T. (2012). Stereotypes and Schadenfreude: Behavioral and physiological markers of pleasure at others' misfortunes. *Social Psychological and Personality Science*, 3, 63–71.

CNBC (2011). World's biggest debtor nations. Available at http://www.cnbc.com/id/30308959?slide= 1 (accessed 13 June 2011).

Conte, A., Davidson, S. & Burchill, R. (2004). *Defining Civil and Political Rights: The Jurisprudence of the United Nations Human Rights Committee*. Burlington, VT: Ashgate.

Crosby, F. J. (1976). A model of egoistical relative deprivation. *Psychological Review*, 83, 85–113.

Crosby, F. J. (1994). Understanding affirmative action. *Basic and Applied Social Psychology*, 15, 13–41.

Crosby, F. J. (2004). *Affirmative Action is Dead; Long Live Affirmative Action*. New Haven, CT: Yale University Press.

Crosby, F. J., Iyer, A., Clayton, S. & Downing, R. (2003). Affirmative action: Psychological data and the policy debates. *American Psychologist*, 58, 93–115.

Cuddy, A. J. C., Fiske, S. T. & Glick, P. (2007). The BIAS Map: Behaviors from intergroup affect and stereotypes. *Journal of Personality and Social Psychology*, 92, 631–648.

Deutsch, M. (1985). *Distributive Justice: A Social Psychological Perspective*. New Haven, CT: Yale University Press.

Dubé, L. & Guimond, S. (1986). Relative deprivation and social protest: The personal-group issue. In J. M. Olson, C. P. Herman & M. P. Zanna (eds.), *Relative Deprivation and Social Comparison: The Ontario Symposium* (vol. 4, pp. 57–77). Hillsdale: Erlbaum.

Duckitt, J. (2001). A cognitive-motivational theory of ideology and prejudice. In M.P. Zanna (ed.), *Advances in Experimental Social Psychology* (vol. 33, pp. 41–113). San Diego: Academic Press.

Duckitt, J. & Sibley, C.G. (2007). Right wing authoritarianism, social dominance orientation and the dimensions of generalized prejudice. *European Journal of Personality*, 21, 113–130.

Ellemers, N. (2001). Individual upward mobility and the perceived legitimacy of intergroup relations. In J. T. Jost and B. Major (eds.), *The Psychology of Legitimacy: Emerging Perspectives on Ideology, Justice, and Intergroup Relations* (pp. 205–222). New York: Cambridge University Press.

Eurostat. (2008). Gender pay gap statistics. Available at http://epp.eurostat.ec.europa.eu/statistics_explained/index.php/Gender_pay_gap_statistics (accessed 16 May 2011).

Feygina, I., Jost, J. T. & Goldsmith, R. E. (2010). System justification, the denial of global warming, and the possibility of 'system sanctified change'. *Personality and Social Psychology Bulletin*, 36, 326–338.

Folkman, S. & Lazarus, R. S. (1980). An analysis of coping in a middle-aged community sample. *Journal of Health and Social Behavior*, 21, 219–239.

Forbes, K. J. (2000). A reassessment of the relationship between inequality and growth. *American Economic Review*, 90, 869–887.

Glick, P. & Fiske, S. T. (1996). The Ambivalent Sexism Inventory: Differentiating hostile and benevolent sexism. *Journal of Personality and Social Psychology*, 70, 491–512.

Glick, P., Lameiras, M., Fiske, S. T., Eckes, T., Masser, B., Volpato, C. & Manganelli, A. M., Pek, J. C. X., Huang, L., Sakalli-Uğurlu, N., Castro, Y. R.,

D'Avila Pereira, M. L., Willemsen, T. M., Brunner, A., Six-Materna, I. & Wells, R. (2004). Bad but bold: Ambivalent attitudes toward men predict gender inequality in 16 ations. *Journal of Personality and Social Psychology*, 86, 713–728.

Greve, F. (2009). America's poor are its most generous givers. *McClatchy Newspapers*. Available at http://www.mcclatchydc.com/2009/05/19/68456/americas-poor-are-its-most-generous.html (accessed 23 July 2011).

Gruenfeld, D. H., Inesi, M. E., Magee, J. C. & Galinsky, A. D. (2008). Power and the objectification of social targets. *Journal of Personality and Social Psychology*, 95, 111–127.

Halevy, N., Chou, E. Y., Cohen, T. R. & Bornstein, G. (2010). Relative deprivation and intergroup competition. *Group Processes and Intergroup Relations*, 13, 685–700.

Ham, J. & van den Bos, K. (2008). Not fair for me! The influence of personal relevance on social justice inferences. *Journal of Experimental Social Psychology*, 44, 699–705.

Heilman, M. E., Block, C. J. & Lucas, J. A. 1992. Presumed incompetent?: Stigmatization and affirmative action efforts. *Journal of Applied Psychology*, 77, 536–544.

Heilman, M. E., Simon, M. C. & Repper, D. P. (1987). Intentionally favored, unintentionally harmed?: The impact of gender based preferential selection on self-perception and self-evaluation. *Journal of Applied Psychology*, 76, 62–68.

Hennigan, K. M., Del Rosario, M. L., Heath, L., Cook, T. D., Wharton, J. D. & Calder, B. J. (1982). Impact of the introduction of television on crime in the United States: Empirical findings and theoretical implications. *Journal of Personality and Social Psychology*, 42, 461–477.

Hogue, M. & Yoder, J. D. (2003). The gender wage gap: An explanation of men's elevated wage entitlement. *Sex Roles*, 56, 573–579.

Jost, J. T. (1997). An experimental replication of the depressed entitlement effect among women. *Psychology of Women Quarterly*, 21, 387–393.

Jost, J. T. & Banaji M. R. (1994). The role of stereotyping in system-justification and the production of false consciousness. *British Journal of Social Psychology*, 33, 1–27.

Jost, J. T., Glaser, J., Kruglanski, A. W. & Sulloway, F. (2003). Political conservatism as motivated social cognition. *Psychological Bulletin*, 129, 339–375.

Jost, J. T. & Hunyady, O. (2005). Antecedents and consequences of system-justifying ideologies. *Current Directions in Psychological Science*, 14, 260–265.

Jost, J. T., Ledgerwood, A. & Hardin, C. D. (2008). Shared reality, system justification, and the relational basis of ideological beliefs. *Social and Personality Psychology Compass*, 2, 171–218.

Jost, J. T., Pelham, B. W., Sheldon, O. & Sullivan, B. N. (2003). Social inequality and the reduction of ideological dissonance on behalf of the system: Evidence of enhanced system justification among the disadvantaged. *European Journal of Social Psychology*, 33, 13–36.

Jost, J. T., & Van der Toorn, J. (2012). System justification theory. In P. A. M. van Lange, A. W. Kruglanski & E. T. Higgins (eds.), *Handbook of Theories of Social Psychology* (pp. 313–343). London: Sage.

Katz, I. & Hass, R. G. (1988). Racial ambivalence and American value conflict: correlational and priming studies of dual cognitive structures. *Journal of Personality and Social Psychology*, 55, 893–905.

Kay, A. C., Gaucher, D., Peach, J. M., Laurin, K., Friesen, J., Zanna, M. P. & Spencer, S. J. (2009). Inequality, discrimination, and the power of the status quo: Direct evidence for a motivation to see the way things are as the way they should be. *Journal of Personality and Social Psychology*, 97, 421–434.

Kay, A. C., Jimenez, M. C. & Jost, J. T. (2002). Sour grapes, sweet lemons, and the anticipatory rationalization of the status quo. *Personality and Social Psychology* Bulletin, 28, 1300–1312.

Kay, A. C. & Jost, J. T. (2003). Complementary justice: Effects of 'poor but happy' and 'poor but honest' stereotype exemplars on system justification and implicit activation of the justice motive. *Journal of Personality and Social Psychology*, 85, 823–837.

Kessler, T. & Mummendey, A. (2002). Sequential or parallel processing? A longitudinal field study concerning determinants of identity-management strategies. *Journal of Personality and Social Psychology*, 82, 75–88.

Kipnis, D. (1972). Does power corrupt? *Journal of Personality and Social Psychology*, 24, 33–41.

Lammers, J., Stapel, D. A. & Galisnky, A. D. (2010). Power increases hypocrisy: Moralizing in reasoning, immorality in behavior. *Psychological Science*, 21, 737–744.

Leach, C. W. (2008). Envy, inferiority and injustice: Three bases of anger about inequality. In R. H. Smith (ed.), *Envy: Theory and Research* (pp. 94–116). Oxford: Oxford University Press.

Leach, C. W. & Spears, R. (2008). 'A vengefulness of the impotent': The pain of in-group inferiority and Schadenfreude toward successful outgroups. *Journal of Personality and Social Psychology*, 95, 1383–1396.

Lerner, M. J. (1980). *The Belief in a Just World: A Fundamental Delusion*. New York: Plenum Press.

Lesko, A. C & Corpus, J. H. Discounting the difficult: How high math identified women respond to stereotype threat. *Sex Roles*, 54, 113–125.

Liu, J. & Huang, L. (2008). Cross-sectional and longitudinal differences in social dominance orientation and right-wing authoritarianism as a function of political power and societal change. *Asian Journal of Social Psychology*, 11, 116–126.

McCoy, S. K. & Major, B. (2007). Priming meritocracy and the psychological justification of inequality. *Journal of Experimental Social Psychology*, 43, 341–351.

Major, B. (1994). From social inequality to personal entitlement: The role of social comparisons, legitimacy appraisals, and group membership. *Advances in Experimental Social Psychology*, 26, 293–355.

Major, B., Gramzow, R. H., McCoy, S., Levin, S., Schmader, T. & Sidanius, J. (2002). Perceiving personal discrimination: the role of group status and legitimizing ideology. *Journal of Personality and Social Psychology*, 82, 269–282.

Mandisodza, A., Jost, J. T. & Unzueta, M. (2006). 'Tall poppies' and 'American dreams': Reactions to rich and poor in Australia and the U.S.A. *Journal of Cross-Cultural Psychology*, 37, 659–668.

Martin, J., Price, R. L., Bies, R. J. & Powers, M. E. (1987). Now that I can have it, I'm not so sure I want it: The effects of opportunity on aspirations and discontent. In B. A. Gutek & L. Larwood (eds.), *Women's Career Development* (pp. 42–65). Beverly Hills, CA: Sage.

Metts, R. (2000). Disability issues, trends, and recommendations for the World Bank. Social Protection Discussion Paper 0007. Washington, DC: World Bank.

Moghaddam, F. M. (2005). The staircase to terrorism: A psychological exploration. *American Psychologist*, 60, 161–169.

Moscatelli, S., Albarello, F. & Rubini, M. (2008). Linguistic discrimination in minimal groups: The impact of status differentials. *Journal of Language and Social Psychology*, 27, 140–154.

Napier, J. L. & Jost, J. T. (2008). Why are conservatives happier than liberals? *Psychological Science*, 19, 565–572.

Newman, J. D. (1989). Affirmative action and the courts. In F. A. Blanchard & F. J Crosby (eds.), *Affirmative Action in Perspective* (pp. 31–49). Springer-Verlag, New York.

Norton, M. I. & Ariely, D. (2011). Building a better America – one wealth quintile at a time. *Perspectives on Psychological Science*, 6, 9–12.

Olsen, J. M., Roese, N. J., Meen, J. & Robertson, D. J. (1995). The preconditions and consequences of relative deprivation: Two field studies. *Journal of Applied Social Psychology*, 25, 944–964.

Pettigrew, T. F. & Tropp, L. R. (2006). A meta-analytic test of intergroup contact theory. *Journal of Personality and Social Psychology*, 90, 751–783.

Pham-Kanter, G. (2009). Social comparisons and health: Can having richer friends and neighbours make you sick? *Social Science and Medicine*, 69, 335–344.

Piff, P., Kraus, M. W., Côté, S., Hayden Cheng, B. & Keltner, D. (2010). Having less, giving more: The influence of social class on prosocial behavior. *Journal of Personality and Social Psychology*, 99, 771–784.

Pratto, F., Sidanius, J., Stallworth, L. M. & Malle, B. F. (1994). Social dominance orientation: A personality variable predicting social and political attitudes. *Journal of Personality and Social Psychology*, 67, 741–763.

Putnam, R. D. (2000). *Bowling alone: The Collapse and Revival of American Community*. New York: Simon and Schuster.

Quinn, D. M. & Crocker, J. (1999). When ideology hurts: Effects of belief in the Protestant ethic and feeling overweight on the psychological well-being of women. *Journal of Personality and Social Psychology*, 77, 402–414.

Rawls, J. (1971). *A Theory of Justice*. Cambridge: Harvard University Press.

Reich, R. (2010). *Aftershock: The Next Economy and America's Future*. New York: Random House.

Saguy, T., Tausch, N., Dovidio, J. F. & Pratto, F. (2009). The irony of harmony: Intergroup contact can produce false expectations for equality. *Psychological Science*, 29, 114–121.

Samuelson, C. D. & Allison, S. T. (1994). Cognitive factors affecting the use of social decision heuristics in resource-sharing tasks. *Organizational Behavior and Human Decision Processes*, 58, 1–27.

Schmitt, M. T., Branscombe, N. R. & Kappen, D. M. (2003). Attitudes toward group-based inequality: Social dominance or social identity? *British Journal of Social Psychology*, 42, 161–186.

Schwarz, S. (1992). Universals in the content and structure of values: Theoretical advances and empirical tests in 20 countries. In M. Zanna (ed.), *Advances in Experimental Social Psychology* (vol. 25. pp. 1–66). San Diego: Academic Press.

Sibley, C. G. & Duckitt, J. (2008). Personality and prejudice: A meta-analysis and theoretical review. *Personality and Social Psychology Review*, 12, 248–279.

Sidanius, J., Levin, S., Federico, C. & Pratto, F. (2001). Legitimizing ideologies: The social dominance approach. In J. Jost and B. Major (eds.), *The Psychology of Legitimacy: Emerging Perspectives on Ideology, Justice, and Intergroup Relations* (pp. 307–331). New York: Cambridge University Press.

Smith, R. H. & Kim, S. H. (2007). Comprehending envy. *Psychological Bulletin*, 133, 46–64.

Stouten, J., De Cremer, D. & van Dijk, E. (2005). All is well that ends well, at least for proselfs: Emotional reactions to equality violation as a function of social value orientation. *European Journal of Social Psychology*, 35, 767–783.

Sutton, R. M., Douglas, K. M., Wilkin, K., Elder, T. J., Cole, J. M. & Stathi, S. (2008). Justice for whom, exactly? Beliefs in justice for the self and various others. *Personality and Social Psychology Bulletin*, 38, 528–541.

Sutton, R. M., Douglas, K. M. & McClellan, L. (2011). Benevolent sexism, perceived health risks, and the inclination to restrict pregnant women's freedoms. *Sex Roles*, 65, 596–605.

Tajfel, H. (1974). Social identity and intergroup behavior. *Social Science Information*, 13, 65–93.

Tajfel, H. (1981). *Human Groups and Social Categories*. Cambridge University Press, Cambridge.

Tajfel, H. (1978). *Differentiation between social groups: Studies in the social psychology of intergroup relations*. London: Academic Press.

Tajfel, H. & Turner, J. C. (1979). An integrative theory of intergroup conflict. In W. G. Austin & S. Worchel (eds.), *The Social Psychology of Intergroup Relations* (pp. 33–47). Monterey, CA: Brooks/Cole.

Tajfel, H. & Turner, J. C. (1986). The social identity theory of intergroup behavior. In S. Worchel & L. W. Austin (eds.), *Psychology of Intergroup Relations* (pp. 7–24). Chicago: Nelson-Hall.

Teachman, J. (1987). Family background, educational resources and educational attainment. *American Sociological Review*, 52, 548–557.

Tougas, F. & Beaton, A. M. (1993). Affirmative action in the work place: For better or for worse. *Applied Psychology: An International Review*, 42, 253–264.

Van den Bos, K. & Lind, E. A. (2001). The psychology of own versus others' treatment: Self-oriented and other-oriented effects on perceptions of procedural justice. *Personality and Social Psychology Bulletin*, 27, 1324–1333.

Van der Toorn, J., Tyler, T. R. & Jost, J. T. (2011). More than fair: Outcome dependence, system justification, and the perceived legitimacy of authority figures. *Journal of Experimental Social Psychology*, 47, 127–138.

Weber, R. & Crocker, J. (1983). Cognitive processes in the revision of stereotypic beliefs. *Journal of Personality and Social Psychology*, 45, 961–977.

Wilkinson, R. & Pickett, K. (2010). *The Spirit Level: Why Equality is Better for Everyone*. London: Penguin.

Wright, S. C. (2001). Restricted intergroup boundaries: Tokenism, ambiguity and the tolerance of injustice. In J. T. Jost & B. Major (eds.), *The Psychology of*

Legitimacy: Emerging Perspectives on Ideology, Justice, and Intergroup Relations (pp.223–254). New York: Cambridge University Press.

Wright, S. & Lubensky, M. (2008). The struggle for social equality: Collective action vs. prejudice reduction. In S. Demoulin, J. P. Leyens & J. F. Dovidio (eds.), *Intergroup Misunderstandings: Impact of Divergent Social Realities* (pp. 291–310). New York: Psychology Press.

Wright, S. C. & Taylor, D. M. (1999). Success under tokenism: Co-option of the newcomer and the prevention of collective protest. *British Journal of Social Psychology, 38,* 369–396.

Wright, S. C., Taylor, D. M. & Moghaddam, F. M. (1990). Responding to membership in a disadvantaged group: From acceptance to collective protest. *Journal of Personality and Social Psychology, 58,* 994–1003.

Yitzhaki, S. (1979). Relative deprivation and the Gini coefficient. *Quarterly Journal of Economics, 93,* 321–324.

Note

1. The second author was supported by National Science Center funds, decision number DEC-2011/01/B/HS6/04637.

6

Social Conflict and Social Protest

Jacquelien van Stekelenburg
and Bert Klandermans

● ●

The place and time is the Netherlands, the last week of November 2007: the situation in Dutch higher education has become a topic of heated debates in the country. Several ambitious reforms have been implemented during the previous decades leaving a widespread feeling that these reforms have generated discontent rather than improvements, especially in secondary education. Some even talked about a crisis in Dutch secondary education (e.g. Ritzen, the former minister of education in the Dutch newspaper *Trouw*, 22 November 2007). In November 2007 secondary education pupils protested against so-called '1040-hours norm'. This norm refers to the number of hours' education that pupils are entitled to receive annually; schools are fined if they fail to deliver. Nonetheless, due to a lack of qualified teachers, quite a few schools were not able to meet these requirements. As a consequence, it could happen, for instance, that mathematics was taught by a physical instructor or that pupils had to sit in a classroom and wait for long periods of time. School management, teachers, students and their parents were all very unhappy with this situation and the time was ripe for mass protests. Some 20,000 secondary schools took to the streets on 23 November at 50 locations scattered all over the country to protest the declining conditions in their education. These protests were initiated by a guy called 'Kevin', a stereotypical 'guy next door' who wrote *one* MSN message that was 'virally' spread via virtual and face-to-face personal networks. One week later, on 30 November, 20,000 pupils again took to the streets, this time mobilized by the national student union, which employed its mobilizing channels supplemented by television, radio and newspapers (see Van Stekelenburg & Klandermans, forthcoming 2012 for a further elaboration on these different campaigns and protests).

Obviously, all protesting pupils were aggrieved and openly contested the established authorities in an attempt to improve the deteriorating quality of their education. However, not all aggrieved pupils protested (cf. Klandermans, 1997). In fact, passivity in the face of imperilled interests or violated values is more often the rule rather than the exception (Marwell & Oliver, 1993). Besides inactivity, there is a vast array of behaviours that people might exhibit as a reaction to experienced grievances. Wright and colleagues (1990) have proposed a framework based on three distinctions: the first between inaction and action, the second between actions directed at improving one's personal conditions (individual action, e.g. opting for another school with better conditions) and actions directed at improving the conditions of one's group (collective action, e.g. signing a petition, demonstrating). The third distinction is between actions that conform to the norms of the existing social system (normative action such as petitioning and taking part in a legal demonstration such as staged by Landelijk Actie Komitee Scholieren (LAKS), National action committee high school students and 'Kevin') and those who violate existing social rules (non-normative action such as illegal protests and civil disobedience).

From a social-psychological viewpoint such taxonomies of participation are relevant because one may expect different forms of participation to involve different motivational dynamics. Motivational dynamics of participation can be distinguished on two dimensions: *time* and *effort* (Klandermans, 1997). Some forms of participation are limited in time or are a once-only kind and involve little effort or risk – giving money, signing a petition, or taking part in a peaceful demonstration such as staged by LAKS and 'Kevin'. Other forms of participation are also short-lived but involve considerable effort or risk – a sit-in, a site occupation or a strike. Participation can also be indefinite but undemanding – paying a membership fee to an organization or being on call for two nights a month. Finally, there are forms of participation that are both enduring and taxing, such as being a member on a committee or a volunteer in a movement organization. This distinction accounts for the motivational dynamics underlying differential forms of participation. Indeed, why does one person go to a demonstration while others stay at home? Or why are many more people prepared to sign a petition than to go on strike? Or why is one person inclined to use violence to pursue the group goals, while others are not? These questions relate to the motivational dynamics of individual protesters and are the core of the social psychology of protest. People – social psychologists never tire of asserting us – live in a perceived world. They respond to the world as they perceive and interpret it. Indeed, this is what a social psychology of protest is about – trying to understand why people who are seemingly in the same situation respond so differently.

Social psychology explores the causes of the thoughts, feelings and actions of people and thus has a lot to offer to the study of social conflict and protest. In this chapter, we will illustrate this point with an overview of the state-of-the-art theoretical approaches and a review of empirical evidence. The main section focuses on social-psychological approaches of mobilization and participation – the *antecedent* of protest. A much smaller section deals with the *consequences* of protest. Mobilization and protest participation are social psychologists' cup of tea, yet surprisingly, the social-psychological consequences of protest are an untouched area in the literature (see for a similar observation Louis, 2009). However, precisely in this process of participation and its aftermath we may be able to find the answers to one of the most intriguing questions in protest participation: that is the paradox of persistent participation (Louis, 2009). Indeed, activism frequently persists despite pessimism regarding the action's ostensible goals (Louis, 2009). Why do people keep on participating in protest although it does not effectuate the demanded political claims? We will discuss how such matters as disengagement, empowerment and increased politicization prevent or promote sustained participation. The chapter closes with a section in which we will try to assess where we stand at the moment and propose directions to proceed for the future.

Mobilization and participation

Successful mobilization brings together what Klandermans (2004) calls 'demand' and 'supply'. *Demand* refers to the will of (a segment) of the population to protest and show its discontent and indignation. The demand side of protest concerns the characteristics of a social movement's mobilization potential (Klandermans, 2012), the grievances and emotions protesters share, and the groups they are embedded in and identify with. *Supply* refers to social-movement organizations and their appeals, and the opportunities staged by organizers to protest. It relates to the characteristics of the movement. Is it strong? Is it likely to achieve its goals at affordable costs? Does it have charismatic leaders? Is it an organization people can identify with? Does it stage activities that are appealing to people? Take for example the secondary education protests: all aggrieved and indignant pupils in the Netherlands are part of the mobilization potential and thus can be potentially mobilized for protests staged by LAKS and 'Kevin'. LAKS and 'Kevin' are both representatives of the supply of protest, albeit different. Demand and supply do not automatically come together. In the market economy, marketing is employed to make sure that the public is aware of a supply that might meet its demand. *Mobilization* can be seen as the marketing mechanism of the social-movement domain. Protest participation is seldom an impulsive act but an act that requires meticulous matching of a 'demand' and 'supply' of protest. Organizers must be willing to invest their resources and time in staging a campaign. Consensus must be mobilized to enlarge the pool of sympathizers. People need to know about an upcoming protest event and need to be motivated to participate (Klandermans & Oegema, 1987).

Mobilization

Mobilization is the process that gets the movement going. Demand and supply would remain as merely potential if processes of mobilization did not bring the two together. Mobilization is a complicated process that can be broken down into several conceptually distinct steps. Klandermans (1988) proposed to break down the process of mobilization into consensus and action mobilization. *Consensus mobilization* refers to dissemination of the views of the movement organization, while *action mobilization* refers to those who adopted the view of the movement and their transformation into active participants. The chairman of LAKS, just 17 years old, played a major role in mobilizing consensus regarding the so-called crisis in Dutch education. This young man – the spokesperson of the pupils – was well-bred good-looking and with an extremely ready tongue; he appeared as a revelation to journalists and aroused a kind of excitement among them. They, in return, enabled him to gain access to the media, thus providing LAKS with a platform for free publicity. This successful consensus mobilization created a large pool of sympathizers that LAKS *and* 'Kevin' could both draw from when they mobilized for action. The more successful the consensus mobilization, the larger the pool of sympathizers that a mobilizing-movement organization can draw from.

In their frame alignment approach to mobilization Snow and Benford and their colleagues elaborated *consensus mobilization* much further (see Benford, 1997 for a critical review; and Snow, 2004 for an overview). Social movements play a significant role in the diffusion of ideas and values: Rochon (1998) makes the distinction between 'critical communities', where new ideas and values are developed, and 'social movements' that are interested in winning social and political acceptance for those ideas and values. He writes: 'In the hands of movement leaders, the ideas of critical communities become ideological frames' (Rochon, 1992, p. 31).

Successful mobilization is a dynamic process that brings together 'supply' and 'demand' (cf. Klandermans and Oegema, 1987). On the supply side, organizations need to pay attention to the following four aspects of mobilization: (1) formation of mobilization potentials, (2) formation and activation of recruitment networks, (3) arousal of motivation to participate, and (4) removal of barriers to participation. On the demand side, individuals go through four synchronous steps towards participation: (1) becoming part of the mobilization potential, (2) becoming a target of mobilization attempts, (3) becoming motivated to participate, and (4) overcoming barriers to participation (see Figure 6.1).

Take for instance the aforementioned 'crisis' in Dutch education. The first step accounts for the successful consensus mobilization by LAKS. This step distinguished the general public into those who sympathize with the cause and those who do not. A large pool of sympathizers is of strategic importance, because for a variety of reasons many sympathizers never become active participants. The second step is equally crucial: it divides the sympathizers into those who have been a target of mobilization attempts and those who have not. The crisis in education was the 'talk of the town'; consequently, 90 per cent of the mobilization potential were targeted by a mobilization attempt (Van Stekelenburg & Klandermans, 2012). The third step concerns the social-psychological core of the process. It divides the sympathizers who have been targeted into those who are motivated to participate in the specific activity and those who are not. Protest activities can be appealing to some but appalling to others, because they deem them to be for instance inefficacious or dangerous. Finally, the fourth step

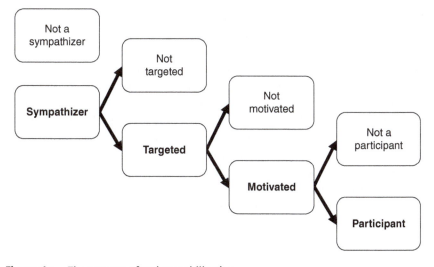

Figure 6.1 The process of action mobilization.
Source: Klandermans & Oegema, 1987.

differentiates the people who are motivated into those who end up participating and those who do not. This last step is about barriers. For instance, the various barriers reported by motivated Dutch pupils who eventually did *not* participate were the weather conditions (it was extremely cold on the day of the protests), illness, and lack of parental consent.

Klandermans and Oegema's mobilization theory is based on a study that examined all four steps of the mobilization process from a mobilization campaign for the peace demonstration in The Hague in 1983, the largest demonstration the Netherlands had ever experienced. The week before the demonstration, they conducted a telephone survey to determine support for the campaign and respondents were asked if they intended to participate in the demonstration. After the demonstration, respondents were asked in a follow-up survey if they had taken part. This pre-event/post-event design appeared to be of utmost importance, as motivations and barriers underlying intended *and* actual participation could be observed. It turned out that the intention to participate was by no means a sufficient condition, as demonstrated by the proportion of motivated individuals that eventually did not participate (60 per cent). In yet another study, Oegema and Klandermans (1994) showed that post-hoc comparison of participants and non-participants would have been inadequate. In this study (with an identical design), they showed that non-participants who reported in the pre-survey that they intended to sign a petition, reported in the post-survey that they never had such intentions. Hence, post-hoc comparison of participants and non-participants is inadequate because people tend to reconstruct the past from the viewpoint of the present.

Another aspect that turned out to be important was the analytical distinction between the four steps. Distinguishing between the steps is justified theoretically because different theories are needed to explain separate aspects of mobilization and participation, and practically relevant as different efforts are required from movement organizations depending on which aspect of the mobilization process they are handling. Analytically distinguishing between the four steps revealed the *process* of mobilization. It made clear that three-quarters of the population felt sympathy for the movement's cause. Of these sympathizers, three-quarters were somehow targeted by mobilization attempts. Of those targeted, one-sixth was motivated to participate in the demonstration. And finally, of those motivated, one-third ended up participating. The net result of these different steps revealed that a small proportion of the general public eventually participated – 4 per cent.

All in all, this study revealed the complexity of mobilization processes and how to go about investigating them. It has shown that mobilization and the final turnout results from a tight interaction between demand and supply factors. For instance, it shows the importance of a large pool of sympathizers, as the net result of the general public who actually participate in the protest is usually a very small proportion. It also shows the importance of the formation of a mobilizing structure: it is via these informal and formal networks that people can be targeted. But, most of all, it revealed the importance of motivation. That is, reducing the costs and increasing the benefits for participation. Indeed, with each step, varying numbers drop out: the better the fit between demand and supply, the smaller the number of people who drop out.

Mobilization with minimal organization

The economic 'demand' and 'supply' metaphor does not entirely translate into protest events, as there can be mobilization with minimal social-movement organization. Walgrave and Manssens (2000) showed that broad mass-based indignation evoked by judicial bias around the Marc Dutroux kidnapping case – and his serial killing of young girls – captivated television and newspaper audiences and functioned as a mobilizing actor. The moral indignation evoked by his crimes was strengthened by a widespread anger and frustration among Belgians induced by investigational errors and a general distrust of the judicial system. This mass indignation formed the basis for the famous White March. Yet, the Belgium White March seems to be an exceptional case. In general, the mobilizing power of the media should not be overestimated (Kingdon, 1984), and *if* they have the power to mobilize it is in case of so-called consensual issues (Verhulst, 2011). Consensual issues root in suddenly imposed grievances to evoke a communal sense of repulsion and indignation. Examples in place are the death of a child caused by drunk-driving (McCarthy & Wolfson, 1996) or senseless violence (Lodewijkx, Kersten & Van Zomeren, 2008). Such tragic events put consensual issues crudely at the top of public and political agendas, and discussions easily converge on a general standpoint. Who, after all, can be against safe roads or safe societies? The salience and high consensus of consensual issues compensate for the lack of organizational brokerage making mobilization via the mass media possible.

Nowadays, we see more mobilization with minimal organization through virtual networks or social media such as Facebook and MySpace. As a message spreads virtually, tens of thousands of people may be reached in a matter of hours or even minutes because people send the message to hundreds of 'friends' at a time. The protests initiated by 'Kevin' are an example of this kind of mobilization (Van Stekelenburg & Boekkooi, 2012; Van Stekelenburg & Klandermans, 2012). These protests took the shape of several protests of relatively small groups geographically scattered and diffused over a longer period of time that were *impromptu* organized and mobilized, and short-lived. 'Kevin's' call for action was 'virally' spread via virtual (e.g. MSN, social-network sites) and face-to-face personal networks. Unrest was uploaded on YouTube and people could watch on their mobile phones. The images of angry empowered pupils enhanced collective efficaciousness of potential protesters and thus triggered their motivation to take part in the protest. These YouTube films facilitated a rapid process of frame-alignment; in nearly real-life time, *potential* protesters came to share grievances, emotions and efficacy with *actual* protesters. Moreover, questions related to expected participation of others were instantly answered by the uploaded films and instant messages. Social media and smartphones, but also YouTube, facilitated organizing without organizations, and thus mobilization without supply.

This case shows that organizing without organizations via informal and virtual networks affects mobilization significantly. The lack of coordination and the loosely coupled informal (virtual) social networks have led to so-called *rhizomatic mobilization* (see Van Stekelenburg & Klandermans, 2012). Rhizomatic mobilization moves from one person to another – individually, as part of a larger cc. list, via a listserv, or via a social network such as Facebook or MySpace. In a process that continues to reproduce itself, the message is copied and redistributed. An original sender cannot know where or when the message stops travelling, stops being copied and redistributed, stops being translated. Messages with higher degrees of resonance will be dispersed in greater densities. The emerging and fluid networks of actions unfold with little planning, are coordinated by ICTs, and are unbounded and uncontrolled. The resulting actions often emerge as simultaneous street demonstrations at multiple locations. Consider, for instance, the Arabian revolutions in the Spring of 2011, scattered from Tunisia to Syria. What seems spontaneous impromptu organized protest at first sight, in hindsight often appears to be more organized than was first presumed. The 'roots' of the Egyptian protests in the Spring of 2011, for instance, can be traced back to a strike of textile workers in 2008. When food prices tripled in 2008, the political temperature began to rise. Textile workers joined forces with other traditional organizations, including student groups, leftist parties, and Islamist organizations, and called a national strike. But the story took a dramatic new turn when Egypt's strikers were joined by a volunteer army of tens of thousands of tech-savvy young people, deploying the interactive media of Facebook, mobile phone text messaging, and YouTube. In the Dutch pupils protest, we observe a similar dynamic, behind the seemingly spontaneous impromptu protests initiated by Kevin appeared LAKS as a successful traditional mobilization 'machine'. Hence, formal organizations still seem important tools to generate large crowds. This word of caution seems therefore appropriate in drawing too hasty conclusions. Indeed, for the time being there are more questions than answers about these 'new' forms of protests.

Participation

Participation brings us to the demand side of protest, which concerns the characteristics of a social movement's *mobilization potential* (Klandermans, 2012). A movement's mobilization potential can be characterized in terms of the grievances and emotions people share and the groups they are embedded in and identify with. Klandermans, speaking of the dynamics of demand, refers to the process of the formation of mobilization potential: grievances and identities politicize, environments turn supportive, and emotions are aroused.

Grievances

Grievances concern the 'outrage about the way authorities are treating a social problem' (Klandermans, 1997, p. 38). At the heart of every protest are grievances, be it the experience of illegitimate inequality, feelings of relative deprivation, feelings of injustice moral indignation, or a suddenly imposed grievance (Klandermans, 1997). Illegitimate inequality is what theories of relative deprivation and social justice are about; suddenly imposed grievances refer to an unexpected threat or inroad upon people's rights or circumstances (Walsh, 1981). Grievances resulting from violated principles refer to moral outrage because it is felt that important values or principles are violated (Van Stekelenburg, Klandermans & van Dijk, 2009). In more general terms, intergroup conflicts can be framed as conflicts of principle or conflicts of interest (Van Stekelenburg & Klandermans, 2009). Evidence suggests that in a conflict of interest people are more inclined to take an instrumental route to protest to enforce changes, whereas a conflict of principle more likely leads to protests in which people express their views and indignation (Van Stekelenburg, Klandermans & van Dijk, 2009).

Classical grievance theories proposed that people participate in protest to express their grievances stemming from relative deprivation, frustration, or perceived injustice (Berkowitz, 1972; Gurr, 1970; Lind & Tyler, 1988). Prominent among grievance theories was relative deprivation theory (Folger, 1986). Feelings of relative deprivation result from a comparison of one's situation with a standard – be it one's past, someone else's situation, or a cognitive standard such as equity or justice (Folger, 1986). If comparison results in the conclusion that one is not receiving what one deserves, a person experiences relative deprivation. Runciman (1966) referred to relative deprivation based on personal comparisons as egoistic deprivation, and to relative deprivation based on group comparisons as fraternalistic deprivation. Research suggests that fraternalistic deprivation is particularly important for engagement in protest (Martin, 1986). Foster and Matheson (1999), however, showed that the relation is more complex. They demonstrate that when the group's experience becomes relevant for one's own experience – i.e. when the personal becomes political – motivation to protest increases; as a consequence, people who experience both personal deprivation *and* group deprivation are the strongest motivated to take on to the streets. On the basis of a meta-analysis, Van Zomeren and colleagues (2008) conclude that the cognitive component of relative deprivation (as reflected in the observation that one receives less than the standard of comparison) has less influence on action participation than the affective component (as expressed by such feelings as dissatisfaction, indignation and discontent about these outcomes).

Identity

Several studies report consistently that the more people identify with a group the more they are inclined to protest on behalf of that group (Klandermans et al., 2002; Mummendey, et al., 1999; Reicher, 1984; Simon & Klandermans, 2001; Simon et al., 1998; Stryker, Owens & White, 2000; van Zomeren, Postmes & Spears, 2008). Take for instance the Dutch pupils: the stronger they identified with other pupils, the higher the chance that they participated in the protests.

Identity is our understanding of who we are and who other people are, and, reciprocally other people's understanding of themselves and others (Jenkins, 2004). If a social identity becomes more salient than personal identity, people are inclined to define their personal self in terms of what makes them different from others, whereas they tend to define their social identities in terms of what makes them similar to others. The redefinition from an 'I' into a 'we' as a locus of self-definition makes people think, feel and act as members of their group and transforms individual into collective behaviour (Turner, 1999).

In the 1970s, a social-psychological identity perspective on protest emerged in the form of social identity theory (Tajfel & Turner, 1979). Tajfel and Turner showed that social categorization according to some trivial criterion such as the 'blue' or the 'red' group suffices to make people feel, think and act as a group member. Compared with this 'minimal group paradigm' real world intergroup conflicts with histories, high emotional intensity attached to them, and socio-political consequences can be seen as 'maximal group paradigms' that bring group membership powerful to mind. Social identity theory proposes that people generally strive for and benefit from positive social identities associated with their groups. Why, then, would people identify with groups that reflect negatively on them (e.g. disadvantaged or low-status groups)? The answer given by social identity theory is that three social structural characteristics affect how people manage their identity concerns. The first social structural characteristic is *permeability of the group boundaries*; the possibilities perceived by the individual to attain membership of a higher-status group. Permeable group boundaries allow disadvantaged group members to leave their group for a higher-status group, whereas impermeable boundaries offer no such 'exit'. When people do not perceive possibilities to join a higher-status group, they might feel commitment to the lower-status group. The second social structural characteristic is *stability*, the extent to which status positions are stable or variable. People who conceive status positions as variable see protest as a possible method to heighten group status, especially when the low group status is perceived as *illegitimate*. Members of a low-status group who perceive the dominant group's position as illegitimate and unstable can use a variety of strategies to obtain a more positive social identity. They may, for instance, redefine characteristics of their own group previously seen as negative; or they may engage in social competition of which protest is the clearest expression.

Why is group identification such a powerful motivational push to protest? First, identification with others is accompanied by an awareness of similarity and shared fate with those who belong to the same category. Furthermore, the 'strength' of an identity comes from its affective component (Ellemers, 1993). The more 'the group is in me' the more 'I feel for us' (Yzerbyt et al., 2003) and the stronger I am motivated to participate on behalf of the group. Social identification, especially the more politicized form of it, intensifies feelings of efficacy (see Simon et al., 1998, Van Zomeren, Postmes & Spears, 2008). Next to shared fate, shared emotions and enhanced efficaciousness, identification with others involved generates a felt inner obligation to behave as a 'good' group member (Stürmer et al., 2003). When self-definition changes from personal to social identity, the group norm of participation becomes salient; the more one identifies with the group, the more weight this group norm will carry and the more it will result in an 'inner obligation' to participate on behalf of the group. Together these dynamics explain why group identification is such a powerful motivational push to protest.

Politicized identity

Collective identities must politicize in order to become the engine of protest. Typically, politicization of identities begins with the awareness of shared grievances. Next, an external enemy is blamed for the group's predicament, and claims for compensation are levelled against this enemy. Unless appropriate compensation is granted, the power struggle continues. Politicization of identities and the underlying power struggle unfold as a sequence of politicizing events that gradually transform the group's relationship to its social environment. If, in the course of this struggle, the group seeks to win the support of third parties such as more powerful authorities (e.g. the national government) or the general public, identities fully politicize (Simon & Klandermans, 2001). The more politicized the group members are, the more likely they will engage in protest directed at the government or the general public. To return to our secondary-educational pupils, for a fully politicized identity they should share the idea that the quality of their education is detoriating, blame the government rather than their own study efforts, and level their claims to this government while winning the support of the general public. LAKS and 'Kevin' played a key role in this process.

Dual and multiple identities

Recent work on multiple identities (see Kurtz, 2002) emphasizes that people hold many different identities at the same time, which may push in the same direction or may come into conflict. When two of the groups people identify with end up on opposite sides of a controversy (for example, union members who are faced with the decision to strike against their company), people might find themselves under cross-pressure. Indeed, workers who go on strike, or movement activists who challenge their government, are often accused of being disloyal to the company or the country. González & Brown (2003) coined the term 'dual identity' to point to the *concurrent* workings of identities. These authors argue that identification with a subordinate entity (e.g. ethnic identity) does not necessarily exclude identification with a supraordinate entity (e.g. national identity). In fact, they hold that a 'dual identity' is the desirable configuration as it implies sufficient identification with one's own group to experience some basic security, and sufficient identification with the overarching identity to preclude divisiveness. There is evidence that immigrants who display a dual identity are more inclined to take to the streets on behalf of their group (Simon & Ruhs, 2008). This is further specified by Klandermans and colleagues (2008) who report that immigrants who display a dual identification tend to be more satisfied with their situation than those who do not display such identity, but *if* they are dissatisfied they are more likely to participate in protest.

Emotions

The study of emotions has become a popular research area in the social psychology of protest. Such was not always the case. As compared to rational approaches, emotions were often regarded as a peripheral 'error term' in motivational theories.

Group-based appraisal theories of emotions have reintroduced emotions to the social psychology of protest. People are continuously evaluating or *appraising* the relevance of their environment for their well-being. After a quick and automatic evaluation of an event's implications for one's well-being and of one's ability to cope with the situation, other appraisal dimensions are evaluated. How does the event influence my goals? Who or what caused the event? Do I have control and power over the consequences of the event? Are the consequences of the event compatible with my personal values and (societal) norms? As a consequence, two persons can appraise the same event differently and have different emotional responses (see Roseman, Antoniou & Jose, 1996 for an overview of different appraisals).

Appraisal theory was developed to explain emotions experienced by individuals. If group membership becomes part of the self, events that harm or favour an ingroup by definition harm or favour the self, and the self might thus experience emotions on behalf of the ingroup. With such considerations in mind, Devos and colleagues (2002) developed a model of intergroup emotions predicated on social identification with the group. The main postulate of intergroup emotion theory is that when a social identity is salient, situations are appraised in terms of their consequences for the ingroup, eliciting specific intergroup emotions and behavioural intentions. Thus, people experience emotions on behalf of their group when the social category is salient *and* they identify with the group at stake (Devos, Silver & Mackie, 2002).

Anger is seen as the prototypical protest emotion (Van Stekelenburg & Klandermans, 2007; van Zomeren et al., 2004). For those of us who have been part of protest events or watched reports on protest events in the news media, this is hardly surprising. Indeed, it is hard to conceive of protest detached from anger. Van Zomeren et al. (2004) show that group-based anger is an important motivator of protest participation of disadvantaged groups.

Anger appears to be related to efficacy: people who perceive the ingroup as strong are more likely to experience anger and desire to take action;

people who perceive the ingroup as weak are more likely to feel fearful and to move away from the outgroup (Devos, Silver & Mackie, 2002; Klandermans, Van der Toorn & Van Stekelenburg, 2008). Anger moves people to adopt a more challenging relationship with authorities than subordinate emotions such as shame and despair (Taylor, 2012) or fear (Klandermans, Van der Toorn & Van Stekelenburg, 2008). In explaining different tactics, efficacy appears to be relevant, too. Group-based anger is mainly observed in normative actions where efficacious and thus hopeful people protest (Sturmer & Simon, 2009). However, in non-normative violent actions, contempt appears to be the more relevant emotion (Fischer & Roseman, 2007; Tausch et al., 2008). This suggests two emotional routes to protest. The anger route is based on efficacy and is related to normative action. The contempt route is more likely when legitimate channels are closed (Wright, Taylor & Moghaddam, 1990) and the situation is seen as hopeless, invoking a 'nothing to lose' strategy and non-normative protest (Kamans, Otten & Gordijn, 2010).

Emotions function as *accelerators* or *amplifiers* of protest motives (Van Stekelenburg & Klandermans, 2007). Accelerators make things move faster, and amplifiers make them sound louder. In the world of protest, *accelerating* means that emotional motives to join a social movement translate into faster action, while amplifying means that these motives are stronger.

An integrating framework

Strikingly, so far a comprehensive framework integrating grievances, identities and emotions into a single model of collective action participation was lacking. We have been working on such a model over the last few years (Van Stekelenburg, Klandermans & Van Dijk, 2009, 2011). The model we have developed and begun to test assigns a central, integrating role to processes of identification. In order to develop the shared grievances and shared emotions that characterize a movement's mobilization potential, a shared identity is needed (see Figure 6.2).

The dependent variable of the model (*the strength of the motivation to participate in protest*) results from emotions and grievances shared with a group that the individual participants identify with. Grievances may originate from interests and/or principles that are felt to be threatened. The more people feel that the interests of the group and/or principles that the group values are threatened, the angrier they feel and the more they are motivated to take part in protest to protect their interests and/or to express their indignation. The model reveals that people participate in protest because they see it as an opportunity to change a state of affairs they are unhappy with (*instrumental route*), or because they identify with the others

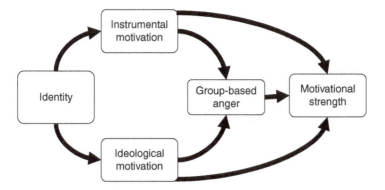

Figure 6.2 Integrative model accounting for protest motivation.
Source : Van Stekelenburg et al., 2009; 2011.

involved (*identification route*), or because they want to express their values and their anger with a target that violated their values (*ideology route)* (cf Klandermans, 2004).

We developed this model of an integrating framework in the context of our demonstration studies (for more information see www.protestsurvey. eu). In these studies, data are collected during *and* after demonstrations. Some protesters are interviewed on the spot, others are given questionnaires to take home and return to the university after they fill them out. Participants are thus sampled at the actual demonstration, in the heat of the battle. Contrary to controlled studies conducted in a laboratory, this kind of field research is conducted in a crowded, unpredictable and erratic environment. To guarantee representativeness of the findings, we rely on two techniques developed, tested and refined by Walgrave and colleagues (Van Aelst and Walgrave 2001).The first technique is a device to make sure that every protester in the area where the protest event takes place has an equal chance of being selected by one of the interviewers, who are positioned on the outer edge of the protest event. They are instructed to select a protester on the outer circle, followed by another, ten steps inwards, and so on until the centre of the circle is reached. The second technique implies conducting short face-to-face interviews during the demonstrations, comprising questions identical to some in the postal survey. As we reach response rates close to 100 per cent for the face-to-face interviews, these can serve to assess response bias of the postal survey data, and thus provide proper sampling of the interviewees.

The model addresses the question as to why people are prepared to participate in protests. Such participation cannot be taken for granted. Why, after all, would people contribute to the production of a public good if one can consume it anyway? The model identifies two reasons why people are prepared to overcome this so-called free-riders dilemma. The literature suggests efficacy (Klandermans, 1984; Olson, 1965) as the logics of action in the instrumental route. The feeling to be able to make a difference helps increase the benefits of participation and lower the personal cost of taking part. Social incentives – i.e. commitment, respect, honour and the pleasure of doing things communally – are the logic of action in the identification route (Stürmer et al., 2003). Moral incentives function as the logic of action in the ideological route. Violated (sacred) values generate moral outrage propelling people into action to express their views (Jasper, 1997). The more that a political or social 'wrong' is against people's principles and values, the more they feel obliged to defend their subjective moral boundaries (Van Stekelenburg, Klandermans & van Dijk, 2009). In taking the instrumental route, people have to overcome the free-riders' dilemma, but the identification and ideological route generate an inner obligation that helps to overcome this dilemma – even though the two routes create an inner obligation for different reasons. Maintaining one's moral integrity may incite an inner moral obligation to *oneself*, versus the inner *social* obligation to other group members incited by group identification (Stürmer et al., 2003). These obligations release an energizing force if, and only *if*, one participates: therefore make free-riding less likely. Hence, one might take a free-ride on the production of a *collective* good, but one cannot take a free-ride on one's own *inner felt obligation*. Successful mobilization requires an ever-changing mix of instrumental, social and moral incentives that work together to overcome free-rider problems.

Social cleavages and protest

Grievances are not randomly dispersed in society, but rooted in social cleavages. A social cleavage is an important division within society (Lipset & Rokkan, 1967). Such a division must fulfill three defining requirements to be called a cleavage. First, it must involve one of the primary determinants of social identity, for example religion, class, gender or ethnicity. Second, the (usually two) groups opposed by the cleavage must be aware of and prepared to act on the basis of their conflicting identities. Third, the social division must lead to the creation of organizations/formal institutions (e.g. trade unions, political parties), which represent and defend the collective identity, and confront those organizations that inherently or explicitly represent the opposing identity across the cleavage. Cleavages therefore operate as fault lines along which opposing identities and grievances emerge and organizational fields break up; cleavages thus generate a demand and supply for protest. When a social-movement organization and its allies begin to mobilize, chances are that in response its 'natural' opponents begin to mobilize as well. Why socio-political conflicts so easily erupt in the context of social cleavages, will be explained in terms of embeddedness and shared fate, and salience.

Embeddedness and shared fate

Simon and colleagues (1998) describe identity as a 'place' in society. A place is a metaphorical expression and concerns people's social embeddedness; that is, the networks, organizations, associations, groups and categories of which they are members. People are not randomly embedded in society. Social cleavages affect social embeddedness. People share interests, and identify and associate almost exclusively with other members of 'their' group. Cleavages create a place shared with others, which leads to shared experiences, grievances and emotions and the creation of a collective identity; social cleavages thus determine people's place in society and give rise to shared fate. Hence, cleavages create 'communities of shared fate', and 'sameness' within cleavages and 'distinctiveness' between cleavages: and, as such, create shared identities *and* opposing identities (referred to as ingroups and outgroups in social identity theory).

Social embeddedness – the quantity and types of relationships with others – includes formal relationships such as being a member of the labour union (cf. Klandermans, Van der Toorn & Van Stekelenburg, 2008); informal relationships such as friends, family and colleagues; and virtual relationships such as active participation in blogs, social media, etc. (Van Stekelenburg & Boekkooi, 2012). As such, the internet has created an additional public sphere; people are embedded in virtual networks in addition to formal and informal *physical* networks.

Social embeddedness plays a pivotal role in the context of protest participation. Social networks function as communication channels; discursive processes take place to form consensus that makes up the symbolic resources in collective sense-making (Gamson, 1992; Klandermans, 1988), and people are informed of upcoming events and social capital as trust and loyalty accumulate in networks to provide individuals with the resources needed to invest in protest (Klandermans, Van der Toorn & Van Stekelenburg, 2008). The effect of interaction in networks or the propensity to participate in politics is contingent on the amount of political discussion that occurs in social networks and the information that people are able to gather about politics as a result (McClurg, 2003). Being integrated in a network increases the chances that one will be targeted with a mobilizing message and that people are kept to their promises to participate (Klandermans & Oegema, 1987). For example, people with friends or acquaintances who are already active within social movements are more likely to take part in movement actions than those who do not have acquaintances in this domain (Klandermans, 1997). Klandermans and colleagues (2008) provide evidence for such mechanisms. For instance, efficacious Moroccan-Dutch and Turkish-Dutch were more likely to participate in protest in the Netherlands provided that they were embedded in social networks, especially ethnic networks (for instance, the Turkish labour association, which offers an opportunity to discuss and learn about (Dutch) politics). In other words, this is where people talk politics and, thus, where the factuality of the socio-political world is constructed and people are mobilized for protest.

Salience. The more salient a cleavage the more dense the multiorganizational field linked to that cleavage, and the more 'ready' its mobilization potential is to act in response to that cleavage. In fact, the salience of a cleavage reflects in a strongly elaborated supply and a well-defined demand of protest. Hence, identities rooted in cleavages are often organized identities, and organized identities are more likely to mobilize than unorganized identities. According to Klandermans and de Weerd (2000) being organized implies communication networks, access to resources, interpersonal control, information about opportunities (when, where and how to act), and all the things that make it more likely that intentions materialize. Organizers play a crucial role in this transformation of 'readiness' into action (Boekkooi, Klandermans & van Stekelenburg, 2011). In order to mobilize potential constituencies, organizers must develop 'master frames' that link a conflict to 'their' cleavage. Hence, organizers may frame the same conflict in different terms. Inequality, for instance, can be framed in terms of 'class' or 'ethnicity'. The more salient a cleavage and the better the organizers align the conflict to 'their' cleavage – the more their frames 'resonate' – the more successful their mobilization attempts.

Should I stay or should I go: sustained participation and disengagement

Most research on protest concerns a comparison of participants and non-participants in a specific instance of participation at a specific point in time – be it a demonstration, a boycott, a sit-in, a rally or a petition. In terms of our typology of forms of participation, this concerns short-term and mostly low-risk or little-effort participation. We have argued that such short-term activities have different motivational dynamics than sustained participation.

Sustained participation is nearly absent in social-movement literature. This is surprising, given that long-term participants keep the movement going. A movement has only a limited number of core activists. For example, 5–10 per cent of the membership of the Dutch labour unions are core activists. Empirical evidence suggests that most core activists are perfectly aware of the fact that they are giving 90 per cent or more of the movement's supporters a free ride, but do not care. On the contrary, this is what seems to motivate them to take the job (Oliver, 1984). They are the true believers who care so much for the movement's cause that they are prepared to make that effort knowing that most others will not. Indeed, for 29 per cent of the core activists within Dutch unions, this was the single most important motivation for their sustained participation.

The dynamics of sustained participation

Activism frequently persists despite pessimism regarding the action's ostensible goals (Louis, 2009). Why do people continue participating in movements even if it does not effectuate their claims? Drury and Reicher (2009) suggest that participation generates a 'positive social-psychological transformation'. They argue that participation strengthens identification and induces collective empowerment. The emergence of an inclusive self-categorization as 'oppositional' leads to feelings of unity and expectations of support. This empowers people to oppose authorities. Such action creates *collective self-objectification:* that is, it defines the participant's identity opposite the dominant outgroup (Drury & Reicher, 2009). Protest participation strengthens empowerment and politicization, paving the path to sustained participation.

Sustained participation need not necessarily take the form of the same activity all the time. People often go from one activity to another, sometimes from one movement to another and, in so doing, build activist careers. Paths leading to sustained participation may vary. *Biographical continuity*, for instance, describes a life history whereby participation appears as the logical result of political socialization from someone's youth onwards, as in a right-wing extremist who is raised in a xenophobic milieu.

Conversion, on the other hand, implies a break with the past. For instance after someone is fired, s/he may decide to join an extreme Right organization. Critical events are supposed to play a crucial role in both situations. In the context of biographical continuity, the event means the last push or pull in a direction in which the person is already going, whereas in the context of conversion the event means an experience that marks a change of mind. Obviously, such conversion does not come out of the blue. It is rooted in a growing dissatisfaction with life as it is. The critical event is the last push towards change. Teske (1997) describes the example of a journalist who ends up in front of the gate of a nuclear weapons plant and whose experience with the authorities' suppressive response to that demonstration turns him into an activist. The story of this journalist made clear that, on the one hand, it was no accident that he ended up at that gate. On the other hand, however, had the demonstration not taken that dramatic turn it would not have had this impact on his life.

Becoming a long-term activist is to a large extent a matter of biographical availability. Sustained participation, after all, requires discretionary time for an extended period. The concept of biographical availability was proposed by McAdam (see Goldstone & McAdam, 2001) in his study of participation in the Mississippi Freedom Summer. This project was a campaign launched in June 1964 to attempt to register as many African-American voters as possible in Mississippi, which had historically excluded most blacks from voting. More than 1,000 students, mostly from universities such as as Yale and Stanford, participated in this project. In his study, McAdam shows that even though college students are free of life-course impediments to activism, the Freedom Summer applicants were freer still, while the actual volunteers were the freest of all (Goldstone & McAdam, 2001). Indeed, participants in the Mississippi Freedom Summer Campaign were students who were biographically available. But in terms of a life history, there is also *mental* availability: that is, susceptibility for the ideas a movement is propagating. For instance, consider the aforementioned White March in Belgium in response to the case of Dutroux. One can imagine that the parents of young children, in particular, were *mentally* available to agree with the injustice claims – *This cannot be true!* – made in the newspapers. The dynamics of sustained participation in social movements have a clear counterpart: namely, the dynamics of disengagement. Indeed, the sustainability of a fit between demand and supply is by no means obvious.

The dynamics of disengagement

Why do people defect from the movement they have worked so very hard to support? Surprisingly little attention has been given to that question. Compared with the abundant literature on why people join movements, literature on why they exit is almost nonexistent. The guiding principle of our discussion on disengagement centres around the following simple model (see Figure 6.3).

Insufficient gratification in combination with declining commitment produces a growing intention to leave. Eventually, some critical event tips the balance and makes the person quit. Obviously, the event itself only triggers the final step, yet its impact may be overestimated. After all, it was the decline in gratification and commitment that caused defection: the critical event only precipitated matters.

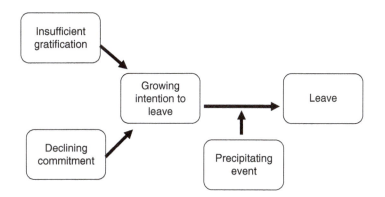

Figure 6.3   The dynamics of disengagement.
Source: Klandermans, 1997.

Insufficient gratification

In the previous sections we distinguished three fundamental motives to participate: instrumental, identification and ideological motivations. Social movements may supply the opportunity to fulfill these demands and, the more they do, the more movement participation turns into a satisfying experience. However, movements may also fall short on each of these motives. Most likely it is for movements to fall short in terms of instrumentality. Although it is difficult to assess the effectiveness of social movements, it is obvious that for many a movement goal is never reached. Opp (1988) has argued that people are very well aware of the fact that movement goals are not always easy to achieve, but that they reason that if no one participates then nothing happens. However, sooner or later some success must be achieved in order for the instrumental motivation to continue to fuel participation. Not only do movement goals often fail to be achieved, but they may lose their attraction to people. They may lose their urgency on the societal agenda. Finally, the individual costs or risks of participation may be too high compared with the attraction of the movement's goals. Repression adds to the costs and might make participation too costly for people (Tilly, 1978).

Movements offer the opportunity to act on behalf of one's group; this is attractive if people identify strongly with their group. But the composition of a movement may change – for instance from self-help groups around battered women to radical feminist-ideology groups – and, as a consequence, people may feel less akin to the others in the movement (Whittier, 1997). Schisms are another reason why movements fail to satisfy identity motives. Sani and Reicher (1998) demonstrate that schisms result from fights over the core identity of a movement; people who leave no longer feel that they can identify with the movement. Finally, people occupy a variety of positions in society, and consequently identify with a variety of collectives. A change in context may make the one collective identity more salient and the others less so, and, therefore identification with a movement may wither. For example, in a study of farmers' protest in the Netherlands and Spain, Klandermans et al. (2002) observed that in Spain during a campaign for local and provincial elections the identification with other farmers declined. In the rural areas of Basque country, the farmers' identity is a highly salient one; however, in times of elections, the most important politicized identities in Spain – Partido Popular and PSOE – suppresses the farmers' identification with each other.

Declining commitment

Movement commitment does not last by itself. It must be maintained via interaction with the movement, and any measure that makes that interaction less gratifying helps to undermine commitment. One way to maintain interaction is to provide *selective incentives*, benefits that participants – participants only – derive from the activity itself, irrespective of whether they manage to provide the public good or not. Unions and other movement organizations have developed all kinds of services for their members in order to make membership more attractive. Although selective incentives may seldom be sufficient reasons to participate in a movement, they do increase commitment. Insufficiently provided selective incentives, however, may undermine commitment. Downton and Wehr (1997) discuss five mechanisms of social bonding which movements apply to maintain commitment: leadership, ideology, organization, rituals and social relations; the most effective is, of course, a combination of all five. Although not all of these mechanisms are equally well researched, each are known from the literature on movement participation as factors that foster people's attachment to movements. For example, it is known from research on union participation that involving members in decision-making processes increases commitment to a union (Klandermans, 1992), while Taylor and Whittier (1995) demonstrate how rituals in lesbian movement-groups strengthen the membership's bond to the movement.

The role of precipitating events

When gratification falls short and commitment declines, the participant develops an intention to leave. Yet, this intention to leave does not necessarily result in leaving. Many participants maintain a marginal level of participation for extended periods until some event makes them finally quit. For example, Goslinga (2002) calculated that a stable 25 per cent of the membership of Dutch labour unions considered leaving. As 'the event' is the immediate cause of disengagement it draws disproportionate attention as explanation of exit behaviour, but note that the event only has this impact in the context of an already present readiness to leave. Such critical events can have many different appearances, and sometimes even appear trivial. When some decades ago Dutch labour unions changed to a different system of dues collection and members had to sign to agree with the new system quite a few members chose not to sign. Changing address may be seized as an opportunity to leave the movement, simply by not renewing contacts in the new place of residence. More substantial reasons might be a conflict with others in the organization, disappointing experiences in the movement, a failed protest, and so on. Such events function as the last drop that makes the cup run over.

Disengagement versus radicalization

When a movement is in decline, many activists quit. But becoming inactive is not the only response to movement decline. Indeed, radicalization has been described as an alternative response to movement decline (della Porta, 1995). Although violence tends to appear from the very beginning of a protest cycle, the more dramatic forms of violence seem to occur when the mass phase of the protest cycle is over (della Porta, 1995). Such violence as mobilization declines, is attributed to people's dissatisfaction with protest outcomes and their attempts to compensate for the 'reduction in numbers' with increased radicalism (della Porta, 1995), reinforced by a repression apparatus that becomes more effective towards the end of a cycle. In light of a declining movement and many 'exiters', sustained participation can take the form of radicalization. For instance, consider the violent Black Panthers that played a short but important part in the American Civil Rights Movement. They believed that the non-violent campaign of Martin Luther King had failed and that any promised changes to their lifestyle via the 'traditional' civil rights movement would take too long to be implemented or simply not be introduced. Hence, in light of the declining civil right movement, both disengagement *and* radical sustained participation were observed.

Conclusion

The Arab Spring protests in Greece and Spain, the Tea Party in the US, the riots in London: these are certainly contentious times. Many people ask the question: why do these people protest? An answer is often provided in terms of grievances. In this chapter, while discussing socio-psychological mechanisms of protest, we have tried to counter the idea that people protest *because* they are aggrieved. Obviously, we did not try to say that those protesters were *not* aggrieved, but we argued that grievances on their own do not provide a sufficient reason to participate in protest. Indeed, although many people may have recognized the grievances and sympathized with the goals of the protests, only a small proportion of those who were aggrieved ended up as participants in those protests. Hence, although protests bring socio-political conflicts into the open, they do not form more than the tip of the iceberg of larger masses who feel that their interests or values are violated. We have therefore argued that the key social-psychological question to address is: why do some aggrieved people protest, while others do not? Throughout this chapter we have shown that protest participation is seldom an impulsive act but an act that requires matching of a 'demand' and 'supply' of protest. Organizers must work hard to turn grievances into claims, to point out targets to be addressed, to create moral outrage and anger, and to stage events where all this can be vented. Consensus must be mobilized to enlarge the pool of sympathizers. People need to know about an upcoming protest event and need to be motivated to participate. And, after the protest, dashed hopes need to be turned into willingness to continue the fight for the good cause. Hence, the act of taking part in protest is a dynamic process, and it might well be that with each step of the mobilization process grievances become less and less important in answering the question as to why people protest.

Practical task for readers

Social conflicts are a fundamental element of our societies and as 'carriers of meaning' and 'suppliers of protest' social movements are the main carriers of these conflicts. Understanding the dynamics of protest is therefore crucial in understanding social conflicts. Compared with 25 years ago, the social psychology of protest has become richer, more sophisticated, and as such has a lot to offer to the study of protest participation. However, there are still a lot of issues unresolved. We want you to consider three issues in more depth.

(1) The explanatory models of protest participation described in this chapter are rather static. We see room for improvement in a focus on dynamics and processes. A move from the static individual level of analyses to the processes underlying protest is therefore necessary. We need to acknowledge that

Continued

the characteristics of mobilization potential we discussed are mutable and vary over time and place; comparative studies are therefore needed to register this variation and its impact on protest participation. We need to examine the formation of demand and its transition into action, and the erosion of demand and its transition into disengagement.

(a) In contrast to static approaches, dynamic approaches account for the element of time. This provides the opportunity to study concepts such as identification, participation motives, efficacy, emotions and feelings of injustice as consequence and antecedent of collective action. Please go through the 'Demand' section and try to imagine how the concepts described can be made more dynamic.

(b) A dynamic approach also offers the opportunity to examine the development of these concepts and their interrelation. This is not easy, as Ellemers observes: 'From an investigational point of view, it is difficult to deal with a variable that, at the same time, can be a dependent and an independent variable, can develop over time or change across contexts' (Ellemers, Spears & Doosje, 1999, p. 3). Design a study in which the development of 'Demand' can be investigated.

(2) Imagine how the dynamics of supply and demand are shaped by the socio-political context. Remember that conflicts root in a socio-political context and are fought out in this context. So far, social-psychological research has hardly focused on the subjective experience of these meso- and macro-level factors. Try to reason how political opportunities or constraints, or the strength or weakness of social-movement organizations – or their proposed tactics – affect the routes that people take towards protest.

(a) What variables at the meso- or macro-level could be important in affecting peoples' *subjective* interpretations of their collective disadvantages?

(b) How would you conceptualize *and* measure these variables? How would they affect people's willingness to participate in collective action?

Continued

(3) A lot of scholars and journalists describe the so-called Facebook or Twitter protests. However, so far, very little empirical evidence is reported. Basic questions as to how they differ from traditional protests, whether they bring a different crowd to the streets, and what is the role of traditional organizations, remain unanswered.

(a) Think of traditional and rhizomatic mobilization. Describe how they differ in terms of the mobilizing actors, the mobilizing structures, mobilizing channels and the kind of events they wage.
(b) To what extent will the protest participants differ in the traditional and rhizomatic campaigns? Describe this in terms of socio-demographics, their motives and their social embeddedness.

Suggested readings

For more information, we would like to suggest two books. The handbook edited by Klandermans and Roggeband (2007) provides an interesting overview of how different disciplines (sociology, political science, social geography, anthropology and social psychology) approach social movements. Klandermans (1997) provides an overview of the first two decades of the social psychology of protest. We also recommend a special issue of *Journal of Social Issues* (2009) on the 'Social and Psychological Dynamics of Collective Action', edited by van Zomeren and Iyar. On emotions in the context of protest we suggest Mackie & Smith (2002); on identity, Stryker, Owens and White (2002) – an interesting interdisciplinary overview on identity in the context of social movements.

References

Benford, R. (1997). An insider's critique of the social movement framing perspective. *Sociological-Inquiry*, 67, 409–430.

Berkowitz, L. (1972). Frustrations, comparisons, and other sources of emotion aroused as contributors to social unrest. *Journal of Social Issues*, 28, 77–92.

Boekkooi, M., Klandermans, B. & van Stekelenburg, J. (2011). Quarrelling and protesting: How organizers shape a demonstration. *Mobilization*, 16, 498–508.

della Porta, D. (1995). *Social Movements, Political Violence and the State*. Cambridge: Cambridge University Press.

Devos, T., Silver, L. A. & Mackie, D. M. (2002). Experiencing intergroup emotions. In D. M. Mackie & E. R. Smith (eds.), *From Prejudice to Intergroup Emotions: Differentiated Reactions to Social Groups* (pp. 111–134). Philadelphia, PA: Psychology Press.

Downton, J., Jr. & Wehr, P. (1997). *The Persistent Activist: How Peace Commitment Develops and Survives*. Boulder, CO & London: Westview.

Drury, J. & Reicher, S. (2009). Collective Psychological Empowerment as a Model of Social Change: Researching Crowds and Power. *Journal of Social Issues*, 65, 707–725.

Ellemers, N. (1993). The influence of socio-structural variables on identity management strategies. In W. Stroebe & M. Hewston (eds.), *European Review of Social Psychology* (vol. 4, pp. 27–58). Chichester: Wiley.

Ellemers, N., Spears, R. & Doosje, B. (1999). Introduction. In N. Ellemers, R. Spears & B. Doosje (eds.), *Social identity: Context, Commitment, Content* (pp. 1–5). Oxford: Basil Blackwell.

Fischer, A. & Roseman, I. (2007). Beat them or ban them: The characteristics and social functions of anger and contempt. *Journal of Personality and Social Psychology*, 93, 103–115.

Folger, R. (1986). Rethinking equity theory: a referent cognitions model. In H. W. Bierhoff, R. L. Cohen & J. Greenberg (eds.), *Justice in Social Relations* (pp. 145–162). New York: Plenum.

Foster, M. D. & Matheson, K. (1999). Perceiving and responding to the personal/group discrimination discrepancy. *Personality and Social Psychology Bulletin*, 25, 1319–1329.

Gamson, W. A. (1975). *Strategy of Social Protest*. Homewood, Illinois: The Dorsey Press.

Gamson, W. A. (1992). *Talking Politics*. New York: Cambridge University Press.

Goldstone, J. & McAdam, D. (2001). Placing contention in demographic and life-course context. In R. Aminzade, J. Goldstone, D. McAdam, E. Perry, J. William Sewell, S. Tarrow & C. Tilly (eds.), *Silence and Voice in the Study of Contentious Politics* (pp. 195–221). New York and London: Cambridge University Press.

González, R. & Brown, R. (2003). Generalization of positive attitudes as a function of subgroup and superordinate group identifications in intergroup contact. *European Journal of Social Psychology*, 33, 195–214.

Goslinga, S. (2002). Binding aan de vakbond (Union Commitment). Unpublished doctoral dissertation. Vrije Universiteit, Amsterdam.

Gurr, T. (1970). *Why Men Rebel*. Princeton: Princeton University Press.

Jasper, J. (1997). *The Art of Moral Protest. Culture, Biography, and Creativity in Social Movements*. Chicago: The University of Chicago Press.

Jenkins, R. (2004). *Social Identity*. Oxon, Canada: Routledge.

Kamans, E., Otten, S. & Gordijn, E. H. (2010). Threat and power in intergroup conflict: How threat detremines emotional and behavioral reactions in powerless groups. Manuscript.

Kingdon, J. W. (1984). *Agendas, Alternatives and Public Policies*. New York: Harper Collins.

Klandermans, B. (1984). Mobilization and participation: Social-psychological expansions of resource mobilization theory. *American Sociological Review*, 49, 583–600.

Klandermans, B. (1988). The formation and mobilization of consensus. In B. Klandermans, H. Kriesi & S. Tarrow (eds.), *From Structure to Action: Comparing Social Movement Research across Cultures* (vol. 1, pp. 173–196). Greenwich, CT: JAI Press.

Klandermans, B. (1992). The social construction of protest and multiorganizational fields. In A. D. Morris & C. M. Mueller (eds.), *Frontiers in Social Movement Theory* (pp. 77–103). New Haven, CT: Yale University Press.

Klandermans, B. (1997). *The Social Psychology of Protest*. Oxford: Blackwell.

Klandermans, B. (2004). The demand and supply of Participation: Social-psychological correlates of participation in social movements. In D. A. Snow, S. A. Soule & H. Kriesi (eds.), *The Blackwell Companion to Social Movements* (pp. 360–379). Oxford: Blackwell Publishing.

Klandermans, B. (2012). The dynamics of demand. In B. Klandermans, J. van Stekelenburg & C. M. Roggeband (eds.), *Advances in Social Movement Theory*. Minnesota: University of Minnesota Press.

Klandermans, B., & de Weerd, M. (2000). Group identification and political protest. In S. Stryker, T. J. Owens & R. W. White (eds.), *Self, identity, and social movements* (pp. 68–92). Minneapolis: University of Minnesota Press.

Klandermans, B., & Oegema, D. (1987). Potentials, networks, motivations, and barriers: Steps toward participation in social movements. *American Sociological Review*, 52, 519–531.

Klandermans, B. & Roggeband, C. M. (2007). *Handbook of Social Movements Across Disciplines*. New York: Springer.

Klandermans, B., Sabucedo, J. M., Rodriguez, M. & Weerd, M. D. (2002). Identity processes in collective action participation: farmers' identity and farmers' protest in the Netherlands and Spain. *Political Psychology*, 23, 235–251.

Klandermans, B., Van der Toorn, J. & Van Stekelenburg, J. (2008). Embeddedness and identity: How immigrants turn grievances action. *American Sociological Review*, 73, 992–1012.

Kurtz, S. (2002). *All Kinds of Justice: Labor and Identity Politics*. Minneapolis: University of Minnesota Press.

Lind, E. A. & Tyler, T. R. (1988). *The Social Psychology of Procedural Justice*. New York: Plenum Press.

Lipset, S. M. & Rokkan, S. (1967). Cleavage structures, party systems, and voter alignments: an introduction. In S. M. Lipset & S. Rokkan (eds.), *Party Systems and Voter Alignments: Cross-National Perspectives* (pp. 1–64). New York: Free Press.

Lodewijkx, H. F. M., Kersten, G. L. E. & Van Zomeren, M. (2008). Dual pathways to engage in 'silent marches' against violence: Moral outrage, moral cleansing and modes of identification. *Journal of Community and Applied Social Psychology*, 18, 153–167.

Louis, W. (2009). Collective action—and then what? *Journal of Social Issues*, 65, 727–748.

Mackie, D. M. & Smith, E. R. (2002). *From Prejudice to Intergroup Emotions: Differentiated Reactions to Social Groups*. Philadelphia, PA: Psychology Press.

Martin, J. (1986). The tolerance of injustice. In J. M. Olson, C. P. Herman & M. P. Zanna (eds.), *Relative Deprivation and Social Comparison: The Ontario Symposium* (vol. 4, pp. 217–242). Hillsdale, NJ: Lawrence Erlbaum.

Marwell, G. & Oliver, P. (1993). *The Critical Mass in Collective Action: A Micro-Social Theory*. Cambridge: Cambridge University Press.

McCarthy, J. D. & Wolfson, M. (1996). Resource mobilization by local social movement organizations: Agency, strategy, and organization in the movement against drinking and driving. *American Sociological Review*, 61, 1070–1088.

McClurg, S. D. (2003). Social networks and political participation: The role of social interaction in explaining political participation. *Political Research Quarterly*, 56, 448–464.

Mummendey, A., Kessler, T., Klink, A. & Mielke, R. (1999). Strategies to cope with negative social identity: Predictions by social identity theory and relative deprivation theory. *Journal of Personality and Social Psychology*, 76, 229–245.

Oegema, D. & Klandermans, B. 1994. Why social movement sympathizers don't participate: erosion and nonconversion of support. *American Sociological Review* 59, 703–722.

Olson, M. (1965). *The Logic of Collective Action: Public Goods and the Theory of Groups*. Cambridge, MA: Harvard University Press.

Opp, K. D. (1988). Grievances and social movement participation. *American Sociological Review*, 53(6), 853–864.

Reicher, S. (1984). The St. Paul's riot: An explanation of the limits of crowd action in terms of a social identity model. *European Journal of Social Psychology*, 14, 1–21.

Rochon, T. R. (1998). *Culture Moves: Ideas, Activism, and Changing Values*. Princeton, NJ: Princeton University Press.

Roseman, I. J., Antoniou, A. A. & Jose, P. E. (1996). Appraisal determinants of emotions: constructing a more accurate and comprehensive theory. *Cognition and Emotion*, 10(3), 241–278.

Runciman, W. G. (1966). *Relative Deprivation and Social Justice*. London: Routledge.

Sani, F. & Reicher, S. (1998). When consensus fails: An analysis of the schism within the Italian Communist Party (1991). *European Journal of Social Psychology*, 28, 623–645.

Simon, B. & Klandermans, B. (2001). Towards a social psychological analysis of politicized collective identity: Conceptualization, antecedents, and consequences. *American Psychologist*, 56(4), 319–331.

Simon, B., Loewy, M., Sturmer, S., Weber, U., Freytag, P., Habig, C., Kampmeier, C., Spahlinger, P. (1998). Collective identification and social movement participation. *Journal of Personality and Social Psychology*, 74, 646–658.

Simon, B. & Ruhs, D. (2008). Identity and politicization among Turkish migrants in Germany: The role of dual identification. *Journal of Personality and Social Psychology*, 95, 1354–1366.

Snow, D. (2004). Framing processes, ideology and discursive fields. In D. A. Snow, S. A. Soule & H. Kriesi (eds.), *The Blackwell Companion to Social Movements* (pp. 380–412). Oxford: Blackwell Publishing.

Stryker, S., Owens, T. J. & White, R. W. (eds.). (2000). *Self, Identity, and Social Movements* (vol. 13). Minneapolis: Minnesota Press.

Stürmer, S., Simon, B., Loewy, M. & Jörger, H. (2003). The dual-pathway model of social movement participation: The case of the fat acceptance movement. *Social Psychology Quarterly*, 66, 71–82.

Sturmer, S., & Simon, B. (2009). Pathways to Collective Protest: Calculation, Identification, or Emotion? A Critical Analysis of the Role of Group-Based Anger in Social Movement Participation 65, 4, 681–705.

Tajfel, H. & Turner, J. C. (1979). An integrative theory of intergroup conflict. In S. Worchel & W. G. Austin (eds.), *The social psychology of intergroup relations* (pp. 33–47). Chicago: Nelson-Hall Publishers.

Tausch, N., Becker, J., Spears, R. & Christ, O. (2008). *Emotion and Efficacy Pathways to Normative and Non-Normative Collective Action: A Study in the Context of Student Protests in Germany.* Paper presented at the Intra- and Intergroup processes' pre-conference to the 15th General Meeting of the EAESP (Invited paper), Opatija, Croatia.

Taylor, V. (2012). Social movement participation in the Global Society: Identity, networks and emotions. In J. van Stekelenburg, C. M. Roggeband & B. Klandermans (eds.), *The Changing Dynamics of Contention*. Minnesota: University of Minnesota Press.

Taylor, V. & Whittier, N. E. (1995). Analytical approaches to social movement culture: The culture of the women's movement in social movements and culture. In H. Johnston & B. Klandermans (eds.), *Social Movements and Culture*. (pp. 163–187). Minneapolis: University of Minnesota Press.

Teske, N. (1997). *Political activists in America: The identity construction model of political participation*. New York: Cambridge University Press.

Tilly, C. (1978). *From Mobilisation to Revolution*. Reading, MA: Addison-Wesley Publishing Company.

Turner, J. C. (1999). Some current themes in research on social identity and self-categorization theories. In N. Ellemers, R. Spears & B. Doosje (eds.), *Social Identity: Context, Commitment, Content* (pp. 6–34). Oxford: Blackwell.

Van Aelst, P., & Walgrave, S. (2001). Who is that (wo)man in the street? From the normalisation of protest to the normalisation of the protester. *European Journal of Political Research, 39*, 461–486.

Van Stekelenburg, J. & Boekkooi, M. (2012). Mobilizing for change in a changing society. In B. Klandermans, J. van Stekelenburg & C. M. Roggeband (eds.), *Advances in Social Movement Theory*. Minnesota: University of Minnesota Press.

Van Stekelenburg, J. & Klandermans, B. (2007). Individuals in movements: A social psychology of contention. In C. M. Roggeband & B. Klandermans (eds.), *The Handbook of Social Movements Across Disciplines* (pp. 157–204). New York: Springer.

Van Stekelenburg, J. & Klandermans, B. (2009). Social movement theory: past, present and prospect. In I. van Kessel & S. Ellis (eds.), *Movers and Shakers: Social Movements in Africa* (pp. 17–44). Leiden: Brill.

Van Stekelenburg, J., Klandermans, B. & van Dijk, W. W. (2009). Context matters. explaining why and how mobilizing context influences motivational dynamics. *Journal of Social Issues*, 65(4), 815–838.

Van Stekelenburg, J., Klandermans, B. & van Dijk, W. W. (2011). Combining motivations and emotion: The motivational dynamics of collective action participation. *Revista de Psicologìa Social*, 26(1), 91–104.

Van Stekelenburg, J., & Klandermans, B. (forthcoming 2012). Uploading unrest. Comparing mobilization and participation in traditional and rhizomatical mobilized protest.

Van Zomeren, M., & Iyer, A. (2009). Toward integrative understanding of the social and psychological dynamics of collective action. *Journal of Social Issues*, 65, 645–660.

van Zomeren, M., Postmes, T. & Spears, R. (2008). Toward an integrative social identity model of collective action: A quantitative research synthesis of three socio-psychological perspectives. *Psychological Bulletin*, 134, 504–535.

van Zomeren, M., Spears, R., Fischer, A. H. & Leach, C. W. (2004). Put your money where your mouth is! Explaining collective action tendencies through group-based anger and group efficacy. *Journal of Personality and Social Psychology*, 87, 649–664.

Verhulst, J. (2011). *Mobilizing Issues and the Unity and Diversity of Protest Events.* UA, Antwerpen, Belgium.

Walgrave, S., & Manssens, J. (2000). The making of the white march: the mass media as a mobilizing alternative to movement organisations. *Mobilization*, 5, 217–239.

Walsh, E. J. (1981). Resource mobilization and citizen protest in communities around Three Mile Island. *Social Problems*, 29, 1–21.

Whittier, N. E. (1997). Political generations, micro-cohorts, and the transformation of social movements. *American Sociological Review*, 62, 760–778.

Wright, S., C., Taylor, D. M. & Moghaddam, F. M. (1990). The relationship of perceptions and emotions to behavior in the face of collective inequality. *Social Justice Research*, 4, 229–250.

Yzerbyt, V., Dumont, M., Wigboldus, D. & Gordijn, E. (2003). I feel for us: The impact of categorization and identification on emotions and action tendencies. *British Journal of Social Psychology*, 42, 533–549.

7

Obedience and Tyranny in Psychology and History

*Stephen D. Reicher and
S. Alexander Haslam*

● ●

Tyranny and obedience in the Holocaust

Adolf Eichmann and the Nazi death camps

Ever since the reality of the Nazi Holocaust was revealed to a horrified world some 70 years ago, social thought in general – and social psychology in particular (see Bilewicz & Vollhardt, this volume) – has been preoccupied with the question of how people can act with such inhumanity towards their fellow human beings. What is it that makes people act tyrannically, support tyrants and obey even the most appalling of their commands?

Before we consider the way that psychologists have addressed these issues of obedience and tyranny, let us first consider what has been learnt from historical studies of the Nazi killers – and no one had more of an impact on our understanding of perpetrator psychology than Adolf Eichmann.

Eichmann was the key bureaucrat of the Holocaust. He was one of those present at the Wannsee Conference of 20 January 1942, where plans for the systematic murder of the Jewish people were agreed (Roseman, 2003). He was the man who then arranged for Jews to be deported to the death camps. Most particularly, he was associated with the deportation of some 400,000 Hungarian Jews to Auschwitz in May 1944. Eichmann survived the war and fled to Argentina, where he posed as a refugee called Ricardo Klement. However, he was captured by Israeli agents and taken to Jerusalem where, in 1961, he was put on trial for his crimes (Cesarani, 2004).

The picture of Adolf Eichmann sitting in a glass booth in a Jerusalem courtroom has become one of the most famous images associated with the Holocaust. Present in the courtroom at the start of the trial was the renowned philosopher Hannah Arendt. Like others around her, she waited with bated breath to actually see Eichmann in the flesh. She describes her anticipation, expecting to see an extraordinary figure – for surely some-one who had committed such monstrous deeds would look different from normal folk. In some way, he would bear the mark of his evil. He would surely look like a monster. But what she saw instead was a nondescript figure: a balding, hunched, fastidious middle-aged man who took careful notes of all that was going on and who looked to Arendt and the world like any other anonymous clerk. Arendt wrote a book about the trial in which, on reflection, she concluded that his nondescript nature was actu-ally far more frightening than had he been immediately identifiable as evil (Arendt, 1963/1994). It meant that you could not see him (or others like him) coming. It suggested that perhaps such people are not so differ-ent from ordinary folk after all. It raised the uncomfortable possibility that we, too, might have it in us to do unspeakable things and it raised the ques-tion of how and when that might happen. All this was encapsulated in the phrase with which Arendt concluded her book. For her, the Eichmann trial was 'the lesson of the fearsome, word-and-thought defying *banality of evil* (Arendt, 1963/1994, p. 252, emphasis in the original).

Arendt's phrase – the banality of evil – has outlived her and has had a massive impact on our understanding not only of Eichmann and the Holocaust, but also of the human capacity for inhumanity in general. The problem, however, is that the term has been widely misused and misunder-stood (Newman, 2001). Accordingly, it is important to appreciate exactly what Arendt herself means by the term, and here several points need to be clarified (Haslam & Reicher, 2007).

The first of these is that Arendt is not claiming that evil acts themselves are banal. She is arguing that the perpetrators are not exceptional people. They are run-of-the-mill folk just like us.

The second point has to do with the mechanisms by which ordinary peo-ple can commit extraordinarily inhumane acts. The problems arise, argues Arendt, when people stop thinking about the wider repercussions of their actions and focus on the details of a task: when they focus on doing the job well rather than on what the job is doing. Nazi bureaucrats focused on getting the trains running on time to the camps, on ensuring that the right amount of Zyklon B was available, that the capacity of the ovens matched that of the gas chambers. They concentrated on the smooth running of the machinery and ignored the fact that this was a machinery of murder. This is what Arendt meant when she wrote that: 'Eichmann...had no motives at all. He merely, to put the matter colloquially, never realized what he was doing' (Arendt, 1963/1994, p. 287).

As we shall see presently, these ideas have been directly translated into psychological literature through Stanley Milgram's (1974) work on obedience. What is more, Arendt's historical and philosophical analysis has been used explicitly to lend additional authority to Milgram's analyses. It is therefore important to note that recent historical research has increasingly challenged the picture of Eichmann that Arendt presents. In particular, close examination of Eichmann's career reveals him to have been anything but a faceless bureaucrat (Cesarani, 2004). He was a committed and proud Nazi who thought up new and creative ways of intimidating, expropriating and expelling the Jewish community. A telling example of this arose late in the war when he found himself in conflict with his boss, Heinrich Himmler, while in Budapest on a mission to expel the Hungarian Jews. Himmler could see that Germany was losing the war and he wanted to cut a deal with the allies – Jewish lives in return for military equipment. Eichmann was furious. He was committed to exterminating the Jews and rejected any such deals, leading him to challenge Himmler directly and openly (Cesarani, 2005).

For Eichmann, what mattered was not the detail of the job, but the larger picture. He knew that he was involved in the mass murder of Jews and he went ahead because it was something he believed in. Indeed, after the war he said in confidence to a fellow ex-Nazi that, had they been able to kill every Jew on the planet, he would have been satisfied and said: 'All right. We have exterminated an enemy' (cited in Cesarani, 2004, p. 219).

Speaking on the issue of Eichmann's appearance in court, Cesarani shows that it was part of the defence strategy for Eichmann to appear more like the humble clerk than the proud Nazi – precisely in order to undermine the credibility of the prosecution about his demonic career. As Vetlesen caustically comments on Arendt: 'in suggesting that he was 'merely thoughtless', she in fact adopts the very self-presentation he cultivated' (2005, p. 5). In short, these authors argue that Eichmann's appearance was a calculated deception, to which Arendt unwittingly fell prey.

There is just one more point to be made here. Eichmann was not alone amongst 'Hitler's bureaucrats' in his ideological convictions, his creativity, his knowledge of what he was doing, and his commitment to genocide. Indeed, it was a principle of Nazi organization that the 'desk murderers' should be exposed to the realities of the camps so that they could not subsequently disavow their acts (Lozowick, 2002). These 'desk murderers' were energetic and zealous, working hard to perfect the processes of extermination.

On this basis, Lozowick counters Arendt's analysis with a phrase that rivals her banality of evil, contending that: 'Eichmann and his ilk did not come to murder Jews by accident or in a fit of absent-mindedness, nor by blindly obeying orders or by being small cogs in a big machine. They worked hard, thought hard, took the lead over many years. They were *the alpinists of evil.*' (Lozowick, 2002, p. 279, emphasis added).

Ordinary men and the Einsatzgruppen

The large-scale Nazi extermination of the Jews began immediately after the Nazi invasion of Russia on 22 June 1941. The Nazis formed four (later five) special 'task groups' or Einsatzgruppen numbering some 20,000 men. They followed behind the combat groups, rounding up the Jewish populations in newly occupied towns and cities and then shooting them (Browning, 1993).

This chapter of the Holocaust is perhaps less well known than the story of the death camps, but in many ways it is more brutal and more shocking. The murderers were not separated from their victims by industrial machinery. Rather, relentlessly and all day long, members of the Einsatzgruppen would line up Jewish men, women and children, put a gun to their heads and fire. Christopher Browning quotes Heinrich Bocholt, an Einsatzgruppen member and a witness to one of the countless massacres that took place:

> From my position I could now observe how the Jews were driven naked from the barracks by other members of our battalion...I definitely remember that the naked Jews were driven directly into the graves and forced to lie down quite precisely on top of those who had been shot before them. The shooter then fired a burst at these prone victims. I can give no details about the number of victims, but there were an awful lot of them.
>
> (Browning, 1993, p. 139)

Because their actions were so blatant, and their consequences so gruesome, even more than Eichmann, then, one might expect these perpetrators to be somehow different from the rest of us – sadists, psychopaths, ideological fanatics, monsters. But Browning's detailed analysis of just one of the units involved – Reserve Police Battalion (RPB) 101 – suggests a rather different picture. It is captured in the title of his book *Ordinary Men* (1993). The unit was composed of middle-aged, mostly working-class police reservists from Hamburg. The percentage of Nazi party members (25 per cent) was certainly high for such a population, but beyond broad ideology there is nothing to suggest that these people were specially selected for their suitability as killers. Indeed, if anything, they were selected as a rather inept unit that was unsuitable for more demanding front-line duties.

Browning shows that only a minority of the unit were enthusiastic killers. A greater number were unenthusiastic; they did not volunteer to shoot people and indeed they were deeply troubled by the killings – especially of women and children. Moreover, they avoided killing if no one was watching. This attitude extended to the battalion commander, Major Wilhelm Trapp. Trapp was the antithesis of the Nazi leadership ideal of the strong, unbending authority who commands his men to complete the most demanding of tasks. Before the first massacre at Józefów, Trapp was reduced to tears and told his men that they need not participate if they did not want to. Later, he even protected men who had refused the orders of other officers to kill. Indeed, one of the striking aspects of Browning's analysis is the revelation that the men in RPB 101 had a choice over what they did. It might not have helped their careers if they refused to participate in the massacres. But equally, any such refusal met with no dire consequences.

And yet, despite this, the men in RPB 101 did kill. In their 16 months in Russia between July 1942 and November 1943 they took part in some 13 massacres, murdering at least 38,000 Jewish people. They also rounded up some 45,000 more Jews and sent them to the death camps. What is more, even if many of these men were reluctant to participate, some 80–90 per cent of them did participate; no more than 20 per cent exercised their option to say 'no' (Browning, 1993).

Browning argues that if we are to understand what turned these 'ordinary men' into mass murderers we need to focus on the field in which they were operating. He quotes approvingly from Philip Zimbardo's famous Stanford prison study (Zimbardo, 2007, which we shall discuss in detail below) in order to highlight the power of situations in shaping what people do. Yet when it comes to explaining the precise processes through which context impacts on us, Browning offers a nuanced and multi-causal account. In particular, he acknowledges the importance of authority but notes that, in light of Major Trapp's ambivalence, one cannot claim that his men were simply following orders. He stresses the role of racism and a genocidal culture, which allowed people to avoid responsibility for their actions (see also Goldhagen, 1996). He stresses the importance of group norms, of peer pressure, of the desire to fit in and be accepted by others. He notes the cumulative impact of all these factors without ever slipping into a deterministic explanation which implies that people were bound to end up as killers – after all, some did manage to say no, even if they were a minority.

In this way, Browning stresses that: 'The story of ordinary men is not the story of all men.... The reserve policemen faced choices, [and...] those who killed cannot be absolved by the notion that anyone in the same situation would have done as they did.' (Browning, 1993, p. 188). Nonetheless, he finishes his book with the chilling question '(i)f the men of Reserve Police Battalion 101 could become killers under such circumstances, what group of men cannot?' (1993, p. 189).

Classic studies of obedience and tyranny

As should be clear by now, the history of the Holocaust and psychological studies of obedience and tyranny are inextricably intertwined to the extent that it is hard to refer to the one without invoking the other. However, this does not mean that historical and psychological understandings are identical. As we argue below, for instance, Browning's attempt to elaborate a rich multi-causal account of how ordinary men become killers – which seeks to take account of contextual pressures without removing choice and responsibility from the perpetrators – is at odds with the explicit theoretical claims of those psychologists he draws upon. However, before outlining these theories it is important to provide some details of the scientific context in which they emerged.

As we discussed in the case of Adolf Eichmann, the most obvious response to Nazi atrocities was to conjecture about the nature of the individuals who were involved. Can one identify something specific about the perpetrators that explains how they were capable of doing what they did? In this vein, in the immediate aftermath of the Second World War, the dominant approach was to look for a personality type that marks a person as being prone to discrimination and to hostility towards outsiders. In this regard, the work of Theodor Adorno and his colleagues on the authoritarian personality was extremely influential (Adorno et al., 1950).

Adorno and his colleagues present a highly sophisticated and nuanced analysis that looks at the interplay between society, experience, ideology and personality. Over time, however, authoritarian-personality research became increasingly simplified and increasingly one-dimensional (at least within the psychological literature), until it ended up advancing the idea that there is a simple stable personality type that is prone to support authoritarian social systems. This analysis holds that those who possess this personality type (a) desire a rigid hierarchical society, (b) show deference and unquestioning obedience to those they perceive to be their superiors, and (c) display contempt and hostility towards those they consider their inferiors and especially those who are viewed as deviant (Billig, 1976; see also Cohrs & Kessler, this volume).

However, from the late 1940s onwards a series of bold, imaginative and powerful field studies challenged and ultimately usurped this view. The first of these studies was by Muzafer Sherif who showed that, when divided into groups and put into competition with each other, the most placid and well-adjusted of individuals can become hostile and aggressive (Sherif & Sherif, 1969). Sherif's key conclusion was that, if we want to understand social conflict, explanations in terms of individual-level factors such as personality will not suffice. We can only understand how members of one group treat members of another group by considering the nature of the relationship between the two groups. This general insight was applied more specifically to issues of obedience and tyranny in two subsequent pieces of field research: Stanley Milgram's 'Obedience to Authority' studies and Philip Zimbardo's 'Stanford prison experiment'.

Milgram's obedience studies

Milgram's studies are among the best known psychology studies of all time. Moreover, they have been publicized so many times in the press, on radio and on television that their broad findings (if not the exact details) are known not only to psychologists but to the public at large. As Muzafer Sherif said in 1975: 'Milgram's obedience experiment is the single greatest contribution to human knowledge ever made by the field of social psychology, perhaps psychology in general' (cited in Takooshian, 2000, p.10).

Stanley Milgram was born to Jewish parents of Hungarian and Romanian backgrounds on 15 August 1933. He grew up during the Nazi period and, even at a very young age, he was acutely aware of the fate of his fellow Jews in Europe. His concerns were reflected in his bar mitzvah speech at the age of 13: 'As I come of age and find happiness in joining the ranks of Israel, the knowledge of the tragic suffering of my fellow Jews throughout war-torn Europe makes this also a solemn event' (cited in Blass, 2004, p. 8). Milgram himself acknowledged later: '(t)he impact of the Holocaust on my own psyche energized my interest in obedience and shaped the particular form in which it was examined' (Blass, 2004, p. 62).

Milgram's early research drew on the famous conformity studies of Solomon Asch (Asch, 1955) in which people were asked to judge which of several lines was the same length as a target stimulus. When several peers (actually accomplices of the experimenter) gave the wrong response, would other participants go along with them and give the same wrong response? About one-third of them did. Milgram's specific interest lay in whether or not levels of conformity vary from country to country. But he soon grew dissatisfied with the paradigm. He wanted to address forms of conformity that were more obviously relevant to the genocidal phenomena that interested him. As he wrote, '[I wanted] to think of a way to make Asch's conformity experiment more humanly significant. I was dissatisfied that the test of conformity was a judgement about *lines*.... At that instant, my thought shifted... Just how far *would* a person go under the experimenter's orders? It was an incandescent moment...' (Milgram, 1975, p. 318).

And so the 'obedience' studies gradually took shape. Eventually, his aim was to look at levels of obedience in Germany (see Blass, 2004) but he would start off in the US. However, such was the power of what he found there, that he never took his studies abroad.

The obedience paradigm is well known. The participant is brought into the laboratory, where he meets the experimenter and another participant (actually an accomplice of the experimenter). They are told they are about to take part in a learning study, where one of them will be the teacher and the other the learner, and that the goal of the study is to investigate the effects of punishing failure on subsequent learning. They then draw lots, which are rigged so that the real participant is always the teacher. The learner's task is to remember a set of words. The teacher then tests the learner and, if an error is made, the teacher has to administer an electric shock using a large and impressive machine (though, in reality, no shocks are delivered). For each error, the level of shock increases in 15-volt increments all the way up to 450 volts. Just to make the implications even clearer, the numbers on the machine are linked to verbal labels that start with 'slight shock' and go through 'moderate shock', 'strong shock', 'very strong shock', 'intense shock', 'extreme intensity shock' and 'danger, severe shock', finishing with a sinister 'XXX' (in an earlier version, Milgram labelled the end of the scale 'lethal', but dropped this as it was too explicit; see Russell, 2011).

There are more than 20 variants of the study (in his 1974 book, Milgram describes 18 of these, but there are a number of others he merely alludes to as 'pilots'). The one that is most often cited is the 'standard', 'baseline' or 'voice feedback' condition (which is Study 5 in Milgram's 1974 book). In this condition, the 'teacher' is physically separated from the 'earner' and hears the latter's responses through an intercom. As the shock level increases, the learner expresses increasing levels of distress and demands to be released from the study. This includes references to the fact that he has a heart condition (which is what differentiates this variant from an earlier, and otherwise identical, baseline study; Study 2 in the 1974 book).

Initially, Milgram did not really expect people to show much obedience. He certainly did not expect them to go all the way to the end of the scale and deliver what would have been lethal shocks, had they been real. Indeed, when he found that the elite students from Yale University who he used in his pilot studies did tend to obey the experimenter, he dismissively responded that this was just because they were 'Yalies' (see Milgram, 2000). Surely ordinary American adults would not behave likewise? It seemed, however, that they did. In the baseline condition 26 out of 40 (65 per cent) of participants obeyed the experimenter to the very end. Milgram sensed that he had stumbled upon something quite extraordinary. He had discovered the 'phenomenon of great consequence' that he had always sought (Russell, 2011).

Having found his phenomenon, Milgram proceeded, in his own terms, to 'worry it to death' (cited in Blass, 2009, p. 40). He looked at how variations in the set-up would impact on what people did. What if the study was run in downtown offices rather than the prestigious laboratories of Yale University? What if the teacher sat face to face with the learner? What if there were two experimenters who argued with each other, or other teachers who refused to obey?

As we have indicated already, even if textbooks often refer to the Milgram *experiment* (in the singular) and describe only the one (baseline condition), one should properly refer the Milgram *experiments* (in the plural). If one does this and looks at the full range of variants, one discovers that the studies tell a much richer and a much more nuanced story than is commonly supposed (for a recent discussion, see Reicher, in press). The thing that stands out is just how much the levels of obedience vary. Indeed, if one includes one of the pilot studies that Milgram describes only in passing (where 'teachers' have no feedback of any sort from the 'learner'), then the percentage of those who go all the way to 450 volts goes from 100 per cent (in one pilot study where teachers have no feedback of any sort from the learner) to 0 per cent (in three studies; e.g. where the experimenters argue with each other). This means that our question needs to shift, subtly but importantly, from '*why* do people obey' to '*when* do people obey' – and hence also, '*when* do people *disobey*'. It is important not to develop a one-sided focus on conformity. We must also look at resistance.

The danger of seeing Milgram's studies simply as demonstrations of obedience (and thereby succumbing to what Moscovici, 1976, referred to as 'conformity bias') relates not only to the way that his findings are described, but also to the way that they are explained. In Milgram's early papers (e.g. 1963, 1965a, 1965b) he discusses his findings in a subtle and nuanced manner. He portrays the participant as torn between competing obligations to the experimenter and the learner, and addresses the multiple factors that might prioritize one over the other. He even addresses the spatial configuration of the set-up, observing that where the experimenter and participant are in the same room and separated from the learner they may be more likely to become bound together and act as a group (Milgram, 1965a).

Some of these points are repeated in Milgram's 1974 book. But they are overshadowed by the notion of an 'agentic state', which Milgram uses to explain his studies and which he clearly derived from Arendt's *Eichmann in Jerusalem*. Thus, in introducing the research, Milgram states that:

> After witnessing hundreds of ordinary people submit to the authority in our own experiments, I must conclude that Arendt's conception of the *banality of evil* comes closer to the truth than one might dare imagine. The ordinary person who shocked the victim did so out of a sense of obligation – a conception of his duties as a subject – and not from any peculiarly aggressive tendencies.
>
> (1974, p. 6, emphasis in the original)

In other words, Milgram suggests that people enter a distinctive mental state when subjugated to authority. They lose sight of what they are doing, they focus narrowly on doing what they are told as well as they can. What matters is being a good functionary, not being a good person. As we have already mentioned, Arendt's notion that Eichmann in particular did not realize what he was doing is here translated into the general claim that humans in general cannot see what they are doing when authorities instruct them.

There are many problems with the agentic state explanation. Even Milgram's staunchest supporters acknowledge that it seems almost like an afterthought (after all, Milgram only published the idea in 1974, 13 years after he conducted the studies) with little to recommend it (see, for instance Blass, 2004; Miller, 2009) – though few are as harsh as Darley (1992) who writes that he was: 'startled and appalled by ... the odd and pseudoscientific concept of the agentic state ... And I continue to be' (p. 207).

To start with, the notion of agentic state simply does not explain the differences in obedience between the different studies. Certainly people do not lose a sense of their own responsibility in those conditions where they obey more (Mantell & Panzarella, 1976). Linked to this, close examination of what people actually do and say during trials of the studies gives no indication of a narrow focus on 'doing one's duty'. People agonize over what they are doing, they seek to justify their acts, they remonstrate and argue with the experimenter. Milgram had devised a series of prompts that the experimenter should use to urge them on. Only one was an explicit order: 'You have no other choice, you must go on.' Milgram himself gives an example of how one participant responded to this order: 'if this were Russia, maybe, but not in America. *The experiment is terminated*' (Milgram, 1974, p. 48, emphasis in the original). More recently, Burger (2009) has replicated some of Milgram's studies and shown that every time this prompt was given, participants refused to go on.

In other words, and in striking contrast to the received wisdom, the studies do not show that people blindly follow orders. Indeed, when stark orders are given they *do not* obey willingly and automatically (which is not to deny that they might comply if a gun were put to their head). As we have observed elsewhere (Reicher & Haslam, 2011), we need some other explanation of obedience. One that explains both when people obey and when they do not obey. This brings us to the greatest problem with the 'agentic state' explanation: its one-sidedness. It is about explaining obedience, about a state where one cannot help but obey. And, as a result, it excludes disobedience from the picture. It suggests that people have no choice and no responsibility for what they do in this state. In this sense, it contradicts Browning's crucial dictum that the story of ordinary men is not the story of all men. Indeed it almost serves to exonerate those ordinary men who did choose to become killers. At this point the argument becomes morally as well as scientifically problematic.

To summarize the significance of the obedience studies, we can do no better than paraphrase Ross (1998). There is no doubt that Milgram's research uncovers a phenomenon of the utmost importance. Yet 50 years after the experiments were conducted, we still have no clear understanding of why people acted as they did. That is, we await a compelling explanation of Milgram's compelling phenomena. What is more, it must be an explanation of when and why people choose to disobey as well as to obey – with *choice* as a critical term in the analysis.

Zimbardo's Stanford prison experiment

Zimbardo is best known for his Stanford prison experiment, which can be seen as taking the 'obedience' studies one step further. Milgram was concerned with the extent to which people would obey the explicit demands of an authority figure. Zimbardo was concerned with the extent to which people would obey the implicit demands associated with a particular social position, even without anyone present to enforce them.

What Zimbardo did to address this question is well known – as well known as Milgram's studies and, like those earlier studies, known also beyond psychology. He randomly divided 24 young men into prisoners and guards, then staged a mock police raid in which the prisoners were picked up and put under the charge of the guards in a simulated prison that had been constructed in the basement of the psychology department at Stanford University.

Very quickly the prisoners became passive and disturbed – or, in Zimbardo's more graphic language, 'zombie-like in yielding to the whims of the ever-escalating guard-power' (Zimbardo, 2007, p. 196). By contrast, the guards become oppressive and brutal. They imposed harsh and often humiliating punishments on the prisoners. They abused and demeaned those in their charge. The combined outcome was so dramatic that the study (scheduled to last two weeks) had to be stopped early. Zimbardo explained that: 'At the end of only six days we had to close down our mock prison because... human values were suspended, self-concepts were challenged, and the ugliest, most base, pathological side of human nature surfaced.' (1971, p. 154).

For Zimbardo, what happened was a dramatic illustration of the power of the uniform – and of the role requirements that it carries – over human behaviour. Indeed, he went so far as to suggest that this power is irresistible. Put a guard's uniform on the back of a young man, and even the most liberal of individuals cannot help acting as a tyrant. To cite Zimbardo once more, the abuses of the Stanford prison experiment came about: 'as a 'natural' consequence of being in the uniform of a 'guard' and asserting the power inherent in that role' (Haney, Banks & Zimbardo, 1973, p. 12).

While the precise details may differ, Zimbardo's conceptual approach has much in common with Milgram's. Both researchers suggest that the context induces a state in which people lose critical insight into what they do. Both imply that people have no choice, that conformity is inevitable. Hence that perpetrators have limited responsibility for their actions. If this is implicit in Milgram's work it is absolutely explicit in the way that Zimbardo has since applied his analysis of brutality in the Stanford prison experiment to a number of real-life cases, most notably the torture of prisoners at Abu Ghraib prison in Iraq. Here, he has argued that the 'basic psychological dynamics... are comparable in both' (2007, p. 378). That is: 'bad systems [prisons], create bad situations [brutal regimes], create bad apples [brutal guards], create bad behaviour [abuse of prisoners]' (2007, p. 445).

Indeed, most recently, this analysis led Zimbardo to act in court for Ivan 'Chip' Frederick, one of the soldiers accused of prisoner abuse in Abu Ghraib. As he sets it out, the soldiers were 'fine young men and women who had been sent overseas by the Pentagon' (Zimbardo, 2007, p. 324) but who had – through no fault of their own – been brought low by the situation into which they were thrust. It should be added that Zimbardo's claims were rejected by the judge, who sentenced Frederick to nine years' detention. The judge seems to have been more swayed by the army prosecutor, Christopher Graveline, who pointed out that, even in the toxic atmosphere of Abu Ghraib, only some guards became abusers. The judge thus concluded that, while the situation is clearly important: 'to say that bad action becomes inevitable negates the responsibility, free will, conscience and character of the person' (Graveline & Clemens, 2010, p. 179).

As with the obedience studies, we do not question the power of the Stanford prison experiment to confirm that ordinary people can be turned into oppressors (what Zimbardo, 2007, refers to as the 'lucifer effect'). But we do question Zimbardo's explanation of how this happens and, in particular, his one-sided focus on conformity to role requirements. Still more, we question the notion that such conformity is natural and inevitable. These conceptions do not account for what happened in the Stanford prison experiment itself, let alone the larger instances of tyranny and abuse in the world at large.

The first issue concerns Zimbardo's claim that the young men in his study acted without any guidance whatsoever. As he puts it: 'participants had no prior training in how to play the randomly assigned roles' (Zimbardo, 2004, p. 39). Yet it is hard to square this with the briefing that Zimbardo provided for his guards. As noted in *The Lucifer Effect* (2007), in this they were told:

> We can create in the prisoners feelings of boredom, a sense of fear to some degree, we can create a notion of arbitrariness that their life is totally controlled by us, by the system, you, me....they'll have no freedom of action, they can do nothing, or say nothing that we don't permit, we're going to take away their individuality in various ways.
>
> (Zimbardo, 2007, p. 55)

What is significant about this quotation is not simply that Zimbardo clearly tells the guards how to behave, but also that he talks several times of 'we' and 'us', thus positioning himself as part of the guard's groups in opposition to the prisoners (who are referred to as 'they'). From this perspective, Zimbardo's study can be seen as more similar to Milgram's than is often supposed. For, at core, both are studies of leadership. By the same token, our critique of the obedience studies becomes even more applicable to the Stanford prison experiment. We argue that even despite the demands of leadership, people do not always obey, and even when they do, they do not obey mindlessly (see Haslam, Reicher & Platow, 2011, for an extended discussion of this point).

When one goes beyond the broad textbook outlines, one discovers that the Stanford prison experiment was replete with examples of resistance as well as conformity (for a recent discussion see Haslam, in press). At the start of the study, the prisoners challenged the guards, refused to obey their orders and mocked their authority. At the end of the first day, the prisoners were in the ascendancy while the guards were deflated and felt humiliated. Things only changed when one prisoner (#8612) was removed from the cells, taken before Zimbardo, and left with the impression that he was unable to exit the study. After this point, some prisoners still continued to resist the guards but the resistance became ineffective because it was not collective.

Equally, many of the guards resisted their role. As will be recalled from the comments of Christopher Browning, and as Zimbardo notes in *The Lucifer Effect*, there were three types of guard: those who sided with the prisoners, those who were firm but fair, and those (who have received the bulk of attention) who were brutal. No numbers are put on these various categories, but in the available material it is a single brutal guard who stands out – an individual who, because of his swagger and drawl was dubbed 'John Wayne'. But even if John Wayne went along with Zimbardo's general instructions, he was no mere cipher who acted automatically. In an interaction with one of his victims after the study (which also appears in *Quiet Rage* – Zimbardo's own video of his study, 1989), the latter reproaches John Wayne primarily for the *creative* ways in which he tormented those in his charge. When John Wayne asks a prisoner what he would have done had he been a guard, the prisoner replies: 'I don't know. But I don't think I would have been so *inventive*. I don't think I would have applied as much *imagination* to what I was doing.'

None of this fits with the notion that people slip helplessly into the roles to which they are assigned. Neither does it fit with the idea that those who do bad things are mere victims of bad situations. Accordingly, Zimbardo's role account fares little better than Milgram's agentic state explanation. The compelling phenomena that both studies bring to our attention are still in want of compelling explanations.

Social identity, compliance and resistance

Summarizing the above account, we argue that there are two narratives of obedience and oppression, both of which bring together historical and psychological evidence to form a strong and coherent whole. The principal difference is that, in the one case this coherence is overt and this helps render the narrative dominant. In the other case, the coherence is hidden and the narrative is therefore subordinate.

The overt and dominant narrative coheres around Arendt's notion of the 'banality of evil'. This draws on historical evidence that the perpetrators of the Holocaust were largely technocrats who acted thoughtlessly. This is combined with psychological evidence that people conform mindlessly and automatically to authorities and/or to social roles. The psychologists draw on the historians to give a larger significance to their findings ('what happens in our studies can explain what happens in the world at large') and the historians draw upon the psychologists in order to make their claims plausible ('what we are saying happened here reflects what we know about human nature'). The two disciplinary strands intertwine to make a narrative thread that is far stronger than could be achieved by either strand alone.

Yet, at the same time, there is reason to doubt the claims from both disciplines. The subordinate narrative supported by recent historical evidence suggests that while ordinary people did become perpetrators, others chose not to do so. It also suggests that perpetrators acted knowingly and were even proud of their acts. This matches re-analyses of the psychological evidence which shows that people do not conform to authorities either automatically or thoughtlessly. Indeed, there is as much resistance as there is conformity and, whatever people do, they retain a critical awareness of their acts. In particular, those who harm others work hard and work creatively at what they do. To reprise those we have already cited, they are both alpinists and artists of evil (Haslam & Reicher, 2007).

The weakness of this second, subordinate narrative, however, is that the critics in each discipline are largely ignorant of doubts in the other, and this makes it harder for them to challenge the dominant narrative. After all, the historians might doubt what fellow historians are telling them, but how can they challenge what psychology tells them (and the same goes, in reverse, for the doubters in psychology)? It is critical, then, to bring the shared nature of the criticisms into the open. More importantly, perhaps, it is important for psychologists to develop a model that can explain when people conform and when people resist the status quo.

Social identity theory

A good place to start in finding such a model is the social identity approach – under which we include both social identity theory (Tajfel & Turner, 1979) and its development into self-categorization theory (Turner et al., 1987). Over the past thirty years or so, this has grown to become the dominant approach to group phenomena in social psychology. Amongst many other things, the theory suggests that people do not automatically act in terms of any given group membership, but rather that they only do so to the extent that they *identify* with the relevant group. What is more, even when they do identify, this does not mean that they act like automatons in terms of their ascribed social position. Rather, group identities and collective identities are the basis on which people can challenge as well as endorse the status quo.

The starting point for social identity research is that people not only think of themselves in terms of their personal characteristics and what makes them distinct from other individuals (their *personal identity*) but also in terms of their membership of social groups and what makes these distinct from other groups (*social identity*). For social identity theory, we are motivated to see our groups (and hence ourselves as group members) in positive terms and we do this by stressing the things we value about the group which make it better than our rivals. But while this might be a general aspiration, it is not one that can always be achieved. For in reality, many people are members of groups that are devalued in our unequal world: black people in a racist world, working-class people in a class-divided world, women in a sexist world (see also Sutton, Cichocka & van der Toorn, this volume). The concern of social identity theory is to explain how people deal with this predicament.

For the theory, the first relevant factor is whether people consider it possible to advance in society despite their group membership (*permeable* boundaries) or whether they are necessarily limited by this membership (*impermeable* boundaries). In the former case, they will seek advance by downplaying the group and insisting on their individual qualities. But, in the latter case, advance is only possible by tying oneself to the group and seeking to change the standing of the group as a whole.

Exactly how one seeks to change the group's position depends upon a further factor: how secure the existing inequality is seen to be. When security is high (either because the inequality is seen as legitimate or else because one cannot conceive of any way of changing it) one is likely to try to find creative new ways of valuing the group. But when security is low (because the system is seen to be illegitimate and weak) then people are more likely to confront the intergroup inequality directly and try to overturn it (see also van Stekelenburg & Klandermans, this volume).

Overall, the power of these ideas is that they retain the notion that we need to explain social behaviour at the group level but without suggesting that there is something about the group context which makes us inherently less thoughtful and more prone to inhumanity. Group processes, in and of themselves, do not make us more thoughtful or less thoughtful, more compliant or more resistant, more brutal or more humane. For how we behave as group members depends not only (a) on how much we identify with the group, but (b) upon the norms and values of the relevant group (what it means to be British, or German, or a woman or whatever), and also (c) on the structural position of the group as compared with others. In terms of the more specific issue of how we respond to a powerful and brutal authority, this means that our response will be a matter of whether we identify with the authority or if we stand in opposition to it. If we are in opposition, group support will be a critical factor in determining whether or not we are able to resist the demands of authority (Haslam & Reicher, 2011).

There is a wealth of research to support the general tenets of the social identity approach (for a recent review, see Reicher, Spears & Haslam, 2010). However, most of this research is either based on laboratory experimentation or field observation. For a long time, there was no field experiment on the scale or with the drama of either the obedience studies or the Stanford prison experiment. As a consequence, the perceived application of social identity ideas to the phenomena invoked by Milgram and Zimbardo was limited. It is for that reason that, a decade ago, we formulated the BBC prison study – so named because it was filmed and broadcast as four documentaries on BBC television (Koppel & Mirsky, 2002).

The BBC prison study

The BBC prison study adopted the same overall paradigm as the Stanford prison experiment. Fifteen men were divided into psychologically matched groups of guards and prisoners, and placed in a specially designed mock prison environment. The guards had better conditions, better resources and control over the prisoners, who were placed in basic cells. However, in contrast to the Stanford experiment, we built in some interventions designed to address the key variables of permeability and security, as specified within social identity theory. We also were very careful to avoid siding with one of the groups in the study. We simply told the guards to run the prison and make it work smoothly. We did not tell them what to do (see Reicher & Haslam, 2006a).

In order to look at the effects of permeability we told participants that, if one of the prisoners showed the qualities necessary to be a guard, he would be promoted. On the third day of the experiment there was a promotion, but from then on no more changes would be made. The system therefore moved from being permeable to being impermeable. As for security, we had intended to manipulate this by introducing a prisoner who, while as naïve to the others about our hypotheses, was a senior trades unionist. On this basis, we expected him to offer a different perspective and to provide the organizational skills to achieve it. We did indeed introduce this prisoner but, as we shall see, by then the internal dynamics of the study had made the prisoners see the guards' position as highly insecure.

We predicted that the guards, given all the advantages associated with their position, would identify with the group and impose their authority. By contrast, we expected the prisoners to identify as a group only after the system was made impermeable, and only to challenge the guards once it was made insecure. What actually happened was a little more complex and a lot more interesting.

Findings – Phase 1

The prisoners acted just as we expected. At first some wanted to advance their position through promotion, while others did not. But immediately after the promotion, they realized that their only option was to challenge the system and, from that point on, they worked together highly effectively to achieve this. The more they believed the guards to be weak, the more they confronted them with an ever-escalating set of challenges.

By contrast, the guards did not identify as we expected. Many were uncomfortable with their position, and, while individually they put in sterling efforts to run the prison, they had very different ideas as to what to do. They squabbled, undermined each other, and failed to achieve any form of meaningful organization. They also began to feel increasingly despondent and burnt out, since their efforts came to nothing and the prisoners were beginning to run rings around them.

These two factors together – the identification and organization of the prisoners combined with the disidentification and disorganization of the guards – led to a gradual shift of power from guards to prisoners. At first, the reluctance of the guards to exert their power was what gave the prisoners a sense that the prison system was insecure. Over time, it gave rise to a sense that anything was possible. Ultimately, as the guards withdrew from trying to impose their authority, the prisoners broke out of their cells and took over the guards' quarters. And as a result of this revolt, the original prison system collapsed.

Findings – Phase 2

Once the system we had devised was defunct, the participants got together and proposed to us a new system that they believed in – in their words 'a self-governing, self-disciplining commune'. Since it was a system of equality that they believed in, not surprisingly, people identified with the 'commune' and, at first it worked well. People put in greater effort than ever before in carrying out chores and observing rules. But quite soon it became clear that there were dissenters. These dissenters were skilled enough to make the others believe that we, the experimenters, were against them (which was not true) and that the system could not work. As a result, people soon lost faith in their democratic system. The psychometric measures we took on a daily basis show that the 'communards' were becoming rapidly more authoritarian.

At this point, the dissenters got together and proposed a new system modelled on the original guard–prisoner divide – only this time harsher, more brutal and more tyrannical. These self-styled 'new guards' wanted to impose their new regime in order to make the prison work 'the way it should have done from the start', and to do so they were insistent that those in their charge should toe the line. And their enthusiasm for this project lent itself to a range of concrete proposals: a series of strictures for inmates, a request for military uniforms and an authoritarian manifesto.

The striking thing was that, while those who favoured the commune were not enthusiastic about this new regime, they also did not oppose it with any enthusiasm. Their attitude was one of resignation. They had lost faith in democracy. At this point, the study was brought to a close for ethical and practical reasons. The striking thing was that the self-same men who had earlier rejected a relatively mild system of inequality were, by the end, on the brink of accepting a far more draconian system.

Lessons from the study

To adapt an old cliché, this was very much a study of two halves. The first half tells us about the consequences of identification. It fleshes out the ways in which shared social identification allows people to work together and to organize in order to achieve their group aims and objectives, what we call *collective self-realization*. Lack of social identification impedes the ability of people to work together in order to achieve such goals (see Reicher & Haslam, 2006b). As we have previously stressed, whether these behaviours are pro-social or anti-social will depend on the group position and group norms. In this study, the lack of identification with a dominant authority group and the identification with a subordinate anti-authority group both undermined the imposition of authority and the survival of the status quo.

By contrast – and this is what was both unexpected and new – the second half tells us about the conditions under which people are prepared to identify with an oppressive and undemocratic group. It shows that it is the ineffectiveness of one's own group, specifically a democratic group, which leads people to accept others imposing a system – specifically an anti-democratic system – upon them.

The emergence of tyranny, together with people's developing support for it, are a product of prior group failure. Moreover, we see that tyranny is promoted and sustained by a leadership whose effectiveness derives not from mindless conformity or passive obedience, but from *active identification with a social project* and the engagement, enthusiasm, creativity and conviction that this fuels. This is a critical point and, we suggest, it reflects the historical evidence. Notably, it accords with the recent evidence about Eichmann that we discussed above: Eichmann, the proud and committed Nazi who believed so firmly in the extermination of the Jewish people that he was even prepared to confront Himmler in order to get his way.

In this sense, the dissemination of models (such as Zimbardo's) which tell us that groups are inherently bad for us and lie at the root of abusive systems, may become a self-fulfilling prophecy. For they lead us to fear the exertion of group authority, to stand aside, like the 'communards' when progressive group values are challenged, and hence to create the conditions where reactionary systems can emerge. The idea that tyranny emerges through a form of collective absent-mindedness is equally dangerous. It blinds us to the active role that leaders play in promulgating identification with oppressive systems of belief, and to the active role that followers play in bringing those systems to bloody fruition.

Conclusion

In this chapter, while discussing socio-psychological mechanisms of tyranny and obedience, we have challenged the idea of the 'banality of evil' in both its historical and psychological guises. We have challenged the notion that ordinary people do great evil because, due to situational (notably group) influences, they become helpless and unaware of what they do. We have argued instead: (a) that people do have a choice and that they resist as well as obey inhumane influences; (b) that when people do obey, they are well aware of what they are doing, they are frequently creative in their inhumanity, and that they generally believe in (and even glorify) what they are doing; and (c) that the group is a critical resource in allowing people to resist malevolent authority.

We have argued that, however powerful the phenomena produced by the classic psychological studies of obedience and tyranny, we await an adequate theoretical explanation of these phenomena. We have also argued that the social identity approach provides the basis for such an explanation. In essence, our argument is that inhumane action depends upon identification with a powerful group with group beliefs that sanction the abusive treatment of others. We have neither had the space, nor has it been our intention here, to examine in detail the nature of such beliefs. However, elsewhere we have focused on the question of what sort of group belief system can represent genocide as somehow acceptable, or even glorious (Reicher, Haslam & Rath, 2008; see also Bilewicz & Vollhardt, this volume).

The flipside of our argument is that resistance to inhumane authority also depends upon identification, but this time with a subordinate group that stands against authority. It is precisely where one has the support of the collective that one can stand up and say 'no' to those who call on us to insult, injure or even kill others (see also van Stekelenburg & Klandermans, this volume). In this regard, one central problem with received understandings of classic studies of obedience and oppression is that they typically pathologize the group, and see it as the core source of our social failings. Accordingly, commentators such as Zimbardo (2007) routinely urge citizens to act as individual heroes in order to repel group influences. As we have shown, the irony of this analysis is that by perpetrating a fear of groups, it robs us of the single most effective resource for resisting tyranny. Our ultimate message, then, is not that we have nothing to fear from groups, but that this fear is itself both corrosive and toxic.

Practical task for readers

The final challenge is to see how our perspective accounts for the findings of Milgram and Zimbardo. And that is a challenge we pass back to you, the reader. Or rather, we challenge you to consider the case of Milgram, where such exhaustive detail is provided in the published papers and in the 1974 book that we can make a judgement (as opposed to Zimbardo's work which was never published in a peer-reviewed psychology journal and where much of the detail is missing).

Your tasks are as follows:

- First, read the transcripts that Milgram provides of the study sessions. Ask yourself whether or not these indicate that the participant is only concerned with being an obedient subject. Consider the types of argument that allow the participant to continue delivering shocks and those which lead to them stopping. Do these indicate that participants are unaware of what they are doing, or do they suggest that participants are

---

Continued

> seeking a rationale as to whether the right thing is to shock (or not to shock)?
> - Second, read the descriptions of the studies listed in Milgram's 1974 book. On a scale of 0 to 100, then estimate for each study how much the participants would have identified with the experimenter (as a scientist involved in carrying out a valuable scientific task) and how much he would have identified with the 'learner' (as an ordinary member of the general public who has volunteered for this study). To anchor your judgements, let us say that in the most well-known variant of Milgram's experiment, identification with the experimenter as a scientist is high, and judge this to have a value of 80 on a scale from 0 to 100. Let us also say that in this variant, identification with the learner as a member of the general public is moderate, and judge this to have a value of 50 on a scale from 0 to 100. Next subtract the latter from the former in order to calculate the relative identification with the experimenter. When you have done this, correlate the relative identification for each study with the percentage of participants who continued giving shocks up to the maximum level (this is provided by Milgram in the book). If you are feeling particularly virtuous you could get a number of friends to do this and then calculate the average correlation for all of them. If social identity processes are at work and explain the results of the Milgram paradigm we would expect to find a significant positive correlation between relative identification with authority and the level of obedience. To help you, the study descriptions and a response sheet (Table 7.1) are provided in appendix 1.

Suggested readings

You can read more in Haslam & Reicher (2007), Milgram (1974), Reicher & Haslam (2006a and 2006b).

References

Adorno, T. W., FrenkLel-Brunswik, E., Levinson, D. J. & Sanford, R. N. (1950). *The Authoritarian Personality*. New York: Harper & Brothers.

Arendt, H. (1963/1994). *Eichmann in Jerusalem: A Report of the Banality of Evil*. Harmondsworth: Penguin.

Asch, S. E. (1955). Opinions and social pressure. *Scientific American*, 193, 31–35.

Baumann, Z. (1991). *Modernity and the Holocaust*. Oxford: Polity.

Billig, M. (1976). *Social Psychology and Intergroup Relations*. London: Academic Press.

Blass, T. (2004). *The Man who Shocked the World*. New York: Basic Books.

Blass, T. A. (2009). From New Haven to Santa Clara: A historical perspective on the Milgram obedience experiments. *American Psychologist*, 64, 1–11.

Browning, C. R. (1993). *Ordinary Men: Reserve Police Battalion 101 and the Final Solution in Poland*. New York: Harper Perennial.

Burger, J. (2009). *In Their Own Words: Explaining Obedience Through an Examination of Participants' Comments* Paper presented at the Meeting of the Society of Experimental Social Psychology, Portland, ME, October 15–17.

Cesarani, D. (2004). *Eichmann: His Life and Crimes*. London: Heinemann.

Darley, J. M. (1992). Social organization for the production of evil. *Psychological Enquiry*, 3, 199–218.

Goldhagen, D. (1996). *Hitler's Willing Executioners: Ordinary Germans and the Holocaust*. New York, NY: Knopf Doubleday Publishing Group.

Graveline, C. & Clemens, M. (2010). *The Secrets of Abu Ghraib Revealed: American Soldiers on Trial*. Dulles, VA: Potomac Books.

Haney, C., Banks, C. & Zimbardo, P. (1973). A study of prisoners and guards in a simulated prison. In E. Aronson (ed.), *Readings about the Social Animal* (3rd edn, pp.52–67). San Francisco, CA: Freeman.

Haslam, S. A. (in press). Tyranny: Beyond Zimbardo's Stanford Prison experiment. In Smith, J. R. & Haslam, S. A. (eds.), *Refreshing Social Psychology: Beyond the Classic Studies*. London: Sage.

Haslam, S. A. & Reicher, S. D. (2007). Beyond the banality of evil: Three dynamics of an interactionist social psychology of tyranny. *Personality and Social Psychology Bulletin*, 33, 615–622.

Haslam, S. A., Reicher, S. D. & Platow, M. J. (2011). *The New Psychology of Leadership: Identity, Influence and Power*. New York and Hove: Psychology Press.

Koppel, G. (Series producer) & Mirsky, N. (Executive producer) (2002, May 14, 15, 20, 21). *The Experiment*. London: British Broadcasting Corporation.

Lozowick, Y. (2002). *Hitler's Bureaucrats: The Nazi Security Police and the Banality of Evil* (trans. H. Watzman). London: Continuum.

Mantell, D. M. & Panzarella, R. (1976). Obedience and responsibility. *British Journal of Social and Clinical Psychology*, 15, 239–245.

Milgram, A. (2000). My personal view of Stanley Milgram. In T. Blass (ed.) *Obedience to Authority: Current Perspectives on the Milgram Paradigm*. Mahwah, NJ: Lawrence Erlbaum.

Milgram, S. (1963). Behavioral study of obedience. *Journal of Abnormal and Social Psychology*, 67, 371–378.

Milgram, S. (1965a). Liberating effects of group pressure. *Journal of Personality and Social Psychology*, 1, 127–134.

Milgram, S. (1965b). Some conditions of obedience and disobedience to authority. *Human Relations*, 18, 57–76.

Milgram, S. (1974). *Obedience to Authority*. New York: Harper & Row.

Milgram, S. (1975). *Psychology in Today's World*. New York: Educational Associates.

Miller, A. G. (2009). Reflections on 'replicating Milgram'. *American Psychologist*, 64, 20–27.

Moscovici, S. (1976). *Social Influence and Social Change*. London: Academic Press.

Newman, L. S. (2001). The Banality of Secondary Sources: Why Social Psychologists have Misinterpreted Arendt's Thesis. Unpublished manuscript. Syracuse University.

Reicher, S. D. (in press). Obedience: Beyond Milgram's shock experiments. In J. R. Smith & S. A. Haslam (eds.), *Refreshing Social Psychology: Beyond the Classic Studies*. London: Sage.

Reicher, S. D. & Haslam, S. A. (2006a). Rethinking the psychology of tyranny: The BBC Prison Study. *British Journal of Social Psychology*, 45, 1–40.

Reicher, S. D. & Haslam, S. A. (2006b). On the agency of individuals and groups: Lessons from the BBC Prison Study. In T. Postmes & J. Jetten (eds.) *Individuality and the Group: Advances in Social Identity* (pp. 237–257). London: Sage.

Reicher, S. D. & Haslam, S. A. (2011). After shock? Towards a social identity explanation of the Milgram 'obedience' studies. *British Journal of Social Psychology*, 50, 163–169.

Reicher, S. D, Haslam, S. A. & Rath, R. (2008). Making a virtue of evil: A five-step social identity model of the development of collective hate. *Social and Personality Psychology Compass*, 2, 1313–1344.

Reicher, S. D., Spears, R. & Haslam, S. A. (2010). The social identity approach in social psychology. In M. S. Wetherell & C. T. Mohanty (eds.) *Sage Handbook of Identities*. London: Sage.

Roseman, M. (2003). *The Villa, the Lake, the Meeting: Wannsee and the Final Solution*. London: Penguin.

Ross, L. D. (1988). Situationist perspectives on the obedience experiments. *Contemporary Psychology*, 33, 101–104.

Russell, N. J. (2011). Milgram's obedience to authority experiments: Origins and early evolution. *British Journal of Social Psychology*, 50, 140–162.

Sherif, M. & Sherif, C.W. (1969) *Social Psychology*. New York: Harper & Row.

Tajfel, H. & Turner, J. C. (1979). An integrative theory of intergroup conflict. In W. G. Austin & S. Worchel (eds.), *The Social Psychology of Intergroup Relations*. Monterey, CA: Brooks/Cole.

Takooshian, H. (2000) How Stanley Milgram taught about obedience and social influence. In T. Blass (ed.) *Obedience to Authority: Current Perspectives on the Milgram Paradigm*. Mahwah, NJ: Lawrence Erlbaum.

Turner, J. C,. Hogg, M. A., Oakes, P. J., Reicher, S. D. & Wetherell, M. S. (1987). *Rediscovering the Social Group: A Self-Categorization Theory*. Oxford: Blackwell.

Vetlesen, A. J. (2005). *Evil and Human Agency*. Cambridge: Cambridge University Press.

Zimbardo, P. G. (1971). The psychological power and pathology of imprisonment. Hearings before Subcommittee No. 3 of the Committee on the Judiciary House of Representatives Nonety-Second Congress, First session on corrections – Part II, Prisons, prison reform, and prisoners' rights : California (Serial No. 15, 25 October). Washington DC: US Government Printing Office.

Zimbardo, P. G. (1989). *Quiet Rage: The Stanford Prison Study Video*. Stanford CA: Stanford University.

Zimbardo, P. G. (2004). A situationist perspective on the psychology of evil: Understanding how good people are transformed into perpetrators. In A. Miller (ed.), *The Social Psychology of Good and Evil.* New York: Guilford.

Zimbardo, P. G. (2007). *The Lucifer Effect: How Good People Turn Evil.* London: Random House.

Appendix 1

Description of variants (from Milgram, 1974)

1. *L Remote Feedback* (p. 49) No vocal complaint is heard from the learner. He is placed in another room where he cannot be seen by the participant, nor can his voice be heard; his answers flash silently on the signal box. However, at 300 volts the laboratory walls resound as he pounds in protest.
2. *L Voice Feedback* (p. 51) This is identical to the first except that vocal protests were introduced. As in Variant 1 the learner was placed in an adjacent room, but his complaints could be heard clearly through the walls of the laboratory.
3. *L Proximal* (p. 51) The victim was placed in the same room as participant (the teacher), a few feet from him. Thus he was visible as well as audible.
4. *L Touching* (p. 51) Thevictim received a shock only when his hand rested on a shock plate. At the 350-volt level the victim refused to place his hand on the shock plate. The experimenter ordered the participant to force the victim's hand on to the plate.
5. *New Baseline* (p. 73) The experiment was moved out of the Yale Interaction Laboratory to more modest quarters in the basement of the same building. The learner would respond not merely with cries of anguish, but would introduce remarks about a heart problem (at 150, 195 and 310 volts).
6. *New Experimenters* (p. 75) In order to speed up the running of the experiments [there was] a new team consisting of a new experimenter and a new learner. Whereas previously the experimenter had been hard and technical looking, and the learner soft, avuncular and innocuous, the new experimenter was rather soft and unaggressive, and the learner in contrast was played by a man with a hard bony face and prognothic jaw.
7. *Experimenter absent* (pp. 76–77) After giving initial instructions, the experimenter left the laboratory and gave his orders by telephone.

8. *Women* (p. 80) All participants were female. The experimenter and learner were still male.

9. *Limited contract* (p. 81) In the standard variant, participants signed a general release form which stated: 'In participating in this experimental research of my own free will, I release Yale University and its employees from any legal claims arising from my participation.' Typically this release was handled as a matter of routine, but in this variant, after the experiment is outlined the learner demurs. Hovering over the release form, pen in hand, he states that because of his heart condition he can agree to participate in the experiment only on condition that the experiment be halted on his demand. 'I'll agree to be in it, but only on condition that you let me out when I say so; that's the only condition.'

10. *Non-university site* (p. 80) The experiment was moved to an office building in a nearby industrial city, Bridgeport, without any visible tie to the university.

13. *Ordinary man as Experimenter* (p. 111) A rigged telephone call took the experimenter away from the laboratory. Somewhat flustered, but eager to have his experiment completed, the experimenter indicated before departing that the learning information will be recorded automatically and that the participants should go on with the experiment until all the word pairs are learned perfectly. After the experimenter departed, the accomplice, with some enthusiasm, announces that he has just thought of a good system to use in administering the shocks, specifically to increase the level one step each time the learner makes a mistake.

15. *Contradictory Experimenters* (pp. 123–124) When the participant arrived at the laboratory he was confronted with two experimenters, who alternated in reciting the instructions. Their seeming accord came to an abrupt end at the 150-volt level (the point that the victim emits his first truly vehement protest). One experimenter gives the usual command to proceed with the experiment. However, the second experimenter indicates precisely the opposite, directing his remark at the naïve participant. The participant thus found himself confronted with conflicting and equally authoritative commands.

Appendix 1   Continued

16. *Experimenter as Learner* (pp. 126–127) The participant con-
    fronted two experimenters alike in appearance and apparent
    authority. At the outset, while the two experimenters and the
    participant are waiting for the fourth participant to appear, a
    phone call was received in the laboratory. The fourth partic-
    ipant, it appears, had cancelled his appointment. The exper-
    imenter expressed disappointment, indicating that they have
    a particular need to complete the accumulation of data that
    night. One suggested that an experimenter might serve as par-
    ticipant as that would allow them to meet their experimental
    quota. The experimenters flipped a coin to decide which one
    will serve in this way. The loser then drew with the partici-
    pant to determine who will be teacher and who learner. The
    rigged drawing made the experimenter the learner, and he was
    strapped into the chair. He performed like the regular learner.
17. *2 Peers rebel* (p. 134) The participant was placed in the midst of
    two peers (acting as fellow teachers) who defy the experimenter
    and refuse to punish the victim against his will.
18. *Peer shocks* (p. 139) The act of shocking the victim was removed
    from the naïve participant and placed in the hands of another
    participant (a confederate). The naive participant had to per-
    form subsidiary acts which, though necessary in the overall
    progress of the experiment, removed him from the act of
    depressing the lever on the shock generator.

Table 7.1   Response sheet for the practical task

Study number	Brief title	Extent to which variant produces identification with the experimenter *as a scientist* and with the values of the scientific community that he represents	Extent to which variant produces identification with the learner *as a member of the general public* and with the values of the general community that he represents.
0	Standard paradigm		
1	L remote feedback		
2	L voice feedback		
3	Learner proximal		
4	Learner touching		
5	New baseline		
6	New Experimenters		
7	Experimenter absent		
8	Women		
9	Limited contract		
10	Non-university site		
13	Ordinary man as Experimenter		
15	Contradictory Experimenters		
16	Experimenter as learner		
17	2 Peers rebel		
18	Peer shocks		

PART III

INTERGROUP VIOLENCE, EXTREMISM AND TERRORISM

8

Extreme Forms of Ingroup Positivity and their Negative Consequences for Intergroup Relations

Agnieszka Golec de Zavala
and Robert T. Schatz

A quick review of videos posted on YouTube showed us how some young people in London feel compelled to use violence to protect the honour of their 'endz' (administrative areas defined by different postcodes e.g. SE1 versus NW1), which can be disrespected by the mere presence of inhabitants of other postcode defined areas (e.g. http://www.youtube.com/watch?v=tjPl7x-FEKw or http://www.youtube.com/watch?v=xCcVs2KAxKk&feature=related). Also in London, 12-year-old Ben was knifed to death in a fight between two groups of teenagers who identified themselves as 'Greens' or 'Greys' depending on the colour of the rubbish bins on the council estates where they lived. The fight was arranged to establish the group's superiority and Ben is remembered by his gang as a 'fallen soldier'. These examples effectively show how little people need to form an ingroup or 'social' identity and become strongly attached to it. Even such arbitrary cues as the colour of rubbish bins in the area can inspire social identity formation. Moreover, this social identity can generate strong feelings of ingroup loyalty and devotion that are tied to feelings of hostility and aggressiveness towards *outgroups*. Outgroups are other groups differentiated on the same dimension: a different postcode, colour of rubbish bins, colour of the skin or the colours of a flag. The above examples are not limited to the Greater London area. They illustrate dynamics that on a larger scale can involve ethnic groups or nations. Consider the example of the American Nazi Party (ANP) that preaches pride in American white European heritage and opposes politics securing equal rights of ethnic minorities in the US. In a flyer opposing legalization of Mexican immigrants working in the US the party claims that such immigration ('unstoppable plague') 'destabilizes America's White/Gringo status as a Euro/Western nation' (http://anp14.com/support/gifs/mexico2.bmp). The ANP ideological stance emphasizes threat to the desired priviledged status of white European-Americans (e.g. see http://whitehonor.com/white-power/what-does-a-national-socialist-believe/). In early decades of the twentieth century the Nazis in Germany believed their group was threatened because their right for better living space and pure blood was not properly appreciated by other nations. This belief legitimized the Second World War aggression and the Holocaust (e.g. Adorno, 1951).

William Sumner, in his seminal book *Folkways* (1906) observed the commonness of the reciprocal link between love for an ingroup and derogation of outgroups. He wrote '[t]he relation of comradeship and peace in the we-group and that of hostility and war towards other-groups are correlative to each other' (p. 12). Sumner coined the term ethnocentrism, which he defined elsewhere as '[t]he sentiment of cohesion, internal comradeship and devotion to the in-group, which carries with it a sense of superiority to any out-group and readiness to defend the interests of the in-group against the out-group' (Sumner, 1911, p. 11). In 1929, commenting on the commonness of human aggressiveness, Sigmund Freud repeated the observation that ingroup love and loyalty are bound to outgroup hostility: 'It is always possible to bind together a considerable number of people in love, so long as there are other people left over to receive the manifestations of their aggressiveness' (Freud, 1961, p. 114).

Empirical studies in social psychology confirm that the conditions that lead people to discriminate in favour of their ingroup and against an outgroup can be quite minimal. The influential social identity theory proposes that ingroup preference is formed very fast, with little external support but with profound consequences for intergroup relations (Tajfel & Turner, 1986). The famous *minimal group paradigm* experiments used most petty and arbitrary reasons to divide people into ingroups and outgroups. Perhaps the most trivial was a flip of the coin (note the arbitrariness and pettiness similar to the colour of rubbish bins or postcodes) (Tajfel, 1970, 1978; Tajfel et al., 1971). Regardless of the importance of the reasons for the group differentiation, participants generally distributed attractive goods in a way that not only favoured their own (minimal) ingroup but also maximized the positive difference between ingroup and outgroup. This means that people would forego the maximum reward for their ingroup in order to increase the difference between the profits of the ingroup and the outgroup (see also Cohrs & Kessler, this volume).

One of the conclusions derived from social identity theory has been that the strength of positive ingroup feelings should be positively related to outgroup discrimination: the more people love their group, the more they should hate other groups. If ingroup favouritism (and, to some extent, outgroup derogation) can be observed for minimal groups, one would expect that more important and realistic social groups would evoke stronger positive ingroup feelings and elicit negative feelings towards realistic outgroups. However, reviews and meta-analyses of studies investigating the link between positive ingroup identification and outgroup hostility do not support this expectation. The average relationship between the strength of ingroup identification or ingroup positivity and outgroup derogation is close to zero (e.g. Hinkle & Brown, 1990; Jackson, Brown, Brown & Marks, 2001; Pehrson, Vignoles, & Brown, 2009; for discussions why see e.g. Brewer, 1999; ; Crocker & Luhtanen, 1990;; Mummendey et al., 1992). Even before the empirical research shed doubt on the relationship between ingroup positivity and outgroup negativity, some researchers argued that this link does not have to be strong or compulsory (Allport, 1954; Levine & Campbell, 1972). In other words, there seems to be no systematic or necessary link between ingroup love and outgroup hate.

In this chapter we look at literature that differentiates between forms of ingroup love that have more and less destructive consequences for intergroup relations and outgroup attitudes. We review existing research findings inspired by social identity theory and attempt to integrate them with political psychology research that focuses on national identity and feelings. We also discuss the possibility that constructive aspects of ingroup positivity can create bases for positive intergroup relations, which has been largely neglected in psychological research. Our review of the literature highlights the contribution of recent work on 'collective narcissism', an extension of the concept of individual narcissism to the intergroup domain.

When does ingroup love lead to outgroup hate?

Conditions of outgroup hate

Marilynn Brewer (1999) in her review entitled *The Psychology of Prejudice: Ingroup Love or Out-group Hate?* argues that ingroup favouritism (a tendency to favour ingroup over outgroups) is much more common than outgroup derogation and is not a necessary precursor of outgroup hate. However, she proposes that the conditions that make ingroup loyalty and attachment important to people can also facilitate outgroup hostility. In other words, conditions that increase ingroup love are often the same conditions that inspire and escalate outgroup hate. They include: (1) situations of perceived intergroup threat; (2) competition over vital resources or power; (3) intergroup conflict and distrust; (4) perceived irreconcilable differences in worldviews, values and moral codes (see Stephan, this volume, for more details). Although some of these conditions are clearly situational, others may be a matter of *perception* and interpretation of social situations. In fact, some researchers have suggested that the way intergroup situations are perceived (as competitive versus cooperative; threatening versus peaceful etc.) and the intensity of perceived intergroup threat may be embedded in the very definition of one's social identity.

Different types of social identity

Jackson and Smith (1999) explain the inconsistencies in the literature on the relationship between positive affect towards an ingroup and outgroup hate by emphasizing differences in people's definitions of social identity. Social identity has been defined as: 'the part of an individual's self-concept which derives from his knowledge of his membership in a social group (or groups) together with the value and emotional significance attached to that group membership' (Tajfel, 1981, p. 255). Jackson and Smith (1999) differentiate between secure and insecure definitions of social identity. The differences between these two types of social identity have important consequences for attitudes towards outgroups.

Insecure social identity is a combination of positive ingroup affect, perceived common fate with ingroup members (the perception that the well-being of the self and the social group are bound closely together), depersonalization (the perception of self as an interchangeable member of the social group rather than a unique individual), and perception of a competitive intergroup context. *Secure social identity* assumes that positive ingroup affect is accompanied by low perceived common fate, low depersonalization and low perceived intergroup competition. Thus, people can feel strong affective ties with their groups but they may understand their place in the group and the place of their group in the intergroup context quite differently. These perceptions are inherent parts of their social identity, tied to feelings of attachment and positive evaluation of an ingroup. They affect the relationship between ingroup positivity and outgroup negativity. When one controls for the fact that these forms of social identity overlap (because of ingroup positivity inherent in both), only the insecure social identity is related to outgroup derogation, whereas the secure social identity predicts less intergroup bias and sometimes predicts outgroup positivity. In the next section we discuss how recent research in psychology of intergroup relations has been inspired by findings of individual psychology that differentiate between secure versus insecure self-love or self-esteem.

Collective narcissism

In general, positive self-esteem, a realistic pride people take in their strengths (e.g. Kernis, 2005), is related to psychological well-being and happiness (e.g. DeNeve & Cooper, 1998; Diener & Diener, 1995). However, high self-esteem has its 'dark side': narcissism, an inflated view of oneself that requires continual external validation (e.g. Baumeister et al., 2003; Crocker & Park, 2004; Emmons, 1987; Morf & Rhodewalt, 2001; Rhodewalt & Sorrow, 2003). Narcissistic self-esteem is unstable and insecure because it is contingent on continuous admiration by others (e.g. Jordan et al., 2003; Kernis, 2005; Kernis & Waschull, 1995). Narcissists protect their self-image by punishing those who question or threaten their high self-opinion. They respond with anger, interpersonal aggression and hostility to what they perceive as ego threats (Baumeister, Bushman & Campbell, 2000; Baumeister, Smart and Boden, 1996; Bushman & Baumeister, 1998; Raskin, Novacek & Hogan, 1991; Rhodewalt & Morf, 1995).

Recent studies indicate that people also can be narcissistic about groups to which they belong (see e.g. Emmons, 1987). Collective narcissism is defined as 'an in-group identification tied to an emotional investment in an unrealistic belief about the unparalleled greatness of an in-group' (Golec de Zavala et al., 2009, p. 1074). Collective narcissism has been examined with reference to various national groups, ethnic groups, a terrorist group (Tamil Tigers), various groups of college peers, and ideological organizations such as political party, feminist movement or religious group (Cichocka & Golec de Zavala, 2010; Golec de Zavala, Cichocka & Bilewicz, in press; Golec de Zavala et al., 2009; Kruglanski, Orehek, Belanger & Sasota, 2010).

Collective narcissism is contingent on external recognition of the ingroup and involves hypersensitivity to threats to the ingroup's image. It is related to a high regard for an ingroup and a belief that others do not appreciate the ingroup sufficiently. Collective narcissism is also highest among people who explicitly assert high regard for their ingroup but on an implicit level (automatic and most likely beyond cognitive control) they do not prefer this group over other groups. Collective narcissism predisposes group members towards outgroup negativity, especially towards outgroups perceived as threatening.

Collective narcissism is related to inability to forget or forgive any wrongdoings against the ingroup (Golec de Zavala, et al., 2009). Collective narcissists exaggerate and remember even minor outgroup transgressions against the ingroup. Thus, they are likely to see outgroups with which they shared a relationship for some time as threatening. Collective narcissists negatively stereotype such outgroups, report negative feelings towards them, and attribute them with hostile intentions towards the ingroup (Golec de Zavala & Cichocka, 2011). Collective narcissism augments intergroup hostility in response to ingroup image threat such as ingroup criticism (Golec de Zavala & Cichocka, 2012).

Paradoxically, understanding of the mechanism driving the link between narcissistic ingroup love and outgroup hostility sheds new light on the capacity of positive ingroup feelings to inspire positive feelings towards outgroups. Studies show that when the narcissistic aspects of positive ingroup identification are excluded from the analysis, what is left, the non-narcissistic ingroup positivity, predicts *less* negative attitudes towards outgroups (Golec de Zavala. Cichocka & Bilewicz, in press). Thus, understanding the mechanisms of collective narcissistic hostility can expand our understanding of the conditions under which ingroup positivity may be dissociated from narcissistic pride and potentially related to outgroup positivity.

In particular, recent studies show that applying the concept of collective narcissism to the context of national identification and national feelings helps to understand why some forms of national attachment are associated with various expressions of outgroup negativity. In the next section, we discuss the literature that analyzes different forms of national attachment and how they relate to outgroup hostility. This work was developed within political psychology research but it can be linked to findings of social psychology regarding different forms of ingroup positivity. At the end of this section we attempt to integrate the relevant research findings of these two literatures.

Forms of national attachment: are all patriots bigots?

Nations are a potent source of group identity and emotional attachment. Like other groups, nations exist within an intergroup context. As the context in this case is the international world, the relationship between ingroup love and outgroup hostility is of particular concern. Yet as with other forms of social identity, positive national identification does not consistently predict negative outgroup evaluations (e.g. Mummendey, Klink & Brown, 2001). Reicher and Hopkins (2001) argue that the link between national ingroup identification and outgroup sentiment depends on how national members construe the nation, its interests and the relevant international context.

The extensive research on national identity points to systematic differences in: a) the extent to which intergroup comparison is embedded in national identity; b) the content of national ingroup representations and c) modes of national ingroup attachment. These different forms of national attachment relate to different attitudes towards foreigners, immigrants and ethnic minorities, and to militaristic attitudes. (We include militaristic attitudes because in an international context outgroup negativity is often expressed as the necessity for one's own nation to attack or otherwise impose its military might over other nations).

Embedded intergroup comparisons: nationalism versus patriotism

As mentioned earlier, social identity theory proposes that group members seek to compare their ingroup to others in a way that favours the ingroup (Tajfel, 1981; Tajfel & Turner, 1986). Further, positive ingroup identification should be more likely to predict outgroup negativity when it is focused on ingroup versus outgroup differentiation that favours the ingroup (Hinkle & Brown, 1990). This idea underlies the distinction made in the national identity literature between patriotism and nationalism. Kosterman and Feshbach (1989) define patriotism as 'degree of attachment to the nation' (p. 261) commonly expressed as sentiments of love, devotion and pride. They distinguish this construct from nationalism, which they define as 'a perception of national superiority and an orientation towards national dominance' (p. 261). Patriotism then is a form of ingroup identification that focuses on positive feelings towards one's nation. Nationalism, on the other hand is a form of intergroup discrimination that focuses on the boundaries between ingroup and outgroups and on favourable international comparisons.

Scores on measures of patriotism and nationalism correlate positively, suggesting that the constructs overlap in positive attitude towards one's national group. However, research conducted in variety of countries finds that nationalism is the stronger or the sole predictor of outgroup negativity. For example, studies in Canada and the United States show that nationalism, but not patriotism, predicts anti-immigrant attitudes (de Figueiredo & Elkins, 2003; Esses et al., 2005). Studies also find that nationalism predicts ethnic prejudice among whites in the US (Sidanius et al., 1997; Sidanius & Petrocik, 2001), whereas patriotism and prejudice are related less strongly or not at all. An experiment conducted by Mummendy, Klink and Brown (2001) provides direct support for the contention that the intergroup comparison embedded in nationalism elicits negative attitudes towards outgroups. British and German participants generated positive evaluations of their nation either in comparison to other nations or with no comparative reference. They then completed measures of national identification, national evaluation and attitudes towards foreigners. Across four different studies, the national identification and national evaluation scores predicted more negative attitudes towards foreigners for participants primed with the intergroup comparison.

In addition to negative outgroup attitudes, nationalism is linked to an aggressive and controlling international stance. Nationalism predicts support for using military force to implement foreign policy goals (Bliss, Oh & Williams, 2007; McCleary & Williams, 2009). Such attitudes were expressed, for example, by US support for nuclear arms in the 'Cold War' with the Soviet Union (Kosterman & Feshbach, 1989). Later, after 9/11 when international terrorism became the largest threat, militaristic attitudes were expressed in support for the war in Iraq (Federico, Golec & Dial, 2005; Golec, et al., 2004 and military aggression against other countries perceived to support terrorism (Crowson, 2009). Nationalism also predicts higher social dominance orientation scores (Kemmelmeir & Winter, 2008; Pratto et al., 1994; Sidanius et al., 1997), indicating general support for group-based hierarchy and intergroup dominance. Some studies have found that patriotism also predicts militaristic attitudes (Bliss, Oh & Williams, 2007; Golec et al., 2004 Study 2; Kosterman & Feshbach, 1989) and social dominance orientation (Pratto et al., 1994; Sidanius et al., 1997), however, the relationships are weaker than those found for nationalism.

These findings clearly suggest that nationalism is the stronger and more reliable predictor of negative and aggressive attitudes towards outgroups. However, it is not entirely clear what the distinction between patriotic and nationalistic ingroup love really means. Nationalism, by its very definition, is a form of ethnocentrism. Although nationalism items are said to measure a form of positive national ingroup identification, they actually seem to tap favourable intergroup comparisons (e.g. 'Other countries should try to make their governments as much like ours as possible'). Other items on Kosterman and Feshbach's (1989) nationalism measure, such as 'In view of [my country's] moral and material superiority, it is only right that we have the biggest say in deciding United Nations policy' and 'The important thing for the [country's] foreign aid program is to see to it that [the country] gains a political advantage', also assess support for intergroup dominance. Thus, it is not surprising and not particularly enlightening to find out that feelings of national ingroup superiority and support for domination of outgroups are associated with outgroup derogation and hostility. Patriotism on the other hand taps the attachment to one's national group without making direct assumptions as to how it relates to attitudes towards other groups (e.g. 'I love my country', 'I feel great pride in the land that is our [country]') Only when intergroup discrimination is not inherently embedded in the ingroup construct itself can we can begin to understand the aspects of national attachment that may inspire outgroup negativity.

Another problem with the patriotism-nationalism distinction is that it can be construed to suggest that only nationalism is potentially destructive (see e.g. Feshbach, 1994; Kosterman & Feshbach, 1989). Compared with nationalism, patriotism appears relatively innocuous, even benign. Perhaps, then, there is no reason to be concerned about patriotism. However, as Billig (1995) and others have pointed out, this conclusion is misleading. For one thing, patriotism and nationalism correlate positively. For another, when significant relationships between patriotism and outgroup attitudes are found, patriotism, like nationalism, predicts more hostile and aggressive attitudes (albeit less strongly). Empirically then, patriotism and nationalism appear more similar than dissimilar; they differ in degree rather than in kind. It would therefore be a mistake to presume that the relationship between national ingroup attachment and outgroup negativity is unworthy of scrutiny. Rather, we should scrutinize more closely the aspects of national attachment that predict people's attitudes towards outgroups. As we will see below, these aspects are expressed in both the content and the manner of national attachment.

Different content of national identity: ethnic and civic representations

One way of approaching the relationship between national feelings and outgroup attitudes is by looking at the psychological content of national identification. This approach assumes that what people think is most important and defining about their group can determine how they perceive and feel towards outgroups. Research on national identity representations focuses on the distinction between 'ethnic' and 'civic' national identity first introduced by the influential nationalism scholar Anthony Smith (1991). According to Smith, ethnic identity is based in '[g]enealogy and presumed descent ties, popular mobilization, vernacular languages, customs and traditions' (p.12); it emphasizes 'historical and symbolic-cultural attributes... myths of descent and historical memories... [and] cultural differences like religion, customs, language or institutions' (p. 20). Smith characterizes civic identity as based in '[h]istoric territory, legal-political community, legal-political equality of members, and common civic culture and ideology' (p. 12). This conception of national identity emphasizes the rights and obligations of citizenship, commitment to shared national institutions, and civic participation in the life of a country (e.g. voting).

Research examining the impact of these definitions of national identity on outgroup attitudes reveals that ethnic national identity consistently predicts anti-immigrant attitudes. This relationship has been found in studies conducted in England (Pehrson, Brown & Zagefka, 2009), Canada (Esses et al., 2005), Australia (Jones, 1997), Belgium (e.g. Meeus et al., 2010), and in several multinational surveys conducted in more than 30 countries (e.g. Ceobanu & Escandell, 2008; Kunovich, 2009; Pehrson, Vignoles & Brown, 2009; Sides & Citrin, 2007; see Hamilton, Medianu, & Esses, this volume, for more details). Ethnic national identity also has been found to predict prejudice against Aboriginal families living in Australia (Jones, 1997). These relationships were obtained for measures that emphasize different aspects of ethnic national identity, including being born and living most of one's life in the country (e.g. Hjerm, 1998), common ancestry (e.g. Pehrson, Vignoles, & Brown, 2009), common language (e.g. Citrin et al., 1994), and more general concern for shared customs and traditions (e.g. Sides & Citrin, 2007).

Civic national identity scores did not predict negative outgroup attitudes in any of these studies. In fact, two multinational surveys found that civic identity, measured as the importance of national citizenship (Pehrson, Vignoles, & Brown, 2009) and as pride in the nation's democratic, economic and social security institutions (Ceobanu & Escandell, 2008), predicted more positive attitudes towards immigrants. Studies conducted in Germany (Wagner et al., in press) and in Switzerland (Green et al., 2011) also found that pride in national democratic and social welfare systems (labelled as 'patriotism') predicted more positive attitudes towards immigrants.

Pehrson, Brown, and Zagefka (2009) claim that ethnic identity, conceived as blood ties and ancestry, is a particular case of essentialism. National essentialism is based on the belief that the nation possesses a distinct and immutable core underlying nature. This definition emphasizes group boundaries and necessarily excludes outgroups that do not share this nature (e.g. are not of the same blood). Moreover, these groups are perceived as threats to the ingroup's nature. Zagefka et al. (2009) found that Russian and German participants' beliefs in national essentialism predicted greater perceived threat to national identity and distinctiveness. This threat also mediated the negative effect of essentialism on feelings of collective guilt for national atrocities perpetrated against Latvians during the Soviet occupation and against Jews during the Holocaust. Empirical support for the link between essentialist representations of national identity and outgroup exclusion comes also from a study conducted by Li and Brewer (2004) that compared the effects of priming US participants' 'core essence' as Americans or 'common goal' to fight terrorism and help victims in the wake of 9/11. The 'core essence' prime generated a stronger positive correlation between patriotism and nationalism and produced significant negative correlations between patriotism and closeness to blacks and Asians.

Another essentialist aspect of ethnic national identity that helps to explain its relationship with outgroup prejudice is its emphasis on national symbolism. National symbols (such as flags) and symbolic displays of allegiance (such as national anthems) communicate attachment to the nation's core characteristics, values and principles. They make ingroup membership and us-them boundaries highly salient (Billig, 1995; Verkuyten, 1995). Importantly, symbols are affectively charged. They appeal to emotional bonds with the ingroup and inspire potent displays of common allegiance (e.g. Connor, 1993; Durkheim, 1915/1957; Firth, 1989). Empirical studies show that symbolic representations of national identity are correlated with inflexible group loyalty, support for national dominance and rejection of outgroups. Emotional investment in national symbolism predicts staunch, uncritical allegiance to the nation and militaristic attitudes (DeLamater, Katz & Kelman, 1969; Kelman & Hamilton, 1989; Sullivan, Fried & Dietz, 1992). A multinational survey of 16 European countries showed that support for national currency (a salient symbol of national identity during EU integration) predicted nationalism (Müller-Peters, 1998). A US study also showed that support for national symbols predicted nationalistic attitudes, including the belief that the United States should risk war to maintain world power (Schatz & Lavine, 2007). In addition, an investigation of responses to the 9/11 attacks found that more extensive flag display correlated with negative feelings towards new immigrants and Middle Easterners (Skitka, 2005).

Experimental research also suggests that increased salience of national symbols elicits outgroup hostility (see Becker et al., in press; Butz, Plant & Doerr, 2007 for exceptions). Studies conducted in the US show that exposure to national symbols such as a national flag increased participants' nationalism and group dominance tendency (Kemmelmeir & Winter, 2008) and support for the Iraq war (Hassin & Ferguson, 2005, as cited in Butz, 2009). Another study found that participants covertly primed with the American flag were significantly more likely to complete word fragments with aggressive words including 'war' (Ferguson & Hassin, 2007). A recent German study found that exposure to the national flag increased anti-immigrant prejudice among highly nationalistic participants (Becker et al., in press). Even exposure to a national flag on a subliminal level (below the level of conscious awareness) increased implicit prejudice towards blacks in the United States and towards Palestinians in Israel (Hassin et al., 2009). These effects suggest that national symbols activate a representation of the national group that excludes minority subgroups within the nation (US blacks and Israeli Palestinians) as well as non-nationals. Devos and Banaji's (2005) finding that American symbols are associated more quickly with white faces than with black or Asian faces supports this contention.

Why does civic national identity not predict negative attitudes and sometimes predict more positive attitudes towards outgroups? For one, nationality is based on legal citizenship instead of common ancestry and heritage. As the nation is not defined by ethnic homogeneity and distinctiveness, group boundaries are less exclusionary. For another, civic identity representations cast the nation in terms of shared social, political and economic institutions. Because these institutions generate both tangible benefits (e.g. social services, legal rights and protections) and feelings of group pride, national citizens are mutually committed to their well-being. This commitment motivates rational and critical appraisal of the nation's institutional functionality rather than emotional and chauvinistic endorsement of the nation's underlying essence (Rothi, Lyons & Chryssochoou, 2005; Schatz & Lavine, 2007). Civic identity also emphasizes group members' rights and responsibilities to effect change believed to enhance the efficacy of national institutions. In contrast, ethnic national identity guards against change because unchanging historical continuity provides a firm basis for us–them differentiation (Rothi, Lyons & Chryssochoou, 2005). Thus, ethnic content emphasizes permanent and distinctive characteristics of a national group such as ancestral heritage. Civic identity focuses more on the present well-being of a national group and therefore favours positive change even if it alters the group's ethnic composition.

Different ways of being patriotic: blind idealization and critical attachment

Also crucial for our understanding of the destructive aspects of ingroup love is a differentiation between 'blind' and 'constructive' forms of patriotic attachment (Schatz, Staub & Lavine, 1999; Staub, 1997). As explained above, the concept of patriotism focuses on feelings towards a national group rather than the position of the national group within the context of intergroup comparisons. Schatz, Staub & Lavine (1999) define blind patriotism as 'a rigid and inflexible attachment to country, characterized by unquestioning positive evaluation, staunch allegiance, and intolerance of criticism' (p. 153). In contrast, constructive patriotism refers to 'an attachment to country characterized by 'critical loyalty', questioning and criticism of current group practices that are driven by a desire for positive change' (Schatz, Staub & Lavine, 1999, p. 153). Both forms are patriotic in that they are rooted in positive group identification and affective bonds. The key difference is whether ingroup criticism and dissent are rejected as inherently disloyal or embraced as means of group enhancement. Unlike constructive patriotism, blind patriotism rejects the possibility of change and betterment as it threatens an idealized view of the nation.

Whereas blind and constructive patriotism both correlate positively with conventional measures of patriotism (Schatz, Staub & Lavine, 1999) they are only weakly related with each other and the direction of the relationship varies between studies. Only blind patriotism predicts outgroup derogation, including negative evaluations of ethnic, religious and national outgroups (Golec de Zavala, Cichocka & Bilewicz, in press; Parker, 2010) and rejection of immigrants (Schwartz, Caprara & Vecchione, 2010; Spry & Hornsey, 2007). Viki and Calitri (2008) found that scores on a measure composed primarily of blind patriotism items (but referred to as 'nationalism') predicted relatively greater attribution of uniquely human secondary emotions to ingroup (British) over outgroup (American). Blind patriotism also predicts militaristic attitudes (McCleary & Williams, 2009; Oh et al., 2009; Schatz & Staub, 1997; Schatz, Staub & Lavine, 1999; Schwartz, Caprara & Vecchione, 2010), including US support for the war in Iraq (Golec de Zavala et al., 2009; McCleary, Nalls & William, 2009; McFarland, 2005) and in Afghanistan (Sahar, 2008). McFarland (2005) found that the relationship between blind patriotism and support for the Iraq War was mediated by reduced concern for the human cost of the attack. Schatz & Staub (1997) found that blind patriotism was negatively correlated with inclusiveness, or the belief that basic human values transcend group boundaries, and positively correlated with just-world thinking, a belief system that predicts devaluation and derogation of innocent victims (Lerner, 1980), especially members of outgroups (Opotow, 1990). Other findings link blind patriotism with heightened perceptions of threat to national security from foreign nations (Golec de Zavala et al., 2009; McFarland, 2005; Oh et al., 2009; Sahar, 2008; Schatz, Staub & Lavine, 1999; Williams, Foster & Krohn, 2008). Blind patriotism also predicts heightened perceptions of threat to national culture from immigration and adoption of foreign practices (Schatz & Staub, 1997; Spry & Hornsey, 2007). Spry & Hornsey (2007) found that Australian participants' cultural threat perceptions fully mediated the relationship between blind patriotism and reduced support for immigration.

Approximately half of these studies also included a measure of constructive patriotism. Constructive patriotism did not predict more negative outgroup attitudes in any of these studies. In fact, two studies found that constructive patriotism predicted reduced support for militarism (McCleary, Nalls & Williams, 2009; Oh et al., 2009). In addition, a study conducted in Germany found that scores on a measure comprised of constructive patriotism and civic identity items (labelled as 'patriotism') predicted more positive attitudes towards foreigners living in Germany and less anti-Semitism (Blank & Schmidt, 2003). Thus, critical loyalty towards one's national group seems to inhibit outgroup hostility. An experiment conducted by Roccas, Klar & Liviatin (2006) suggests that constructive ingroup criticism can increase feelings of collective guilt for outgroup harm. These researchers compared the effects of priming either *actual* characteristics of Israel that *do generate* positive national identification ('actual ingroup') or *desired* characteristics of Israel that *would generate* positive national identification but presumably are lacking ('ideal ingroup'). Participants exposed to the ideal ingroup prime, who arguably believed that their ingroup should work harder to achieve desirable standards, expressed significantly greater feelings of guilt for Israeli harm to Palestinians. Perhaps then, constructive recognition of the ingroup's shortcomings in achieving desirable standards can encourage group members to bring the nation more closely in line with a desired moral image of the ingroup. If this image includes support for basic and universal human values, its realization should promote more positive intergroup relations (Staub, 1997). The fact that constructive patriotism correlates positively with inclusiveness and with internationalism, in this regard a measure of support for goodwill and cooperation between nations (see Kosterman & Feshbach, 1989) offers some hope (Schatz & Staub, 1997).

Sonia Roccas and her colleagues (2006) argue that the attitude towards national criticism that underlies the blind-constructive distinction reflects the extent to which ingroup members idealize or glorify the nation. Roccas, Klar & Liviatan (2006) define ingroup glorification as:

'viewing the national in-group as superior to other groups and having a feeling of respect for the central symbols of the group such as its flag, rules, and leadership. An individual who is highly identified in this sense believes that the in-group is better and more worthy than other groups and that group members should adhere to all the group's rules and regulations and feels insulted if others do not show the utmost respect for the group's symbols'.

(p. 700)

As this definition includes beliefs in national superiority, it shares the problems of nationalism discussed above. However, the ingroup glorification construct also provides insight into how national group blind idealization operates. Roccas and colleagues' (2006) research indicates that national glorification predicts reduced guilt for past ingroup infractions and suppresses the tendency for positive national identification to predict greater guilt. Exonerating cognitions, beliefs that minimize and justify the severity of the ingroup's infractions (e.g. 'the Arabs would have done [worse] to the Israeli side', p. 702) mediated both of these effects. Leidner et al. (2010) also found that national glorification, but not positive national identification, predicted lesser demands for justice regarding mistreatment of Iraqi war prisoners perpetrated by ingroup members. Further, the effect of national glorification was mediated by minimization of the victim families' suffering and by victim dehumanization.

Together, the research on blind and constructive patriotism and national glorification demonstrate how different modes of ingroup attachment – blind idealization on the one hand and critical attachment on the other – impact the relationship between national attachment and outgroup derogation. Blind idealization of the nation predicts negative and hostile attitudes towards outgroups, especially under conditions of threat. Critical attachment does not predict negative outgroup attitudes, and sometimes predicts more positive attitudes. Note that these two modes of national attachment parallel Jackson and Smith's (1999) distinction between insecure and secure social identities. Blind idealization reflects the insecure combination of positive ingroup affect, perceived common fate with ingroup members, depersonalization and perception of a competitive intergroup context. These factors 'tie personal and group identity close together' (Jackson & Smith, 1999, p. 123) in a way that promotes uncritical ingroup idealization, high identity threat, and negative outgroup attitudes. Critical attachment, on the other hand, reflects the secure combination of positive ingroup affect but relatively low perceived common fate, depersonalization and perceived intergroup competition. These factors permit, if not encourage, constructive ingroup criticism, reduced perceptions of threat and more favourable outgroup attitudes.

The concept of collective narcissism described in the previous section can be used to advance our understanding of the effect of excessive idealization of the national ingroup on outgroup attitudes and intergroup relations. It offers an explanation of the link between inflated ingroup love and outgroup hate. It also provides insight into the conditions under which positive national feelings may help the development of positive outgroup attitudes and harmonious intergroup relations. Collective narcissism predicts negative attitudes towards ethnic minorities, immigrants and negative evaluations of foreign countries (Golec de Zavala & Cichocka, 2012; Golec de Zavala, Cichocka & Bilewicz, in press; Golec de Zavala et al., 2009; Lyons, Kenworthy & Popan, 2010). It also mediates the relationship between blind patriotism and outgroup hostility (Golec de Zavala et al., 2009; Study 1). Most importantly, collective narcissism suppresses the *negative* relationship between constructive patriotism and outgroup hostility (Golec de Zavala, Cichocka & Bilewicz, in press).

Research on national collective narcissism provides compelling evidence linking constructive patriotism to more *favourable* outgroup attitudes. Whereas some studies of constructive patriotism have pointed to such a relationship (e.g. McCleary, Nalls & Williams, 2009; Oh et al., 2009), others have found no relationship between constructive patriotism and outgroup negativity (e.g. Schatz, Staub & Lavine, 1999; Spry & Hornsey, 2007). Studies of national collective narcissism showed that whereas constructive patriotism and outgroup attitude scores were not significantly correlated, after controlling for the overlap between national collective narcissism and constructive patriotism, constructive patriotism predicted less negative outgroup attitudes (Golec de Zavala, Cichocka & Bilewicz, in press). Similar relationships have been found outside the context of national group. For example, narcissistic identification with one's university predicted degradation of students from other universities. However, when the overlap between collective narcissism and positive university attachment was statistically controlled for, non-narcissistic attachment predicted more positive attitudes towards students from other universities (Golec de Zavala, Cichocka & Bilewicz, in press).

Thus, collective narcissism seems to explain a particularly important aspect of belligerent group attachment. It is the only form of 'destructive' group attachment that, when differentiated and controlled for, uncovers the potential for 'benevolent' ingroup love to inspire positive attitudes towards other groups. It seems that positive feelings for one's ingroup may promote positive intergroup relations provided that these feelings are devoid of narcissistic ingroup idealization. This confirms an intuition of romantic poets, writers and philosophers that mature love of one's nation should inspire appreciation for other nations.

Conclusion

Positive ingroup feelings inspire outgroup negativity when (and perhaps because) they overlap with insecure, narcissistic idealization of the ingroup. The line between positive attachment, loyalty and responsibility for the ingroup's well-being, and uncritical idealization of the ingroup, seems to be quite fine. The question of theoretical and applied importance is how to untangle narcissistic from genuine positive group regard in real-life settings. One approach would be to identify situations that increase chances of narcissistic ingroup identification and therefore also increase the overlap between narcissistic and non-narcissistic ingroup positivity. Another approach would be to identify the conditions in which narcissistic rather than non-narcissistic ingroup favouritism is normative. Initial studies indicate that collective narcissism serves a defensive function compensating for loss of control over the ingroup's fate and feelings of uncertainty (Cichocka, Golec de Zavala & Olechowski, 2011). In other words, when people feel personally insignificant, when they feel uncertain as a group member or when they are not sure where their group is heading, they become more narcissistic about their group.

Collective narcissism also increases in response to negative feedback to the ingroup. Such feedback is experienced as personally threatening and leads to an increase in collective narcissism. The only situations in which negative feedback or criticism did not increase collective narcissism was when negative information about the external evaluation of an ingroup was provided together with positive feedback about the ingroup's performance in an unrelated area. For example, university students who read a mock newspaper article presenting their university as having quite a low position in the ranking of universities in the area showed an increase in narcissistic identification with the university. However, narcissistic identification did not increase when the same information was accompanied by another mock article presenting their university as scoring relatively high in the National Student Survey, which indicated that the university is esteemed by its students (Golec de Zavala, 2011). Further studies should examine the social conditions in which narcissistic beliefs about an ingroup become socially acceptable and normative versus conditions in which narcissistic identification with an ingroup is discouraged and marginalized.

Another way of approaching the potentially destructive overlap between narcissistic and non-narcissistic ingroup positivity might be 'neutralization' of collective narcissistic hostility. Studies that examined the link between individual narcissism and aggression offer some suggestions on what kind of interventions may weaken this association. For example, aggressive response to ego-threat characteristic of narcissists was significantly reduced when narcissistic participants were offered an option to self-affirm by ranking values that they treat as guidance in their lives. Reflecting on complexity of self apparently lowers the motivation to defend the threatened self-image typical for narcissists (Thomaes et al., 2009). Asking people to reflect on their values may also provide a humbling experience because it reminds people that they are not always able to follow the guidance of values they render important. The effects of the humbling realization of one's shortcomings in an intergroup context speak to the results of the study by Roccas and her colleagues (2006) described above. In this study, reflecting on the ingroup's imperfections increased participants' feelings of guilt for harm done to the outgroup and neutralized the negative intergroup consequences of ingroup glorification.

The ability to self-reflect and assess the standing of one's ingroup in relation to a desired and ideal state is cognitively advanced and taxing. It requires assuming 'a third person's' perspective in self-assessment (Flavell, Miller & Miller, 1993). Such cognitive ability is achieved relatively late in the course of individual cognitive development and, even when achieved, may not be used (e.g. Golec, 2002). Advanced cognitive skills need to be exercised, and their application to understanding of intergroup situations needs to be encouraged. It has been suggested that different forms of national attachment might form a developmental sequence as well (e.g. Reykowski & Golec de Zavala, 2006). Thus, the ability to form a constructive and critical attachment to one's ingroup can be seen as cognitive developmental achievement.

In fact, all the forms of constructive ingroup attachment that we discussed in this chapter seem to require more cognitive effort than the destructive ones. The destructive forms of ingroup love require little differentiation between self and the ingroup but clear and rather simplistic, black and white differentiation between ingroup and outgroups. The constructive forms of ingroup attachment are based on more complex understanding of the relationship between an individual and an ingroup and between different social groups. They assume critical differentiation of an individual from the group the individual identifies with and cares for. Such differentiation lowers the possibility of using the idealized and inflated group image to protect against individual feelings of insignificance. It also allows for critical assessment of what the group lacks with reference to its standards and encourages betterment typically prevented by blind idealization (e.g. Staub, 1997). It also assumes complex and fluid understanding of group boundaries and foundations.

Thus, factors that promote cognitive development and reinforce cognitive effort are likely to increase the probability that more complex and constructive forms of social identification may develop and be applied in intergroup situations. These factors should thereby reduce the chance that ingroup positivity will be taken to its narcissistic extreme. On the other hand, factors that increase cognitive closure and make cognitive effort difficult are likely to increase the chance that ingroup positivity will be linked to narcissistic, blind idealization of the ingroup. Future studies should advance our understanding of factors affecting the overlap between ingroup positivity and collective narcissism and the link between collective narcissism and outgroup negativity. Such studies would inform interventions aiming at reducing the capacity of ingroup love to inspire outgroup hate. They could also propose how to use the ingroup positivity as a platform for creating positive and tolerant attitudes towards outgroups.

Practical task for readers

Have a close look at the 'letter to America' issued by Osama bin Laden after the terrorist attacks in the US on 11 September 2001. Analyse and describe the narcissistic beliefs about an ingroup that this letter expresses. Pay close attention to how narcissistic rhetoric, and beliefs about the privileged but not recognized status of the ingroup, give justification to intergroup violence.

Suggested readings

To learn more about the topic read Brewer (2007), de Figueiredo and Elkins (2003), Golec de Zavala (2011), Reicher and Hopkins (2001), and Schatz and colleagues (1999).

References

Adorno, T. (1951). Freudian theory and the pattern of fascist propaganda. In M. Bernstein (ed.), *Culture Industry* (pp. 132–158). New York: Routledge.
Allport, G. W. (1954). *The Nature of Prejudice*. Cambridge, MA: Perseus Books
Baumeister, R. F., Bushman, B. J. & Campbell, W. K. (2000). Self-esteem, narcissism, and aggression: Does violence *result* from low self-esteem or from threatened egotism? *Current Directions in Psychological Science*, 9, 26–29.
Baumeister, R. F., Campbell, J. D., Kreuger, J. I. & Vohs, K. D. (2003). Does high self-esteem cause better performance, interpersonal success, happiness, or healthier lifestyle? *Psychological Science in the Public Interest*, 4, 1–44.
Baumeister, R. F., Smart, L. & Boden, J. M. (1996). Relation of threatened egotism to violence and aggression: The dark side of high self-esteem. *Psychological Review*, 103, 5–33.

Becker, J. C., Enders-Comberg, A., Wagner, U., Christ, O. & Butz, D. A. (in press). Beware of national symbols: How flags can threaten intergroup relations. *Social Psychology*.

Billig, M. (1995). *Banal Nationalism*. London: Sage.

Blank, T. & Schmidt, P. (2003). National identity in a United Germany: Nationalism or patriotism? An empirical test with representative data. *Political Psychology*, 24, 289–312.

Bliss, S. L., Oh, E. J. & Williams, R. L. (2007). Militarism and sociopolitical perspectives among college students in the U.S. and South Korea. *Peace and Conflict: Journal of Peace Psychology*, 13, 175–199.

Brewer, M. B. (1999).The psychology of prejudice: Ingroup love or outgroup hate? *Journal of Social Issues*, 55, 429–444.

Brewer, M. B. (2007). The importance of being *We*: Human nature and intergroup relations. *American Psychologist*, 62, 728–738.

Bushman, B. J. & Baumeister, R. (1998). Threatened egotism, narcissism, self-esteem, and direct and displaced aggression: Does self-love or self-hate lead to violence? *Journal of Personality and Social Psychology*, 75, 219–229.

Butz, D. A. (*2009*). National symbols as agents of psychological and social change. *Political Psychology*, 30, 779–804.

Butz, D. A., Plant, E. A. & Doerr, C. E. (2007). Liberty and justice for all? Implications of exposure to the U.S. flag for intergroup relations. *Personality and Social Psychology Bulletin*, 33, 396–408.

Ceobanu, A. M. & Escandell, X. (2008). East is West? National feelings and anti-immigrant sentiment in Europe. *Social Science Research*, 37, 1147–1170.

Cichocka, A. & Golec de Zavala, A. (2011). Kolektywny narcyzm a sprawa polska. [Collective narcissism and the polish issue]. In M. Kofta & M. Bilewicz. *Wobec obcych. Zagrożenia psychologiczne a stosunki międzygrupowe*. [Towards others. Psychological threat and intergroup relations]. Warsaw: PWN.

Cichocka, A., Golec de Zavala, A. & Olechowski, M. (2011). *Defensive and Genuine Group Identification in the Face of Collective Trauma*. Poster presented at the 12th Annual Meeting of the Society for Personality and Social Psychology, San Antonio, Texas.

Citrin, J., Haas, E. B., Muste, C. & Reingold, B. (1994). Is American nationalism changing? Implications for foreign policy. *International Studies Quarterly*, 38, 1–31.

Connor, W. (1993). Beyond reason: The nature of the ethnonational bond. *Ethnic and Racial Studies*, 16, 373–389.

Crocker, J. & Luhtanen, R. (1990). Collective self-esteem and in-group bias. *Journal of Personality and Social Psychology*, 58, 60–67.

Crocker, J. & Park, L. E. (2004). The costly pursuit of self-esteem. *Psychological Bulletin*, 130, 392–414.

Crowson, M. H. (2009). Nationalism, internationalism, and perceived UN irrelevance: Mediators of relationships between authoritarianism and support for military aggression as part of the war on terror. *Journal of Applied Social Psychology*, 39, 1137–1162.

de Figueiredo, R. J. P. & Elkins, Z. (2003). Are patriots bigots? An inquiry into the vices of ingroup pride. *American Journal of Political Science*, 47, 171–188.

DeLamater, J., Katz, D. & Kelman, H. C. (1969). On the nature of national involvement: A preliminary study. *Journal of Conflict Resolution*, 13, 320–357.

Devos, T. & Banaji, M. R. (2005). American = White? *Journal of Personality and Social Psychology*, 88, 447–466.

Durkheim, E. (1957). *Elementary Forms of Religious Life* (J. W. Swain, Trans.). London: Allen & Unwin. (Original work published 1915).

Emmons, R. A. (1987). Narcissism: Theory and measurement. *Journal of Personality and Social Psychology*, 52, 11–17.

Esses, V. M., Dovidio, J. F., Semenya, A. & Jackson, L. (2005). Attitudes towards immigrants and immigration: The role of national and international iden-tity. In D. Abrams, M. A. Hogg & J. M. Marques (eds.), *The Social Psychology of Inclusion and Exclusion* (pp. 317–337). Hove: Psychology Press.

Federico, C. M., Golec, A. & Dial, J. L. (2005). The relationship between the need for closure and support for military action against Iraq: Moderating effects of national attachment. *Personality and Social Psychology Bulletin*, 31, 621–632.

Ferguson, M. J. & Hassin, R. R. (2007). On the automatic association between America and aggression for news watchers. *Personality and Social Psychology Bulletin*, 33, 1632–1647.

Feshbach, S. (1994). Nationalism, patriotism, and aggression: A clarification of functional differences. In R. L. Huesmann (ed.), *Aggressive Behaviour: Current Perspectives* (pp. 275–291). New York: Plenum Press.

Freud, S. (1961). *Civilization and its Discontents*. New York: W. W. Norton Firth, R. (1989). *Symbols: Public and Private*. Ithaca, NY: Cornell University Press.

Flavell, J. H., Miller, P. H., & Miller, S. A. (1993). *Cognitive development*. Englewood Cliffs, NJ: Prentice-Hall.

Golec A. (2002). Cognitive skills as predictor of attitudes toward political conflict: A study of Polish politicians. *Political Psychology*, 4, 731–759.

Golec, A., Federico, C. M., Cislak, A. & Dial, J. (2004). Need for closure, national attachment, and attitudes toward international conflict: Distinguishing the roles of patriotism and nationalism. *Advances in Psychology Research*, 33, 231–251.

Golec de Zavala, A. (2011). *Situations that Increase Narcissistic In-Group Love*. Research report prepared for the completion of the British Academy Small Research Grant (SG090532).

Golec de Zavala, A. & Cichocka, A. (2012). *Collective Narcissism Moderates the Effect of Threat to In-Group's Image on Intergroup Hostility*. Manuscript submitted for publication.

Golec de Zavala, A. & Cichocka, A. (2012). Collective narcissism and Anti-Semitism in Poland. *Group Processes and Intergroup Relations*, 15, 213–229.

Golec de Zavala, A., Cichocka, A. & Bilewicz, M. (in press). The paradox of in-group love: Narcissistic and genuine in-group positivity and out-group attitudes. *Journal of Personality*.

Golec de Zavala, A., Cichocka, A. K., Eidelson, R. & Jayawickreme, N. (2009). Collective narcissism as and its social consequences. *Journal of Personality and Social Psychology*, 97, 1074–1096.

Green, E. G. T., Sarrasin, O., Fasel, N. & Staerklé, C. (2011). Nation-alism and patriotism as predictors of immigration attitudes in Switzerland: A municipality-level analysis. *Swiss Political Science Review*, 17, 369–393.

Hassin, R. R., Ferguson, M. J., Kardosh, R., Porter, S. C., Cater, T. J. & Dudareva, V. (2009). Précis of implicit nationalism. *Annals of the New York Academy of Sciences*, 1167, 135–145.

Hinkle, S. & Brown, R. (1990). Intergroup comparisons and social identity: Some links and lacunae. In D. Abrams & M. A. Hogg (eds.), *Social Identity Theory: Constructive and Critical Advances* (pp. 48–70). New York: Harvester Wheatsheaf.

Hjerm, M. (1998). National identities, national pride and xenophobia: A comparison of four Western countries. *Acta Sociologica*, 41 (4), 335–347.

Jackson, J. W. & Smith, E. R. (1999). Conceptualizing social identity: A new framework and evidence for the impact of different dimensions. *Personality and Social Psychology Bulletin*, 25, 120–135.

Jones, F. L. (1997). Ethnic diversity and national identity. *Journal of Sociology*, 33, 285–305.

Jordan, C. H., Spencer, S. J. & Zanna, M. P. (2005). Types of high self-esteem and prejudice: How implicit self-esteem relates to ethnic discrimination among high explicit self-esteem individuals. *Personality and Social Psychology Bulletin*, 31, 693–702.

Kelman, H. C. & Hamilton, V. L. (1989). *Crimes of Obedience: Toward a Social Psychology of Authority and Responsibility* (pp. 261–306). New Haven: Yale University Press.

Kemmelmeier, M. & Winter, D. G. (2008). Sowing patriotism, but reaping nationalism? Consequences of exposure to the American flag. *Political Psychology*, 29, 859–879.

Kosterman, R. & Feshbach, S. (1989). Toward a measure of patriotic and nationalistic attitudes. *Political Psychology*, 10, 257–274.

Kunovich, R. M. (2009). The sources and consequences of national identification. *American Sociological Review*, 74, 573–593.

Leidner, B, Castano, E., Zaiser, E & Giner-Sorolla R. (2010). Ingroup glorification, moral disengagement, and justice in the context of collective violence. *Personality and Social Psychology Bulletin*, 36, 1115–1129.

Lerner, M. J. (1980). *The Belief in a Just World: A Fundamental Delusion*. New York: Plenum Press.

Levine, R. A. and Campbell, D. T. (1972) *Ethnocentricism: theories of conflict, ethnic attitudes and group behavior*, New York: Wiley.

Li, Q. & Brewer, M. B. (2004). What does it mean to be an American? Patriotism, nationalism, and American identity after 9/11. *Political Psychology*, 25, 727–739.

Lyons, P. A., Kenworthy, J. B. & Popan, J. R. (2010). Ingroup identification and group-level narcissism as predictors of U.S. citizens' attitudes and behaviors toward Arab immigrants. *Personality and Social Psychology Bulletin*, 36, 1267–1280.

McCleary, D. F., Nalls, M. L. & Williams, R. L. (2009). Types of patriotism as primary predictors of continuing support for the Iraq War. *Journal of Political and Military Sociology*, 37, 77–94.

McCleary, D. F. & Williams, R. L. (2009). Sociopolitical and personality correlates of militarism in democratic societies. *Peace and Conflict: Journal of Peace Psychology*, 15, 161–187.

McFarland, S. G. (2005). On the eve of war: Authoritarianism, social domi- nance, and American students' attitudes toward attacking Iraq. *Personality and Social Psychology Bulletin*, 31, 360–367.

Meeus, J., Duriez, B., Vanbeselaere, N. & Boen, P. (2010). The role of national identity representation in the relation between in-group identification and out-group derogation: Ethnic versus civic representation. *British Journal of Social Psychology*, 49, 305–320.

Morf, C. C. & Rhodewalt, F. (2001). Unraveling the paradoxes of narcis- sism: A dynamic self-regulatory processing model. *Psychological Inquiry*, 12, 177–196.

Müller-Peters, A. (1998). The significance of national pride and national iden- tity to the attitude toward the single European currency: A Europe-wide comparison. *Journal of Economic Psychology*, 19, 701–719.

Mummendy, A., Klink, A. & Brown, R. (2001). Nationalism and patrio- tism: National identification and outgroup rejection. *British Journal of Social Psychology*, 40, 159–172.

Mummendey, A., Simon, B., Dietze, C., Grunert., M., Haeger, G., Kessler, S., Lettgen, S. & Schaferhoff, S. (1992). Categorization is not enough: Intergroup discrimination in negative outcome allocations. *Journal of Experimental Social Psychology*, 28, 125–144.

Oh, E. J., Williams, R. L., Bliss, S. L. & Krohn, K. R. (2009). Constructive and blind patriotism: Relationship to emphasis on civil liberties, national secu- rity, and militarism in a Korean and an American university. *Korean Social Science Journal*, 36, 93–121.

Opotow, S. (1990). Moral exclusion and injustice: An overview. *Journal of Social Issues*, 46, 1–20.

Parker, C. S. (2010). Symbolic versus blind patriotism: Distinction without a difference? *Political Research Quarterly*, 63, 97–114.

Pehrson, S., Brown, R. & Zagefka, H. (2009). When does national identification lead to the rejection of immigrants? Cross-sectional and longitudinal evi- dence for the role of essentialist ingroup definitions. *British Journal of Social Psychology*, 48, 61–76.

Pehrson, S., Vignoles, V. L. & Brown, R. (2009). National identification and anti-immigrant prejudice: Individual and contextual effects of national definitions. *Social Psychology Quarterly*, 72, 24–38.

Pratto, F., Sidanius, J., Stallworth, L. M. & Malle, B. F. (1994). Social dominance orientation: A personality variable predicting social and political attitudes. *Journal of Personality and Social Psychology*, 67, 741–763.

Raskin, R., Novacek, J. & Hogan, R. (1991). Narcissistic self-esteem manage- ment. *Journal of Personality and Social Psychology*, 60, 911–918.

Reicher, S. & Hopkins, N. (2001). *Self and Nation*. London: Sage.

Reykowski, J. & Golec de Zavala, A. (2006). Consequences of patriotism: Is ethnocentrism inevitable? In A. Golec de Zavala, K. Skarzynska (eds). *Understanding Social Change: Political Psychology in Poland* (pp. 87–104). Hauppauge, New York: Nova Publishers.

Rhodewalt, F. & Morf, C. C. (1995). Self and interpersonal correlates of the Nar- cissistic Personality Inventory: A review and new findings. *Journal of Research in Personality*, 29, 1–23.

Rhodewalt, F. & Sorrow, D. L. (2003). Interpersonal self-regulation: Lessons from the study of narcissism. In M. R. Leary & J. P. Tangney (eds.), *Handbook of Self and Identity* (pp. 519–535). New York: Guilford Press.

Roccas, S., Klar, Y. & Liviatan, I. (2006). The paradox of group-based guilt: Modes of national identification, conflict vehemence, and reactions to the in-group's moral violations. *Journal of Personality and Social Psychology*, 91, 698–711.

Rothi, D. M., Lyons, E. & Chryssochoou, X. (2005). National attachment and patriotism in a European nation: A British study. *Political Psychology*, 26, 135–155.

Sahar, G. (2008). Patriotism, attributions for the 9/11 attacks, and support for war: Then and now. *Basic and Applied Social Psychology*, 30, 189–197.

Schatz, R. T. & Lavine, H. (2007). Waving the flag: National symbolism, social identity, and political engagement. *Political Psychology*, 28, 329–355.

Schatz, R. T & Staub, E. (1997). Manifestations of blind and constructive patriotism: Personality correlates and individual-group relations. In D. Bar-Tal and E. Staub (eds.), *Patriotism in the Lives of Individuals and Nations* (pp. 229–245). Chicago: Nelson Hall.

Schatz, R. T., Staub, E. & Lavine, H. (1999). On the varieties of national attachment: Blind versus constructive patriotism. *Political Psychology*, 20, 151–174.

Schwartz, S. H., Caprara, G. V. & Vecchione, M. (2010). Basic personal values, core political values, and voting: A longitudinal analysis. *Political Psychology*, 31, 421–452.

Sidanius, J., Feshbach, S., Levin, S., Pratto, F. (1997). The interface between ethnic and national attachment: Ethnic pluralism or ethnic dominance? *Public Opinion Quarterly*, 61, 102–133.

Sidanius, J. & Petrocik, J. R. (2001). Communal and national identity in a multiethnic state: A comparison of three perspectives. In R. D. Ashmore & Jussim (eds.), *Social Identity, Intergroup Conflict, and Conflict Resolution* (pp.101–129). London: Oxford University Press.

Sides, J. & Citrin, J. (2007). European opinion about immigration: The role of identities, interests and information. *British Journal of Political Science*, 37, 477–504.

Skitka, L. J. (2005). Patriotism or nationalism? Understanding post-September 11, 2001, flag-display behavior. *Journal of Applied Social Psychology*, 35, 1995–2011.

Smith, A. D. (1991). *National Identity*. Reno: University of Nevada Press.

Spry, C. & Hornsey, M. (2007). The influence of blind and constructive patriotism on attitudes toward multiculturalism and immigration. *Australian Journal of Psychology*, 59, 151–158.

Staub, E. (1997). Blind versus constructive patriotism: Moving from embeddedness in the group to critical loyalty and action. In D. Bar-Tal & E. Staub (eds.), *Patriotism in the Lives of Individuals and Nations* (pp. 213–228). Chicago: Nelson-Hall.

Sullivan, J. L., Fried, A. & Dietz, M. G. (1992). Patriotism, politics, and the presidential election of 1988. *American Journal of Political Science*, 36, 200–234.

Sumner, W. G. (1911). War and other essays. Freeport: Yale University Press.

Tajfel, H. (1970). Experiments in intergroup discrimination. *Scientific American*, 223, 96–102.

Tajfel, H. (ed.). (1978). *Differentiation Between Social Groups*. London: Academic Press.

Tajfel, H. (1981). *Human Groups and Social Categories: Studies in Social Psychology*. New York: Cambridge University Press.

Tajfel, H., Billig, M., Bundy, R. P. & Flament, C. (1971). Social categorization and intergroup behaviour. *European Journal of Social Psychology*, 2, 149–178.

Tajfel, H. & Turner, J. C. (1986). The social identity theory of intergroup behavior. In S. Worchel & W. C. Austin (eds.), *Psychology of Intergroup Relations* (2nd edn). (pp. 7–24). Chicago: Nelson-Hall.

Thomaes, S., Bushman, B., Orbio de Castro, B., Cohen, G., & Denissen, J. (2009). Reducing narcissistic aggression by buttressing self-esteem: an experimental field study. Psychological Science, 20, 1536–1542.

Verkuyten, M. (1995). Symbols and symbolic representations. *Journal for the Theory of Social Behavior*, 25, 263–284.

Viki, G. T. & Calitri, R. (2008). Infrahuman outgroup or suprahuman ingroup: The role of nationalism and patriotism in the infrahumanization of outgroups. *European Journal of Social Psychology*, 38, 1054–1061.

Wagner, U., Becker, J. C., Christ, O., Pettigrew, T. F. & Schmidt, P. (in press). A longitudinal test of the relation between German nationalism, patriotism, and outgroup derogation. *European Sociological Review*.

Williams, R. L., Foster, L. N. & Krohn, K. R. (2008). Relationship of patriotism measures to critical thinking and emphasis on civil liberties versus national security. *Analyses of Social Issues and Public Policy*, 8, 139–156.

Zagefka, H., Pehrson, S., Mole, R. C. M. & Chan, E. (2009). The effect of essentialism in settings of historic intergroup atrocities. *European Journal of Social Psychology*, 40, 718–732.

9

The Role of Threats in Understanding and Improving Intergroup Relations

Walter G. Stephan

● ●

In a book about applied social psychology, you might not expect to read much about theory since it may seem to you that most psychological theories are not concerned with practical ways of solving social problems. However, one of the fathers of social psychology, Kurt Lewin, made just the opposite argument, saying: 'There is nothing as practical as a good theory.' (Lewin, 1948, p. 12). In this chapter, I will make a case for this argument by focusing on a set of theories about the role that feelings of anxiety, fear and threat play in intergroup relations. I will be relying heavily on my own theories and research to make this argument and, along the way, will show that theory-making, at least in my case, is a highly personal process.

Before I consider Lewin's argument, I would like you to do a thought experiment. Terrorists – particularly radical Muslim terrorists – are among the most hated people in the world today. The question I want you to think about is, 'why'? What are the reasons for this hatred? (see Das et al., 2009 and Oswald, 2005 for some research on this question). What is your personal theory on the causes of hatred against terrorists? How would you go about framing your approach? Can you come up with categories of causes to organize your thoughts? For instance, people may hate terrorists because they pose a threat to their lives, their communities, their society and the global economy. They might also see terrorists as a threat to their religion, their culture and their way of life. Also, they probably strongly disagree with the values the terrorists advocate, as well as the violent means they use to try to achieve their goals. These types of thoughts constitute the beginnings of a theory, but, as we shall see, theories are more abstract and complex than a list of causes.

To return to the question about the practicality of theory in understanding social problems, the best place to start is with a reminder of the definition of a theory. Theories address a domain of interest (e.g. the causes of hatred) and postulate the relationships among a set of concepts that are relevant to that domain. One of the primary functions of theories is to guide us in deciding what causes to examine if we want to deepen our understanding of a given domain of interest. Good theories have clearly defined concepts and specify the ways in which they are related (e.g. which variables cause which other variables or moderate the effects of other variables). The best of them do this with simplicity and elegance. And the best of those have a wide range of applicability.

In applied social psychology, theories help us to understand social issues and solve social problems by providing us with ideas about the causal relations among the variables that create or sustain these problems. When you ask a question such as, 'how do we improve relations between groups in conflict?', it is of enormous value to understand why there are negative relations between some groups in the first place. For instance, if you want to reduce prejudice, it is beneficial to know what causes it. If you know what the causes are, you can address them with an intervention or some type of programme or public policy. To determine what the causes are, it is often necessary to do basic experimental research, because there is no better tool to establish causality. Invariably, research will lead to modifications in the theory – some causal arguments will be wrong, in other cases causality may be bi-directional, and in still other cases, the theory may only hold under certain conditions or for certain types of people.

Next, I would like to illustrate the value of theory in applied social psychology by examining a set of theories I had a major role in developing. I will be focusing on my own work because I can present details about it that I could not present if I used a theory developed by someone else. I will then discuss how they apply to understanding and improving relations between groups that have a history of conflict.

There is, of course, a long history of theories and research on the causes of negative relations between social groups, both in social psychology and in other disciplines (Nelson, 2009). From the early history of social psychology, there is contact theory, the authoritarian personality (Adorno,

1950; Altemeyer, 1981), realistic group conflict theory (LeVine & Campbell, 1972), social identity theory (Scheepers et al., 2006; Tajfel, 1982), and many others. These theories paid scant attention to a set of factors that has always seemed to me to be at the heart of intergroup conflict – anxiety, fear and threat. They were not ignored by earlier theorists – so much as relegated to a minor role. These factors will be the primary focus of this chapter.

Intergroup anxiety theory

At the inception of a new theory, there is always a catalyst that triggers it. My own interest in threat and fear as causes of negative intergroup relations was instigated by an invitation a generation ago to speak at a symposium on school desegregation (i.e. the legally mandated mixing of whites and blacks in American schools). The organizer asked me to try to answer the following question: *Why don't blacks and whites interact together in desegregated schools?* I was asked to address this question because I had been studying the effects of school desegregation on racial attitudes for more than a decade (Stephan, 1978). There are many answers to this seemingly simple question (e.g. the history of conflict between these groups, differences in race and culture, differences in social class), but the one I chose to focus on was psychological in nature. At the symposium, I argued that students feel anxious about, and do not have positive expectations for, interactions with members of other racial/ethnic groups. They worry about being rejected by members of the other group (or sometimes by members of their own group for mixing with the outgroup), being stereotyped by the other group, being taken advantage of, being ridiculed or put down, or being physically harmed. I made these arguments primarily on the basis of my own experiences while working in the schools, but also on my understanding of previous research on black/white relations.

After the conference, I started working with my favourite collaborator, Cookie Stephan, on research to test these ideas. She had helped to develop and test one of the first programmes designed to improve intergroup relations in the schools – a programme that involved students working together cooperatively in small ethnically mixed groups (Blaney et al., 1977). We suspected that the type of anxiety I discussed at the conference presentation extended beyond the issue of black/white relations in American schools, and we began to build a theory around this idea (see Figure 9.1). We postulated that intergroup anxiety occurs when people feel personally threatened by interaction with members of other groups. In this context, threat means that they anticipated that negative consequences

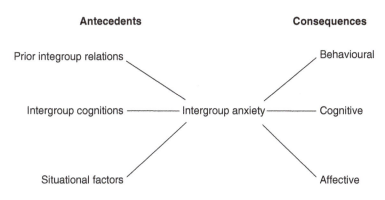

Figure 9.1 Model of intergroup anxiety.

would follow from intergroup interaction. Further, we hypothesized that intergroup anxiety would be highest when prior relations between the groups had been limited or antagonistic, when the groups had negative attitudes and beliefs about each other, when the two groups differed greatly in social status, and when they had little personal contact with members of the other social group. Moreover, we argued that when intergroup anxiety was high, it would lead to cognitive biases in the perception of the other group, extreme emotions and evaluations, and strong behavioural responses (usually negative, but sometimes overly positive responses such as excessive politeness).

At the time we were developing this theory, we were living in New Mexico. Thus it seemed natural to us to try to understand what factors were related to intergroup anxiety in Hispanic college students (Americans with a Latin American background, see Figure 9.2). The results of this study generally confirmed our hypotheses. What we found was that intergroup anxiety was highest among Hispanic students who had the least contact with Caucasians, who perceived the status of Hispanics to be low relative to

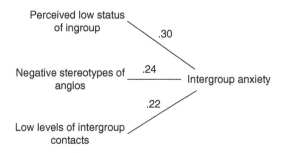

Figure 9.2 Predictors of intergroup anxiety among Hispanics.
Note: The numbers indicate standardized beta weights from multiple regression analysis.

Anglos, and who had the most negative stereotypes of Anglos (Stephan & Stephan, 1985).

It also occurred to us that an especially strong type of intergroup anxiety would arise in relations between individuals from different countries who had little prior contact. To test this idea, we examined the effects of visiting a foreign culture on students' levels of intergroup anxiety (Stephan & Stephan, 1992). The study was conducted using students participating in a Semester-At-Sea programme (an academic programme that takes students on a voyage around the world). We found that a one-week stay in Morocco, a country that few of the students had visited before, lowered their levels of intergroup anxiety towards Moroccans. This study also showed that the students' whose anxiety decreased the most were those who had the most favourable contact experiences with Moroccans.

There have since been hundreds of studies that have examined intergroup anxiety (e.g. Islam & Hewstone, 1993; Littleford, Wright & Sayoc-Parial, 2005; Plant & Devine, 2003). Here is a brief summary of some of the findings from those studies. People who have had little previous intergroup contact or predominantly negative contact tend to have the highest levels in intergroup anxiety. People who expect their interactions with outgroup members to be cooperative, pleasant, personal and voluntary have low levels of intergroup anxiety. A belief that the outgroup is dissimilar to the ingroup is associated with high intergroup anxiety. Negative stereotypes of the outgroup are related to intergroup anxiety. In addition, people who have a strong identification with their ingroup tend to have high intergroup anxiety.

When people experience intergroup anxiety, it leads them to be more prejudiced towards outgroup members (Turner, Hewstone & Voci, 2007). They also tend to perceive that outgroups are homogeneous ('they' are all the same), which prevents them from noticing the individuality of members of other groups. Moreover, people experiencing intergroup anxiety are more likely to rely on their stereotypes of the other group than those who are low in intergroup anxiety (Amodio, 2009). People who are high in intergroup anxiety are also less apt to disclose information about themselves during intergroup interactions than people who are low in intergroup anxiety. In addition, intergroup anxiety often leads people to behave awkwardly during intergroup interactions, because they are uncomfortable. The anticipation of this discomfort can cause people to avoid interacting with outgroup members (Plant, Butz & Tartakovsky, 2008). At its worst, intergroup anxiety may lead ingroup members to behave negatively or aggressively towards outgroup members. However, it can sometimes have just the opposite effect, leading people to behave in unusually positive ways to avoid being seen as prejudiced or ignorant.

Integrated threat theory

After we published our original article on intergroup anxiety, I was contacted by a colleague from Spain who invited me to write an article on attitudes towards immigrants – a problem of increasing importance in Spain and throughout Europe. It seemed clear that intergroup anxiety should apply to this context. Specifically, people who feel very anxious about interacting with immigrants would be expected to have negative attitudes towards them. But the more I thought about it, the more it seemed to me that it was not just feelings of personal threat that led to negative attitudes – other types of threat posed by the outgroup might be relevant as well. So, along with my students and colleagues, I started digging into the literature on the causes of prejudice, looking for theories and research on intergroup threat. This review of the literature launched a new theory that we labelled the integrated threat theory (Stephan, Ybarra & Bachman, 1999). This theory proposes that there are four basic types of intergroup threat: realistic threats, symbolic threats, intergroup anxiety and negative stereotypes (see Figure 9.3).

(1) *Realistic threats* are threats to the ingroup's political power, economic power or physical well-being. The concept of realistic threats is derived from realistic group conflict theory (LeVine & Campbell, 1972), which argues that competition for limited resources causes negative relations between groups. In realistic group conflict theory, limited resources consist of such things as land, natural resources and money. Integrated threat theory takes a broader view of realistic threats and also includes threats to the material and physical well-being of the group and its members. (2) *Symbolic threats* are threats to the ingroup's values, beliefs or worldview. Our concept of symbolic threats is based on ideas found in the works of Allport (1954) and

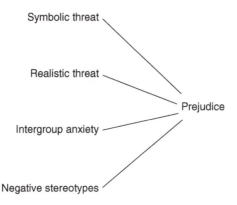

Figure 9.3 Integrated threat theory.

Adorno (1950), as well as the work on symbolic racism (Sears, 1988), and symbolic attitudes (Esses, Haddock & Zanna, 1993). However, our thinking about threats differed from these previous theorists. For instance, Sears (1988) considered symbolic racism to be a type of prejudice, whereas we think of symbolic threats as a cause of prejudice. A good example of what we consider to be a symbolic threat would be the belief held by many minority religious groups that the dominant religious group in their culture wants to suppress their religious beliefs. (3) *Intergroup anxiety*, as already noted, is a threat that arises before or during intergroup interaction due to the expectation of negative outcomes (Stephan & Stephan, 1985). Intergroup anxiety is similar to the concept of anxiety/uncertainty used by Gudykunst (1995) and the concept of negative affect used in aversive racism theory (Gaertner & Dovidio, 1986, p. 63). (4) *Negative stereotypes* create feelings of threat because they lead people to expect outgroup members to behave in ways that may be harmful to the ingroup. The study of stereotypes has a long history in the social sciences, dating back to Katz and Braly (1933). In the integrated threat theory, the focus is only on negative stereotypes. Positive stereotypes pose problems (such as leading to false expectations about members of the other group), but they are usually not thought to pose a threat to the ingroup in the way that most negative stereotypes are. To give but one example, the stereotype that the outgroup is aggressive creates a fear of suffering physical harm at the hands of the outgroup members.

What we were attempting to do was to weave these four disparate threads in the literature into one comprehensive theory of the effects of threat on prejudice. Although we assumed that these threats would be related to one another, we also anticipated that they would make separate contributions to a theory of prejudice. Perhaps a simple analogy will help to understand the relationships among the four threats and prejudice: When you are swimming, the movements of your 2 arms and 2 legs propel you forward. Their movements are coordinated (related to one another) and move you forward, but each arm and each leg makes a separate contribution. So, too, the four threats are conceptually related, but each makes its own distinct contribution to a theory of prejudice.

Now, let us return to the issue of immigration. The realistic threats posed by immigration include competition for scarce jobs; unwanted changes in the host community, including the necessity to provide education, housing, medical and other social services to immigrants; and the threats of crime and increased drug use. Symbolic threats derive from the cultural, religious and other differences in values, beliefs and lifestyles that immigrants and residents have. The fear is that immigrants will change the established ways of the host culture. Intergroup anxiety arises because of differences in language, norms for social interaction, and concerns about being disliked or ill treated. Negative stereotypes of immigrants abound, often based on their countries of origin, their social class backgrounds and their perceived lack of moral values.

Using the four types of threat outlined above – realistic threats, symbolic threats, intergroup anxiety and negative stereotypes – my collaborators and I did a series of nine studies in the US, Spain and Israel to examine attitudes towards immigrants (Stephan, Ybarra & Bachman, 1999; Stephan et al., 1998). The results of regression analyses provided strong support for the idea that threats are closely related to negative attitudes towards immigrants, and made it possible to compare the relative contributions of each threat in explaining negative attitudes towards immigrants. For example, in a regression analysis of attitudes towards Mexican immigrants to the US, we found that all four threats in the theory were significantly related to negative attitudes (see Figure 9.4), but realistic and symbolic threats were the strongest predictors. This last result may be due to the fact that the students in this study interacted with Hispanics on a daily basis so they did not feel personally threatened, but they were concerned about threats posed by immigration from Mexico to their group as a whole.

A review of research on the four basic threats in the theory (done on a compilation of 89 studies with 37,000 participants) also found solid support for the theory (Reik, Mania & Gaertner, 2006). The target outgroups were diverse and included men and women; blacks and whites in the US; Mexicans; Native Canadians and Anglo Canadians; immigrants to the US, Canada, Israel and Europe; AIDS victims; people with terminal cancer; obese people; gays; religious and political outgroups; and the beneficiaries of affirmative action (Riek, Mania & Gaertner, 2006). All four threats

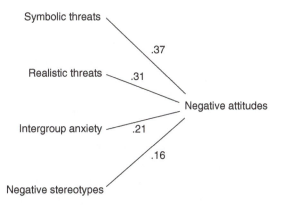

Figure 9.4 Predictors of attitudes towards Mexican immigrants.
Note: The numbers indicate standardized beta weights from multiple regression analysis.

frequently showed up as strong predictors of intergroup attitudes. In one comprehensive analysis, it was found that the threats in the integrated threat theory accounted for 36 per cent of the variance in attitudes towards outgroups. In the social sciences, this is considered to be a very respectable result. However, it does mean that the threats did not predict the remaining variation in attitudes. Thus, additional factors such as those covered in other theories of prejudice, are very important in understanding the causes of prejudice.

So far, all of the studies I have mentioned were correlational in nature. These studies provide strong evidence that threats are *related* to prejudice, but they do not provide direct evidence that threats *cause* prejudice. In order to establish that threats actually cause prejudice, my colleagues and I did a set of experiments in which we aroused intergroup anxiety, negative stereotypes, symbolic threats and realistic threats towards immigrants (Stephan et al., 2005). Using a news article format, we provided students with information that their community would soon be experiencing an influx of immigrants. The article indicated that people in other communities had found interacting with these immigrants to be anxiety-provoking (intergroup anxiety threat), or that the immigrants were characterized by negative traits (negative stereotype threat), or that the immigrants would be competing with local people for jobs (realistic threat), or that the immigrants had different values than most Americans (symbolic threat). We then examined the effects of these threats on prejudice towards immigrants. We found that when students were experiencing these four threats, they reacted by displaying more negative attitudes towards immigrants (in comparison to a control condition in which students received information about the influx of immigrants, but no specific threat information). In these studies, we know exactly what *caused* the students to react with more negative attitudes – the information leading them to think that these immigrants posed threats to them.

Another line of our research focused on the antecedents of threat. In these studies, we examined attitudes towards people with AIDS, attitudes towards cancer victims, attitudes of women towards men, and attitudes of Mexican nationals and Americans towards one another. The most complete study of antecedents to date was done on the interracial attitudes of blacks and whites in the US (Stephan et al., 2002). This study indicated that negative contact with the other racial group, strong identification with one's own racial group, a belief that the two groups were adversaries, and a belief that the status differences between the groups were large consistently predicted threats in both racial groups (see Figure 9.5 for the results for the white participants).

At this point, it is worth mentioning that testing theories requires an incredible amount of time and labour. The study I just cited involved

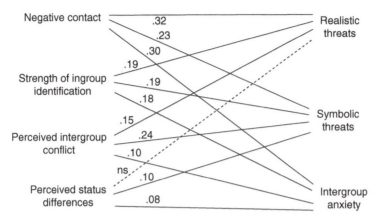

Figure 9.5 Predictors of threat among white students.
Note: The numbers represents standardized path coefficients.

eight authors spending hundreds of hours developing and pre-testing the questionnaire. More than 1,000 participants from five different universities each spent half an hour responding to our questionnaire. Then the analyses and original write-up took an additional several hundred hours. The article was then reviewed by the journal editor and two referees, and finally it was sent to the publisher who edited, printed and distributed it. All that work for one 12-page publication. Is it any wonder that theories are slow to develop?

In addition to examining the relationship between threats and attitudes towards outgroups, we also did studies that looked at the relationship between threats and attitudes towards social policies that favoured the outgroups. Specifically, we did a study of the attitudes of men towards affirmative action policies for women (i.e. the preferential hiring of women when both women and men are equally qualified for a job – a policy designed to redress the under-representation of women in many occupational categories in the US). Here, we found that realistic threats were the strongest predictor of attitudes towards affirmative action (Renfro et al., 2006). In this study, we concluded that for these men, the possibility of losing jobs to women was more relevant to evaluating the social policy of affirmative action than value differences between the sexes, intergroup anxiety or negative stereotypes.

Most social science theories aim to be causal theories, but issues of causality in the social sciences are often quite complicated. Typically, there are multiple causes of any given variable, and in many cases causality is bidirectional. For instance, we found in one study that negative stereotypes fit best in the statistical models if they were considered to be a cause of the other types of threat – suggesting that negative stereotypes cause threat.

This seems logical enough since if negative traits such as aggressiveness are attributed to an outgroup, it makes sense to perceive that group as posing threats. However, it also makes sense to consider threats as a cause of negative stereotypes. If an outgroup is thought to pose realistic threats because of its brutal treatment of its enemies, it could lead to stereotyping its members as aggressive.

Intergroup threat theory

Most social science theories evolve over time and ours is no exception. Usually, this evolution means the theory grows increasingly complex and, again, our theory is not an exception. The evidence from studies of threat, and the issues raised by these studies, led us to develop a new version of the theory (Stephan & Renfro, 2002; Stephan, Ybarra & Rios Morrison, 2009). We tried to broaden the scope of the theory so it would apply to a larger range of groups. We added more antecedents and a wider variety of consequences (see Figure 9.6). The distinction between realistic and symbolic threats is still at the heart of the revised theory. However, we came to believe that the target of the threat was also important. Specifically, we argued that people would react differently to threat depending on whether they felt the threat was directed at their group as a whole or at them personally. We referred to these threats as group threats versus individual threats. Thus, the new theory included four types of threats: realistic group threats, realistic individual threats, symbolic group threats and symbolic individual threats. *Realistic group threats* are threats to the group's power, resources and general welfare. *Realistic individual threats* concern actual physical or material harm to the individual, personal economic loss, and threats to personal safety or health. *Symbolic groups threats* relate to a group's cultural values, religion and ideology. *Individual symbolic threats* concern loss of face, honour, identity or self-esteem.

The conflict between Israelis and Arabs can be used to illustrate the various types of threat. The ever looming possibility of open warfare creates a sense of realistic group threat for both groups. The struggle between the groups also involves other realistic threats concerning control over land, economic issues and water issues, among others. We know from the statements of their leaders, and from interviews and public opinion polls, that members of both groups believe the very existence of their group is at stake. Symbolic group threats are also a pervasive part of the conflict. The two groups have different religions, cultures and languages. Each group worries that the other wishes to destroy its culture and poses a threat to its way of life. Individual threats also abound. On a day-to-day basis,

Antecedents   Consequences

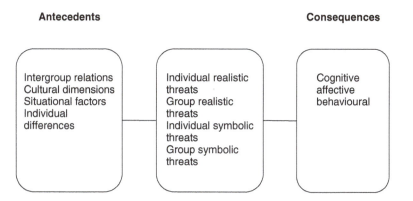

Figure 9.6 Intergroup threat theory.

Israeli Jews worry about their own personal safety from terrorist attacks by Palestinians. For Arabs, realistic individual threats consist of concerns over attacks by Israel in which civilians are sometimes casualties, as well as discrimination in employment and other domains. Palestinians, particularly those in Gaza, may also worry about their own basic needs for food, water, fuel and electricity, which are controlled to some degree by the Israelis. Individual symbolic threats may arise for individual members of either group when they feel dishonoured, disrespected or dehumanized by members of the other group.

In the new version of the theory, which we called *intergroup* threat theory, we also specified many more potential causes of threat. We grouped these into four categories: relations between groups, individual difference variables, dimensions of cultural (or group) difference, and situational factors. Relations between groups include the prior history of conflict and the relative sizes of the groups (Cornielle et al., 2001; Quillan, 1995). We argued that, in general, when there is a history of conflict between two groups, people will feel threatened by the other group and that smaller social groups are likely to feel more threatened than larger groups. Individual difference variables included strength of ingroup identity, social dominance orientation (Sidanius, Devereux & Pratto, 1992) and self-esteem (Crocker & Schwartz, 1985; Luhtanen & Crocker, 1992). The arguments here were that people who strongly identify with their group are the most prone to believe their group is threatened. People who strongly believe in the legitimacy of social hierarchies, such as social class (i.e. those who are high in social dominance orientation), would be expected to be sensitive to threats to the established order. In the case of self-esteem, we argued that people with low self-esteem would be more attuned to threats because they tend to feel less capable of dealing with them.

Among the cultural variables included in the revised theory are individualism/collectivism (Hofstede, 1980, 1991; Triandis, 1995) and cultural tightness versus looseness (Triandis, 1995). Individualistic cultures are those in which the self is defined by its unique characteristics, whereas in collectivistic cultures the self is defined in terms of affiliations with particular groups, such as the family. People in collectivistic cultures, given their emphasis on social groups, may be especially sensitive to threats to the group as a whole. Cultural tightness refers to cultures in which conformity to the rules and norms of society is considered to be important; cultural looseness is the opposite. People from 'tight' cultures feel threatened by nonconformity because they view it as a danger to the integrity of their culture. The situational variables draw on extensions of contact theory (Pettigrew, 1998) and include the degree to which intergroup interactions are structured, and the extent to which norms exist for intergroup relations, in addition to the conditions specified by Allport (1954), such as cooperation between groups, equal status between groups, and the possibility of getting to know outgroup members as individuals.

We also broadened the types of consequences we believed would flow from threats. In addition to prejudice and social policy attitudes, the revised theory suggests that there are a number of other potential outcomes of threat. For example, we suggested that threat leads to greater perceived dissimilarity from the outgroup. We also hypothesized that emotional reactions such as fear and anger would increase in response to threat and that behavioural reactions such as aggression, submission, protests and strikes would also increase. In addition, we suggested that when the ingroup recognizes it possesses less power than the outgroup, threats will more often lead to withdrawal, submission or negotiation than they would in high power groups.

Essentially, the theory argues that intergroup threats function as mediators between a set of antecedent variables and a set of consequences. That is, the antecedents are believed to cause people to feel threatened and these threats are believed to cause the outcomes. Sometimes, however, the antecedents cause the outcomes directly, as well as influencing them indirectly through their effects on threat. For instance, negative contact may cause negative attitudes directly (as well as causing them indirectly by increasing feelings of threat, which then lead to more negative attitudes). Here is how this might work. Suppose that there are substantial numbers of people with Asian backgrounds and people with African backgrounds living in the same community. If the people with African backgrounds often have negative contacts with people from Asian backgrounds (for instance, in their business dealings with them) this could lead them to dislike people from Asian backgrounds. In this case, contact has a direct effect on attitudes towards an outgroup. These same negative experiences may also lead to beliefs that Asians are out to take advantage financially of people from African backgrounds; this perceived realistic threat could then lead to negative attitudes towards people with Asian backgrounds. Here, the effect of contact on prejudice is mediated by a perceived threat.

It is worth noting that while intergroup threat theory focuses one set of variables (the different types of threats) along with their antecedents and consequences, each of the antecedents in the theory has its own set of antecedents (for instance, there are causes of strong identification with the ingroup). Likewise, each consequence has its own consequences (for instance, responding to a perceived threat with aggression will probably create hostility and resentment in the other group).

We have done a number of studies to test aspects of the revised theory. In one study, we used videotaped footage of the 9/11 terrorist attacks on the World Trade Towers to examine people's emotional responses to threat (Davis & Stephan, 2011). As the participants were viewing the videotapes, they were asked to think about 'how Americans felt about these events'. These instructions were designed to get the participants to focus on threats to their ingroup as a whole. Another set of participants was asked to focus on 'their own personal reactions to these events' – here with the intention of evoking individual threats.

Facial electromyography (EMG) was used to capture the participants' emotional reactions as they watched the videotapes. The reactivity of muscles in the face was measured using small electrodes. EMG assesses the emotions people initially register in response to a stimulus. The reactivity of a muscle associated with facial expressions of fear (the frontalis, which controls the wrinkles on your forehead) and a muscle associated with facial expressions of anger (the corrugator, which controls your eyebrows) were examined in this study. You can do a little experiment on yourself by putting your fingers on these muscles and making the facial expressions for fear and anger to see how facial muscles are activated differently by these emotions. We expected people in the group threat condition to be concerned about defending the welfare of their group and to respond with anger. In contrast, we expected people in the individual threat condition to be concerned about their own welfare and to respond with fear. The results supported these predictions (see Table 9.1).

Thus, this study demonstrates that the distinction between group threats and individual threats is a potentially useful one. The study shows that individual and group threats can have different impacts on the emotions people experience in response to threat. These different emotions may then lead to different consequences (although they were not examined in this study). For instance, anger might lead to an aggressive response such as

Table 9.1 Facial muscle reactivity in response to individual and group threat.

	Frontalis muscle (fear)	Corrugator muscle (anger)
Individual threats	.31	−.24
Group threats	−.24	.32

Note: The numbers represent change in muscle reactivity from a baseline measure.

advocating reprisals against Al-Qaeda, whereas fear might lead to a more cautious response such as advocating that the government gather more information before responding.

Reducing intergroup threat

I would like to return to the quote from Kurt Lewin with which I opened this chapter and address the question, 'How useful is this threat theory?' To answer this question, I will review programmes that have been developed to improve intergroup relations with an eye to the types of threat they may reduce. One review of the literature found that there are five basic types of intergroup relations programmes: enlightenment, contact, skill-based, healing and problem-solving (Dovidio et al., 2004).

Enlightenment programmes are based on the idea that ignorance is the primary cause of problems in intergroup relations. These programmes are educational in nature and provide information about the other group's values, norms, beliefs, practices and experiences – as a means of improving intergroup relations. Most rely on written information, along with an array of simulations, role-playing and other interactive exercises. Multicultural education (Banks, 1997, 2002) is an example of such enlightenment programmes. It aims to provide students with the knowledge, attitudes and skills needed to participate in the social, civic and cultural life of diverse nation states (Banks, 1997). It focuses on the history of the various groups in a society, but also strives to increase students' identification with their own racial, ethnic, religious and cultural groups. These types of programmes can reduce threat by providing accurate information about outgroups, undermining stereotypes and increasing intergroup understanding. It is likely that multicultural education is more effective in reducing symbolic threats than realistic threats, because of its focus on increasing intergroup knowledge and understanding.

Contact programmes are based on the assumption that intergroup contact under controlled conditions improves intergroup relations. The use of cooperative intergroup learning programmes in schools is a good example of this approach. One such initiative is the 'jigsaw classroom', which has been widely used in the US and other countries: intergroup contact occurs in small inter-ethnic learning groups in which the task and reward structure involve face-to-face interaction and interdependence (Aronson & Patnoe, 1997). The students can only reach their individual academic goals by working together across group lines. The materials to be learned are the same as those used in the traditional curricula, but the learning occurs in a cooperative environment. It is worth noting that this technique embodies all of the elements of Allport's (1954) contact hypothesis: cooperation towards a common goal, equal status within the workgroup, individualized contact, and support from the relevant authority figures. Contact programmes are likely to reduce intergroup anxiety and other individual threats because they provide participants with personal experiences with outgroup members. However, because contact-based programmes do not directly provide information about ethnic outgroups as a whole, they may not reduce group realistic or group symbolic threats.

Skill-based programmes have as their goal the transmission of skills that promote positive intergroup relations. For example, conflict resolution programmes are designed to help members of conflicting groups resolve disputes (Fisher, 1990). In one programme, the participants are taught mediation skills they can use to deal with their own conflicts or in mediating conflicts between others (Johnson & Johnson, 2006). The approach to learning is highly interactive. The students practice role-playing the resolution of conflicts. When applied to intergroup relations, these programmes involve teaching students to take into consideration the history, culture and characteristics of the groups in conflict. These programmes should reduce individual realistic threats, but may have less impact on other types of intergroup threats.

Healing programmes are designed to address the emotional trauma of people affected by long-term conflict. One example of a healing approach is a programme devised for Jews and Arabs in Israel (Bar-On & Kassem, 2004). College students from both groups met together over the course of a year to share stories about the traumas their families had experienced during the ongoing conflict between their groups. Two leaders, one from each group, facilitated the processing of the participants' responses to the stories. This storytelling approach created empathy for the other group and fostered mutual trust and respect among the participants. This type of programme should decrease individual symbolic and realistic threat because participants meet members of the other group who do not pose threats to them personally, but these reductions in perceived threat might not carry over to the group level.

Problem-solving programmes are oriented towards finding solutions to the problems faced by communities affected by long-term conflict (Kelman,

2010). An example of the problem-solving approach is a workshop conducted with Israeli and Palestinian government advisors, journalists, business leaders and scholars (Kelman, 2010; Kelman & Cohen, 1986). The participants were brought together on neutral ground and the discussions were facilitated by impartial leaders who were well acquainted with the conflict, but who were not members of either group. The facilitators tried to foster a safe environment so that participants could express themselves openly, and encouraged an analytic approach to the conflict. The participants were urged to try to understand the perspective of the other group. Towards the end of the workshop, the participants brainstormed solutions to the conflict: it was expected that they would carry these ideas back to policymakers. This approach is more likely than most of the others to reduce realistic group threats in the long run, since it focuses on changing relations between the entire groups, not just the individual participants in the programme.

It is important to point out that the research literature indicates that, in general, these initiatives are successful in improving intergroup relations (Denson, 2009; Paluck & Green, 2009; Stephan, Renfro & Stephan, 2004). Nonetheless, there is considerable variability in how effective they are and there is still much to be learned about what makes these programmes less or more effective.

I would like to conclude this section with a discussion of a relatively recent initiative that serves as model for how intergroup relations programmes should be evaluated. The 'intergroup dialogue programme' employs small group discussions among members of social groups that have a history of conflict (Gurin, Nagda & Zuniga, in press). The dialogues are facilitated by two trainers, one from each group, and the goals are to increase intergroup understanding, provide participants with the skills needed to interact across group boundaries, and motivate participants to seek greater social justice. Unlike most other programmes, participants are encouraged to address issues over which there is conflict between the groups. Participants are encouraged to express their emotions and discuss their reactions to prejudice, stereotyping and discrimination. Dialogue groups usually involve 10–20 participants. The facilitators guide the discussions and help the participants adhere to norms that are conducive to a productive exchange of feelings and views. Although the facilitators encourage honesty and openness, they also emphasize mutual respect and request that the participants be non-judgemental. The participants are directed to help members of the other group understand their perspective, rather than trying to argue with them about who is right (as they might do in a debate). Initially, the interactions are quite structured, but as the dialogues progress and the participants learn the norms of productive interaction, they become less structured. Simulations, role-playing and other interactive exercises are employed to encourage discussion of significant intergroup issues. The participants also discuss assigned readings. Towards the end of the programme, the participants work together in small mixed groups on projects to promote social justice.

Research on intergroup dialogues has shown that they have a dramatic impact on attitudes, emotions and behaviour. One study involved 56 dialogues which took place at nine universities across the US (Gurin, Nagda & Zuniga, in press). The dialogues lasted one semester and were focused either on race/ethnic relations or gender relations, using an experimental format in which students were randomly assigned to a dialogue or a control group. The students were tested at the beginning of the semester and again at the end, and the results demonstrated that intergroup dialogues led to improvements in intergroup relations, including increases in openness to multiple perspectives, more positive emotions in interactions with members of other groups, increases in empathy for members of other groups, and more positive attitudes towards cultural diversity. The dialogues also had led to positive changes in variables related to social justice and conflict resolution. For instance, they increased motivation to bridge the differences between groups, reduced the degree to which individual factors were used to explain social inequality, improved skills in dealing with intergroup conflicts, and increased participation in campus organizations devoted to promoting social justice. Nearly all of these positive effects were maintained when the students were re-tested one year after the dialogues had taken place.

There are reasons to think intergroup dialogues would reduce realistic and symbolic threats at both the individual and group level. Intergroup dialogues should reduce individual realistic threats because the interactions in dialogue groups take place in a safe environment where participants come to realize that many of their fears about members of other groups are unwarranted. They should reduce individual symbolic threats because the norms of group discussion encourage participants to treat members of other groups with respect and to validate their identities. Intergroup dialogues should also reduce group symbolic threats because participants learn about values that the groups share in common. In addition, the participants come to a better understanding of the other group and their worldview as they listen to the narratives of members of the other group. Finally, the focus on social justice in intergroup dialogues should reduce group realistic threats. Participants learn that it is possible to work together with members of the other group to resolve conflicts between the groups and reduce social inequality.

Psychological processes involved in threat reduction

The next section of this chapter presents some of the psychological processes that help to explain how intergroup relation programmes can reduce intergroup threats. There are three basic domains of psychological processes involved in reducing intergroup threats: affective, cognitive and behavioural processes.

One *affective process* that should reduce threat is *emotional* empathy, the capacity to feel the emotions of outgroup members as one's own (Batson et al., 1997; Dovidio et al., 2004, Finlay & Stephan, 2000; Stephan et al., 2005). Emotional intergroup empathy is often created in contact programmes when participants narrate their own experiences as members of their group. Experiencing emotional empathy humanizes members of the other group and should be especially effective in reducing individual threats.

People sometimes recognize that the attitudes and stereotypes they have towards members of other groups are irrational and that they should not have them. The feelings of guilt generated by this recognition have been labelled 'compunction' in the research literature on intergroup relations (Devine, 1989; Devine & Sharp, 2009). People can learn to counteract their stereotypes and replace them with non-biased responses (see Devine, Plant & Buswell, 2000). This type of learning is probably most likely to occur in educational settings or small group dialogues and workshops. In such settings, people often engage in self-reflection and come to see that their feelings about outgroups are at variance with their values. In some programmes, participants are taught how to recognize and suppress their negative stereotypes and prejudices. Feelings of individual threat should be reduced as participants come to interact with outgroup members as individuals.

When groups have a history of conflict, misinformation and distorted perceptions of other groups are common. Providing *accurate information* about the outgroup counteracts ignorance and should reduce both realistic and symbolic threats. However, the process is not an easy one (Gawronski et al., 2008). For instance, to counteract stereotypes, people must want to change; they must pay close attention to the information that contradicts their stereotypes and attribute the causes of stereotype disconfirming behaviours to internal factors (Crocker, Hannah & Weber, 1983; Mackie, Allison, Worth & Asuncion, 1992). Information-oriented programmes, such as multicultural education, can provide this information, but it may be most effective when it is acquired in face-to-face interactions.

Creating *cognitive empathy* may also lead to threat reduction. Individuals experience cognitive empathy when they take the role of another and view the world from that person's perspective (Shih et al., 2009). It can be fostered by helping people acquire knowledge about the outgroup's worldview and their practices, norms and values. It can be created in educational settings as well as in small group dialogues and workshops. Cognitive empathy should reduce individual threats because viewing the world from the perspective of members of other groups promotes better intergroup understanding.

Perceived threats are often based on the premise that the outgroup is very dissimilar to the ingroup. These beliefs are usually exaggerated and can be reduced through information and personal experiences that contradict them. When members of different groups interact with one another in terms of their individual (rather than their group) identities, it reduces the tendency to make sharp distinctions between groups (Brewer, 2000; Brewer & Miller 1984; Dovidio et al., 1998; Miller, Brewer & Edwards, 1985). Personalizing outgroup members can best be done in one-on-one interactions or in small groups. As members of the other group come to be seen as less dissimilar, they are apt to be liked more (Pilkington & Lydon, 1997) and should be seen as posing fewer symbolic threats as a result.

It may also be possible to reduce feelings of threat by activating aspects of individuals' identities that they share with outgroup members, such as being the same age or gender, coming from the same social class, or sharing similar family and work roles. Like increasing perceived similarity, becoming aware of these unifying identities blurs the sharp distinctions between the ingroup and outgroup and thus should reduce symbolic threats (Crisp & Hewstone, 2007; Dovidio et al., 1998; Dovidio, Kawakami & Gaertner, 2000; Hewstone, Islam & Judd, 1993). Helping people to be aware of their multiple identities is probably most easily done in small group settings.

Another way to reduce distinctions between ingroup and outgroup categories is to encourage members of the two groups to think of themselves as members of one overarching group (Gaertner, et al., 1989; Gaertner et al., 1999), such as the school, the community, the nation state, a unifying religion, or humanity itself. Identifying with a larger group converts enemies into allies and should reduce both realistic and symbolic group threats. Overarching identities can be promoted in community, work and educational settings.

Intergroup anxiety (Pettigrew & Tropp, 2008) and other individual threats can be reduced through face-to-face contact under favourable conditions such as those specified in the contact hypothesis (i.e. cooperation, equal status, and individual contact supported by authority figures). Contact reduces anxiety, primarily because people learn that the negative expectations they have for intergroup interaction are inaccurate. A variety of intergroup relations programmes, such as those relying on cooperative learning and dialogues, create optimal contact conditions, but almost any well-designed programme that brings people from different groups into contact should reduce threats.

Conclusion

My goal in this chapter was to use threat theories to demonstrate Lewin's dictum that theories have practical utility. Along the way, I described the evolution of intergroup threat theory in personal terms because I wanted you to see that theory-making and the research it generates is a very human enterprise. I then applied intergroup threat theory to a variety of intergroup relations programmes in order to show that not only is the theory useful in understanding the causes and consequences of threat, but that it can also be useful in understanding intergroup relations programmes. I ended by describing the ways in which the psychological processes activated by these programmes can reduce feelings of threat and thereby improve intergroup relations.

Practical task for readers

Now, here is a task for you. Think about the most intense intergroup division in your community (e.g. a racial, ethnic, religious or cultural division that is generating conflict). If you were given the opportunity, what suggestions would you make to the leaders in your community about changes in social policies and practices that would help to improve relations between these two groups? This first set of suggestions should be about changes to social institutions (e.g. health care or educational institutions, community agencies, police policies, etc.) that would have a positive effect on people's views of the other group and behaviour towards the other group. Next, what intergroup relations programmes would you suggest be implemented in schools, private-sector work settings, and in government or non-governmental agencies to improve relations between these two groups? After you have come up with some ideas, ask yourself if threat theory, and the other theories you have been reading about, were helpful in doing so. If they were, you should now have a greater appreciation for Lewin's argument that theories have practical utility.

Suggested readings

To learn more, read Devine and colleagues (2000), Dovidio and colleagues (2004), Gurin and colleagues (in press), Johnson and Johnson (2006).

References

Adorno, T. W. (1950). *The Authoritarian Personality*. New York, Harper.

Allport, G. W. (1954). *The Nature of Prejudice*. Cambridge, MA: Addison-Wesley.

Altemeyer, B. (1981). *Right Wing Authoritarianism*. Winnipeg: University of Manitoba Press.

Amodio, D. M. (2009). Intergroup anxiety effects on the control of racial stereotypes: A psychoneuroendocrine analysis. *Journal of Experimental Social Psychology*, 45(1), 60–67.

Aronson, E. & Patnoe, S. (1997) *The Jigsaw Classroom: Building Cooperation in the Classroom* (second edition). New York: Longman.

Banks, J. A. (1997). *Educating Citizens in a Multicultural Society*. New York: Teachers College Press.

Banks, J. A. (2002). *An Introduction to Multicultural Education* (third edition). Boston: Allyn & Bacon.

Bar-On, D. & Kassem, F. (2004). Storytelling as a way to work through intractable conflicts: The German-Jewish experience and its relevance to the Palestinian-Israeli context. *Journal of Social Issues*, 60, 289–306.

Batson, C. D., Polycarpou, M. P., Harmon-Jones, E., Imhoff, H. J., Mitchener, E. C., Bednar, L. L., Klein, T. R. & Highberger, L. (1997). Empathy and attitudes: Can feeling for a member of a stigmatized group improve feelings toward the group? *Journal of Personality and Social Psychology*, 72, 105–118.

Blaney, N., Stephan, C., Rosenfield, D., Aronson, E. & Sikes, J. (1977). Interdependence in the classroom: A field study. *Journal of Educational Psychology*, 69, 121–128.

Brewer, M. B. & Miller, N. (1984). Beyond the contact hypothesis: Theoretical perspectives on desegregation. In N. Miller & M. B. Brewer (eds.), *Groups in Contact: The Psychology of Desegregation* (pp. 281–302). New York: Academic Press.

Brewer, M. B. (2000). Reducing prejudice through cross-categorization: Effects of multiple social identities. In S. Oskamp (ed.), *Reducing Prejudice and Discrimination*. (pp. 165–183). Mahwah, NJ: Lawrence Erlbaum.

Crisp, R. J. & Hewstone, M. (2007). Multiple social categorization. In M. P. Zanna (ed.), *Advances in Experimental Social Psychology* (vol. 39, pp. 163–254). San Diego, CA, US: Elsevier Academic Press.

Cornielle, O., Yzerbyt, V. Y., Rogier, A. & Buidin, G. (2001). Threat and the group attribution error: When threat elicits judgments of extremity and homogeneity. *Personality and Social Psychology Bulletin*, 27, 437–446.

Crocker, J., Hannah, D. B. & Weber, R. (1983). Person memory and causal attributions. *Journal of Personality and Social Psychology*, 44, 55–66.

Crocker, J. & Schwartz, I. (1985). Prejudice and ingroup favoritism in a minimal intergroup situation: Effects of self-esteem. *Personality and Social Psychology Bulletin*, 1, 379–386.

Das, E., Bushman, B. J., Bezemer, M. D., Kerkhof, P. & Vermeulen, I. E. (2009). *Journal of Experimental Social Psychology, 45,* 453–459.

Davis, M. D. & Stephan, W. G. (2011). Electromyographic analysis of responses to threat. *Journal of Applied Social Psychology, 41,* 196–218.

Denson, N. (2009). Do curricular and co-curricular diversity activities influence racial bias? A meta-analysis. *Review of Educational Research, 79,* 805–838.

Devine, P. (1989). Stereotypes and prejudice: Their automatic and controlled components. *Journal of Personality and Social Psychology, 56,* 5–18.

Devine, P. G., Plant, E. A. & Buswell, B. N. (2000). Breaking the prejudice habit: Progress an obstacles. In S. Oskamp (ed.), *Reducing Prejudice and Discrimination* (pp. 185–208). Hillsdale, NJ: Erlbaum.

Devine, P. G. & Sharp, L. B. (2009). Automaticity and control in stereotyping and prejudice. In T. Nelson (ed.), *Handbook of Prejudice* (pp. 61–88). Mahwah, NJ: Lawrence Erlbaum Associates.

Dovidio, J. F., Gaertner, S. L., Isen, A. M., Rust, M. & Guerra, P. (1998). Positive affect, cognition, and the reduction of intergroup bias. In C. Sedikides, J. Schopler & C. A. Insko (eds.), *Intergroup Cognition and Intergroup Behavior* (pp. 337–366). Mahwah, NJ: Lawrence Erlbaum.

Dovidio, J. F., Gaertner, S. L., Stewart, T. L., Esses, V. M., ten Vergert, M. & Hodson, G. (2004). From intervention to Outcome: Processes in the reduction of bias. In W. G. Stephan & W. P. Vogt (eds.), *Learning Together: Intergroup Reations Programs* (pp. 243–265). New York: Teachers College Press.

Dovidio, J. F., Kawakami, K. & Gaertner, S. L. (2000). Reducing contemporary prejudice: Combating explicit and implicit bias at the individual and intergroup level. In S. Oskamp (ed.), *Reducing Prejudice and Discrimination* (pp. 137–163). Mahwah, NJ: Lawrence Erlbaum.

Dovidio, J. F., ten Vergert, M., Stewart, T. L., Gaertner, S. L., Johnson, J. D., Esses, V. M.,Riek, B. M., Pearson, A. R.. (2004). Perspective and prejudice: Antecedents and mediating mechanisms. *Personality and Social Psychology Bulletin, 30*(12), 1537–1549.

Esses, V. M., Haddock, G. & Zanna, M. P. (1993). Values, stereotypes, and emotions as determinants of intergroup attitudes. In D. M. Mackie and D. L. Hamilton (eds.), *Affect, Cognition and Stereotyping: Interactive Processes in Group Perception* (pp. 137–166). Orlando, FL: Academic Press.

Finlay, K. A. & Stephan, W. G. (2000). Reducing prejudice: The effects of empathy on intergroup attitudes. *Journal of Applied Social Psychology, 30,* 1722–1736.

Fisher, R. J. (1990). *The Social Psychology of Intergroup and International Conflict Resolution.* New York: Springer-Verlag.

Gaertner, S. L. & Dovidio, J. F. (1986). The aversive form of racism. In J. F. Dovidio & S. L. Gaertner (eds.), *Prejudice, Discrimination, and Racism* (pp.61–90). Orlando: Academic Press.

Gaertner, S. L., Dovidio, J. F., Nier, J. A., Ward, C. M. & Banker, B. S. (1999). Across Cultural divides: The value of superordinate identity. In D. A. Prentice & D. T. Miller (eds.), *Cultural Divides: Understanding and Overcoming Group Conflict* (pp. 173–212). New York: Russell Sage Foundation.

Gaertner, S. L., Mann, J., Murrell, A. & Dovidio, J. F. (1989). Reducing intergroup bias: The benefits of recategorization. *Journal of Personality and Social Psychology, 57,* 239–249.

Gawronski, B., Deutsch, R., Mbirkou, S., Seibt, B. & Strack, F. (2008). When 'just say no' is not enough: Affirmation versus negation training and the reduction of automatic stereotype activation. *Journal of Experimental Social Psychology*, 44(2), 370–377.

Gudykunst, W. B. (1995). Anxiety/uncertainty management (AUM) theory: Development and current status. In R. L. Wiseman (ed.), *Intercultural Communication Theory* (pp. 8–51). Thousand Oaks, CA: Sage.

Gurin, P., Nagda, B. R. & Zuniga, X. (in press). *Engaging Race and Gender: Intergroup Dialogues in Higher Education.* New York: Russell Sage Foundation.

Hewstone, M., Islam, M. R. & Judd, C. M. (1993). Models of cross categorization and intergroup relations. *Journal of Personality and Social Psychology*, 64, 779–793.

Hofstede, G. (1980). *Culture's Consequences.* Beverly Hills: Sage.

Hofstede, G. (1991). *Cultures and Organizations.* London: McGraw-Hill.

Islam, M. R. & Hewstone, M. (1993). Dimensions of contact as predictors of intergroup anxiety, perceived outgroup variability, and outgroup attitude: An integrative model. *Personality and Social Psychology Bulletin*, 19, 700–710.

Johnson, D. W. & Johnson, R. T. (2006). Conflict resolution, peer mediation, and peacemaking. In C. M. Evertson & C. S. Weinstein (eds.), *Handbook of Classroom Management: Research, Practice, and Contemporary Issues* (pp. 803–832). Mahwah, NJ: Lawrence Erlbaum.

Katz, D. & Braly, K. (1933). Racial stereotypes of one hundred college students. *The Journal of Abnormal and Social Psychology*, 28, 280–290.

Kelman, H. C. (2010). Interactive problem solving: Changing political culture in the pursuit of conflict resolution. *Peace and Conflict: Journal of Peace Psychology*, 16(4), 389–413.

Kelman, H. C. & Cohen, S. P. (1986). Resolution of international conflict: an interactional approach. In S. Worchel & W. G. Austin (eds.), *Psychology of Intergroup Relations* (pp. 323–342). Chicago: Nelson Hall.

LeVine, R.A. & Campbell, D.T. (1972). *Ethnocentrism: Theories of Conflict, Ethnic Attitudes, and Group Behavior.* New York: Wiley.

Lewin, K. (1948). *Resolving Social Conflicts.* New York: Harper & Row.

Littleford, L. N., Wright, M. O. & Sayoc-Parial, M. (2005). White students' intergroup anxiety during same-race and interracial interactions: A multimethod approach. *Basic and Applied Social Psychology*, 27(1), 85–94.

Luhtanen, R. & Crocker, J. (1992). A collective self-esteem scale: Self-evaluation of one's own identity. *Personality and Social Psychology Bulletin*, 18, 302–318.

Mackie, D. M., Allison, S. T., Worth, L. T. & Asuncion, A. G. (1992). Social decision making processes: The generalization of outcome-biased counter-stereotypic inferences. *Journal of Experimental Social Psychology*, 28, 23–42.

Miller, N., Brewer, M. B. & Edwards, K. (1985). Cooperative interaction in desegregated settings: A laboratory analogue. *Journal of Social Issues*, 41, 63–81.

Nelson, T. (ed.), (2009). *Handbook of Prejudice.* Mahwah, NJ: Lawrence Erlbaum Associates.

Oswald, D. L. (2005). Understanding anti-arab reactions post-9/11: The role of threats, social categories, and personal ideologies. *Journal of Applied Social Psychology*, 35, 1775–1799.

Paluck, E. L. & Green, D. P. (2009). Prejudice reduction: What works? A review and assessment of research and practice. *Annual Review of Psychology*, 60, 339–367.

Pettigrew, T. F. (1998). Intergroup contact theory. *Annual Review of Psychology*, 49, 65–85.

Pettigrew, T. F. & Tropp, L. R. (2008). How does intergroup contact reduce prejudice? Meta-analytic tests of three mediators. *European Journal of Social Psychology*, 38, 922–934.

Pilkington, N. W. & Lydon, J. E. (1997). The relative effect of attitude similarity and attitude dissimilarity on interpersonal attraction: Investigating the moderating roles of prejudice and group membership. *Personality and Social Psychology Bulletin*, 23, 107–122.

Plant, E. A., Butz, D. A. & Tartakovsky, M. (2008). Interethnic interactions: Expectancies, emotions, and behavioral intentions. *Group Processes & Intergroup Relations*, 11, 555–574.

Plant, E. A. & Devine, P. G. (2003). The antecedents and implications of interracial anxiety. *Personality and Social Psychology Bulletin*, 29, 790–801.

Quillan, L. (1995). Prejudice as a response to perceived group threat: Population composition and anti-immigrant and racial prejudice in Europe. *American Sociological Review*, 60, 586–611.

Riek, B. M., Mania, E. W. & Gaertner, S. L. (2006). Intergroup threat and outgroup attitudes: A meta-analytic review. *Personality and Social Psychology Review*, 0, 336–353.

Renfro, C. L., Duran, A., Stephan, W. G. & Clason, D. L. (2006). The role of threat in attitudes toward affirmative action and its beneficiaries. *Journal of Applied Social Psychology*, 36, 41–74.

Sears, D. O. (1988). Symbolic racism. In P. A. Katz & D. A. Taylor (eds.), *Eliminating Racism* (pp. 53–84) New York: Plenum.

Scheepers, D., Spears, R., Doosje, B. & Manstead, A. S. R. (2006).The social functions of ingroup bias: Creating, confirming, or changing social reality. *European Review of Social Psychology*, 17, 359–396.

Shih, M., Wang, E., Trahan Bucher, A. & Stotzer, R. (2009). Perspective taking: Reducing prejudice towards general outgroups and specific individuals. *Group Processes & Intergroup Relations*, 12, 565–577.

Sidanius, J., Devereux, E. & Pratto, F. (1992) A comparison of symbolic racism theory and social dominance theory as explanations for racial policy attitudes. *The Journal of Social Psychology*, 132, 377–395.

Stephan, W. G. (1978). School desegregation: An evaluation of predictions made in Brown vs. the Board of Education. *Psychological Bulletin*, 85, 217–238.

Stephan, W. G., Boniecki, K. A., Ybarra, O., Bettencourt, A., Ervin, K. S., Jackson, L. A., McNatt, P. S. & Renfro, C. L. (2002). The role of threats in the racial attitudes of Blacks and Whites. *Personality and Social Psychology Bulletin*, 28, 1242–1254.

Stephan, W. G. & Renfro, C. L. (2002). The role of threats in intergroup relations. In D. Mackie and E. R. Smith (eds.), *From Prejudice to Intergroup Emotions* (pp. 191–208). New York: Psychology Press.

Stephan, W. G., Renfro, C. L., Esses, V. M., Stephan, C. W. & Martin, T. (2005). The effects of feeling threatened on attitudes toward immigrants. *International Journal of Intercultural Relations*, 29, 1–19.

Stephan, W. G., Renfro, L. & Stephan, C. W. (2004). The evaluation of multicultural education programs: techniques and a meta-analysis. In W. G. Stephan and W. P. Vogt (eds.), *Education Programs for Improving Intergroup Relations: Theory, Research and Practice* (pp. 227–242). New York: Teachers College Press.

Stephan, W. G. & Stephan, C. W. (1985). Intergroup anxiety. *Journal of Social Issues*, 41, 157–175.

Stephan, W. G & Stephan, C. W. (1992). Reducing intercultural anxiety through intercultural contact. *International Journal of Intercultural Relations*, 16(1), 89–106.

Stephan, W. G., Ybarra, O. & Bachman, G. (1999). Prejudice toward immigrants: An integrated threat theory. *Journal of Applied Social Psychology*, 29, 2221–2237.

Stephan, W. G., Ybarra, O., Martinez, C., Schwarzwald, J. & Tur-Kaspa. (1998). Prejudice toward immigrants to Spain and Israel: An integrated threat theory analysis. *Journal of Cross-Cultural Psychology*, 29, 559–576.

Stephan, W. G., Ybarra, O. & Rios Morrison, K. (2009). Intergroup threat theory. In T. Nelson (ed.), *Handbook of Prejudice* (pp. 43–59). Mahwah, NJ: Lawrence Erlbaum Associates.

Tajfel, H. (1982). *Social Identity and Intergroup Relations*. Cambridge: Cambridge University Press.

Triandis, H. C. (1995). *Individualism and Collectivism*. Boulder, CO: Westview.

Turner, R. N., Hewstone, M. & Voci, A. (2007). Reducing explicit and implicit outgroup prejudice via direct and extended contact: The mediating role of self-disclosure and intergroup anxiety. *Journal of Personality and Social Psychology*, 93, 369–388.

10

Why Society Members Tend to Support the Continuation of Intractable Conflicts and Resist Peaceful Resolution

Daniel Bar-Tal, Eran Halperin, Roni Porat and Rafi Nets-Zehngut

● ●

On 20 November 1977, Egyptian President Anwar Sadat delivered a speech before the Israeli parliament that marked the beginning of Israeli-Egyptian peace negotiations. After referring to the 'wall' of conflict, he then said:

> Yet there remains another wall: This wall constitutes a psychological barrier between us. A barrier of suspicion. A barrier of rejection. A barrier of fear of deception. A barrier of hallucinations around any action, deed and decision. A barrier of cautious and erroneous interpretation of all and every event or statement. It is this psychological barrier which I described in official statement as constituting 70 percent of this whole problem.
>
> (Rabinovich & Reinarz, 2008, p. 366)

Indeed, we concur with this observation of Sadat, suggesting that conflicts are real and they erupt over disagreements relating to tangible and non-tangible goals, but they could be resolved if not for psychological barriers that play a major role in the resistance to peaceful settlement. This chapter will rely on that assumption with the purpose of revealing the psychological forces that both contribute to the continuation of intractable conflicts and hamper their resolution.

Introduction

Violent conflicts have been an inseparable part of human intergroup interaction throughout history to present times. For example, Sarkees, Wayman and Singer (2003) noted that just from 1816 to 1997 there have been a total of 401 wars (79 interstate, 214 civil and 108 extra-state that involved an actor that is not a state), bringing us to a surprisingly high average of almost 22 wars per decade. Sarkees and colleagues also pointed out that there have been more wars in the twentieth century than in the nineteenth century. Of special interest is the study by Harbom, Hogbladh and Wallensteen (2006), which reported that out of 352 violent conflicts that erupted after the Second World War, only 144 were concluded with peace agreements (see also Bilewicz & Vollhardt, this volume). Thus, the question as to why society members in an intractable conflict have such great psychological difficulty to embark on the road of peace is one of the most challenging issues for human beings in general, and for social scientists in particular.

The response to this question is very wide in scope. In the present chapter, taking a social-psychological perspective, we will try to explain the difficulties in persuading society members to terminate protracted conflicts peacefully, once they have been mobilized to participate in them. However, we will first provide a brief conceptualization and definition of conflicts in general, and intergroup intractable conflicts in particular.

Intergroup conflicts

There are various definitions of a conflict situation (see Coleman, 2003; Kriesberg, 2007; Pruitt & Rubin, 1986; Sherif, 1967). They all focus on incompatibility of goals. We define a conflict as a situation in which two or more parties perceive their goals, intentions and/or actions as being mutually incompatible and act in accordance with this perception (Bar-Tal, in press). This definition applies to any conflict. However, this chapter focuses on very severe and violent intergroup conflicts, so-called intractable because they resist peaceful resolution and last for a long period of time.

The notion of intractability was proposed initially by Kriesberg (Kriesberg, 1993, 1998; Kriesberg, Northrup & Thorson, 1989), who differentiated intergroup conflicts on a tractable–intractable continuum. At one end are *tractable conflicts*, which erupt over goals of low importance and last a short period of time, during which the parties in dispute view them as being of mixed motive nature,[1] solvable, and are interested in resolving them through negotiation.

At the other end of the continuum are *intractable conflicts* (Bar-Tal, 1998, 2007; Kriesberg, 1993, 1998) that hold the following features: (1) They are perceived by the participating societies as total – because they consider the goals as being existential; (2) involve physical violence in which society members are killed and wounded; (3) are perceived by society members as irresolvable; (4) are perceived as zero-sum[2] in nature; (5) are central because they greatly preoccupy the involved society members and appear continuously on the public agenda; (6) demand extensive investment of both the materialistic and psychological domains and (7) are long enduring, lasting at least a generation. The conflicts between Tamil and Sinhalese in Sri Lanka, between Turks and Kurds in Turkey, between Russians and Chechens in Chechnya, between Muslims and Hindus in India's Kashmir, and between Jews and Palestinians in the Middle East, are the prototypical examples of such intractable conflicts.

Violent conflicts in general, and intractable conflicts in particular, demand dramatic sacrifices from involved individuals and collectives. The most salient sacrifices are in terms of human lives, but such conflicts also require vast investments in terms of material, financial, educational and psychological resources. In addition, these conflicts bring suffering, distress, misery, hardship, stress and other negative experiences to the participating societies.

Collectives such as nations, ethnic groups or ideological groups are aware of these high costs and we would expect that they will make enormous efforts to avoid a violent conflict and rally massively to support every attempt to resolve disagreements peacefully. Yet, a brief look into the history of war and peacemaking provides a gloomy snapshot of the nature of mankind (see for example Black, 1998; as well as the war statistics given at the beginning of this chapter). Despite enormous efforts to resolve intergroup violent conflicts, history shows that while societies are mobilized to wars relatively easily and quickly, it is much harder and slower to rally them in support of peace (Foyle, 1999; Russell, 2007; Solomon, 2005).

The cases in the Middle East, Sri Lanka or Kashmir are only a few of the salient examples of how easily people are mobilized to support intergroup violent conflict. For example, Russell (2007) pointed out that in 2000 about 70 per cent of Russians supported the decision of President Putin to launch a war against Chechnya. Another example is the strong public support of Israelis to attack the Gaza Strip in December 2008. A survey conducted a week and half after the launching of the attack revealed that 94 per cent of the Israeli–Jewish public supported the attack (Yaar & Hermann, 2009). At the same time, studies regarding peacemaking in Israel (e.g. Bar-Tal, Halperin & Oren 2010) and in Russia (Russell, 2007) show more polarized views with substantial objection to such steps.

In trying to explain the described paradox, we propose that socio-psychological factors play a major role in the resistance of society members involved in intractable conflict to embark on the road to peace. We suggest that once collectives engage in a conflict and continue it for a long period of time, they develop a socio-psychological repertoire that is functional to meet the various challenges that the harsh and violent context of the conflict poses (Bar-Tal, 2007, 2011, in press). Such a repertoire consists of social beliefs, values, attitudes and emotions. Society members tend to adhere to this repertoire, even when peaceful resolutions to the conflict become a possibility, and there is need to develop an alternative repertoire that facilitates peacemaking and reconciliation (Bar-Tal & Halperin, 2011).

The main goal of this chapter is to provide a number of socio-psychological explanations as to why society members prefer – consciously or unconsciously – to continue the conflict that brings losses, misery and suffering, and why it is so difficult to sway people to adopt an alternative repertoire that advances a peacemaking process. First, we will describe some of the important socio-psychological factors and mechanisms that encapsulate the barriers to peaceful resolution of intractable conflicts.

Barriers to peace

Protected values

Intractable conflicts often concern goals and interests that need to be compromised in order to reach a peace agreement. However, such goals are often viewed as directly related to (or reflecting) the protected values of the individual or the ingroup and therefore cannot be even brought to the negotiation table. According to Tetlock (2003), protected (or sacred) values are defined as 'those values that a moral community treats as possessing transcendental significance that precludes comparisons, trade-offs, or indeed any mingling with secular values' (p. 320). These values may be abstract (e.g. human rights, justice and religious dogma) or symbolized in a tangible asset, such as a holy site or a territory (Skitka,

2002). They can be found in almost every society, and are perceived by its members as fundamental for defining their identities, world views and ideologies. Protected values are regarded as 'moral mandates' (Skitka, 2002) and, accordingly, it is impossible to use rational tools in measuring their utility or substitution. Therefore, they are considered a taboo and any infringement on them is perceived as a violation of the fundamental rules of ethics (Tetlock, 1999, 2003).

Studies have shown that when issues are perceived as moral mandates, people find it difficult to agree on who has the legitimate authority to decide on them, or even agree on the type of process that is necessary for resolving conflicts that involve them (Skitka, Bauman & Sargis, 2005). It is thus not surprising that these issues become protected against any trade-offs, compromise, division, exchange or sharing. Even worse, the mere proposal of trading off a protected value is perceived as a threat to the fundamental identity of the group (Baron & Spranca, 1997; Fiske & Tetlock, 1997).

In cases of intractable conflicts, the core issues under dispute are often perceived by the parties as protected values. That makes them non-negotiable by definition, and society members adopt rigid and stubborn positions in dealing with them (Landman, 2010). Giving up on these issues is perceived as moral bankruptcy; the mere thought of their being compromised evokes moral outrage and emotional resistance (Tetlock, 2003; Tetlock et al., 2000). In such cases, members of the collectives engaged in conflict do not see any possibility of compromising and, as a result, view the conflict as being total, of zero-sum nature and unsolvable. They support one-sided, violent and aggressive actions towards the opponent (Ginges & Atran, 2011).

An example of the impact of protected values is the perception of Jerusalem by the Palestinians: one of the key issues that have to be resolved in the Israeli–Palestinian conflict (Klein, 2001; Amirav, 2009). Palestinians perceive the goal of establishing their capital in Jerusalem and control over the Temple Mount as a sacred one.[3] To Sunni Muslims, Jerusalem is one of the three most important religious cities, primarily due to Muhammad's Night Journey of Ascension. Today, Temple Mount is the location of two Islamic landmarks intended to commemorate the event: Al-Aqsa and the Dome of the Rock mosques. In viewing Jerusalem as sacred, Palestinians insist on placing the capital of their state in the city and having full control of Temple Mount. The Palestinians insisted on this during the Camp David summit in 2000 in which the leaders of both parties negotiated a peace agreement. Eventually, the issue of Jerusalem – the future of the city (and Temple Mount in particular) – has been considered as the primary reason for the failure of the summit, as for both sides Jerusalem in general and Temple Mount specifically are related to the realm of sacred values (Klein, 2001; Sher, 2001; Druker, 2002).

Another example of a protected value pertains to the India–Pakistan conflict over Kashmir. From India's perspective, the goal of holding Kashmir represents the sacred value of secularism. This sacred value allows India to live with considerable Muslim minority, viewing the partition of 1947 as an unfortunate historical act that was done because of religious pressure. In this line, in India's view, new territorial concession based on religious contentions will open a possibility of second partition, negating India's secular sacred value (Bose, 2005; Paul, 2005).

Identity

Another factor that instills intractable conflicts is the fact that many of these conflicts are viewed as involving threats to the most basic foundations of social identities (Cash, 1996; Kelman, 1999, see also Golec de Zavala & Schatz, this volume). According to social identity theory, individuals organize their social world in terms of groups, and form a social identity that reflects their group membership. This identity becomes an extremely important part of their individual and collective being and, when an issue concerning their identity is salient, individuals will think, feel and act on the basis of their group's membership (Tajfel & Turner, 1986). Moreover, social identity is not only related to organization of social world, but also to contents that imbue it with meaning (David & Bar-Tal, 2009). Ashmore, Deaux, & McLaughlin-Volpe (2004) defined contents related to identity as 'the semantic space in which identity resides – a space that can include self-attributed characteristics, political ideology, and developmental narratives' (p. 94). These contents provide a common societal viewpoint that underlies the sense of belonging and identification. Content differs from one collective to another (Bar-Tal, 2000) and in the case of nations each has its own set of contents that defines its identity (Andrews, 2007). These contents enable members of the collective to identify with their unique collective rather than with any other collective (Barthel, 1996; Cairns et al., 1998; Oren, Bar-Tal & David, 2004). Contents of social identity can be related to territory, use of language or cultural myths.

Importantly, when the goals in conflict (such as a particular territory, or practising a tradition of the particular ethnic group) are defined as deeply related to identity, groups have great difficulty to compromise on them (Brewer, 2011; Korostelina, 2006). Rothman (1997) argued that intractable conflicts are 'deeply rooted in the underlying human needs and values that together constitute people's social identities' (p. 6). In such cases, parties in conflict need full achievement of the goals because their deprivation threatens their existence as a collective.

An illustration of the major role of social identity in intractable conflicts is the situation of the Kurds in Turkey. Until the 1990s, Kurdish schools were closed, their cultural heritage was banned, names of geographical places were changed from Kurdish to Turkish, and Kurds were discouraged or prohibited to use Kurdish dialects in broadcasting, religious preaching and education. The state also tried to suppress their religious–traditional practices, aiming to promote a secular, Westernized citizenship of modern Turkey. Since all the suppressed cultural expressions are an essential part of Kurdish social identity, the oppressive policies of the Turkish state raised Kurdish resentment and anger and contributed to the violent escalation of the Kurdish–Turkish conflict (Loizides, 2010; Ocarlar, 2009).

Another example relates to the role of the Tamil identity, centralized over the Tamil language for the Tamil minority in Sri Lanka. In 1956, the Sinhalese majority in the parliament enacted a law that made their language, Sinhala, the sole official language. Tamils were suddenly called upon to obtain proficiency in a language that was alien to them in order to secure employment in the public sector, hold jobs in government services and receive promotions. Most importantly, Tamils felt that the bases of their social identity were threatened – as their language is its central part. Not surprisingly, Tamils protested fiercely against this legislation and, after being rejected, turned to militant activities against the Sinhalese majority (Bandarage, 2008; Kearney, 1978).

Basic needs

The goals of those involved in intractable conflicts are often related to ful-filment of basic needs that every individual and collective aims to satisfy (e.g. basic needs to be able to feed the family or for safety). Maslow's (1954) seminal theory of hierarchy of needs refers to the needs of individuals and arranges them in order of importance. However, in the current chapter we focus more on collective needs. We suggest that although the needs are experienced on the individual level, group members may share needs and care about (or personalize) the needs that concern their whole collective. Various types of needs can be relevant with respect to societies involved in intractable conflicts. First, conflicts can be related to unequal distribu-tion of economic resources and wealth along lines of groups' boundaries, when some groups experience a very high level of poverty (Ledgerwood, Liviatan & Carnevale, 2007; see also Sutton, Cichocka & van der Toorn, this volume). These groups may pose a goal, via conflict, of achieving equal division of wealth. Next in importance to needs of physical survival are the collective needs of safety and security. Many groups define the goals they hope to achieve through conflict in terms of assuring secure existence. Finally, collectives express needs related to positive self-esteem and self-actualization such as positive social identity, or collective self-expression and self-determination.

Deprivation of these needs (or at least one of them) can mobilize efforts to satisfy them. Azar (1990) suggested that the basic conditions for eruption of protracted conflicts are deprivation of the basic living needs that relate to collectives. Collectives have great difficulty to compromise on goals that they consider to be essential to the satisfaction of their basic needs. In many cases, groups believe that the continuation of the conflict ensures the satisfaction of their needs and that its ending might change that situation.

Jewish society illustrates the need in security and safety that is well-embedded into the Israeli goals of the Israeli–Arab/Palestinian conflict. Because Israeli Jews perceive their history as a continuum of persecutions, culminating with the Holocaust, they share a collective need in establishing secure existence (Bar-Tal, Jacobson & Klieman, 1998; Bar-Tal, Magal & Halperin, 2009). Individual and collective security became an ultimate goal that for Israeli Jews has to be satisfied in any peace agreement with the Arab states and the Palestinians. Since the security demands are very far-reaching (e.g. demanding parts of the Palestinian and Syrian territories), they play a major role in the current stalemate in the Israeli–Palestinian and Israeli–Syrian peace processes.

Another example relates to the basic needs of economic survival. The Mayan Indians in Guatemala have suffered enormous economic and political deprivation because of the unequal distribution of the wealth, resources and power that favoured greatly the upper classes – white-skinned descendants of European immigrants to Guatemala. The poverty and very low living standards of the Mayan Indians in comparison to the ruling class led to the eruption of the civil war in 1960, initiated by various Mayan insurgent groups (Paige, 1983; Reeves, 2006). It was very difficult to terminate this conflict because the goals of the Mayans related to the satisfaction of their basic needs and thus required major restructuring of the society.

Conflict supporting societal beliefs

Another factor that obstructs peacemaking is the conflict-supporting socio-psychological beliefs that societies involved in intractable conflicts share with great confidence. These societal beliefs are part of the repertoire that society members develop to meet the challenges that conflicts pose (see Bar-Tal, 2007, in press). The repertoire helps to satisfy unfulfilled needs, facilitates coping with threat and plays a major role in the attempts to withstand the enemy. Yet, at the very same time, this repertoire – due to its selective, biased and distortive nature – prevents society members from identifying opportunities to resolve the conflict. Thus, it preserves the conflict because it prevents an alternative view about the conflict and/or the opponent.

It was suggested that this repertoire consists of two elements (Bar-Tal, 2007 2011, in press).[4] These are as follows:

a. *Collective memory* which includes a coherent and meaningful constructed narrative about the history of the conflict that has some basis in actual events (Cairns & Roe, 2003; Halbwachs, 1992; Liu & Hilton, 2005), but typically is significantly biased, selective and distorted in ways that meets the present needs of the society (Nets-Zehngut, 2011a, 2011b).

b. *Ethos of conflict* which is defined as the configuration of shared, central-societal beliefs that provide a particular dominant orientation to a society at present and for the future (Bar-Tal, 2000, 2012). It is composed of eight major themes about issues related to the conflict, the ingroup, and its adversary: (1) societal beliefs about the justness of one's own goals, which outline the contested goals, indicate their crucial importance, and provide their explanations and rationales; (2) societal beliefs about security stress the importance of personal safety and national survival, and outline the conditions for their achievement; (3) societal beliefs of positive collective self-image concern the ethnocentric tendency to attribute positive traits, values and behaviour to one's own society; (4) societal beliefs of victimization concern the self-presentation of the ingroup as the victim of the conflict; (5) societal beliefs of delegitimizing the opponent concern beliefs that deny the adversary's humanity; (6) societal beliefs of patriotism generate attachment to the country and society, by propagating loyalty, love, care and sacrifice; (7) societal beliefs of unity refer to the importance of ignoring internal conflicts and disagreements during intractable conflicts to unite the society's forces in the face of an external threat; (8) societal beliefs of peace refer to peace as the ultimate desire of the society (Bar-Tal, 2000, 2007; Rouhana & Bar-Tal, 1998).

The described two elements of the repertoire permeate with time into the fabric of the society, and can be referred to as an ideology that a society involved in an intractable conflict conforms to. It is widely shared by society members and is maintained by societal institutions and channels of communication. It contributes to the formation, maintenance and strengthening of the social identity (Bar-Tal, 2000, 2001, 2007, 2012; Nets-Zehngut, 2008, 2011a; Rouhana & Bar-Tal, 1998) and serves as a pillar for the emerged culture of conflict (Bar-Tal, 2012). Thus, the conflict-supporting societal beliefs serve as the epistemic basis to imbue social identity with meaning (Barthel, 1996; Cairns et al., 1998; Gillis, 1994; Oren, Bar-Tal & David, 2004) and provide the major contents that constitute the foundations of a 'culture of conflict'. As such, it serves as a major obstacle to resolve the conflict peacefully (Bar-Tal & Halperin, 2011).

Halperin and Bar-Tal (2011) found that adherence to the ethos of conflict led Israeli Jews to oppose compromises for peace and to reject any possibility to be exposed to positive information about Palestinians. Porat, Halperin and Bar-Tal (2012) found that when faced with a new peace proposal, Jews in Israel who hold high levels of ethos of conflict were more prone to acquire negative information about the implications of that proposal. This negative information ultimately led those who believed in the ethos of the conflict to reject the proposal. Thus, empirical data confirms that the repertoire of the conflict inhibits penetration of new and positive information into the individual and the societal cognitive sphere.

Another example relates to the impact of the Irish Catholic collective memory of the long conflict in Northern Ireland, which glorifies events such as the opposition to the oppression under the British rule, the 1916 Easter Rising against the British, the 1964–1972 civil rights campaign, and the 1972 Bloody Sunday in which 14 unarmed Catholic protestors were killed by the British. Such memories were a significant obstacle in reaching a peace agreement in this conflict (Feldman 1998; Rolston, 2010; Walker, 1996). First, the societal beliefs of the collective memory intensified feelings of threat, mistrust and a sense of victimhood. Second, making peace with compromises was viewed as violating the memories of the fallen: as many Irish Catholics died in order to achieve the ultimate goal of uniting Northern Ireland with the Republic of Ireland (Shaw, 1972).

Centrality of perceived threat

The next factor is the centrality of threat and its emotional consequences, namely fear, anxiety and angst (see also Stephan, this volume). Threat is experienced when human beings detect danger to themselves personally, to their kin in the wide sense and/or to their collective (Cohen, 1979, Rousseau, 2006). This detection implies possible harm in various domains: physical or economic harm (to individuals or their properties), as well as symbolic harm to values, ideology, dogmas or specific beliefs (Stephan & Renfro, 2002).

The context of every intractable conflict is characterized with the chronic perception of threat. These threatening cues tend to be amplified in human minds because, as suggested in evolutionary psychology, human beings are more tuned to threats than to positive signs (Bigelow, 1969; Ross, 1991). It means that negative information in conflict situations receives more weight: is more attended, remembered and considered. This phenomenon, which has been coined the 'negativity bias', is an inherent characteristic of the negative motivational system (Cacioppo & Bernston, 1994; Cacioppo, Gardner & Bernston, 1999; Jordan, 1965; Kanouse & Hanson, 1972; Lewicka, Czapinski & Peeters, 1992; Peeters, 1971; Peeters & Czapinski, 1990; Rozin & Royzman, 2001; Taylor, 1991). It explains why people have difficulty in disregarding, or at least minimizing, the influence of the negative information that motivates continuation of the conflict, and thus have difficulty focusing on the positive information that signals the possibility and advantages of peacemaking. The negative motivational system is structured to respond more intensely than the positive motivational system to comparable levels of motivational activation (Cacioppo & Gardner, 1999).

In addition, negative information strongly impacts evaluation, judgement and action (Cacioppo & Berntson, 1994; Christianson, 1992; Lau, 1982; Peeters & Czapinski, 1990 and studies by Ito et al., 1998; Wagenaar & Groeneweg, 1990). A similar bias has also been noted within the literature on persuasion. Negative events and information tend to be more closely attended, better remembered and more able to produce attitude change than positive events and information (Brehm, 1956; Cacioppo & Bernston, 1994; Patchen, Hofman & Davidson, 1976).

Also according to prospect theory (Kahneman & Tversky, 1979), people are more reluctant to lose what they already have than they are motivated to gain what they do not have (Tversky & Kahneman, 1986). Put differently, the value function is steeper on the loss side than on the gain side. Consequently, the negativity bias has two implications: (1) during evaluation of new opportunities, information about potential harm is weighted more heavily than positive information about peace opportunities; (2) when making a decision under risky conditions, potential costs are more heavily weighted than potential gains (Kanouse & Hanson, 1972).

Direct evidence regarding the role of threat in preserving conflicts was presented by Maoz and McCauley (2008). Their study showed that perceived threat by Israeli Jews in the context of the Israeli–Arab/Palestinian conflict led them to higher support of retaliatory aggressive policies against the Palestinians – their transfer or coercive operations against them, as well as resistance to compromising views regarding the solution of the conflict.

The enduring perceived threat leads individuals who are involved in intractable conflict to chronic experience of fear (Bar-Tal, 2001), which predisposes people to react to threatening cues and leads to overestimation of danger and threat. Increased sensitivity to threat facilitates the selective retrieval of information related to fear and increases accessibility of procedural knowledge that was effective in coping with threatening situations in the past (Clore, Scharz & Conway, 1994; Isen, 1999; Lazarus & Folkman, 1984; LeDoux, 1995, 1996; Öhman, 1993). Moreover, once fear is evoked, people tend to adhere to known situations and avoidance of risky, uncertain and novel ones. Thus, fear leads to cognitive freezing: it reduces openness to new ideas and increases resistance to change (Clore, Scharz & Conway, 1994; Isen, 1999; Jost et al., 2003; LeDoux, 1995, 1996; Öhman, 1993). These effects of fear not only apply to individuals, but also to collectives who, in the context of intractable conflict, form collective emotional orientation of fear (Bar-Tal, 2001; Halperin, Sharvit & Gross, 2011; Jarymowicz & Bar-Tal, 2006).

The collective fear orientation tends to limit perspective by binding the present to past experiences related to the conflict, and by building expectations for the future exclusively on the basis of the difficult past (Bar-Tal, 2001). This seriously hinders the disassociation from the past needed to allow creative thinking about new alternatives that may resolve the conflict peacefully. Collective fear, if deeply entrenched in the psyche of society members, as well as in their culture, inhibits the evolvement of their hope for peace (see Jarymowicz & Bar-Tal, 2006). Society members then have difficulty freeing themselves from the domination of fear to construct hope for peace.

Another angle explaining the central role of threat and fear in the continuation of intractable conflicts derives from the psychological theory of *terror management* (Pyszczynski, Greenberg & Solomon, 1997; Solomon, Greenberg & Pyszczynski, 1991). This theory suggests that an innate anxiety of annihilation, combined with the human knowledge of inevitable death, creates an ever-present potential for terror. According to the theory, a central defence mechanism used by society members in this situation is validation and maintenance of cultural worldviews that instil meaning, order and stability. In the case of intractable conflict, signals of threats increase salience of mortality. This salience leads to the adherence to conflict-supporting societal beliefs (ethos of collective memory and conflict) that are hegemonic worldviews in this context, as part of the culture of conflict. In addition, collectives may turn to violent means in order to defend these societal beliefs, as well as trying to defeat or annihilate rival outsiders who are viewed as threatening the dominant worldview and the society itself (Hirschberger & Pyszczynski, 2010).

In fact, perceptions of threat and fear are continuously present in all intractable conflicts that typically involve violence and destruction of various kinds. The Russian perception of the Chechens provides a specific example to the effect of threat and salience of mortality. Since the beginning of the fighting in the mid-1990s, the Russians suffered casualties not only on the battlefields but also, and most significantly, at home – as a result of terror attacks against the civilian population. Such incidents included the taking of hostages at Budennovsk (1995) and Kizlyar (1996), the 'Black September' bombings in various cities (1999), the Nord-Ost theatre siege (2002), and the 'Black Widow' suicide bombings throughout 2003. These traumatic events caused fear and alarm among the majority of Russians, swinging public mood decisively against the Chechens (as the theory of terror-management would predict). Indeed, as a result, the Chechens have been widely dehumanized; perceived as terrorists, bandits, spooks, thieves, wild, dangerous and mad. But of special importance was the effect of threat on the intensified feelings of insecurity and intolerance of any opposition to drastic counterinsurgency measures, support of military means against Chechens and resistance to compromising solutions to the conflict (Russell, 2002, 2005).

Habituation to conflict

Through the years of intractable conflict, individuals as well as collectives learn how to deal with situations and conditions of violent confrontations and how to adapt to them. They learn how to understand meaningfully the conflict situation, how to organize new information and experiences, and what to expect from the rival (Bar-Tal, 2007, in press). They also learn how to deal with the threatening situation, how to develop institutionalized ways to cope with the stress and how to withstand the rival. As a result, society members live with the feeling that the conflict context is meaningful, unambiguous, predictable and even bearable.

Peacemaking requires profound changes of well-established ways of coping and adaptation. It requires moving into an unknown realm and taking risks. Such changes arouse uncertainty, unpredictability and ambiguity. For example, it is never certain that the opponent really means to engage in the peacemaking process. It is always possible that he may try to gain time to regroup and collect resources for the continuation of the conflict. Thus, society members prefer to continue the known, certain and predictable reality of the conflict instead of moving into the unknown peace process that causes new stress and threat (Kelman, 2007; Mitchel, 2005; Mitzen, 2006). This choice can be understood: as during peacemaking processes there are still many signs of conflict. Often the violence continues, as well as hostile rhetoric. Thus people are hesitant to change their approach to the ongoing conflict too quickly.

The above analysis is illustrated in the conflict between the Greek Cypriots and the Turkish Cypriots. In the recent referendum on the Kofi Annan Plan held in 2004, Greek Cypriots rejected the plan to resolve the conflict. Various explanations can be given for this result, but one of them pertains to the habituation process. The majority of Greek Cypriots preferred the familiar conflictive situation over the proposed new, unknown situation of peace. Being habituated to the conflict, refusing to accept the proposed compromises led to the continuation of the conflict (Michael, 2007; Yilmaz, 2005).

Another example relates to the attitude of nationalists (Catholics) in Northern Ireland regarding the new police force. Familiar with police persecution by the enemy (i.e. the Protestants) in the past, they find it hard to cooperate with the new police force and to obey its orders. Policing is a contentious issue for them, since they continue to see the police as a political force, and therefore many are resistant to changing their suspicious and antagonistic attitude towards the police. Consequently, they effectively interfere with its operation, and many of them (e.g. members of Sinn Fein, the largest republican political party) do not join the police force (Wilson & Stapleton, 2007).

Profiteers and their motivation

Resistance to peacemaking is also observed among various societal sectors, groups and individuals who consciously or unconsciously are motivated by their gains from the conflict situation. Consciously means that these society members and sectors are well aware of their gains and act upon those interests, while unconsciously means that they support the continuation of the conflict without being completely aware of how they benefit from it, instead expressing various ideological or other arguments for its continuation.

One segment in society that often has a motivation to continue the conflict is the military sector itself. During intractable conflict, this sector gains tremendous influence in the decision-making process as its members are the professionals who carry the burden of the confrontation. Furthermore, because prolonged and violent conflicts impinge on every domain of collective life, the military elite extends its influence also to other domains. Because of their high status, prestige and sacrifices, they also gain easy access to major positions in either the public service or the private sector after their retirement (Cohen, 1995). Eventually, the military elite as an agent of conflict, exercises significant influence to continue it, acting at times as a spoiler of the peace process when this possibility appears.

A example of this relates to the conflict in El Salvador between the military-led government and the Farabundo Martí National Liberation

Front (FMLN). The Salvadorian army had significant gains from the continuation of the conflict: it acquired major power and status in the state's administration and elite as their alleged protector from the revolutionaries. In addition, senior officers gained wealth from extortion they conducted during the war, and payments received by the elite. Consequently, some of them had an interest in the continuation of the conflict and tried to obstruct its resolution (Deane, 1996; Huge, 1996).

Another example is that of the Israeli-Jewish settlers who received from the Israeli government land to build their houses, infrastructure and tax benefits, gaining much from the continuation of the conflict. Peaceful resolution of the Israeli–Palestinian conflict that will necessitate dismantling many settlements will lead to the loss of some of these gains. This is one of the reasons why some of the settlers lead a well-orchestrated campaign to prevent peaceful resolution of the conflict (Hever, in press; Zertal & Eldar, 2007).

Human losses

Another socio-psychological factor that often inhibits peacemaking is the weight of losses suffered by the societies involved. The sanctity of life is a universal value, therefore killing is considered as the most serious violation of the moral code (Donagan, 1979; Kleinig, 1991). Societies engaged in intractable conflict frequently suffer heavy human losses of both soldiers and civilians. Death of society members as a result of hostile activities of the rival increases the emotional involvement of the parties (Bar-Tal, 2003; Nets-Zehngut, 2009).

Moreover, human losses generate rituals, ceremonies and monuments that are dedicated to preserving the memory of the fallen. They glorify battles and wars, the heroism of the fallen, the malevolence of the enemy, and the necessity to continue the struggle in fulfilment of the patriotic 'will' of the fallen. Thus, they inspire society members to continue the conflict against the enemy (Arviv-Abromovich, 2011). A vivid example is the words of a young Israeli Jew who explained his objection to withdrawal from the territories seized by Israel in the Six Day 1967 War: 'Now, I...I'm not in favor to give up territories for...for peace. It pains me because people fought, people died there for that territory, so why are you returning them? Do you know how much Jewish blood there is there?' (Fuxman, 2011). Furthermore, people feel obliged to revenge these losses in retribution for the violence inflicted (Silke, 2006; Turner-High, 1949), or because they know that it is impossible to compensate close relatives for the loss of a life (Bar-Tal, 2003; Scheff, 1994).

In addition, people who have lost their dear ones often urge society to adhere to its original goals and object to any peace move that results in compromise. This stand is motivated by the feeling that by compromising the goals the sacrifice was in vein. Similarly, a peace settlement that could have been achieved in the past and was not arouses the feeling that it would have been possible to avoid the sacrifices made. There is an assumption that early compromises could have saved lives, but since the society has decided to adhere to its original goals – and has sacrificed compatriots in the conflict – there should be continuation of this adherence. Moreover, supporting peace might cause a cognitive dissonance, since adhering to new goals is inconsistent with the sacrifice made in continuing the conflict. People who loose their dear ones exert a strong influence on the decision to continue the conflict and refuse to reach compromises that could settle the conflict peacefully.

Empirical data from the Israeli-Jewish society shows that those who were personally exposed to or suffered from terrorism expressed more radical positions towards Palestinians (Canetti-Nisim et al., 2009). For example, the Israeli-Jewish hawkish non-governmental organization Almagor was founded by relatives of victims of Palestinian terror attacks, with the goal of exerting pressure against the release of Palestinians captured by Israel and held as prisoners. It conducts wide-scale activity against the Palestinians such as demonstrations, lobbying in Israeli parliament and abroad, and giving lectures – all about delegitimizing the Palestinians and trying to decrease public support for making the compromises needed for peace such as the release of Palestinian prisoners (Almagor, 2011).

Similarly, relatives of nationalist victims in the conflict in Northern Ireland demanded during the 1990s peace negotiations that the responsibility of the British Army for the death of their loved ones should be investigated, and that in case of illegal killings, the responsible soldiers should be prosecuted. This demand was rejected by the British and presented an obstacle in the peace process (Lundy & McGovern, 2010).

Conclusion

This chapter has focused on intractable intergroup conflicts and attempts to provide an answer to a key question related to these conflicts: why is it so difficult to end them? In other words, why is it so difficult for societies involved in intractable conflicts to change towards peacemaking? The chapter reviews socio-psychological mechanisms and dynamics that play a central role in the process of preserving protracted conflicts. We have argued that people and collectives in conflicts tend to adhere to their repertoire of goals, motivations, beliefs, attitudes, emotions and patterns of behaviours that support the continuation of the conflicts.

Obviously, socio-psychological factors are not the only factors that make conflict resolution so difficult. Arrow et al. (1995), in their seminal work about barriers to peace, mention also tactical, strategic, structural and organizational types of barrier. Nevertheless, the main focus of our argument here is on the socio-psychological obstacles and, along these lines, the main challenge is to suggest ways to overcome all the above-described barriers and motivate society members to adopt a new repertoire that supports peaceful resolution.

Embarking on the road of peace often begins when a number of society members begin to think that the conflict should be resolved peacefully, and then begin to realize this idea. Once such an idea emerges – and is propagated by society members – a process of moving the society towards resolving the conflict peacefully begins. There are various ways to illuminate this process. It is possible to divide it into different phases or to look at it from various angles. In essence, however, it is a long process of societal change; of building a new repertoire that allows reaching an agreement with the opponent, and then constructing a new ethos and collective memory that serve as a new foundation in the emerging new culture of peace.

This process involves all types of society members, from the grass roots to leaders. Fundamental views about the conflict have to change: the definition of group goals, the perception of the opponent and the relationship with them, the beliefs about the group and about its past, and more. This process usually involves bottom-up and top-down processes where, together with the extensive activities of peace organizations (representatives of the bottom-up, the grass roots) that impart the new ideas, there is also need to involve leaders from the top who eventually lead the negotiations. This process is gradual, long and complex because societal change is not a simple matter. The above mentioned barriers are well entrenched in the society and powerful forces guard that they will not change easily.

Also, the process towards peace is not necessarily linear but may have fluctuations that sometimes lead to re-escalation of the conflict and then again to its de-escalation. The process described above may begin, but may not necessarily end with the new peace-supporting repertoire, or with peaceful conflict settlement. Furthermore, en route to a peace agreement, the process may stop at a certain point for a long period of time. Nevertheless, it is obvious that lasting peace requires a long process of reconciliation and the evolution of a culture of peace. This process does not only change the nature of relations between two rivals, it also transforms the nature of the societies that lived under the shadow of intractable conflict, sometimes through many generations. A new context of peace can influence many different aspects of life in different domains. It may change relations and power structure between different segments of the society, and so on. The cases of peacemaking in El Salvador, Algeria, South Africa or even Northern Ireland testify that the process of peacemaking is possible. It is our mission to find ways to strengthen the weak part of the presented asymmetry in order move societies out of the destructive intractable conflicts and into the light of peace and prosperity.

Practical task for readers

This chapter has attempted to present major socio-psychological barriers that play a role in intractable intergroup conflicts, preventing their peaceful resolution. In the analysis, we referred to a number of notable intractable intergroup conflicts such as the conflict between Jews in Israel and Palestinians, between Russians and Chechens in Russia, the intra-societal conflicts in El Salvador and Guatemala, inter-ethnic conflicts between Kurds and Turks in Turkey, or between Tamil and Sinhalese in Sri Lanka, or between Turkish and Greek Cypriots in Cyprus, as well as between Catholics and Protestants in Northern Ireland. Please select one of these conflicts, describe its history and background and then analyse all the socio-psychological barriers that played a major role in preventing its resolution. Finally, propose ways to overcome these barriers. (If you wish you may select another intractable intergroup conflict for this analysis as well.)

Suggested readings

To learn more about the topic of this chapter see Ross and Ward (1995), Halperin (2011), Kelman (2007), Bar-Tal and Halperin (2011 and 2009).

References

Almagor (2011). Almagor Terror Victims Association's website. Available at http://www.al-magor.com/index.htm (accessed 27 March 2011).

Amirav, M. (2009). *Jerusalem Syndrome: The Palestinian-Israeli Battle for the Holy City*. Eastbourne: Sussex Academic Press.

Andrews, M. (2007). *Shaping History: Narrative of Political Change*. Cambridge, England: University Press.

Anwar S. & Menachem B. (2008). Speeches to Knesset, November 20, 1977. In I. Rabinovich & J. Reinarz (eds.), *Documents and Readings on Society, Politics and Foreign Relations, Pre-1948 to the Present* (second edition pp. 363–372). Lebanon, NH: Brandeis University Press.

Arrow, K., Mnookin, R., Ross, L., Tversky, A. & Wilson, R. (eds.), (1995). *Barriers to Conflict Resolution*. New York: Norton.

Arviv Abromovich, R. (2011). *Societal Beliefs About Israeli-Arab Palestinian Conflict Transmitted in National Ceremonies 1948-2006*. Doctoral dissertation submitted to Tel Aviv University (in Hebrew).

Ashmore, R. D., Deaux, K. & McLaughlin-Volpe, T. (2004). An organizing framework for collective identity: Articulation and significance of multidimensionality. *Psychological Bulletin*, 130, 80–114.

Azar, E. (1990). *The Management of Protracted Social Conflict: Theory And Cases*. Dartmouth: Aldershot, Hampshire, England and Brookfield.

Bandarage, A. (2008). *The Separatist Conflict in Sri Lanka: Terrorism, Ethnicity, Political Economy*. London: Routledge.

Baron, J. & Spranca, M. (1997). Protected values. *Organizational Behavior and Human Decision Processes*, 70(1), 1–16.

Bar-Tal, D. (1998). Societal beliefs in times of intractable conflict: The Israeli case. *The International Journal of Conflict Management*, 9, 22–50.

Bar-Tal, D. (2000). *Shared Beliefs in a Society: Social Psychological Analysis*. Thousand Oaks, CA: Sage.

Bar-Tal, D. (2001). Why does fear override hope in societies engulfed by intractable conflict, as it does in the Israeli society? *Political Psychology*, 22, 601–627.

Bar-Tal, D. (2003). Collective memory of physical violence: Its contribution to the culture of violence. In E. Cairnes & M. D. Roe, *The Role of Memory in Ethnic Conflict* (pp. 77–93). Houndmills: Palgrave Macmillan.

Bar-Tal, D. (2007). Sociopsychological foundations of intractable conflicts. *American Behavioral Scientist*, 50, 1430–1453.

Bar-Tal, D. (2011). Introduction: Conflicts and social psychology. In Bar-Tal, D. (ed.), *Intergroup conflicts and their resolution: Social psychological perspective* (pp.1-38). New York: Psychology Press.

Bar-Tal, D. (in press). *Intractable Conflicts: Socio-psychological Foundations and Dynamics*. Cambridge: Cambridge University Press.

Bar-Tal, D. & Halperin, E. (2009). Overcoming psychological barriers to peace process: The influence of beliefs about losses. In M. Mikulincer & P. R. Shaver (eds.), *Prosocial Motives, Emotions and Behaviors: The Better Angels of Our Nature* (pp. 431–448). Washington DC: American Psychological Association.

Bar-Tal, D. & Halperin, E. (2011). Socio-psychological barriers to conflict resolution. In D.Bar-Tal (ed.), *Intergroup Conflicts and Their Resolution: A Social Psychological Perspective* (pp.217–240). New York: Psychology Press.

Bar-Tal, D., Halperin, E. & de Rivera, J. (2007). Collective emotions in conflict: Societal implications. *Journal of Social Issues*, 63, 441–460.

Bar-Tal, D., Halperin, E., & Oren , N. (2010). Socio-psychological barriers to peace making: The case of the Israeli Jewish society. *Social Issues and Policy Review*, 4, 63–109.

Bar-Tal, D., Jacobson, D. & Klieman, A. (eds.) (1998). *Security Concerns: Insights from the Israeli Experience*. Stamford, CT: JAI.

Bar-Tal, D., Magal, T. & Halperin, E. (2009). The paradox of security views in Israel: Socio-psychological explanation. In G. Scheffer & O. Barak (eds.), *Existential Threats and Civil Security Relations* (pp. 219–247). Lanham MD: Lexington Books.

Barthel, D. (1996). *Historic Preservation: Collective Memory and Historical Identity*. New Bruswick, NJ: Rutgers University Press.

Bigelow, R. (1969). *The Dawn Warriors: Man;s Evolution Towards Peace*. Boston: Little Brown.

Black, J. (1998). *Why Wars Happen*. London: Reaktion Books.

Bose, S. (2005). *Kashmir: Roots of Conflict, Paths to Peace*. Cambridge: Harvard University Press.

Barbalet, J. M. (1998). *Emotion, Social Theory, and Social Structure: A Macrosociological Approach*. Cambridge: Cambridge University Press.

Brehm, J. (1956). Post-decision changes in desirability of alternatives. *Journal of Abnormal and Social Psychology*, 52, 384–389.

Brewer, M. B. (2011). Identity and conflict. In D. Bar-Tal (ed.), *Intergroup Conflicts and Their Resolution: A Social Psychological Perspective* (pp.125–143). New York: Psychology Press.

Cacioppo, J. T. & Berntson, G. G. (1994). Relationship between attitudes and evaluative space: A critical review with emphasis on the seperability of positive and negative substrates. *Psychological Bulletin*, 115(3), 401–423.

Cacioppo, J. T. & Gardner, W. L. (1999). Emotions. *Annual Review of Psychology*, 50, 191–214.

Cacioppo, J. T., Gardner, W. L. & Bernston, G. G. (1999). The affect system has parallel and integrative processing components: Form follows function. *Journal of Personality and Social Psychology*, 76, 839–855.

Cairns, E. & Roe, M. D. (2003). *The Role of Memory in Ethnic Conflict*. New York: Palgrave Macmillan.

Cairns, E., Lewis, C. A., Mumcu, O. & Waddell, N. (1998). Memories of recent ethnic conflict and their relationship to social identity. *Peace and Conflict: Journal of Peace Psychology*, 4, 13–22.

Canetti-Nisim, D., Halperin, E., Sharvit, K. & Hobfoll, S. (2009). A new stress-based model of political extremism: Personal exposure to terrorism, psychological distress and exclusionist political attitudes. *Journal of Conflict Resolution*, 53, 363–389.

Cash, J. D. (1996). *Identity, Ideology and Conflict*. Cambridge: Cambridge University Press.

Christianson, S. A. (1992). Remembering emotional events: Potential mechanisms. In S. A. Christianson, *The Handbook of Emotion And Memory* (pp. 307–340). Hillsdale, NJ: Lawrence Erlbaum.

Clore, G. L., Scharz, N. & Conway, M. (1994). Affective causes and consequences of social information processing. In R. S. Wyer & T. K. Strull, *Handbook of Social Cognition* (vol. 1, pp. 323–417). Hillsdale, NJ: Lawrence Erlbaum.

Cohen, A. S. (1995). The Israeli Defense Forces (IDF): From a 'people's army' to a 'professional military' – causes and implications. *Armed Forces and Society*, 21(2), 237.

Cohen, R. (1979). *Threat Perception in International Crisis*. Madison, WI: University of Wisconsin Press.

Coleman, P. T. (2003). Characteristics of protracted, intractable conflict: Towards the development of a metaframework - I. *Peace and Conflict: Journal of Peace Psychology*, 9(1), 1–37.

David, O. & Bar-Tal, D. (2009). A socio-psychological conception of collective identity: The case of national identity. *Personality and Social Psychology Review*, 13, 354–379.

Deane, S. (1996). *The Protection Racket State: Elite Politics, Military Extortion, and Civil War in El Salvador*. Philadelphia: Temple University Press.

Donagan, A. (1979). *The theory of morality*. Chicago: University of Chicago Press.

Drucker, R. (2002). *Hrakiri*. Tel Aviv: Miscal (in Hebrew).

Feldman, A. (1998). Retaliate and punish: Political violence as a form of memory in Northern Ireland. *Eire-Ireland*, 33, 195–235.

Fiske, A. P. & Tetlock, P. E. (1997). Taboo trade-offs: Reactions to transactions that transgress the spheres of justice. *Political Psychology*, 18(2), 255–297.

Foyle, D. C. (1999). *Counting the Public In, Presidents, Public Opinion, and Foreign Policy*. New York: Columbia University Press.

Fuxman, S. (2011). *Learning the Past, Understanding the Present and Expecting the Future: Israeli Adolescents' Narratives of the Conflict*. Doctoral dissertation submitted to Harvard University.

Gillis, J. (1994). *Commemorations: The politics of National Identity*. Princeton: Princeton University Press.

Ginges, J. & Atran, S. (2011). War as a moral imperative (Not just practical policy by other means). *Proceedings of the Royal Society: Biological Sciences*. Online first publication, 16 February 2011.

Halbwachs, M. (1992). *On Collective Memory*. Chicago: University of Chicago Press.

Halperin, E. (2008). Group-based hatred in intractable conflict in Israel. *Journal of Conflict Resolution*, 52, 713–736.

Halperin, E. (2010). The emotional roots of intergroup violence – The distinct role of anger and hatred. In M. Mikulincer & P. R. Shaver, *Human Agression and Violence: Causes, Manifestations, and consequences*. Washington, DC: American Psychological Association.

Halperin, E. (2011). Emotional barriers to peace: Negative emotions and public opinion about the peace process in the Middle East. *Peace and Conflict: Journal of Peace Psychology*, 17, 22–45.

Halperin, E. & Bar-Tal, D. (2011). Socio-psychological barriers to peace making: An empirical examination within the Israeli Jewish society. *Journal of Peace Research*, 48, 637–657.

Halperin, E., Sharvit, K. & Gross, J. J. (2011). Emotions and emotion regulation in intergroup conflict: An appraisal based framework. In D. Bar-Tal (ed.), *Intergroup Conflicts and their Resolution: A Social Psychological Perspective* (pp. 83–124). New York: Psychology Press.

Harbom, L., Hogbladh, S. & Wallensteen, P. (2006). Armed conflict and peace agreements. *Journal of Peace Research*, 43(5), 617–631.

Hever, S. (in press). Economic cost of the ooccupation to Israel. In D. Bar-Tal and I. Schnell (eds.), *Effects of Lasting Occupation: Lessons from the Israeli Society*. New York: Oxford University Press.

Hirschberger, G. & Pyszczynski, T. (2010). Killing with a clean conscience: Existential angst and the paradox of mortality. *Social Psychology of Mortality: Exploring the Causes of Good and Evil*. Hertzliya: IDC.

Huge, B. (1996). *El Salvador's Civil War: A Study of Revolution*. Boulder, CO: Lynne Rienner.

Isen, A. M. (1999). Positive affect. In T. Dalgleish & M. Power, *Handbook of Cognition and Emotion* (pp. 521–539). New York: Wiley.

Ito, T. A., Larsen, J. T., Smith, N. K. & Cacioppo, J. T. (1998). Negative information weighs more heavily on the brain: The negativity bias in evaluative categorizations. *Journal of Personality and Social Psychology*, 75, 887–900.

Jarymowicz, M. & Bar-Tal, D. (2006). The dominance of fear over hope in the life of individuals and collectives. *European Journal of Social Psychology*, 36, 367–392.

Jordan, N. (1965). The asymmetry of liking and disliking. A phenomenon meriting further reflection and research. *Public Opinion Quarterly*, 29, 315–322.

Jost, J. T., Glaser, J., Kruglanski, A. W. & Sulloway, F. J. (2003). Political conservatism as motivated social cognition. *Psychological Bulletin*, 129, 339–375.

Kahneman, D. & Tversky, A. (1979). Prospect theory: An analysis of decision under risk. *Econometrica*, 47, 263–291.

Kanouse, D. E. & Hanson, L. R. (1972). Negativity in evaluations. In E. E. Jones D. E. Kanouse, H. H. Kelley, R. A. Nisbett, S. Valins, & B. Weiner (eds.), & et al., *Attribution: Perceiving the Causes of Behavior*. Morristown, NJ: General Learning Press.

Kearney, R. (1978). Language and the rise of Tamil separatism in Sri-Lanka. *Asian Survey*, 18, 521–534.

Kelman, H. C. (1999). The interdependence of Israeli and Palestinian identity: The role of the other in existential conflicts. *Journal of Social Issues*, 55, 581–600.

Kelman, H. C. (2007). Socio-psycological dimensions of international conflicts. In W. Zartman, *Peacemaking in International Conflicts: Methods and Techniques* (pp. 61–110). Washington, D.C.: United States Institute of Peace.

Kemper, T. D. (1990). *Research Agendas in the Sociology Of Emotions*. Albany, NY: State University of New York Press.

Klein, M. (2001). *Jerusalem: The Contested City*. New York: New York University Press.

Kleinig, J. (1991). *Valuing life*. Princeton: Princeton University Press.

Koistinen, P. A. (1980). *The Military-Industrial Complex: A Historical Perspective*. Westport, CT: Praeger.

Korostelina, K. (2006). National identity formation and conflict intentions of ethnic minorities. In M. Fitzduff & C. E. Stout (eds.), *The Psychology of Resolving Global Conflicts: From War to Peace* (vol. 2, pp. 147–170). Westport CT: Praeger Security International.

Kriesberg, L. (1993). Intractable conflict. *Peace Review*, 5, 417–421.

Kriesberg, L. (1998). Intractable conflict. In E. Weiner, *The Handbook of Interethnic Coexistence* (pp. 332–342). New York: Continuum.

Kriesberg, L. (2007). *Constructive Conflicts: From Escalation to Resolution*. Lanham, MD: Rowman & Littlefield.

Kriesberg, L., Northrup, T. A. & Thorson, S. J. (1989). *Intractable Conflicts and their Transformation*. Syracuse: Syracuse University Press.

Landman, S. (2010). Barriers to peace: Protected values in the Israeli-Palestinian conflict. In Y. Bar-Siman-Tov, *Barriers to peace: The Israeli-Palestinian conflict* (pp. 135–177). Jerusalem: Jerusalem Institute for Israel Studies.

Lau, R. R. (1982). Negativity in political perception. *Political Behavior*, 4, 353–377.

Lazarus, R. S. & Folkman, S. (1984). *Stress, Appraisal, and Coping*. New York: Springer.

Ledgerwood, A. L., Liviatan, I., & Carnevale, P. (2007). Group-identity completion and the symbolic value of property. *Psyhcological Science*, 18, 873–878.

LeDoux, J. E. (1995). Emotion: Clues from the brain. *Annual Review of Psychology*, 1, 209–227.

LeDoux, J. E. (1996). *The Emotional Brain: The Mysterious Underpinnings of Emotional Life*. New York: Touchstone.

Lewicka, M., Czapinski, J. & Peeters, G. (1992). Positive-negative asymmetry or 'when the heart needs a reason'. *European Journal of Social Psychology*, 22, 425–434.

Liu, J. H. & Hilton, D. J. (2005). How the past weighs on the present: Social representations of history and their in identity poliltics. *British Journal of Social Psychology*, 44, 537–556.

Loizides, N. (2010). State ideology and the Kurds in Turkey. *Middle Eastern Studies*, 46(4), 513–527.

Lundy, P. & McGovern, M. (2010). The politics of memory in post-conflict Northern Ireland. *Peace Review*, 13(1), 27–33.

Mackie, D. M. & Smith, E. R. (2002). *From Prejudice to Intergroup Emotions: Defferentiated Reactions to Social Group*. Philadelphia, PA: Psychological Press.

Maoz, I. & McCauley, C. (2008). Threat, dehumanization, and support for retaliatory aggressive polices in asymmetric conflict. *Journal of Conflict Resolution*, 52, 93–116.

Maslow, A. H. (1954). *Motivation and Personality*. New York: Harper & Row.

Michael, M. (2007). The Cyprus peace talks: A critical appraisal. *Journal of Peace Research*, 44(5), 587–604.

Mintz, A. (1983). The military-industrial complex: The Israeli case. *Journal of Strategic Studies*, 6, 103–127.

Mitchel, C. (2005). *Conflict, Social Change and Conflict Resolution. An Enquiry*. Berghof Research Center for Constructive Conflict Managment.

Mitzen, J. (2006). Ontological security in world politics: State identity and the securty dilemma. *European Journal of International Relations*, 12, 341–370.

Nets-Zehngut, R. (2008). The Israeli National Information Center and collective memory of the Israeli-Arab conflict. *The Middle East Journal*, 62(4), 653–670.

Nets-Zehngut, R. (2009). Passive healing of the aftermath of intractable conflicts. *The International Journal of Peace Studies*, 14, 39–60.

Nets-Zehngut, R. (2011a). Origins of the Palestinian refugee problem: Changes in the historical memory of Israelis/Jews 1949–2004. *Journal of Peace Research*, 48, 235–248.

Nets-Zehgut, R. (2011b). Palestinian autobiographical memory regarding the 1948 Palestinian exodus. *Political Psychology*, 32, 271–295.

Ocarlar, N. (2009). *Between Majority Power and Minority Resistance: Kurdish Linguistic Rights in Turkey*. Lund: Lund University.

Öhman, A. (1993). Fear and anxiety as emotional phenomena: Clinical psenomenology, evolutionary perspectves, and information processing mechanisms. In M. Lewis & J. M. Haviland, *Handbook of Emotions* (pp. 511–536). New York: Guilford Press.

Oren, N., Bar-Tal, D. & David, O. (2004). Conflict, identity and ethos; The Israeli-Palestinian case. In Y. T. Lee, C. R. McCauley, F. M. Moghaddam & S. Worchel, *Psychology of Ethnic and Cultural Conflict* (pp. 133–154). Westport, CT: Greenwook.

Paige, P. (1983). Social theory and peasant revolution in Vietnam and Guatemala. *Theory and Society*, 12, 699–737.

Patchen, M., Hofman, G. & Davidson, J. D. (1976). Interracial perceptions among high school students. *Sociometry*, 39, 341–354.

Paul, T. V. (2005). Causes of the India-Pakistan enduring rivalry. In T. V. Paul (ed.), *The India-Pakistan Conflict: An Enduring Rivalry* (pp. 3–24). Cambridge: Cambridge University Press.

Peeters, G. (1971). The positive-negative asymmetry: On cognitive consistency and positivity bias. *European Journal of Social Psychology*, 1, 455–474.

Peeters, G. & Czapinski, J. (1990). Positive-negative asymmetry in evaluations: The distinction between affective and informational effects. In W. Stroebe & M. Hewstone, *European Review of Social Psychology* (vol. 1, pp. 33–60). New York: Wiley.

Porat, R., Halperin, E. & Bar-Tal, D. (2012). *Socio-Psychological Barriers to Peace-Making: Conception and Empirical Evidence*. Manuscript Submitted for Publication.

Pruitt, D. G. & Rubin, J. Z. (1986). *Social Conflict: Escalation, Stalemate and Settlement*. New York: Random House.

Pyszczynski, T., Greenberg, J. & Solomon, S. (1997). Why do we need what we need? A terror management perspective on the roots of human motivation. *Psychological Inquiry*, 8, 1–20.

Reeves, R. (2006). *Ladinos with Ladinos, Indians with Indians: Land, Labor, and Regional Ethnic Conflict in the Making of Guatemala*. Stanford, CA: Stanford University Press.

Rolston, B. 2010. 'Trying to reach the future through the past': Murals and memory in Northern Ireland. *Crime Media Culture*, 6, 285–307.

Ross, L. & Ward, A. (1995). Psychological barriers to dispute resolution. *Advances in Experimental Psychology*, 27, 255–304.

Ross, M. H. (1991). The role of evolution in ethnocentric conflict and its management. *Journal of Social Issues*, 47, 167–185.

Rothman, J. (1997). *Resolving Identity-based Conflict in Nations, Organizations, and Communities*. San Fransisco: Josey-Bass.

Rouhana, N. & Bar-Tal, D. (1998). Psychological dynamics of intractable conflicts: The Israeli-Palestinian case. *American Psychologist*, 53, 761–770.

Rousseau, L. D. (2006). *Identifying Threats and Threatening Identities*. California: Stanford University Press.

Rozin, P. & Royzman, E. B. (2001). Negativity bias, negativity dominance, and contagion. *Personality and Social Psychology Review*, 5, 296–320.

Russell, J. (2002). Mujahedeen, mafia, madmen: Rusian perspectives of Chechens during the wars in Chechnya, 1994–96 and 1999–2001. In R. Fawn and S. White (eds.), *Russia in Retrospect: Ten Years since the End of the USSR* (pp. 73–96). London: Frank Cass.

Russell, J. (2005). Terrorists, bandits, spooks and thieves: Russian demonisation of the Chechens prior to and since 9/11. *Third World Quarterly*, 26, 101–116.

Russell, J. (2007). *Chechnya – Russia's 'War on Terror'*. New York: Routledge.

Sarkees, M. R., Wayman, F. W. & Singer, J. D. (2003). Inter-state, intra-state, and extra state wars: A comprehensive look at their distribution over time, 1816–1997. *International Studies Quarterly*, 49, 49–70.

Scheff, T. J. (1994). *Bloody Revenge: Emotions, Nationalism, and War*. Boulder, CO: Westview Press.

Shaw, F. (1972). The canon of Irish history: A challenge. *Studies*, 61, 115–153.

Sher, G. (2001). *Within Reach: The Peace Negotiations: 1999–2001*. Tel Aviv: Yedioth Aharonot (in Hebrew).

Sherif, M. (1967). *Group Conflict and Cooperation*. London: Routledge & Kegan Paul.

Silke, A. (2006). The role of suicide in politics, conflict, and terrorism. *Terrorism and Political Violence*, 18, 35–46.

Skitka, L. J. (2002). Do the means justify the ends, or do the ends justify the means? A test of the value protection model of justice. *Personality and Social Psychology Bulletin*, 28, 588–597.

Skitka, L. J., Bauman, C. W. & Sargis, E. G. (2005). Moral conviction: Another contributer to attitude strength or something more? *Journal of Personality and Social Psychology*, 88, 895–917.

Solomon, N. (2005). *War Made Easy, How Presidents and Pundits Keep Spinning Us to Death*. New Jersey: John Wiley & Sons.

Solomon, S., Greenberg, J. & Psyzczynski, T. (1991). Terror management theory of self-esteem. In C. R. Snyder, Forsyth & R. Donelson, *Handbook of Social and Clinical Psychology: The Health Perspective, Pergamon General Psychology Series* (pp. 21–40). Elmsford, NY: Pergamon Press.

Stephan, E. G. & Renfro, C. L. (2002). The role of threat in intergroup relations. In D. Mackie & E. Smith, *From Prejudice to Intergroup Emotions* (pp. 191–207). Philadelphia, PA: Psychology Press.

Tajfel, H. & Tunner, J. C. (1986). The social identity theory of intergroup behavior. In S. Worchel & W. Austin, *Psychology of Intergroup Relations* (pp. 7–24). Chicago: Nelson-Hall.

Taylor, S. E. (1991). Asymmetrical effects of positive and negative events: The mobilization-minimization hypothesis. *Psychological Bulletin*, 110, 67–85.

Tetlock, P. E. (1999). Coping with tradeoffs: Psychological constraints and poliltical implications. In A. Lupia, M. D. McCubbins & S. L. Popkins, *Elements of Reason: Cognition, Choice, and the Bounds of Rationality* (pp. 239–263). Cambridge: Cambridge Universiy Press.

Tetlock, P. E. (2003). Thinking the unthinkable: Sacred values and taboo cognitions. *Trends in Cognitive Science*, 7, 320–324.

Tetlock, P. E., Kristel, O. V., Elson, S. B., Green, M. C. & Lerner, J. F. (2000). The psychology of the unthinkable: Taboo trade-offs, forbidden base-rates, and heretical counterfactuals. *Journal of Personality and Social Psychology*, 78, 853–870.

Turner-High, H. H. (1949). *General Anthropology*. TY: Crowell Co.

Tversky, A. & Kahneman, D. (1986). Rational choice and the framing of decisions. *The Journal of Business*, 59, 251–278.

Wagennar, W. A. & Groeneweg, J. (1990). The memory of concentration camp survivors. *Applied Cognitive Psychology*, 4, 77–87.

Walker, B. (1996). *Dancing to History's Tune: History, Myth and Politics in Northern Ireland*. Belfast: Institute of Irish Studies.

Wilson, J. & Stapleton, K. (2007). The discourse of resistance: Social change and policing in Northern Ireland. *Language in Society*, 36, 393–425.

Yaar, E. &. Hermann, T. (2009). *Peace Index: January 2009*. Tel Aviv: The Tami Steinmetz Center for Peace Research.

Yilmaz, M. (2005). The Cyprus conflict and the Annan plan: Why one more failure? *Edge Academic Review*, 5, 29–39.

Zertal, I. & Eldar, A. (2007). *Lords of the Land: The War over Israel's Settlements in the Occupied Territories, 1967-2007*. New York: Nation Books.

Notes

1. Mixed motive approach denotes that the parties in conflict realize that their fate is interdependent and therefore take into consideration the needs and goals of the other group too.
2. Zero-sum approach denotes unwillingness by the parties to consider compromises, focuses only on own needs and goals, and holds a belief suggesting that any gain by the rival is own loss and any loss by the rival is own gain.
3. This is a religious site in the Old City of Jerusalem, considered as a very holy place by Jews and Muslims.
4. The third element is *collective emotional orientation* with an emphasis on a number of particular emotions that appear in times of intractable conflict (Bar-Tal, 2012, Bar-Tal, Halperin & de Rivera, 2007; Barbalet, 1998; Kemper, 1990; Mackie & Smith, 2002) – the most notable are fear, hatred, humiliation and despair (see also, for example, Bar-Tal, 2001; Halperin, 2008, 2010; Halperin, Sharvit, & Gross, 2011).

11

Evil Transformations: Social-Psychological Processes Underlying Genocide and Mass Killing

Michał Bilewicz and Johanna Ray Vollhardt

• •

In the preface to his re-issued, widely acclaimed book *At the Mind's Limits*, Jean Améry, a survivor of Auschwitz, wrote:

> Between the time this book was written and today, more than thirteen years have passed. They were not good years. One need only follow the reports from Amnesty International to see that in horror this period matches the worst epochs of a history that is as real as it is inimical to reason. Sometimes it seems as though Hitler has gained a posthumous triumph. Invasions, aggressions, torture, destruction of man in his essence.
>
> (1998, p. vii)

Améry's observation could be applied to most decades of modern world history. The genocides in Rwanda, Cambodia, Bosnia and Herzegovina, and Sudan, mass killings in Uganda and the Congo, the cultural revolution in China and great famine in Soviet Ukraine, political murders in Argentina and Chile – these are just some examples of organized bloodsheds in different periods of the twentieth century. Philosophers and sociologists have suggested that genocide might be considered a result of normal modernization processes (Bauman, 1989). Acknowledging the universality of this extreme social problem, some social psychologists have undertaken efforts to explain the processes leading to genocide and mass killings (Newman & Erber, 2002; Staub, 1989; see also Golec de Zavala & Adler, 2010). Yet, overall, social-psychological research and writing on this issue has been rather scarce.

The term 'genocide', first coined by the Polish-Jewish lawyer Raphael Lemkin (1944), is defined by the UN Convention on the Prevention and Punishment of the Crime of Genocide from 1948 as 'acts committed with intent to destroy, in whole or in part, a national, ethnical, racial or religious group'. However, there has been a lot of political debate and controversy about the definition of specific events as genocide – in part due to the difficulty in proving 'intent'. Therefore, many psychologists use broader terms such as 'genocidal mass murder' (Chirot & McCauley, 2006) in order to include events that are not officially acknowledged as genocide.

Psychological and historical scholarship on genocide and mass killings has moved away from a pathologizing view on the perpetrators that had focused on psychological dissociation, pathological personality traits, or early childhood problems as root causes of genocidal acts (e.g. the 'authoritarian personality' concept proposed by Adorno et al., 1950; Lifton, 1986; see also Browning, 2002). Instead, the main focus has shifted towards the analysis of underlying, basic human – psychological and social – processes. This shift has occurred through interdisciplinary cross-fertilization, with psychologists, philosophers and historians influencing each other and responding to events of the time. In particular, Eichmann's trial in Jerusalem in 1961 gave rise to Hannah Arendt's influential book on 'the banality of evil' (published in 1963). It also inspired, to some extent, psychologist Stanley Milgram's famous experiments on obedience (first published in 1963 and further elaborated in Milgram, 1974). With their distinct disciplinary approaches, both scholars responded to the findings of the trial, suggesting that ordinary psychological and organizational processes may have been more important than previously assumed (Arendt, 1963; Milgram, 1974). However, Reicher and Haslam (this volume) discuss that Milgram's studies showed great variability in obedience across different situations. Milgram's work later greatly influenced the historian Christopher Browning (1992), who further highlighted the role of basic social-psychological processes such as obedience to authority and peer pressure that facilitated genocidal acts. In response to Browning's assertion, Goldhagen (1996) wrote his controversial book *Hitler's Willing Executioners*.

This book explicitly disregarded the social-psychological explanation of genocide and stressed the influence of cultural beliefs and historical anti-Semitism, allegedly specific to the German context. Nevertheless, these interdisciplinary debates illustrate the increasing importance of applying social-psychological knowledge to understand and explain genocide and mass killing.

In this chapter, we discuss the social-psychological processes that contribute to genocide and allow ordinary human beings to become perpetrators and passive bystanders of mass killings, as well as psychological processes that inhibit resistance among victims. We discuss the misconceptions that exist in the literature regarding the stability of the social roles in genocide. We argue that in times of genocide and mass killing, social-psychological transformations occur that enable these atrocities. This includes the transformation of stereotypes of the victim groups in early and later stages of genocide; moral transformations among perpetrators and bystanders; and motivational transformations among victims, bystanders and perpetrators. We conclude with a discussion of constructive processes that can counteract these destructive transformations and are important for interventions and the prevention of genocide.

The perpetrator–victim–bystander triangle

Raul Hilberg's book on the Holocaust (1993) has shaped the stereotypical triangle of social roles in the genocide literature: perpetrators, victims and bystanders. At the same time, for many researchers this typology became too narrow. For example, some genocide scholars stressed differences between *internal bystanders* – members of the perpetrating group who did not act against the crimes – and *external bystanders*, members of other national groups who did not intervene to prevent the actions of the perpetrating nation (Staub, 1997). Furthermore, *instigators* of genocide (such as Adolf Hitler, Joseph Stalin or Pol-Pot) can be differentiated from the *followers* who obeyed their orders to kill outgroup members (e.g. SS officers, NKVD agents or Khmer Rouge members; Mandel, 2002; Staub, 2002). Distinctions have even been drawn between victims of genocide. For example, while some victim groups formed armed resistance (Tec, 1993), others sought survival by joining the perpetrators as members of the Judenräte in ghettoes and concentration camps (Trunk, 1972), the ghetto police (Perechodnik, 1996), or even secret services (Haska, 2008).

Similarly, Oliner and Oliner (1988) distinguish resistance fighters who rescued Jews during the Holocaust from those who did not engage in rescuing acts. Complicating things even further, historical research reveals several cases of non-Jewish resistance fighters involved in killings of Jews during the Holocaust, for example the execution of Jews by the Opatów section of the Polish underground Home Army (Skibińska & Libionka, 2008), or killings of Jews in the Haberbusch-Schiele breweries during the Warsaw Uprising by Polish resistance fighters (Cichy, 1994). In all these cases, members of victimized, Nazi-occupied nations acted as perpetrators against other victim groups. Another example of the complexity of social roles in genocide comes from the region of the Naliboki forest in Belarus, portrayed in a widely read historical book (Tec, 1993) and popular film (*Defiance*). Here, the local Jewish partisan unit that consisted mainly of former ghetto-survivors fought as part of the Soviet underground and raided Belorussian and Polish villages, searching for food to supply Jewish survivors in the forest (Tec, 1993). The perceived need for self-defence against such raids led the formerly anti-fascist local branch of the Polish Home Army to collaborate with the Nazi police in killings of hidden Jews (Głuchowski & Kowalski, 2009; Grossman, 1988). In response, Soviet anti-fascist partisans, including Jewish survivors, took part in the killings of Polish civilians in some villages of this region (Perelman, 2003). This complex situation shows how the deprivation of basic needs (for food or personal security) in occupied territories placed some groups simultaneously into all possible roles of the perpetrator–victim–bystander triangle.

Although most of the scholarship on the complicated relations between these roles is based on the Holocaust, this complexity is also apparent in other genocides, such as the Rwandan genocide. For example, not all Hutus were perpetrators, and some moderate Hutus and those who did not participate in the killings or even protected Tutsis also became victims (Des Forges, 1999). Moreover, in the last phase of the genocide and in its immediate aftermath some Tutsis (mostly members of the Rwandan Patriotic Front) killed Hutus in self-defence or revenge (Prunier, 2009; Verwimp, 2003). Thus, social roles during the Rwandan genocide are not as clear-cut as the national narrative would like to present them, creating a challenge for the justice process and for official commemorations in Rwanda. In particular, the victimization of some Hutus during the genocide and in its immediate aftermath is silenced and does not receive public acknowledgement (Doná, 2011).

Because of the complexity of these extreme situations, we focus on the psychological processes – above all, motivations – and situational forces that *transform* people into taking up certain roles during genocide and mass killing. In particular, rather than merely discussing individual-level processes and individual differences, we pay attention to the interaction between societal (macro- and meso-level) conditions and individual (micro)-level processes that jointly give rise to destructive or maladaptive attitudes and behaviours. Thus, whenever we use the terms 'bystander', 'victim', or 'perpetrator', we do not imply stability of these social roles. Rather, we use these terms to describe the specific psychological processes that may drive human behaviour in certain roles in the situation of genocide or mass killings. In the following we address cognitive, moral and motivational changes that are responsible for the evolution of a conflict or of oppression into genocide (Staub, 1989).

Stereotype transformations in genocide and mass killing

In genocide and mass killings, the legal and socio-political situation of the victims gradually changes over time (e.g. Friedlander, 1997; Staub, 1989). The victims are first classified and distinguished from the rest of the society, stigmatized and discriminated in economic, legal and political life, and finally deprived of basic human rights (Stanton, 1998). Many victims suffer hunger, illness and forced migration. Mass killing and organized genocide are usually the last stages of this destructive process.

As the status of the victims in society changes in different stages of genocide, the stereotypes and dominant representations of the victims are also transformed. Numerous studies show that stereotypes are associated with specific emotions towards outgroup members (Alexander, Brewer & Livingston, 2005; Cuddy, Fiske & Glick, 2007; Mackie, Devos & Smith, 2000). For example, the BIAS (Behaviors from Intergroup Affect and Stereotypes) map model proposed by Cuddy, Fiske & Glick (2007) posits that the specific contents of stereotypes, emotions and discriminatory tendencies towards outgroup members coordinate in a functional, systematic and predictable way (for a more general discussion of this model see Cohrs & Kessler, this volume). The two main dimensions of stereotypes (warmth and competence) determine typical reactions to a given group, such that the warmth dimension is linked with active reactions (e.g. harassment versus help) and the competence dimension with passive reactions (e.g. exclusion versus association). For genocide, two specific forms of prejudice seem to be of greatest relevance – envious prejudice (against groups that are perceived as high in competence and low in warmth, an example from basic research being rich people: Glick, 2002), and dehumanizing prejudice (against groups that are perceived as low in competence and low in warmth, an example from basic research being beggars and homeless people: Harris & Fiske, 2009). As we will discuss below, these two forms of stereotypes appear in almost all genocides, albeit in different stages. They are often disseminated through propaganda and other forms of hate speech.

The main aim of propaganda during genocide is to engage the per-petrators' society in active support for genocidal policies and to further reduce potential helping-behaviour among bystanders that could limit the cruel effectiveness of genocide. In order to achieve these goals, specific stereotypes are used in propaganda against the targeted group.

Stereotypes in early stages of genocide

The goal of gaining support for destructive policies is particularly impor-tant during the early stage of the genocidal process. Peter Glick (2002, 2005) has suggested that envious prejudice is the basic ideology underlying scapegoating, which occurs when outgroups that are seen as powerful and influential are blamed for societal problems. When people are faced with serious political and economic deprivation, their basic psychological needs are frustrated (Staub, 1989). Under these conditions, ideologies gain popu-larity that depict the targeted outgroup as highly competent and strong (high competence), and as harbouring negative intentions towards the ingroup (low warmth). These ideologies serve as a naïve explanation of the ingroup's misfortunes and externalize blame and responsibility. The instigators of genocide use this logic to legitimize their power and mobilize the ingroup against the stereotyped outgroup (Glick, 2002). For example, in the last years of the Ottoman Empire during the First World War, Turks accused Armenians of collaborating with their enemy, the Russian Empire. The stereotype of Armenians as strong, cunning and dangerous collabora-tors of Russia was widespread in the Ottoman Empire before and during the genocide of Armenians (Bloxham, 2005). In Rwanda, the radio propa-gated the stereotype of Tutsis as external enemies exploiting the country (Rothbart & Bartlett, 2008). In the early stages of the Holocaust, Jews were depicted in Nazi propaganda as controlling the world markets, global politics and local German economy (see Figures 11.1 and 11.2).

Some key personalities in German politics and economy (such as Walther Rathenau, a German Jew, foreign minister of the Weimar Republic and the president of the large company AEG) were repeatedly used in Nazi propa-ganda as examples of Jewish power (Friedlander, 1997). Content analyses of 'The protocols of the elders of Zion' (an anti-Semitic propaganda pam-phlet) and the fascist Italian magazine *La Difesa della Razza* (The Defense of the Race) show that the prevalent image of Jews linked high com-petence and low warmth (Durante, Volpato & Fiske, 2010; Volpato & Durante, 2009). Conspiracy theories depicting Jews as highly powerful and conspiring against the ingroup also appeared in times of political mobi-lization and economic depression in other parts of the world (Bilewicz & Krzemiński, 2010; Kofta & Sedek, 2005). Finally, because victimized groups

Figure 11.1 Cover of the anti-Semitic book *The Eternal Jew*, published in 1937 in Munich.

Source: Calvin German Propaganda Archive.

Figure 11.2 Propaganda picture from Ernst Hiemer's *Der Giftpilz* – an educational Nazi publication from Nuremberg, 1938.

Source: Calvin German Propaganda Archive.

are perceived as powerful, they are often blamed by the perpetrators for their own fate – this was true both in Nazi Germany and in the Ottoman Empire (Melson, 2002).

Another important component of the stereotypes of targeted groups in the early stage of genocide is an essentialist view of social groups. Several lines of psychological research show that essentialist thinking leads to increased stereotyping and prejudice (e.g. Keller, 2005; Prentice & Miller, 2007). This essentialist view is based on the perception of the ingroup as a coherent entity, rooted in common biological essence – a link of blood rather than common citizenship (Keller, 2005). This belief allows singling out the victims of genocide even if they are assimilated and integrated in the society, a process referred to as 'genocidal classification' (Stanton, 1998). Ziya Gökalp, the founding father of Turkish nationalism, wrote that 'Greeks, Armenians who lived in Turkey would remain a foreign body in the national Turkish state' (Melson, 2004, p. 77). Only a few years later, the genocide of Armenians occurred in the country, and a few decades later Greeks became victims of the Istanbul Pogrom that resulted in the nearly total disappearance of these two ethnic groups from Turkish society.

Stereotypes in later stages of genocide

In the later stages of genocide, the other part of the 'BIAS map' (Cuddy, Fiske & Glick, 2007) that focuses on perceptions of both low competence and low warmth best describes the dominant attitude towards the victim group. When the victims are spatially segregated and economically deprived, the main aim of the perpetrators is to reduce the potential for possible intervention and rescue by internal and external bystanders (Staub, 1997). To achieve this goal, the Nazis used a different image of Jews in their propaganda for occupied territories in the 1940s (Grabowski, 2009; Herf, 2006). As the genocide advanced, Jews were not any more depicted as strong and cunning villains. Instead, dehumanizing images of Jews as vermin, rats and lice were disseminated (see Figures 11.3 and 11.4). Similarly, Tutsis were often referred to as *inyenzi* (cockroaches) and sometimes also as rats or snakes during the Rwandan genocide (Straus, 2006).

During this phase, victims of genocide are clearly depicted as cold and incompetent. According to the stereotype content model, this depiction elicits our disgust and contempt, which is further amplified by dehumanizing images of animals that are associated with filth and known as transmitters of infectious diseases. Disgust motivates distancing, rejecting, and expelling reactions (Roseman, Wiest & Swartz, 1994) and reduces the potential for helping and empathizing (Piliavin, Rodin & Piliavin, 1969).

Figure 11.3   A propaganda poster used in Nazi-occupied Poland stating: 'Jews-lice-typhus'.
Source: The National Library of Poland – Biblioteka Narodowa.

Recent neuroscientific research provides insight into the underlying mechanism of these stereotypes (Harris & Fiske, 2009). The activation of the medial prefrontal cortex (mPFC) is related to our ability to understand mental states of others (Singer, 2006). Activation of this part of our brains is also related to person perception rather than object perception. Lasana Harris and Susan Fiske (2009) demonstrated that when participants viewed pictures of members of social groups that are stereotyped as low in warmth and competence (such as homeless people, drug addicts), their medial prefrontal cortex was less activated than when they viewed pictures of members of social groups stereotyped differently (e.g. middle-class: high on competence and warmth; older people: low on competence but high on warmth; or rich people: high on competence but rather low on warmth). Viewing pictures of groups that are perceived as cold and incompetent activated participants' amygdala and insula – regions responsible for processing information about disgust and regulating avoidant behaviour (Calder et al., 2007). In other words, information about dehumanized outgroups is processed in different brain regions than is information about other human beings.

Comparing victims of genocide to animals, as in the examples of Nazi or Hutu propaganda, is a clear case of dehumanization. Experimental

Figure 11.4   A propaganda poster used in Nazi-occupied Poland stating: 'Jews return with Bolshevism'.
Source: Courtesy of the Jewish Historical Institute, Warsaw, Poland.

social-psychological research provides further insight into the processes of dehumanization. People deny animals emotions and mental states that are typical of and unique for humans (Bilewicz, Imhoff & Drogosz, 2011). The denial of 'uniquely human' emotions, known as infrahumanization (Leyens et al., 2001), is often used as a strategy to distance oneself from the victims. Castano and Giner-Sorolla (2006) showed that participants who learn that their group committed crime against outgroup members were less likely to recognize 'uniquely human' emotions of the victims. The more animalistic comparisons that are presented, the less likely the helping reaction among bystanders becomes, and the easier it is for people to participate in harm-doing against other human beings (Bandura, 1999; Opotow, 2001; Staub, 1989).

Moral transformations in genocide among perpetrators and bystanders

The transformation of outgroup stereotypes to dehumanized images has an important function for moral transformation in genocide and mass killing. Dehumanization of victims is one of the mechanisms that enables human beings to morally disengage from atrocities (Bandura, 1999; Stanton, 1998). Specifically, moral disengagement allows bystanders and members of the perpetrator group to maintain a positive image of themselves and of their group that is consistent with their self-concept as moral human beings (Bandura, 1999). Apart from dehumanization, social psychologist Albert Bandura describes several other mechanisms of moral disengagement that also all seem to apply to genocide. (1) *Moral justification of atrocities*, for example, occurred among Hutu perpetrators who were convinced that they had to kill Tutsis so that Hutus would not be extinguished themselves (Mironko, 2006; Straus, 2006). (2) *Sanitizing or euphemizing language* includes, for example, the use of the word 'Final solution' instead of mass murder of Jews in gas chambers during the Holocaust (Staub, 1989). (3) *Advantageous comparisons* might have been involved when alleged Jewish attempts to control the world were contrasted with the harm committed against Jews in a limited geographic region, which by comparison may have been seen as less severe (Herf, 2006). (4) *Displacement of responsibility* as well as *diffusion of responsibility* occurred when high-level Nazi perpetrators claimed that they had merely carried out orders (Arendt, 1963). (5) *Distortion of harmful consequences* of the ingroup's actions is apparent for example in the denial of the Armenian genocide by Turkish officials through minimization of the number of deaths and mislabelling of the massacres (Akçam, 2006). These social-psychological processes are not only supported by historical case studies across various genocides, but are also corroborated by anthropological work on the Cambodian genocide, describing the moral transformation of society from a 'gentle ethic' to a 'violent ethic' as well as individual moral transformations into a 'genocidal self' that was enabled through mechanisms of dehumanization, the use of euphemisms, moral restructuring, and denial of responsibility for one's actions (Hinton, 1996).

Importantly, these examples illustrate that the transformation of morality in genocide consists in the inclusion of destructive practices into pre-existing moral schemata and beliefs. To external observers of genocide, morality seems to be completely lacking, or at least radically transformed. However, perpetrators and bystanders of genocide often use mechanisms of moral disengagement in order to present harmful acts against others as consistent with (previous) moral beliefs, and as in fact moral.

Additionally, mechanisms of stereotyping and dehumanization as described earlier result in the exclusion of the victims from the realm of those to whom regular moral values are applied. Susan Opotow (2001) refers to this process as the *moral exclusion* of victims. Previous moral standards are maintained for ingroup members but not extended to dehumanized outgroup members. The scope of morality becomes narrower.

Moreover, in times of genocide, harmful actions against the dehumanized outgroup may become 'the right thing to do' (Staub, 2011, p. 172), perceived even as a pro-social act aimed at protecting the ingroup (Cohen, Montoya & Insko, 2006; Mironko, 2006; Monroe, 2008). The belief that the killing of outgroup members was moral because it would contribute to the well-being of the nation was expressed by perpetrators of the Armenian genocide (Akçam, 2006), the Cambodian genocide (Hinton, 1996), the Holocaust (Staub, 1989), the Rwandan genocide (Straus, 2006) and many others.

Motivational transformations in genocide

In order to better understand what enables human beings to participate in or passively witness violence, it is necessary to consider not only cognitive and moral transformations, but also the transformations of psychological motives that shape the attitudes and behaviour of perpetrators, bystanders and victims. Social psychology has proposed several theories about motivations underlying prejudice and intergroup conflicts (e.g. Duckitt & Sibley, 2009, Tajfel & Turner, 1979; see also Cohrs & Kessler, this volume). In the next section we discuss those that seem specific to genocide and mass killings.

Motivational transformation among perpetrators

The psychological process of becoming a perpetrator is usually gradual and does not occur as an unexpected eruption of cruelty. Ervin Staub (2011), summarizing his previous work, writes in his recent book that 'genocide and mass killing are, perhaps without exception, the outcome of an evolution of progressive increase in hostility and violence' (p. 6). He refers to this evolution as 'steps along the continuum on destruction' – applicable to genocides in Rwanda, Ottoman Empire, the Holocaust and other contexts (Staub, 1989, 2002).

In order to explain what pushes entire groups and nations along this continuum, psychologists have examined several motivating factors (Frey & Rez, 2002; Staub, 2002). Roy Baumeister (1997, 2002; Baumeister & Vohs, 2004) focused on stable, personality-based motivations and distinguished four root causes of mass violence: *instrumentality* (violence as means to an end), *egotism* (violence in response to self-esteem threats), *idealism* (a misguided effort to achieve a virtuous society) and *sadism* (violence as a source of pleasure). These four motives are apparent in biographies of instigators of genocides and mass murders (e.g. Hitler and Eichmann in Nazi Germany, Pol-Pot in Cambodia, Stalin in Soviet Russia), revealing ideologies that treated human life as a tool to achieve abstract utopian (or from an outside point of view rather: dystopian) societies (Arendt, 1963; Bullock, 1993). Several of these leaders could be described as narcissistic, having highly elevated but unstable self-esteem (Baumeister, 2002). It has been recently suggested that narcissism can also occur on the collective level, among ordinary citizens. People who perceive their ingroup in a highly positive manner, but whose collective self-esteem is vulnerable and unstable are most prone to prejudice. They also perceive outgroup members as a threat to their idealized picture of the ingroup (Golec de Zavala et al., 2009; see also Golec de Zavala & Schatz, this volume).

While sadism can be considered a rather stable personality trait, the other three motivations proposed by Baumeister and colleagues might be affected by situational forces: egotism, idealism and instrumentality arise in certain developmental and cultural contexts (Adorno et al., 1950). In other words, individual-level motives interact with situational factors and specific societal conditions that can reinforce these motives and transform their outcomes to a destructive level. One such genocide-catalyzing condition is collective and individual *loss of control*.

Most genocides occurred in societies that had faced a tremendous loss of control in many important aspects of social and individual lives. Genocide of Armenians took place during the First World War, when the Ottoman Empire was declining and the future fate of the Turkish nation was unclear. The Nazi Holocaust occurred during deep economic crisis, after a lost war as well as humiliation through the treaty of Versailles (Friedlander, 1997). The situation of war stressed the sense of uncontrollability on the most basic, existential level – the control over one's own life and the lives of close ones. In an analysis of all genocides that occurred since 1955, Harff (2003) describes political upheaval (including internal war and regime collapse) as a 'necessary condition' for genocide. Similarly, Staub (1989, 2011) identifies sudden political or economic deterioration and extreme social changes that create personal and collective uncertainty and perceived control loss as the starting points of mass violence.

Societal conditions that result in loss of control can give rise to psychological reactions that, in turn, negatively affect political outcomes and intergroup relations. People who feel they have lost control over their lives tend to prefer simple solutions over complex ones and delegate control to strong leaders (Frey & Rez, 2002). Research on group-control restoration shows that in all cases of control deprivation (by thinking about uncontrollable mortality, job loss, or breakdown of personal relationships) people are motivated to defend their ingroup's norms (Fritsche, Jonas & Fankhänel, 2008). Moreover, thoughts about one's (uncontrollable) mortality make people think in more exclusive ways about the ingroup and be more vigilant against potential traitors within the ingroup (Castano, 2004). In sum, situational forces might elevate idealism, (collective) egotism, sadism and instrumentalism, gradually pushing entire nations into genocide as a perceived solution to its problems.

People in unstable societal circumstances are likely to be attracted to ideologies that offer a restoration of control. This was a common characteristic of the nationalistic ideologies promoted by perpetrators of genocides against the Armenians, Jews and Tutsis (Staub, 2002). In all these cases, genocidal ideology was most popular in societies where the situation deteriorated in a relatively short time. This might have given rise to the feeling of relative deprivation in comparison to other groups and compared with the ingroup's past situation. Relative deprivation – the perception of one's position as illegitimately worse than the position of others – is an important source of prejudice and discriminatory intentions (Fiske, 1998; Vanneman & Pettigrew, 1972). People who perceive their situation as deteriorating also tend to perceive injustice against their ingroup, and as a result express higher levels of prejudice towards immigrants (Pettigrew et al., 2008). Similarly, instigators of genocide often instrumentalize perceptions of the group's past – imagined or real – victimization (Mamdani, 2001; Paxton, 2004) and resulting humiliation (Lindner, 2009) in order to motivate followers to participate in violence against the perceived enemies. Cultural conceptions of revenge, as discussed in anthropological work in the context of the Cambodian genocide (Hinton, 2002b), can then contribute to disproportionate revenge and escalate the impact of these beliefs.

The instigators of genocidal policies offer actions that seemingly regain control and change the power structure in the society, thereby ostensibly improving the situation of the group. If leaders are able to provide economic successes for the ingroup (as was Hitler: Bullock, 1993), their followers are likely to attribute this improved situation to the destructive policies implemented against ethnic minorities and political enemies. This reinforces support for and participation in the destructive processes of genocide.

Motivational transformation among bystanders

The social context in which mass killings are perpetrated creates different kinds of *bystanders*, defined by Staub (2011) as 'witnesses who are in a position to know what is happening and to take action' (p. 195). There are internal bystanders – individuals who are members of the society that is perpetrating genocide but who themselves are neither perpetrators nor targeted. There are also external bystanders, such as other nations. Passive bystanders who do not intervene are differentiated from active bystanders who attempt to intervene (Staub, 1989, 2002). In the case of the Rwandan genocide, the Twa, a historically marginalized ethnic group, mostly remained passive during the killing of Tutsis by Hutu (Gourevitch, 1998). They were internal passive bystanders. Hutus who did not participate in the genocide and paid the génocidaires so that they would not be forced to participate in the killings (Straus, 2006) were also internal passive bystanders; as were many churches in the country that remained passive during the genocide, refusing to shelter Tutsi victims (Prunier, 1995). The international community failed to intervene in most genocides, thereby becoming external bystanders. The UN personnel could be considered an external passive bystander, a bystander by formal appointment (Vetlesen, 2000). Finally, all spectators passively watching the crimes broadcasted worldwide bear responsibility for not forcing their governments to intervene (Vetlesen, 2000), and can therefore be considered external passive bystanders.

In explaining the psychological processes that transform people into passive bystanders, social-psychological theories have a lot to offer. The literature suggests that non-intervention is a general human reaction to a crime, since intervening may be costly and difficult. Latané and Darley (1970) describe a sequence of decisions that precede any prosocial intervention in an emergency. People need to be present at the place of a crime, define the event as an emergency, assume their responsibility and decide what can be done. However, this process is interrupted by *social influence, audience inhibition* and *diffusion of responsibility*.

The strongest form of social influence during genocide is the threat of direct and severe punishment for intervening on behalf of the victims. For example, in some Nazi-occupied territories in Europe, helping Jews was punished with the death penalty. Similarly, Muslims who protected Armenians during the Armenian genocide were executed (Akçam, 2006). Because of these severe and realistic threats, passive bystandership becomes a likely, dominant response. In turn, when people witness abuse and killings on a daily basis, rationalization of these acts and habituation to violence are likely to occur (Staub, 1989). Moreover, diffusion of responsibility and perceived lack of agency to intervene will inhibit taking action (Monroe, 2008). Thereby, passive bystandership is reinforced in a vicious circle.

Helping is even less probable if the suffering victim is perceived as dissimilar (Crosby, Bromley & Saxe, 1980). During genocide, conditions related to the persecution – such as starvation and expropriation leading to extreme poverty, spatial segregation, identifying clothing or other symbols

(Stanton, 1998) – build walls of difference between victims and bystanders. The perpetrators create a situation in which even the physical appearance distinguishes victims from bystanders and the differences between 'us' and 'them' are intentionally enhanced (Piliavin, Rodin & Piliavin, 1969).

Additionally, the poor economic conditions often experienced by ordinary citizens during genocide may motivate bystanders to treat victims as a source of material wealth. For example, Nazi rulers of occupied Europe tried to reinforce instrumental motivations of bystander nations to participate in violence (Baumeister, 2002). They created a situation in which thousands of Ukrainians, Poles, Greeks and Lithuanians were able to financially exploit Jewish genocide victims (Gross, 2012).

Motivational transformation among victims

Finally, an important question that has often been asked – at times bearing the sense of victim-blaming – is why victims did not show more resistance during genocide. In our view, one of the key factors underlying the motivational transformation of human beings into obedient victims is *positivity bias*. The literature on reasoning shows that people often ignore negative information (Lewicka, Czapiński & Peeters, 1992). Self-serving mechanisms such as unrealistic optimism – a generalized belief about one's positive fate (Helweg-Larsen & Shepperd, 2001) – are adaptive in times of peace and stability. However, they may contribute to passivity among bystanders and victims in times of conflict and violence.

Hannah Arendt, in her controversial book on the Eichmann trial (Arendt, 1963), suggested that without the collaboration of victims – embodied in the figures of Judenrat officers in the ghettoes – the scale of Nazi crimes could have been reduced. While this point is not supported by evidence collected by historians and sociologists (Bauman, 1989; Trunk, 1972), these scholars all stress the importance of the obedience and collaboration of the victims' groups in galvanizing the potential of revolts or armed struggle. Analyzing several such cases, sociologist Zygmunt Bauman coined the metaphor of the 'save what you can' game. Many group members sought individual survival strategies instead of collective action (in order to understand preconditions necessary for collective action, refer to van Stekelenburg & Klandermans, this volume). For example, some tried to change their official racial status (especially those with mixed ethnic background, referred to as 'passing' in many other contexts) or rejected group solidarity to obtain personal or group privileges (Bauman, 1989). In order to facilitate the killing process, perpetrators often cruelly appealed to unrealistic optimism in victims and suggested alleged individual survival strategies (such as collaboration, attempts to corrupt officials, or 'resettlement' to the East). However, in the end these were usually unsuccessful for the victims and did not guarantee their survival.

A tragic example of the belief in individual rescue strategies is the case of the ghetto policeman Calek Perechodnik, who obeyed the Nazis' orders, trusting that his and his family's lives would be saved. He even went so far as to assist the deportation of his wife and daughter from the Otwock ghetto to the Treblinka death camp. At all stages of his conformity with the perpetrators, Perechodnik stressed his positive illusions about the chances for his and his relatives' survival as the motivation that biased his thinking (Perechodnik, 1996). Another such example is the history of Hotel Polski. This Nazi-organized shelter in Warsaw was established after the liquidation of the Warsaw ghetto for Jews who could afford to buy foreign affidavits or passports, ostensibly to save their life in occupied Europe. Most people who stayed there were later killed in the camps of Auschwitz, Bergen-Belsen and the Pawiak Prison, after giving all their property to the perpetrators. Authors writing about this history emphasize that all people involved in the Hotel Polski affair – victims as well as agents organizing it – were motivated by positivity illusions, trusting that this strategy would end successfully for them (Haska, 2008). Finally, in a comparative analysis of the ghettoes in Łódź and Warsaw, Tiedens (1997) found that the inhabitants of the Warsaw Ghetto – where a large uprising took place – had less hope for the future and were less optimistic than the residents of the Łódź Ghetto, where no such revolt was organized.

Importantly, resistance to the perpetrators' destructive plans cannot be understood without considering the extreme threat and danger of the situation. The victims' potential to take action in times of genocide was limited by the heavy risks involved. Many testimonies from the Holocaust describe how risky it was to leave the ghetto and move to the 'Aryan side'. The danger was not only due to the German police (Gestapo) or SS, but also because of potential blackmailers among members of the occupied nations. Basic psychological research on decision-making sheds some light on psychological processes among victims of genocide under these conditions. Of particular importance is the finding that people weigh costs more heavily than gains in making risky decisions (Kahneman & Tversky, 1979). By envisioning the dangers of their potential future fate elsewhere, victims during the Holocaust often decided to stay in the environment they already knew and therefore perceived – unrealistically – as more secure (Paulsson, 2003).

Yet, there were important resistance movements during the Holocaust by those who believed in collective rather than individual solutions to victimization (Grossman, 1988). Social-psychological research on collective action shows that people are motivated to act collectively against the enemy only if they perceive collective efficacy of their group and if they strongly identify with this group in a politicized way (van Zomeren, Postmes & Spears, 2008; see also van Stekelenburg & Klandermans, this volume). Accordingly, historical sources show that many Jewish resistance fighters during the Holocaust had previously been very active in socialist, Zionist or communist Jewish movements (Grossman, 1988). This political involvement in large numbers likely strengthened perceptions of collective efficacy, even in such extreme circumstances.

Constructive transformations that contribute to intervention and genocide prevention

Social-psychological theories can help us explain not only the destructive processes contributing to genocide and mass killing, but also constructive processes that can transform the situation and contribute to the prevention of such violence. Even the classical studies of obedience (Milgram, 1974) and conformity (Asch, 1956), that were often used to explain the Holocaust, also tell an equally interesting story about disobedience and nonconformity that can be observed in times of genocide (Hodges & Geyer, 2006; see also Reicher & Haslam, this volume). Thus, social psychologists can address the potentially positive role of the *active* bystander – an important key to the prevention of genocide (Staub, 1989, 2002, 2011). Specifically, social-psychological theories can illuminate which factors may facilitate action on behalf of the victims of genocide. Based on what we know to date, these involve, above all, processes of social (re-)categorization and moral inclusion that counteract moral, motivational and cognitive transformations in times of genocide.

A key factor that motivates bystanders to become active on behalf of victims during genocide is the inclusion of victims in a shared identity. Levine et al. (2005) show in experimental studies conducted in ordinary contexts that inducing a common identity among bystanders and victims significantly increases the probability of helping. In the context of the Holocaust, Reicher et al. (2006) demonstrated through archival research that a common identity between Christian and Jewish Bulgarians (stressing nationality and shared culture rather than religion and ethnicity) was invoked to mobilize Bulgarians against the deportation of Jews. However, there are limitations of the positive effect of commonality on helping. Victims who are able to stress a common identity shared with the bystanders (e.g. being a member of the same nation), rather than a dual identity (e.g. being a member of the nation *and* the ethnic group), are more appealing to potential helpers and receive greater support from the majority group (Dovidio et al., 2009). This is in line with the historical finding that Jews who survived the Holocaust hiding on the 'Aryan side' were mostly assimilated people who were able to appeal to a common Polish, Hungarian or Czech identity (Paulsson, 2003).

One form of perceived commonality that may also increase helping in times of genocide is shared fate or perceived similarities of experiences. This is often mentioned by heroic helpers during the Holocaust. For example, a man from Parczew in Poland, whose family was active in sheltering Jews during the Holocaust, expressed this idea: 'My father was a prisoner of war and they were also discriminated, so the brotherhood of misery linked him with them [Jews]. (...) People who are repressed just stick to each other' (Dąbrowska, 2008). These and similar accounts reflect inclusive victim beliefs (Vollhardt, 2009a), which have been described as one of the underlying motivations of 'altruism born of suffering' that occurs even in extreme situations of collective violence (Vollhardt, 2009b; see also Staub & Vollhardt, 2008; Vollhardt & Staub, 2011).

Another important factor that facilitates intergroup helping is the ability to take the perspective of an outgroup member (Davis & Maitner, 2009). Research shows that participants motivated to take the perspective of a suffering victim have a greater affective response to observing a victim experiencing pain (Lamm, Batson & Decety, 2007). However, the effects of perspective-taking on the willingness to help outgroup members are limited by power relations between groups. People who perceive their own group as more powerful are often not motivated to help, even if they are forced to take the perspective of outgroup members (Bilewicz, 2009). The extreme status differences in the context of genocide, where victims are derogated and deprived of all their property as well as their civil rights, might therefore constrain the willingness to take the perspective of the suffering neighbours.

When the process of negative stereotyping of the victim group is too far evolved to persuade majority group members that the minority is part of a common ingroup, it may be more effective to appeal to (narrowly defined, national) ingroup interests. For example, one might emphasize the harm that will occur to the ingroup by persecuting a minority (Reicher et al., 2006), or material costs that occur by engaging in violent conflict (see, for example, the US website costsofwar.org: Costs of War, n.d.).

In sum, research aimed at identifying personality characteristics responsible for actions of heroic helpers during the Holocaust concluded with the statement that 'they were and are "ordinary" people' (Oliner & Oliner, 1988, p. 260). In other words, it was not any special religious beliefs, personality traits, political attitudes or professions that led to heroic acts of rescuing during genocide, but rather situational forces and the values and norms learned from parents, friends and colleagues that enabled those people to help the victims of genocide. Thus, every human being has the potential to be transformed not only into a perpetrator or a passive bystander, but also into a helper – even if those who actually risk their life during genocide to help the victims are only a small proportion of the population.

Constructive processes (such as altruism born of suffering and inclusive victim beliefs: Staub & Vollhardt, 2008; Vollhardt, 2009a, 2009b) can transform the very same processes that feed into support for violence (such as past victimization: Mamdani, 2001; Paxton, 2004), into pro-social attitudes and behaviours towards outgroup victims. Similarly, processes of categorization can be used to exclude or include victims from the moral realm, resulting either in further dehumanization or in pro-social behaviour towards outgroup members (Dovidio et al., 2009). Therefore, more research on these constructive processes is needed, as well as on parallel processes that could potentially transform perpetrators – an even more understudied topic.

Conclusion

To summarize, several social-psychological theories can be applied to understand the extreme social problem of genocide and mass killing. Social-psychological theories also provide insight into constructive processes that may potentially counteract the escalation of violence. However, it is necessary to realize the limitations of conventional social-psychological research in applications to such extreme and complex societal processes. In order to better understand processes of mass violence and genocide, we need to integrate social-psychological theories with work on these topics in history (e.g. Bloxham, 2005; Herf, 2006), sociology (e.g. Bauman, 1989), political science (e.g. Harff, 2003; Straus, 2006) and anthropology (e.g. Hinton, 2002a, b), as we have attempted to do in this chapter. It is also necessary for social psychologists studying genocide and mass violence to expand our methodological toolbox and include methods and materials that are underutilized in mainstream social psychology, such as interviews, oral history, written testimonies and other archival data. In this way, social psychologists can enrich their theorizing, and perform a 'reality check' of the processes we know about – from times of relative stability and peace – to test which of them apply to more extreme situations.

Social-psychological scholarship on genocide requires great attention to the societal context and to situational factors that interact with individual motives and other psychological processes. The reactions we observe in times of extreme violence are, at least in part, the result of responses to social cues that people receive (such as instability and lack of control over important domains of life, propaganda aimed at creating perceptions of threat, as well as dehumanizing images of outgroup members). Only by considering both the social context and all possible individual reactions to it can we understand when and how violence evolves. As scholars writing on these topics have demonstrated, and as we have described in this chapter, genocide and mass violence occurs through gradual transformation of individuals and of societal conditions (Stanton, 1998; Staub, 1989; Zimbardo, 2007). Therefore, to increase our knowledge on prevention, it is important to examine the early stages that can result in genocide, and how these processes can be effectively counteracted. This requires a greater focus not only on the destructive processes, but also on the – understudied – positive, constructive processes that occur as well in the context of mass violence and its aftermath.

Last but not least, we would like to emphasize that identifying the ordinary responses people often have in reaction to societal and other situational factors does not mean that these processes are inevitable. As we have shown throughout this chapter, in every given situation there are alternative choices people can make. People as well as groups respond in different ways – constructively or destructively – to the same situation. Future social psychological research can contribute to our understanding of the individual-level and situational factors that interact with contexts that are characterized by societal instability and confrontations with others' suffering, as well as with dehumanized outgroups. Through this knowledge we can learn how to strengthen constructive processes that may counteract some of these most destructive and devastating moments of humanity.

Practical task for readers

Choose a current ethnic conflict that is covered in mass media (TV, Internet sources, newspaper articles, radio broadcasts). Examine political speeches, blogs and images from a conflict region. Concentrate on images used in political propaganda, in particular the stereotypes of groups that are used. Evaluate potential threats to control loss and identity threats of groups participating in the conflict. For each category listed in the response sheet below, try to assess whether there is no risk, moderate risk, or high risk for destructive transformation of the conflict into genocidal processes leading to the justification of (mass) violence against certain social groups (using Table 11.1). Based on your observations, try to assess the overall potential for genocide in this given conflict.

Continued

Table 11.1   Response sheet for the practical task

RISK FACTORS	YOUR OBSERVATIONS OF THE CONFLICT	LEVEL OF RISK (CHECK ONE)
Sources of shared humiliation- threats to ingroup image and identity?		• No risk • Moderate risk • High risk
Societal conditions that feed into subjective loss of control in everyday life?		• No risk • Moderate risk • High risk
Stereotypes of minority groups in propaganda – envious or dehumanizing depictions?		• No risk • Moderate risk • High risk
Behaviour of bystanders (institutions, other nations and citizens) – active? passive? harming?		• No risk • Moderate risk • High risk

Discuss your findings with others and try to compare your description with what was observed for other parts of the world. Together, try to develop a map of 'genocidal risk' in the current world.

Suggested readings

To learn more about issues discussed in this chapter read Bauman (1989), Newman and Erber (2002), Oliner and Oliner (1988) and Staub (1989).

References

Adorno, T., Frenkel-Brunswick, E., Levenson, D. & Sanford, R. (1950). *The Authoritarian Personality*. New York: Harper & Row.
Akçam, T. (2006). *A Shameful Act. The Armenian Genocide and the Question of Turkish Responsibility*. New York: Holt.

Alexander, M., Brewer, M. & Livingston, R. (2005). Putting stereotype content in context: image theory and interethnic stereotypes. *Personality and Social Psychology Bulletin*, 31, 781–794.

Améry, J. (1998). *At the Mind's Limits. Contemplations by a Survivor on Auschwitz and its Realities*. Bloomington: Indiana University Press.

Arendt, H. (1963). *Eichmann in Jerusalem: A Report on the Banality of Evil.* New York: Viking.

Asch, S. E. *(1956)*. Studies of independence and submission to group pressure: I. A minority of one against a unanimous majority. *Psychological Monographs*, 70, 417.

Bandura, A. (1999). Moral disengagement in the perpetration of inhumanities. *Personality and Social Psychology Review*, 3, 193–209.

Bauman, Z. (1989) *Modernity and the Holocaust*. Cambridge: Polity.

Baumeister, R. (1997). *Evil: Inside Human Violence and Cruelty*. New York: Holt.

Baumeister, R. (2002). The Holocaust and the four roots of evil. In L. Newman & R. Erber (eds.), *Understanding Genocide: The Social Psychology of the Holocaust* (pp. 241–258). New York: Oxford University Press.

Baumeister, R. & Vohs, K. (2004). Four roots of evil. In A. G. Miller (ed.), *The Social Psychology of Good and Evil: Understanding Our Capacity for Kindness and Cruelty* (pp. 85–101). New York: Guilford Press.

Bilewicz, M. (2009). Perspective taking and intergroup helping intentions: The moderating role of power relations. *Journal of Applied Social Psychology*, 39, 2779–2786.

Bilewicz, M., Imhoff, R. & Drogosz, M. (2011). The humanity of what we eat. Conceptions of human uniqueness among vegetarians and omnivores. *European Journal of Social Psychology*, 41, 201–209.

Bilewicz, M. & Krzemiński, I. (2010). Anti-Semitism in Poland and Ukraine: The belief in Jewish control as a mechanism of scapegoating. *International Journal of Conflict and Violence*, 4, 234–243.

Bloxham, D. (2005). *The Great Game of Genocide: Imperialism, Nationalism, and the Destruction of the Ottoman Armenians*. Oxford: Oxford University Press.

Browning, C. (1992). *Ordinary Men: Reserve Police Battalion 101 and the Final Solution in Poland*. New York: Harper Collins.

Browning, C. (2002). Introduction. In L. S. Newman & R. Erber (eds.), *Understanding Genocide: The Social Psychology of the Holocaust* (pp. 3–7). New York: Oxford University Press.

Bullock, A. (1993). *Hitler and Stalin: Parallel Lives*. New York: Vintage Books.

Calder, A., Beaver, J., Davis, M., van Ditzhuijzen, J., Keane, J. & Lawrence, A. (2007). Disgust sensitivity predicts the insula and pallidal response to pictures of disgusting foods. *European Journal of Neuroscience*, 25, 3422–3428.

Castano, E. (2004). In case of death, cling to the ingroup. *European Journal of Social Psychology*, 34, 375–384.

Castano, E. & Giner-Sorolla, R. (2006). Not quite human: Infrahumanization in response to collective responsibility for intergroup killing. *Journal of Personality and Social Psychology*, 90, 804–818.

Chirot, D. & McCauley, C. (2006). *Why Not Kill Them All? The Logic and Prevention of Mass Political Murder*. Princeton, NJ: Princeton University Press.

Cichy, M. (1994). Polacy – Żydzi: czarne karty Powstania. *Gazeta Wyborcza*, p. 13.

Cohen, T., Montoya, R. & Insko, C. (2006). Group morality and intergroup relations: Cross-cultural and experimental evidence. *Personality and Social Psychology Bulletin*, 32, 1559–1572.

Costs of War. (n.d.). Available at http://costofwar.org (accessed 4 February 2012).

Crosby, F., Bromley, S. & Saxe, L. (1980). Recent unobtrusive studies of black and white discrimination and prejudice: A literature review. *Psychological Bulletin*, 87, 546–563.

Cuddy, A., Fiske, S. & Glick, P. (2007). The BIAS map: Behaviors from intergroup affect and stereotypes. *Journal of Personality and Social Psychology*, 92, 631–648.

Dąbrowska, A. (ed.). (2008). *Światła w ciemności. Sprawiedliwi wśród Narodów Świata. Relacje [Light in the Darkness. Righteous among the Nations in Relations]*. Lublin, Poland: Brama Grodzka/Teatr NN.

Davis, M. & Maitner, A. (2009). Perspective taking and intergroup helping. In S. Stürmer & M. Snyder (eds.), *The Psychology of Prosocial Behavior: Group Processes, Intergroup Relations, and Helping* (pp. 175–190). Oxford: Wiley-Blackwell.

Des Forges, A. (1999). *Leave None to Tell the Story: Genocide in Rwanda*. New York: Human Rights Watch.

Doná, G. (2011). Researching children in evolving socio-political contexts. In J. Pottier, L. Hammond & C. Cramer (eds.), *Caught in the Crossfire: Ethical and Methodological Challenges to Researching Violence in Africa* (pp. 39–59). Leiden, The Netherlands: Brill Publishers.

Dovidio, J., Gaertner, S., Shnabel, N., Saguy, T. & Johnson, J. D. (2009). Recategorization and prosocial behavior: Common identity and a dual identity. In S. Stürmer & M. Snyder (eds.), *The Psychology of Prosocial Behavior: Group Processes, Intergroup Relations, and Helping* (pp. 191–208). Oxford: Wiley-Blackwell.

Duckitt, J. & Sibley, C. (2009). A dual process motivational model of ideology, politics, and prejudice. *Psychological Inquiry*, 20, 98–109.

Durante, F., Volpato, C. & Fiske, S. (2010). Using the stereotype content model to examine group depictions in fascism: An archival approach. *European Journal of Social Psychology*, 40, 465–483.

Fiske, S. (1998). Stereotyping, prejudice, and discrimination. In D. Gilbert, S. Fiske & G. Lindzey (eds.), *The Handbook of Social Psychology* (vols. 1 and 2, 4th edition, pp. 357–411). New York: McGraw-Hill.

Frey, D. & Rez, H. (2002). Population and predators: Preconditions for the Holocaust from a control-theoretical perspective. In L. Newman & R. Erber (eds.), *Understanding Genocide: The Social Psychology of the Holocaust* (pp. 188–221). New York: Oxford University Press.

Friedlander, S. (1997). *Nazi Germany and the Jews*, vol. 1: *The Years of Persecution, 1933–1939*. New York: Harper Collins.

Fritsche, I., Jonas, E. & Fankhänel, T. (2008). The role of control motivation in mortality salience effects on ingroup support and defense. *Journal of Personality and Social Psychology*, 95, 524–541.

Glick, P. (2002). Sacrificial lambs dressed in wolves' clothing: Envious prejudice, ideology, and the scapegoating of Jews. In L. Newman & R. Erber (eds.), *Understanding Genocide: The Social Psychology of the Holocaust* (pp. 113–142). New York: Oxford University Press.

Glick, P. (2005). Choice of scapegoats. In J. Dovidio, P. Glick & L. Rudman (eds.), *On the Nature of Prejudice: Fifty Years After Allport* (pp. 244–261). Malden, MA: Blackwell.

Głuchowski, P. & Kowalski, M. (2009). *Odwet. Prawdziwa historia braci Bielskich [Revenge. The True Story of Bielski Brothers]*. Warsaw, Poland: Agora.

Goldhagen, D. J. (1996). *Hitler's Willing Executioners: Ordinary Germans and the Holocaust*. New York: Knopf.

Golec de Zavala, A. &. Adler, J. (2010). Aetiology of genocide. In J. Adler & J. Gray (eds.), *Forensic Psychology: Concepts, Debates and Practice* (second edition, pp. 264–282). New York: Willan Publishing.

Golec de Zavala, A., Cichocka, A., Eidelson, R. & Jayawickreme, N. (2009). Collective narcissism and its social consequences. *Journal of Personality and Social Psychology*, 97, 1074–1096.

Gourevitch, P. (1998). *We Wish To Inform You That Tomorrow We Will Be Killed With Our Families. Stories from Rwanda*. New York: Farrar, Strauss, and Giroux.

Grabowski, J. (2009). German anti-Jewish propaganda in the General government, 1939–1945: Inciting hate through posters, films, and exhibitions. *Holocaust and Genocide Studies*, 23, 381–412.

Gross, J. (2012). *Golden Harvest*. Oxford: Oxford University Press.

Grossman, C. (1988). *The Underground Army: Fighters of the Bialystok Ghetto*. New York: Holocaust Library.

Harff, B. (2003). No lessons learned from the Holocaust? Assessing risks of genocide and political mass murder since 1955. *American Political Science Review*, 97, 57–73.

Harris, L. & Fiske, S. (2009). Social neuroscience evidence for dehumanised perception. *European Review of Social Psychology*, 20, 192–231.

Haska, A. (2008). Adam Żurawin, a hero of thousand faces. *Holocaust: Studies and Materials*, 1, 123–146.

Helweg-Larsen, M. & Shepperd, J. (2001). Do moderators of the optimistic bias affect personal or target risk estimates? A review of the literature. *Personality and Social Psychology Review*, 5, 74–95.

Herf, J. (2006). *The Jewish Enemy: Nazi Propaganda during World War II and the Holocaust*. Cambridge, MA: Harvard University Press.

Hilberg, R. (1993). *Perpetrators, Victims, Bystanders: the Jewish Catastrophe 1933–1945*. New York: Harper Perennial.

Hinton, A. L. (1996). Agents of death. Explaining the Cambodian genocide in terms of psychosocial dissonance. *American Anthropologist*, 98, 818–831.

Hinton, A. L. (ed.) (2002a). *Genocide. An Anthropological Reader*. Malden, MA: Blackwell.

Hinton, A. L. (2002b). A head for an eye: revenge in the Cambodian genocide. In A. L. Hinton (ed.), *Genocide. An Anthropological Reader* (pp. 254–285). Malden, MA: Blackwell.

Hodges, B. H. & Geyer, A. (2006). A nonconformist account of the Asch experiments: Values, pragmatics, and moral dilemmas. *Personality and Social Psychology Review*, 10, 2–19.

Kahneman, D. & Tversky, A. (1979). Prospect theory: An analysis of decisions under risk. *Econometrica*, 47, 313–327.

Keller, J. (2005). In genes we trust: The biological component of psychological essentialism and its relationship to mechanisms of motivated social cognition. *Journal of Personality and Social Psychology*, 88, 686–702.

Kofta, M. & Sedek, M. (2005). Conspiracy stereotypes of Jews during systematic transformation in Poland. *International Journal of Sociology*, 35, 40–64.

Lamm, C., Batson, C. & Decety, J. (2007). The neural substrate of human empathy: effects of perspective-taking and cognitive appraisal. *Journal of Cognitive Neuroscience*, 19, 42–58.

Latané, B. & Darley, J. (1970). *The Unresponsive Bystander: Why Doesn't He Help?* New York: Appleton-Century-Crofts.

Lemkin, R. (1944). *Axis Rule in Occupied Europe: Laws of Occupation, Analysis of Government, Proposals for Redress*. Washington DC: Carnegie Endowment for International Peace, Division of International Law.

Levine, M., Prosser, A., Evans, D. & Reicher, S. (2005). Identity and emergency intervention: How social group membership and inclusiveness of group boundaries shape helping behavior. *Personality and Social Psychology Bulletin*, 31, 443–453.

Lewicka, M., Czapiński, J. & Peeters, G. (1992). Positive-negative asymmetry or 'When the heart needs a reason.' *European Journal of Social Psychology*, 22, 425–434.

Leyens, J., Rodriguez-Perez, A., Rodriguez-Torres, R., Gaunt, R., Paladino, M., Vaes, J. & Demoulin, S. (2001). Psychological essentialism and the differential attribution of uniquely human emotions to ingroups and outgroups. *European Journal of Social Psychology*, 31, 395–411.

Lifton, R. J. (1986). Reflections on genocide. *Psychohistory Review*, 14, 39–54.

Lindner, E. (2009). Genocide, humiliation, and inferiority. An interdisciplinary perspective. In N. Robins & A. Jones (eds.), *Genocides by the Oppressed. Subaltern Genocide in Theory and Practice* (pp. 138–158). Bloomington: Indiana University Press.

Mackie, D., Devos, T. & Smith, E. R. (2000). Intergroup emotions: Explaining offensive action tendencies in an intergroup context. *Journal of Personality and Social Psychology*, 79, 602–616.

Mamdani, M. (2001). *When Victims Become Killers*. Princeton, NJ: Princeton University Press.

Mandel, D. R. (2002). Instigators of genocide: Examining Hitler from a social-psychological perspective. In L. Newman & R. Erber (eds.), *Understanding Genocide: The Social Psychology of the Holocaust* (pp. 259–284). New York: Oxford University Press.

Melson, R. (2002). *On the Uniqueness and Comparability of the Holocaust: A Comparison with the Armenian Genocide*. Erevan: Republic of Armenia Academy of Sciences.

Melson, R. (2004). Provocation or nationalism: A critical inquiry into the Armenian Genocide of 1915. In R. Hovannisian (ed.), *Armenian Genocide in Perspective*. New Brunswick, NJ: Transaction Publishers.

Milgram, S. (1963). Behavioral study of obedience. *The Journal of Abnormal and Social Psychology*, 67, 371–378.

Milgram, S. (1974). *Obedience to Authority: An Experimental View*. New York: Harper and Row.

Mironko, C. K. (2006). Ibitero: means and motives in the Rwandan Genocide. In S. E. Cook (ed.), *Genocide in Cambodia and Rwanda. New Perspectives* (pp. 163–189). New Brunswick, NJ: Transaction Publishers.

Monroe, K. (2008). Cracking the code of genocide: The moral psychology of rescuers, bystanders, and Nazis during the Holocaust. *Political Psychology*, 29, 699–736.

Newman, L.S. & Erber, R. (eds.). (2002). *Understanding Genocide: The Social Psychology of the Holocaust*. New York: Oxford University Press.

Oliner, S. & Oliner, P. (1988). *The Altruistic Personality. Rescuers of Jews in Nazi Europe*. New York: Free Press.

Opotow, S. (2001). Reconciliation in times of impunity: challenges for social justice. *Social Justice Research*, 14, 149–170.

Paulsson, G. (2003). *Secret City: The Hidden Jews of Warsaw, 1940–1945*. New Haven: Yale University Press.

Paxton, R. (2004). *The Anatomy of Fascism*. New York: Knopf.

Perechodnik, C. (1996). *Am I a murderer? Testament of a Jewish Ghetto Policeman Calel Perechodnik*. Boulder, CO: Westview Press.

Perelman, M. (2003). Poles open probe into Jewish role in killings. *The Forward*. Available at http://www.forward.com/articles/7832/ (accessed 24 April 2012).

Pettigrew, T., Christ, O., Meertens, R., Van Dick, R. & Zick, A. (2008). Relative deprivation and intergroup prejudice. *Journal of Social Issues*, 64, 385–401.

Piliavin, I., Rodin, J. & Piliavin, J. (1969). Good Samaritanism: An underground phenomenon? *Journal of Personality and Social Psychology*, 13, 289–99.

Prentice, D. & Miller, D. (2007). Psychological essentialism of human categories. *Current Directions in Psychological Science*, 16, 202–206.

Prunier, G. (1995). *The Rwanda Crisis: History of a Genocide*. New York: Columbia University Press.

Prunier, G. (2009). *Africa's World War. Congo, the Rwandan Genocide, and the Making of a Continental Catastrophe*. New York: Oxford University Press.

Reicher, S., Cassidy, C., Wolpert, I., Hopkins, N. & Levine, M. (2006). Saving Bulgaria's Jews: An analysis of social identity and the mobilsation of social solidarity. *European Journal of Social Psychology*, 36, 49–72.

Roseman, I., Wiest, C. & Swartz, T. (1994). Phenomenology, behaviors, and goals differentiate discrete emotions. *Journal of Personality and Social Psychology*, 67, 206–211.

Rothbart, D. & Bartlett, T. (2008). Rwandan radio broadcasts and Hutu/Tutsi positioning. In F. Moghaddam, R. Harré & N. Lee (eds.), *Global Conflict Resolution Through Positioning Analysis* (pp. 227–246). New York: Springer.

Singer, T. (2006). The neuronal basis and ontogeny of empathy and mind reading: Review of literature and implications for future research. *Neuroscience & Biobehavioral Reviews*, 30, 855–863.

Skibińska, A. & Libionka, D. (2008). 'I swear to fight for a free and mighty Poland, carry out the orders of my superiors, so help me God.' Jews in the Home Army. An episode from Ostrowiec Świętokrzyski. *Holocaust. Studies and Materials*, 1, 235–269.

Stanton, G. (1998). *The Seven Stages of Genocide*. New Haven, CT: Yale Center for International and Area Studies.

Staub, E. (1989). *The Roots of Evil: The Origins of Genocide and Other Group Violence*. New York: Cambridge University Press.

Staub, E. (1997). The psychology of rescue: perpetrators, bystanders and heroic helpers. In J. Michalczyk (ed.), *Resisters, Rescuers and Refugees: Historical and Ethical Issues*. Kansas City, MO: Sheed and Ward.

Staub, E. (2002). The psychology of bystanders, perpetrators, and heroic helpers. In L. Newman & R. Erber (eds.), *Understanding Genocide: The Social Psychology of the Holocaust* (pp. 11–42). New York: Oxford University Press.

Staub, E. (2011). *Overcoming Evil. Genocide, Violent Conflict, and Terrorism*. New York: Oxford University Press.

Staub, E. & Vollhardt, J. (2008). Altruism born of suffering: The roots of caring and helping after experiences of personal and political victimization. *American Journal of Orthopsychiatry*, 78, 267–280.

Straus, S. (2006). *The Order of Genocide: Race, Power and War in Rwanda*. Ithaca, NY: Cornell University Press.

Tajfel, H. & Turner, J. (1979). An integrative theory of intergroup conflict. In W. Austin & S. Worchel (eds.), *The Social Psychology of Intergroup Relations*. Monterey, CA: Brooks-Cole.

Tec, N. (1993). *Defiance. The Bielski Partisans*. New York: Oxford University Press.

Tiedens, L. (1997). Optimism and revolt of the oppressed: a comparison of two Polish Jewish ghettos of WWII. *Political Psychology*, 18, 45–69.

Trunk, I. (1972). *Judenrat: The Jewish Councils in Eastern Europe under Nazi Occupation*. New York: Macmillan.

Vanneman, R. & Pettigrew, T. (1972). Race and relative deprivation in the urban United States. *Race*, 13, 461–486.

van Zomeren, M., Postmes, T. & Spears, R. (2008). Toward an integrative social identity model of collective action: A quantitative research synthesis of three socio-psychological perspectives. *Psychological Bulletin*, 134, 504–535.

Verwimp, P. (2003). Testing the double-genocide thesis for Central and Southern Rwanda. *Journal of Conflict Resolution*, 47, 423–442.

Vetlesen, A. J. (2000). Genocide: A case for responsibility of the bystander. *Journal of Peace Research*, 37, 519–532.

Vollhardt, J. R. (2009a). The role of victim beliefs in the Israeli-Palestinian conflict: Risk or potential for peace? *Peace and Conflict: Journal of Peace Psychology*, 15, 135–159.

Vollhardt, J. R. (2009b). Altruism born of suffering and prosocial behavior following adverse life events: A review and conceptual integration. *Social Justice Research*, 22, 53–97.

Vollhardt, J. R. & Staub, E. (2011). Inclusive altruism born of suffering: The effects of past suffering on prosocial behavior toward outgroups. *American Journal of Orthopsychiatry, 81*, 307–315.

Volpato, C. & Durante, F. (2009). Empowering the 'Jewish threat': The protocols of the Elders of Zion. *Journal of US-China Public Administration*, 6, 23–36.

Zimbardo, P. (2007). *The Lucifer Effect: Understanding how Good People Turn Evil*. New York: Random House.

12

The Social Psychology of Terrorism: Individual, Group and Organizational Processes

Keren Sharvit and Arie W. Kruglanski

● ●

On 6 April 2008, Jeyaraj Fernandopulle, Sri Lanka's minister of highway and road development, was about to flag off a marathon race when a suicide bomber belonging to the Liberation Tigers of the Tamil Eelam (LTTE) blew himself up, killing the minister and several runners and spectators. Fourteen people were killed and 83 injured. On 1 September 2004, Chechen rebels took over a school in Beslan, North Ossetia, Russia, and held approximately 1,200 children, parents and teachers hostage. In the fight that ensued between the rebels and Russian commandoes, more than 300 people were killed and hundreds were injured. On 11 September 2001, Al-Qaeda activists hijacked four commercial passenger-jet airlines in the United States. They intentionally crashed two planes into the World Trade Center buildings in New York City and one plane into the Pentagon building near Washington, DC. The fourth plane crashed near Shanksville, Pennsylvania, as passengers and crew tried to retake control of it. Nearly 3,000 people were killed and thousands more were injured. On 15 August 1998, members of the Real Irish Republican Army left a car full of explosives in a crowded shopping area in Omagh, Northern Ireland. The car exploded a short while later, killing 29 people and injuring more than 200.

The above are but few very different examples of terrorist incidents from the past 15 years. The phenomenon of terrorism has developed and proliferated the latter part of the twentieth century, and understanding it is of major interest to researchers. One reason for this interest is that the willingness of individuals to commit mass murder of innocents, as in the above examples, and to occasionally take their own lives in the process, is a bizarre phenomenon that begs a scientific explanation. But more importantly, a scientific understanding of terrorism can potentially contribute to the development of effective strategies for countering terrorism.

Terrorism is both a psychological and a social phenomenon. It is psychological because it is a behaviour carried out by humans, albeit one that falls outside the range of what most would consider as normative, civilized or socially sanctioned behaviour. It is psychological also because it attempts to influence its audience by psychological means, namely by spreading terror and fear (e.g. Ganor, 2005b; Hoffman, 1998; Marsella, 2004). Terrorism is a social phenomenon, too, because the individuals who carry out terrorist attacks often do so in the name of a social or political agenda and attempt to influence an audience that is broader than the direct victims of the attacks. In fact, many scholars consider the existence of a political agenda to be a defining feature of terrorism (Arce & Sandler, 2005; Ganor, 2005a; Hoffman, 1998; LaFree & Dugan, 2007; Schmid & Jongman, 1988). In addition, the individuals who carry out attacks often represent, or claim to represent, social groups and/or organizations. Hence, social psychology can offer important insights into the processes that underlie terrorism. We begin the present chapter by discussing the challenges of defining what constitutes terrorism. We then offer a social-psychological perspective on terrorism, which considers three levels of analysis: the individual, the group and the organization. In the concluding section, we discuss the implications of our analysis for countering terrorism.

The challenge of defining terrorism

Despite the vast scholarly interest in terrorism, researchers have not been able to arrive at a consensual definition of the term. One comprehensive review (Schmid & Jongman, 1988) listed no less than 109 different definitions, but this did not even purport to be exhaustive. One reason for the difficulty is that the term 'terrorism' is highly pejorative, and may be used at times to distinguish forms of aggression that one wishes to condemn from those that one considers legitimate. Consequently, the chosen definition for terrorism varies as a function of perspective and motivation (Carr, 2002; Kruglanski & Fishman, 2006). Indeed, one party's terrorist is often another party's freedom fighter.

Nevertheless, it is possible to identify certain defining elements that are included in many commonly used definitions of terrorism. Most definitions refer to the use of force or violence as a defining feature, as well as the targeting of noncombatant victims (see review in Schmid & Jongman, 1988). Other frequently cited defining features include the use of terror and fear in order to exert influence, and having a political agenda and/or attempting to influence an audience that is broader than the direct victims (see above).

The latter two defining features imply that terrorism is a means to a goal, specifically one of exerting influence in support of a broader social or political goal. While possibly instrumental to the social or political goals that it intends to advance, terrorism is often highly detrimental to other goals (e.g. preservation of human life, upholding moral values). Therefore, terrorism is typically employed when the goal that it is meant to promote is considered more important than other goals (Kruglanski & Fishman, 2006). High commitment of group members to focal collective goals can lead to the suppression of other goals (Shah, Friedman & Kruglanski, 2002), and consequently increase the likelihood of choosing terrorism as a means of promoting the focal goals. In addition, group members may be inclined to use terrorism if they believe that alternative means of promoting their goals are not available or are inefficient (Kruglanski & Fishman, 2006). In the following sections, we present a detailed discussion of the processes that lead individuals, groups and organizations to opt for terrorism as a means of promoting their goals.

Terrorism and individual psychology

Terrorism often involves extreme atrocities that are far removed from socially sanctioned conduct, such as deliberate and indiscriminate killing of multiple noncombatants. These acts naturally bring to mind the hypothesis that terrorist activities result from some form of psychopathology. Indeed, early research on the psychology of terrorists focused on attempts to identify the psychopathological features or unique personality of terrorists (Silke, 2003). This line of research, however, yielded few positive results. Numerous systematic studies of members of various terrorist-employing groups from different regions of the world (including the German Red Army

Faction, the Italian Red Army Brigades, the Basque ETA operating in Spain and several Palestinian groups) found nothing particularly striking about the psychological make-up of these individuals (Horgan, 2003; Victoroff, 2005).

Having failed to identify dispositional or psychopathological factors that might contribute to terrorism, scholars turned their attention to aspects of the social environment that might constitute 'root causes' of terrorism. Potential 'root causes' that have been suggested include low socio-economic status, young age, lack of education, frustration, relative deprivation, religious faith and political repression (see e.g. Ehrlich & Liu, 2002; Newman, 2006; Ross, 1993). But just as in the case of the terrorist personality hypothesis, empirical studies did not reveal a consistent relationship between any of the potential 'root causes' and terrorism. Furthermore, research on 'root causes' of terrorism suffers from the fundamental conceptual problem of specificity (Sageman, 2004). Although many people may be exposed to the same hardships in life or share similar backgrounds, very few of them actually become terrorists. In other words, none of the proposed 'root causes' can be considered a sufficient and necessary condition for terrorism.

The foregoing arguments hardly imply that personality traits or environmental conditions are *irrelevant* to terrorism. Although no single factor of those suggested may qualify as a 'root cause' of terrorism, many could serve as contributing factors. Unlike 'root causes', contributing factors may predict individuals' support for or involvement in terrorism *if the right conditions exist* (see also Silke, 2003). The question remains, however, what are the specific conditions that could lead some persons, but not others, to opt for terrorism as a preferred course of action? This question has to do with terrorists' motivations.

Terrorists' motivation

Several recent analyses of terrorism devoted considerable attention to terrorists' motivations (e.g. Bloom, 2005; Pedahzur, 2005; Sageman, 2004; Stern, 2003). Some authors emphasized a *singular* critical motivation. Sageman (2004), for instance, emphasized the *quest for emotional and social support* by Muslims of European diasporas, who felt rejected by and alienated from their local societies. Pape (2005) highlighted *resistance to foreign occupation* as a main motivating force. Spekhard and Akhmedova (2005) assigned this role to *personal loss and trauma*. Finally, Hassan (2001) concluded that Hamas terrorists' main motivation concerned entering paradise, meeting Allah and the prophet Muhammad, and reaping the rewards of participating in a holy war.

Other scholars listed a potpourri of motives, including but not limited to honour, dedication to the leader, social status, personal significance, group pressure, humiliation, injustice, vengeance, exposure to violence, lack of alternative prospects, modernization, poverty, moral obligation, simplification of life, and glamour (see Bloom, 2005; Stern, 2003). Ricolfi (2005) suggested that 'the motivational drive to engage in suicide missions is likely to be found in a *cocktail of feelings*, which include desire for revenge, resentment, and a sense of obligation towards the victims' (p. 106, emphasis added).

A reasonable step in dealing with such a heterogeneity is to aggregate the diverse motives into fewer, more general categories. Several authors have hinted at such a classification, typically based on a distinction between *ideological* and *personal* motivations (Pedahzur, 2005; Taarnby, 2005). Personal motives have to do with the individual's life circumstances and experiences, whereas ideological motives pertain to broader social, political or religious goals that transcend the particular individual. For example, alienated individuals' quest for social and emotional support may be considered a personal motive (Sageman, 2004), while liberation of one's land or carrying out God's will may be seen as ideological motives (Atran, 2004, 2006).

A third motivational category, pertinent to suicidal attacks in particular, involves a sense of *duty and obligation*, whether internalized or induced by social pressure. This is apparent in data on Japanese kamikaze pilots, who accepted suicide missions because they believed that refusing to do so would bring upon them shame and dishonour in the eyes of others (Ohnuki-Tierney, 2006). Concern with duty and obligation has been identified as relevant to present-day suicidal terrorism as well (Bloom, 2005; Gambetta, 2005; Stern, 2003). This can be considered a social motivation, because the individual is responding to social norms and expectations rather than personal experiences or beliefs.

Classification of terrorist motives into *ideological, personal* and *social* is helpful, yet insufficient, and leaves several questions unanswered. For instance, are any of these motive categories unique to terrorism, or could they foster alternative activities in alternative circumstances? The answer seems obvious. Alienation, pain and trauma could foster numerous nonviolent activities. To reduce alienation, for example, one could get involved in a group that works to promote pro-social causes. The same holds for ideological objectives and social pressures. Mahatma Ghandi's ideological commitment, for example, identified non-violence as the supreme means for the pursuit of freedom from foreign rule (Bondurant, 1988). Similarly, social pressures and a sense of duty and obligation are capable of inducing any kind of commitment, not necessarily commitment to violence.

For example, one could become committed to helping those less fortunate out of a sense of obligation. Thus, the question is what precise role do these motives play in terrorism, and under what circumstances might they instigate it?

It is also of interest to ask whether all three motivational categories constitute authentic forces that drive terrorism. Some scholars regard personal circumstance factors as the *true* explanations of terrorists' behaviour and view their ideological statements as *post hoc justifications* (Sageman, 2004; Spekhard & Akhmedova, 2005). Other authors, however, have greater faith in terrorists' idealism as the true motivation for militant activities (Atran, 2004; Gunaratna, 2006; Pape, 2005). Yet other authors propose a differentiation whereby some individuals carry out terrorist acts for ideological reasons, whereas others do so because of personal crises (e.g. Pedahzur, 2005).

In an attempt to synthesize the widely dispersed literature on terrorists' motivations, Kruglanski and colleagues have recently proposed that a central motivation underlying most terrorist attacks is the quest for personal significance (Kruglanski, Chen, Dechesne, Fishman & Orehek, 2009). Such quest has been hailed by psychologists as a major motivational force, having to do with transcendence of the self and attachment to larger causes. According to Victor Frankl (2000), the ability to transcend immediate survival concerns and to believe that there are persons, ideas or values that are worth fighting for is the essence of human existence. Maslow's (1943) theory of motivation identifies self-esteem and self-actualization as top-level human strivings.

Frankl (1963) and others (e.g. Antonovsky, 1987; Moos & Schaefer, 1986; Taylor, 1983) have linked the search for meaning and significance to processes of coping with adversities. Consistent with this notion, recent analyses of human motivation (Greenberg, Koole & Pyszczynski, 2004) have implied that among humans the need for physical survival is intimately linked to the quest for personal significance. Humans' awareness of their own mortality implies a threat of insignificance, and consequently motivates people to 'do well' in culturally prescribed ways, and to be 'good' members of society. Living up to the cultural standards carries the promise of literal immortality (i.e. life after death) or symbolic immortality, which is achieved by identifying with entities that are larger and longer lasting than the individual.

A supreme demonstration of one's 'goodness' as a society member is the readiness to sacrifice oneself for the group in an hour of need. Therefore, times of crisis to the group present an opportunity for enormous significance gain, often coupled with a potential for considerable significance loss in case one fails to respond to the challenge. We propose, therefore, that the underlying motivation for terrorist acts involves the coupling of a quest for significance with a collective crisis situation, entailing perceived threat to one's group, and a terrorism-justifying ideology whereby terrorist attacks are portrayed as heroic acts, lending one's existence and potential demise an aura of supreme glory. As Crenshaw (2007) recently summarized it:

> the [terrorist] act is not just about dying and killing. The expectation of gaining status and respect as a martyr for the cause is important, so that individual action is linked to anticipation of both popular approval and collective political success... Sacrifice for the cause is both personally redemptive and a mark of honor, a way of becoming a hero and part of an exalted elite... It [contrasts sharply with] *an otherwise insignificant or disappointing life.*
>
> (p. 153)

The theory of significance quest has several testable implications. First, if reminders of one's own mortality convey one's potential insignificance, then such reminders should augment the quest for significance as defined by one's cultural norms and accepted ideological frames. Indeed, hundreds of studies based on Terror Management Theory (TMT) provided support for the idea that reminders of one's own mortality motivate individuals to embrace their group's culture and ideals (see review in Greenberg, Solomon & Pyszczynski, 1997). One recent study (Pyszczynski et al., 2006) looked at the effect of mortality salience on Iranian students' support for martyrdom attacks against the United States. In the absence of death reminders, these students evaluated a fellow student who opposed martyrdom attacks more favourably than a student who supported such attacks. However, after answering questions about their own death, Iranian students rated the student who supported martyrdom more favourably than the one who opposed it. This study demonstrates that reminders of one's mortality can lead individuals to support acts of terrorism, if these acts are believed to serve an ideological cause that is valued by their culture.

In real life outside the laboratory, mortality reminders can come in the form of personal trauma occasioned by the loss of a loved one. Spekhard and Akhmedova (2005) studied Chechen and Palestinian suicide terrorists via interviews with their significant others and hostages that they had captured. They found that all the interviewees mentioned traumatic events – such as witnessing death, beating, torture or incarceration of loved ones – as factors that appeared to have motivated the fallen terrorists to engage in terrorism. Of even greater interest, the authors observed that their subjects sought ideological inspiration in response to their personal trauma.

The theory of significance quest also suggests that adoption of cultural causes that lend one a sense of personal significance should reduce death-anxiety. Accordingly, Durlak (1972) found that 'purpose in life' defined in terms of commitment to cultural objectives was negatively related to fear of death. That is, the higher the sense of purpose in one's life, the lower is the fear of death. Arndt et al. (1997) found that reminders of death increased the accessibility of death thoughts, which later declined after an opportunity to defend the cultural norm.

Mortality salience is by no means the only route to significance loss. The theory suggests that perceived loss of significance through events other than mortality-reminders should also fuel efforts at significance *restoration*. Feelings of isolation and disenfranchisement by Muslim youth in European diasporas (Sageman, 2004) could be of this ilk. So could social shame and ostracism to which one might be subjected by failing to live up to the norms of one's society. There are cases in which the perpetrators of terror attacks appeared to be motivated by the need to compensate for their deviant status in the community. Women bombers in particular have often been reported to be on a mission to redeem themselves in the eyes of the community for such shame-bestowing occurrences as divorce, infertility, extramarital sex or rape (Bloom, 2005; Pedahzur, 2005).

In sum, the notion of significance-quest affords an integration of seemingly disparate motivational contexts of terrorism, involving personal traumas, ideological reasons and social pressures. All of these factors represent *significance loss*, motivating the quest for *significance restoration*, resulting from the constant human yearning for significance (Frankl, 2000) that is arguably born of awareness of our temporality (Greenberg, Koole & Pyszczynski, 2004). When direct restoration of one's sense of significance seems impossible, individuals may seek to achieve this indirectly through identification with a collective cause that affords a path to renewed significance via militancy and terrorism. Yet significance loss brought about by personal hardships seems neither sufficient nor necessary for motivating terrorism. Terrorism may also arise from a perceived opportunity for *significance gain* that offers individuals a rare shot at immense 'stardom' (Sprinzak, 2001). It could also stem from the desire to avert *future significance loss*, as illustrated by the kamikaze pilots of the Second World War who sought to avert the shame and dishonour of mission refusal (Ohnuki-Tierney, 2006). Thus, rather than explaining terrorism by a 'fatal mix' of motives that does not distinguish between the different ingredients of the 'cocktail' (Crenshaw, 2007; Ricolfi, 2005), our analysis emphasizes the crucial motivational nucleus of the phenomenon, namely, *ideologically based adoption of terrorism as means of promoting a collective cause that lends individuals a sense of personal significance*. Other motivational and cognitive processes are seen as factors that may drive individuals towards the adoption of such a cause.

Terrorism and group processes

Ideology and indoctrination

If individuals' involvement in terrorism is motivated by the desire to gain significance or prevent its loss, then the role of the collective, or group, is to supply ideologies that elucidate what constitutes significance gain according to the group and what means are acceptable in order to prevent significance loss. By ideology, one usually means a belief system centred around some social or collective ideal based on collectively valued causes such as justice or inalienable rights. Ideology's motivating power resides in its identifying a *discrepancy* from an ideal state and offering a means of removing the discrepancy through action. A terrorism-justifying ideology identifies a culprit presumed responsible for the discrepancy and portrays violence against that culprit as an effective and justified means for moving towards the ideal state. In this way, acts of terrorism involving extreme violence appear legitimate rather than deviant (Moghaddam, 2005). For example, the ideal state identified by the Salafi-Jihadist ideology is the establishment of a Muslim caliphate based on shari'a (strict Islamic law) on all Muslim lands ranging between North Africa and East Asia. According to proponents of this ideology, many of these lands have been taken over by infidels; hence a discrepancy exists between the present state and the ideal state. The culprits identified as responsible for the discrepancy are the infidels, specifically Western nations and Arab governments that have allied with the West. According to this ideology, Islam is under attack by the West, and therefore it is the duty of all devout Muslims to take up arms and join a Jihad to defend Islam (Kepel, 2003; Moghaddam, 2005).

It should be noted, however, that from a psychological perspective, an ideology that glorifies terrorism need not be of any particular kind or content. It can be religious, ethno-nationalist or socialist as long as it portrays terrorist missions on behalf of the collective as means to the end of significance. Indeed, one can find examples of terrorism used by groups advancing various ideologies. These include socialist or Marxist groups, such as the Red Army Faction in Germany, the Weathermen in the United States, the Shining Path in Peru and the Revolutionary Armed Forces of Columbia (FARC); right-wing or reactionary groups such as the Ku Klux Klan in the United States, the Afrikaner Resistance Movement in South Africa and the Ulster Defence Association in Northern Ireland; National-separatist groups, such as the LTTE in Sri Lanka, the Basque ETA in Spain, and the Palestinian Fatah; and religiously motivated groups such as Hizballah in Lebanon and Al-Qaeda (see review in Miller, 2007).

To be willing to commit such extreme acts as terror attacks in the name of a collectively valued cause, one must be very strongly committed to the ideology that justifies the cause and the use of violence in its service. Therefore, terrorist groups invest considerable efforts in imparting their ideology to their members and creating a shared reality (Hardin & Higgins, 1996) in which the group's ideology appears to be the only valid belief system.

The process begins with the *creation of an ensconced culture*, isolated from the larger society. Isolation is particularly important in the early stages of the ideology acquisition. Exposure to contradicting views from outside the terrorist groups may instil doubt in the terrorists' minds concerning the validity of their ideological beliefs. To prevent such external influences, terrorist groups often reduce their members' contact with outside sources in the early stages of training. They create a unique culture wherein the terrorism-justifying ideology is repeatedly highlighted. In some cases, the isolation process is social rather than physical. That is, the terror activists are not physically removed from mainstream society, but their social contacts are restricted and they have little interaction with others who do not share their ideological convictions (Moghaddam, 2005).

Once they have joined a militant group, activists are cast into a social reality that forcefully affirms their 'newborn' identities as fighters for the cause. They undergo a process of indoctrination, which involves extensive anti-enemy propaganda, glorification of their own group, and affirmation of their own superior status within the group (Moghadam, 2003).

The ideological beliefs that are imparted to recruits portray the enemies as inhuman, comparing them to animals (e.g. 'sons of dogs and monkeys') or to supernatural but evil beings (e.g. demons, monsters). Enemies may also be analogized to groups known for their immorality (e.g. Nazis) or destructiveness (e.g. Barbarians, Vandals), or referred to as despicable criminals such as murderers or rapists (Bar-Tal, 1990). These labels derogate and diminish the targets of one's aggression, and essentially exclude them from the category of human groups acting within acceptable norms and/or values. Therefore, the enemies are seen as undeserving of the basic respect, empathy, consideration and rights accorded to other human beings (Bandura, 1999; Bar-Tal, 1990).

The indoctrination process also involves glorification of the terrorist group and the cause for which it is fighting. Few would commit extreme acts for pragmatic reasons such as middle-class tax cuts or prescription drugs for seniors. The will of God, however, or the liberation of one's ethnic or national group, are reasons enough to go to extremes and endure sacrifices (Moghadam, 2003; Neria et al., 2005; Pape, 2005).

To be sure, strategies of enemy delegitimization and ingroup glorification are not unique to terrorists. They are quite common among groups that are involved in intense conflicts (Bar-Tal, 1998) and may be often part and parcel of any aggressive behaviour towards fellow humans. The unique aspect of terrorist indoctrination is that the would-be terrorists are led to believe that they have the unique privilege to act in order to promote the collective cause. In radical Islamist groups, for instance, would-be suicide bombers are depicted as 'living martyrs' (*al Shahid al hai*). The attack is portrayed as a tremendous act of self-sacrifice, for which the martyrs will be rewarded in the afterlife and their families in the present life (Brooks, 2002; Moghadam, 2003). The indoctrination process also emphasizes the duty and obligation of would-be terrorists to their own values, family, community or religion, as well as the honour in having been selected for the mission (Brooks, 2002; Hafez, 2006).

Epistemic authority

To say that ideology is important hardly means that every 'foot soldier' about to carry out a terror attack is an expert on religious or political ideology. More likely, the 'rank and file' activists put their trust in certain 'epistemic authorities', defined as sources of information on whom individuals rely in their knowledge-formation process because their judgement is believed to be valid beyond doubt (Kruglanski et al., 2005). These sources explain to individual activists what the ideology asks of them at a given time. One type of 'epistemic authority', namely expert authority, has received particular attention in the social-psychological literature (e.g. Chaiken, Lieberman & Eagly, 1989; Petty & Cacioppo, 1986). According to French and Raven (2001), expertise is a power base through which individuals can exert influence on others, leading to change of behaviour, opinions, attitudes, goals, needs or values. Expert influence occurs because the influenced individual believes that the agent exerting the influence knows the truth and can be trusted to tell the truth. In other words, the agent is considered an epistemic authority.

The role of expert authority in terrorism is illustrated by the contribution of Sayid Muhammad Husayn Fadlallah, the supreme spiritual leader of Hizballah, a Lebanese Shi'ite Muslim group, to the suicide bombings first employed by this organization in 1983. Fadlallah had initially voiced moral reservations about suicidal tactics, but subsequently gave them his fullest possible endorsement short of an explicit *fatwa*. This provided the needed spiritual 'seal of approval' for unleashing a wave of suicide attacks that have been widely emulated since (see e.g. Helmer, 2006). Similarly, religious authorities inside and outside Palestine have depicted 'martyrdom operations' (i.e. suicide attacks) as 'the highest and noblest form of resistance and one that is most effective' (Hafez, 2006, p. 179).

Community support

The group or community may also represent a trusted 'epistemic authority'. That is, individuals may consider certain ideas as valid and use them as a basis for judgement because the majority of members of their community accept these ideas as fact. The group consensus can then determine for individuals whether or not terrorist acts are considered legitimate and desirable.

In addition to its epistemic authority function, a sympathetic community may also considerably enhance terrorist groups' operational capacities. Community support can provide logistical backing, which may include funding, transportation, safe housing, intelligence and explosives or weapons expertise (Saggar, 2009). Moreover, a sympathetic community can serve as a source of recruitment for new terror activists (Flanigan, 2006; McCauley, 2004).

Revolutionary terrorist groups, such as the Red Army Faction in Germany, the Weathermen in the United States and the Shining Path in Peru, typically advocate dramatic societal change and therefore do not receive broad community support (Miller, 2007). As a result, their operational capabilities are severely limited and they are ultimately apprehended and/or defeated (Kruglanski, Golec de Zavala & Chen, 2008). In contrast, national-separatist groups often enjoy considerable support from the minority communities that they purport to represent, which allows them to persist in their activities despite attempts of suppression. Illustrating the importance of community support, a recent study found that increases in Palestinian public support for violent struggle, as assessed in public opinion polls over time, predicted increases in the incidence of terror attacks by Palestinian groups against Israeli targets between 2000 and 2006 (Sharvit et al., 2010).

Terrorism and organizational processes

Terrorist groups vary immensely in their organizational characteristics. Some well-known organizations such as the Red Army Faction in Germany or the Weathermen in the US have had relatively few active members, while other organizations, such as Hizballah in Lebanon or Al-Qaeda, are estimated to have an active membership of thousands. Terrorist groups also vary in their organizational structures, ranging from very tight structures to diffuse networks. Hizballah, for instance, is often likened to a well-disciplined military (Bar, 2007), whereas Al-Qaeda operates through an expansive transnational network of connections among relatively independent cells (Farley, 2003; Kepel, 2003). In addition, some terrorist organizations have a structure that is centred around a single leader. Examples of a leader-centred structure can be found in the Kurdistan Workers' Party (PKK), a Kurdish group operating in Turkey, which had centred around the leader Abdullah Öcalan until his capture in 1999. Another example is the Peruvian Shining Path, which had centred around the leader Abimael Guzmán. Other organizations, such as the Palestinian Islamic Jihad or Hamas, have a less centralized structure.

The organizational level is of utmost importance to understanding terrorism. Although some cases of terror attacks by 'lone wolves' have been reported, in most cases individual terrorists represent organizations with certain social or political agendas. Some militant organizations have been able to create very efficient mechanisms for activist recruitment by relying on a considerable intuitive understanding of psychological principles. Furthermore, it is the organizations that decide when and where to launch terrorist attacks and what tactics to use in ways that best serve the organizations' political agenda. We present below a detailed discussion of recruitment and decision-making processes that take place in terrorist organizations.

Recruitment

Personal connections

The mechanism of introduction through a personal connection is a frequent feature of the recruitment of activists to terrorist groups (Horgan, 2005; Reinares, 2001; Sageman, 2004; Weinerg & Eubank, 1987). An individual has a relationship with a family member, friend or romantic partner, who is already a member of a terrorist group and considers this membership as central to their social identity. It may be difficult to maintain the relationship with this person without sharing their important values and concerns (Heider, 1958). This activates the individual's motivation to seek membership in the terrorist group and buy into its ideology. A group socialization process may then ensue (Moreland & Levine, 1982) in which members acquire increasing centrality in the group and in which group membership becomes increasingly central to their social identity.

Terrorism-promoting institutions

Whereas recruitment through personal connections can be thought of as a bottom-up process, commencing with individuals' social relationships, organizations can initiate top-down recruitment processes. This form of recruitment may take place at institutions whose climate and/or explicit objectives concern ideological indoctrination.

In the case of Islamic radicalization, for example, one important institution of recruitment has been the mosque. Post, Sprinzak and Denny (2003) conducted interviews with 35 incarcerated terrorists from the Middle East, the majority of which belonged to Palestinian groups. They found that most of the Palestinian interviewees were initially introduced to the Palestinian cause at a mosque. Authority figures from the mosque were prominent in all of the interviews, and most dramatically so for members of the Islamist organizations.

Self-recruitment

Self-recruitment via the Internet is another important source of top-down recruitment. Coolsaet (2005) characterized this process as: '... the result of an individual track of self-radicalization outside usual meeting places ... It mixes a psychological process of personal *reidentification* ... implying searching ... for others with a similar world view ... In this process groupthink gradually eliminates alternative views [and] simplifies reality' (pp. 6–7).

Experts agree that the Internet is playing an important role in radicalization and self-recruitment into terrorist groups. US Army Brigadier General John Custer, who is head of intelligence at central command, responsible for Iraq and Afghanistan, has stated that: 'Without doubt, the Internet is the single most important venue for the radicalization of Islamic youth' (cited in Schorn, 2007). Indeed, Al-Qaeda's websites urge Muslim Internet professionals to spread and disseminate news and information about the Jihad through email lists, discussion groups and their own websites (Bergen, 2008; Weimann, 2006). It should be noted that different recruitment processes are inextricably intertwined. Internet messages furnish the ideological arguments, while personal relations provide access to and validation of terrorist ideologies as well as social motivation to buy into the ideologies (Taarnby, 2005).

Decision-making and the rationality of terrorism

As noted above, terrorism may be thought of as a means to the attainment of organizational goals (Kruglanski & Fishman, 2006). Hence, the launching of terrorist attacks requires a deliberate decision by an organization, based on the belief that spreading fear among a target population will advance their objectives. In other words, terrorist organizations decide whether or not to launch attacks and what type of tactics to use according to their assessment of what best serves their goals under given political, social and economic conditions (Berman & Laitin, 2008; Hafez, 2006; Krueger & Laitin, 2008). Psychological analyses of goal-pursuit suggest that terrorist organizations may have different goals that may be activated at different times (Kruglanski et al., 2002). Hence, the decision whether or not to launch attacks and the choice of a particular tactic are products of a cost-benefit analysis that depends on the specific goals that are activated at a given time. For instance, Helmer (2006) suggests that Hizballah's decision to launch suicide attacks against American, French and Israeli forces in Lebanon during the 1980s was based on practical considerations. The organization preferred suicide attacks to other tactics only when they believed that the benefits of the former would outweigh the costs. The following quote from Fadlallah illustrates this rationale:

> We believe that suicide operations should only be carried out if they can bring about a political or military change in proportion to the passions that incite a person to make of his body an explosive bomb. As such, the operations launched by Moslems against Israeli intelligence centers in Tyre or Metulla were successful in that they significantly harmed the Israelis. But the present circumstances do not favor such operations anymore, and attacks that only inflict limited casualties (on the enemy) and destroy the building should not be encouraged, if the price is the death of the person who carries them out.
>
> (cited in Helmer, 2006, p. 78)

Indeed, several authors have commented on the cost-effectiveness of suicide attacks as a tactic in the context of asymmetric warfare (Atran, 2006; Berman & Laitin, 2008; Bloom, 2005; Hafez, 2006; Moghadam, 2003; Pape, 2005). According to Pape (2005), suicide attacks 'amount to just 3 percent of all terrorist incidents from 1980 through 2003, but account for 48 percent of all fatalities' (p. 6). Suicide terrorism is also cost-effective in financial terms. The 9/11 attacks, for example, cost less than US$100,000 and inflicted damage amounting to billions of dollars. In addition, the use of suicide tactics minimizes the concern that the operatives will reveal damaging information if caught, and eliminates the need for complex and costly escape plans (Kruglanski, Golec de Zavala & Chen, 2008).

The rational organizational-decision processes that lead to the use or to the cessation of terror attacks have implications for the concept of deterrence, which denotes a threat of aggression against an actor contingent on the latter carrying out some undesirable activity (Schelling, 1960/2007). Although individual terrorists are often willing to die for the cause and are therefore less susceptive to threats of aggression, terrorist organizations do have material vulnerabilities. The larger the organization, the greater are its needs in terms of territory and infrastructure. These can be threatened and targeted, making continued terrorist activities potentially costly for the organization. Furthermore, territory and infrastructure often require (tacit or explicit) support from organized states. State sponsors of terrorism can also become targets of threats or attacks and consequently withdraw their support, which is also costly to the terrorist organizations. Libya's late leader, Muammar Gaddafi, for instance, had essentially got out of the terrorist business despite his earlier enthusiasm for it, out of concern that his country might be targeted (Pillar, 2003).

Implications or counter-terrorism

Given the threat that terrorism poses to individuals, societies and nations, the question arises how understanding the social-psychological processes involved in terrorism can contribute to its reduction or prevention. Each of the levels of analysis we have considered above offers possibilities for countering terrorism.

The individual level

On the individual level, our analysis suggests that counter-terrorist efforts should focus on terrorists' motivations rather than their ability to launch attacks. Without attention to motivation, efforts to reduce terrorists' *ability* to launch attacks may have a temporary effect, lasting only until the ability has been recovered or alternative tactics have been discovered (Brophy-Baermann & Conybeare, 1994; Enders & Sandler, 1993).

Thus, counter-terror efforts at the individual level may address the motivational base for terrorism, namely, the desire to gain personal significance through commitment to terrorism-justifying ideologies and acceptance of terrorist missions. This may require the alleviation of personal significance loss-prompting circumstances, especially those that are widespread and amenable to policy initiatives. For example, foreign-policy undertakings, immigration programmes and educational campaigns may address the alienation and embitterment of immigrant adolescents. Such programmes can help integrate these adolescents into the host society, for example by facilitating positive contact with members of the host society

(Victoroff, 2005) or by encouraging strong anti-discrimination norms in the host society, which may reduce immigrant adolescents' sense of alienation and their readiness to regain significance by turning to terrorism (Kepel, 2004). An additional way to steer individuals away from terrorism is to provide alternative means to significance gain. Sageman (2004) noted that peaceful fundamentalist Muslim groups attract the same clusters of alienated young men as the Salafi-Jihad, a radical and militant understanding of Islam advocated by terrorist groups such as Al-Qaeda. Hence, peaceful groups may provide individuals with a means of realizing their religious faith and gaining a sense of significance without resorting to terrorism.

The present emphasis on the ideological warrants for terrorism suggests another route to countering terrorism at the individual level, namely, undermining the commitment to terror-justifying ideologies through credible communication efforts. Recently, such efforts have been launched in several countries with sizable Muslim populations, including Singapore, Saudi Arabia, Egypt and Jordan. In Singapore, clerics are sent to detention centres where members of the radical Islamist terrorist group Jamaah Islamiyah are incarcerated. These clerics engage the detainees in religious discussions and attempt to counter-argue, from a Muslim religious perspective, the legitimacy of militancy and the killing of civilians. The Saudi enterprise is comprised of several elements including outreach to security prisoners by Muslim clerics and jurists, online dialogue with extremists, distribution to the public of statements by religious figures condemning terrorism, and a media campaign denouncing terrorism and calling for national unity (Ansary, 2008). These counter-terrorist efforts represent attempts to counter individuals' ideological beliefs through use of 'epistemic authorities' from outside the terrorist organization (Kruglanski et al., 2005).

The group level

Counter-terrorist efforts at the group level may attempt to forge a shared reality opposed to radicalization, militancy and terrorism. Lewin (1958) argued that persuasion attempts focused exclusively on individuals are likely to be less effective than ones directed at their important reference groups. Hence, counter-terrorist efforts focused exclusively on individual activists may not have long-term effects if these activists continue to live in a community that is sympathetic to terrorism. Indeed, the de-radicalization projects presently under way in Singapore and Saudi Arabia involve not only interventions with detainees, but also material assistance to the detainees' families, and youth workshops in the community.

Social-psychological principles could contribute to the development and improvement of such community interventions. For instance, it may be possible to incorporate principles of persuasion-resistance into these interventions, which may immunize participants against persuasion and recruitment attempts by advocates of terror-justifying ideologies (McGuire, 1961, 1964). It may also be important to identify the communities' opinion leaders and direct the persuasive efforts to them in particular (Katz, 1973; Katz & Lazarsfeld, 1955; Lazarsfeld, Berelson & Gaudet, 1944), since these leaders function as epistemic authorities for other members of their communities.

The organizational level

Counter-terrorist measures may take into account the structure of the organization and its objectives. A highly hierarchical structure with a clearly identified leader affords an opportunity to cripple the organization by arresting and putting pressure on the leader. For example, the PKK in Turkey and the Peruvian Shining Path considerably reduced their terrorist activities for years after their leaders, Ocalan and Guzman, had been arrested. A less centralized structure, however, reduces the likelihood that strikes against leaders would impede the organization's operational capabilities. Recent studies have found that targeted strikes against leaders of Palestinian groups (e.g. Fatah, Hamas and Palestinian Islamic Jihad), which have a less centralized structure, did not reduce these groups' terrorist activities and in fact increased it (Kaplan et al., 2005; Sharvit et al., 2010).

The understanding of terrorism as means to an end, and the proposition that terror attacks are a product of rational decision-processes in terrorist organizations, suggest that effective counter-terrorism may require persuading organizations that (a) terrorism is ineffectual given their objectives; (b) that there exist alternative, more effective means to their ends; and (c) that terrorism hinders the attainment of other important objectives. For example, the Gama'a Islamiyyah, which was the most prominent terrorist group that has operated in Egypt, decided in 1997 to renounce violence, after harsh repression and persuasive attempts by the government had convinced the group's leaders that violence was not conducive to their objectives.

Terrorism, beside its presumed advancement of the organization's *ideological* objectives, affords the *emotional* satisfaction of watching the enemies suffer. In this sense, terrorism is a 'multi-final' means, that is, a means that serves several goals simultaneously. This increases the appeal of terrorism, as compared with other 'unifinal' means, which do not serve additional goals (Kruglanski et al., 2002). Consequently, policies such as 'ethnic profiling' or the inadvertent 'collateral damage' inflicted during anti-terrorist campaigns might backfire by amplifying the goal of vengeance (Atran, 2003). However, the notion of multi-finality could also be exploited to benefit counter-terrorist efforts. Rekindling alternative objectives that are incompatible with terrorism may dissuade organizations from using terrorism and lead them to prefer other 'multi-final' means that are instrumental to their alternative goals. For instance, many terrorism-using organizations have political objectives of gaining power and influence within their respective communities. If terrorism is seen as incompatible with the organization's political objectives, its appeal may be reduced. For example, the conflict between Protestants and Catholics in Northern Ireland had for years involved violent activities by paramilitary groups on both sides, including the Irish Republican Army (IRA) on the Catholic side and the Ulster Defence Association on the Protestant side. Over the years, the paramilitary factions increased their political involvement, and this led to a reduction in their militant activities (Fitzduff, 2002).

Nevertheless, it may be important to distinguish between terrorist organizations that use terrorism as a means to an end and those that are committed to terrorism as a goal due to its intrinsic properties, such as the sense of power it bestows or the appeal of violence (Gunaratna, 2002). It is unlikely that anything short of a total defeat will convince the latter groups to relinquish terrorism. The situation is rather different for groups for whom terrorism represents one among several available instruments. Organizations such as Hamas, Hizballah or Sinn Fein, though hardly shy of using terrorism, have other means at their disposal (e.g. diplomacy, media campaigns) as well as other goals of political or social variety. Therefore, they may desist from the use of terrorism when it appears that their goals would be best served by doing so.

Conclusion

The present chapter reviewed social-psychological factors that play a role in terrorism at all its relevant levels of analysis: the individual, group and organizational levels. Though we have treated the different levels separately, it is important to note that in reality they are all inextricably intertwined. Processes of belief and attitude-formation at the individual level determine the degree of support for a terrorist cause among any given population, thus affecting the recruitment potential of terrorist organizations. Recursively, an organization's potency may increase its status as a trusted 'epistemic authority', and consequently increase social acceptance of its ideology and the development of a social reality that encourages individuals to join the fight for the cause as a way of attaining personal significance.

The role of psychological process in terrorism affords suggestions for effective counter-terrorist strategies. It is important to note, however, that an evaluation of the utility of a given counter-terrorist measure should take into consideration all the relevant levels of analysis. Counter-terrorist activities that may appear desirable at a given analytic level may prove to be detrimental at another level. For instance, the use of military force against vulnerable organizational targets may impede an organization's ability to operate, but at the same time fuel the outrage of the affected community and increase individuals' motivation to support the terrorists and buy into their ideology. In deploying psychology in aid of counter-terrorism, it is important to be aware of such trade-offs and paradoxes.

Underlying our discussion of the social psychology of terrorism is the fundamental notion that terrorism is a means to a goal. This approach implies that terrorism is likely to be utilized when perceived as effective for the attainment of important objectives, and that it might be relinquished when its perceived efficacy is undermined, when alternative superior means to the same ends appear feasible, and/or when it is seen as undermining other significant goals. Psychologically, all of these strategies refer to perceptions that members of terrorist organizations may form about their ends and available means. Understanding what those perceptions are and how they might form and change in specific instances represents a major challenge for the psychological researcher seeking to understand contemporary terrorism and ways of counteracting it.

Practical task for readers

Some scholars argue that coercive strategies, involving military attacks against terrorist targets, are the most efficient means of reducing terrorism. These strategies, they argue, undermine terrorist groups' operational capacities and serve as deterrents, demonstrating that terror attacks will necessarily lead to tangible losses to those responsible. They cite the examples of the Peruvian Shining Path and Egyptian Islamic Jihad groups, which considerably reduced their militant activities in response to coercion. Others scholars maintain that conciliatory approaches involving negotiation and persuasion are more effective. According to this view, conciliatory approaches directly address terrorists' grievances and consequently eliminate the

---

Continued

motivation to launch attacks. Canada, for example, made considerable attempts to address the grievances of the French-speaking minority, following which the militant group Québec Liberation Front ceased its activities.

Can you think of explanations for why different approaches are effective in different situations? Is it possible that their effectiveness depends on certain conditions? Referring to the individual, group and organizational levels of analysis, can you suggest under which conditions each would be more effective?

Suggested readings

To learn more read Crenshaw (2007), Ganor (2005b), Kruglanski et al. (2009), Miller (2007) and Moghaddam (2005).

References

Ansary, A. F. (2008). Combating extremism: A brief overview of Saudi Arabia's approach. *Middle East Policy*, 15, 111–142.

Antonovsky, A. (1987). *Unraveling the Mystery of Health: How People Manage Stress and Stay Well*. San Francisco: Jossey-Bass.

Arce M. D. G. & Sandler, T. (2005). Counterterrorism: A game-theoretic analysis. *Journal of Conflict Resolution*, 49(2), 183–200.

Arndt, J., Greenberg, J., Solomon, S., Pyszczynski, T. & Simon, L. (1997). Suppression, accessibility of death-related thoughts, and cultural worldview defense: Exploring the psychodynamics of terror management. *Journal of Personality and Social Psychology*, 73, 5–18.

Atran, S. (2003). Genesis of suicide terrorism. *Science*, 299, 1534–1539.

Atran, S. (2004). Mishandling suicide terrorism. *The Washington Quarterly*, 27, 67–90.

Atran, S. (2006). The moral logic and growth of suicide terrorism. *The Washington Quarterly*, 29, 127–147.

Bandura, A. (1999). Moral disengagement in the perpetration of inhumanities. *Personality and Social Psychology Review*, 3, 193, 209.

Bar-Tal, D. (1990). Causes and consequences of delegitimization: Models of conflict and ethnocentrism. *Journal of Social Issues*, 46, 65–81.

Bar-Tal, D. (1998). Societal beliefs in times of intractable conflict: The Israeli case. *International Journal of Conflict Management*, 9, 22–50.

Bar, S. (2007). Deterring nonstate terrorist groups: The case of Hizballah. *Comparative Strategy*, 26, 469–493.

Bergen, P. (2008). Al Qaeda, the organization: A five-year forecast. *The Annals of the American Academy of Political and Social Science*, 618, 14–30.

Berman, E. & Laitin, D. D. (2008). Religion, terrorism and public goods: Testing the club model. *Journal of Public Economics*, 92, 1942–1967.

Bloom, M. M. (2005). *Dying to Kill: The Allure of Suicide Terrorism*. New York: Columbia University Press.

Bondurant, J. V. (1988). *Conquest of Violence: The Ghandian Philosophy of Conflict*. Princeton, NJ: Princeton University Press.

Brooks, D. (2002). The Culture of Martyrdom: How suicide bombing became not just a means but an end. *The Atlantic Monthly, 289*(6), 18.

Brophy-Baermann, B. & Conybeare, J. A. C. (1994). Retaliating against terrorism: Rational expectations and the optimality of rules versus discretion. *American Journal of Political Science*, 38, 196–210.

Carr, C. (2002). *The Lessons of Terror: A History of Warfare Against Civilians*. New York: Random House.

Chaiken, S., Lieberman, A. & Eagly, A. (1989). Heuristic and systematic information processing within and beyond the persuasion context. In J. S. Uleman & J. A. Bargh (eds.), *Unintended Thought* (pp. 212–252). New York: Guilford Press.

Coolsaet, R. (2005). Between al-Andalus and a failing integration: Europe's pursuit of a long-term counterterrorism strategy in the post-al Qaeda era. *Egmont Paper 5*. Brussels: Royal Institute for International Relations (IRRI-KIB).

Crenshaw, M. (2007). Explaining suicide terrorism: A review essay. *Security Studies*, 16, 133–162.

Durlak, J. A. (1972). Relationship between individual attitudes toward life and death. *Journal of Consulting and Clinical Psychology*, 38, 460–473.

Ehrlich, P. R. & Liu, J. (2002). Some roots of terrorism. *Population and Environment*, 24(2), 183–192.

Enders, W. & Sandler, T. (1993). The effectiveness of antiterrorism policies: A vector-autoregression-intervention analysis. *American Political Science Review*, 87, 829–844.

Farley, J. D. (2003). Breaking Al Qaeda cells: A mathematical analysis of counterterrorism operations (a guide for risk assessment and decision making). *Studies in Conflict & Terrorism*, 26, 399–411.

Fitzduff, M. (2002). *Beyond Violence: Conflict Resolution Process in Northern Ireland*. Tokyo, Japan: United Nations University Press.

Flanigan, S. T. (2006). Charity as resistance: Connections between charity, contentious politics, and terror. *Studies in Conflict & Terrorism*, 29, 641–655.

Frankl, V. E. (1963). *Man's Search for Meaning*. New York: Washington Square Press.

Frankl, V. E. (2000). *Man's Search for Ultimate Meaning*. New York: Perseus Publishing.

French, J. R. P. & Raven, B. (2001). The bases of social power. In I. G. Asherman & S. V. Asherman (eds.), *The Negotiation Sourcebook* (second edition, pp. 61–74). Amherst, MA: HRD Press.

Gambetta, D. (ed.). (2005). *Making Sense of Suicide Missions*. Oxford: Oxford University Press.

Ganor, B. (2005a). *The Counter-Terrorism Puzzle: A Guide for Decision Makers.* Herzlia, Israel: The Interdisciplinary Center for Herzlia Projects.

Ganor, B. (2005b). Terrorism as a strategy of psychological warfare. *Journal of Aggression, Maltreatment and Trauma, 9,* 33–43.

Greenberg, J., Koole, S. L. & Pyszczynski, T. (eds.). (2004). *Handbook of Experimental Existential Psychology.* New York: Guilford Press.

Greenberg, J., Solomon, S. & Pyszczynski, T. (1997). Terror management theory of self-esteem and cultural worldviews: Empirical assessment and conceptual refinements. In M. Zanna (ed.), *Advances in Experimental Social Psychology* (vol. 30, pp. 61–139). San Diego: Academic Press.

Gunaratna, R. (2002). *Inside Al Qaeda: Global Network of Terror.* New York: Columbia University Press.

Gunaratna, R. (2006). Strategic counter-terrorism: Getting ahead of terrorism. Part I: Understanding the threat *The Jebsen Center for Counter-Terrorism Studies Research Briefing Series* (vol. I, pp. 2–8).

Hafez, M. M. (2006). Rationality, culture, and structure in the making of suicide bombers: A preliminary theoretical synthesis and illustrative vase study. *Studies in Conflict and Terrorism, 29,* 165–185.

Hardin, C. & Higgins, E. T. (1996). Shared reality: How social verification makes the subjective objective. In R. M. Sorrentino & E. T. Higgins (eds.), *Handbook of Motivation And Cognition: The Interpersonal Context* (vol. 3, pp. 28–84). New York: Guilford.

Hassan, N. (2001). An arsenal of believers: Talking to the 'human bombs'. *The New Yorker.*

Heider, F. (1958). *The Psychology of Interpersonal Relations.* New York: Wiley.

Helmer, D. (2006). Hezbollah's employment of suicide bombing during the 1980's: The theological, political, and operational development of a new tactic. *Military Review, 86*(4), 71–82.

Hoffman, B. (1998). *Inside Terrorism.* New York: Columbia University Press.

Horgan, J. (2003). The search for the terrorist personality. In A. Silke (ed.), *Terrorists, Victims and Society: Psychological Perspectives on Terrorism and its Consequences* (pp. 3–28). Chichester: John Wiley & Sons.

Horgan, J. (2005). *The Psychology of Terrorism.* London: Routledge.

Kaplan, E. H., Mintz, A., Mishal, S. & Samban, C. (2005). What happened to suicide bombings in Israel? Insights from a terror stock model. *Studies in Conflict & Terrorism, 28,* 225–235.

Katz, E. (1973). The two-step flow of communication: An up-to-date report of a hypothesis. In B. M. Enis & K. K. Cox (eds.), *Marketing Classics* (pp. 175–193). Colombus, OH: Allyn & Bacon.

Katz, E. & Lazarsfeld, P. F. (1955). *Personal Influence.* New York: The Free Press.

Kepel, G. (2003). The origins and develoment of the Jihadist movement: From anti-communism to terrorism. *Asian Affairs, 14,* 91–108.

Kepel, G. (2004). *The Ear for Muslim Minds: Islam and the West.* Cambridge, MA: Harvard University Press.

Krueger, A. B. & Laitin, D. D. (2008). Kto kogo?: A cross-country study of the origins and targets of terrorism. In P. Keefer & N. Loayza (eds.), *Terrorism, Economic Development, and Political Openness* (pp. 148–173). Cambridge: Cambridge University Press.

Kruglanski, A. W., Chen, X., Dechesne, M., Fishman, S. & Orehek, E. (2009). Fully committed: Suicide bombers' motivation and the quest for personal significance. *Political Psychology*, 30(3), 331–357.

Kruglanski, A. W. & Fishman, S. (2006). The psychology of terrorism: 'Syndrome' versus 'tool' perspectives. *Terrorism and Political Violence*, 18, 193–215.

Kruglanski, A. W., Golec de Zavala, A. & Chen, X. (2008). Individual motivations, the group process and organizational strategies in suicide terrorism. *Journal of Policing, Intelligence and Counter Terrorism*, 3, 70–85.

Kruglanski, A. W., Raviv, A., Bar-Tal, D., Raviv, A., Sharvit, K., Ellis, S., Bar. R, Pierro, A. & Mannetti, L. (2005). Says who? Epistemic authority effects in social judgment. In M. P. Zanna (ed.), *Advances in Experimental Social Psychology* (vol. 37, pp. 346–392). New York: Academic Press.

Kruglanski, A. W., Shah, J. Y., Fishbach, A., Friedman, R., Chun, W. Y. & Sleeth-Keppler, D. (2002). A theory of goals systems. In M. P. Zanna (ed.), *Advances in Experimental Social Psychology* (vol. 34, pp. 331–378). New York: Academic Press.

LaFree, G. & Dugan, L. (2007). Introducing the global terrorism database. *Terrorism and Political Violence*, 19, 181–204.

Lazarsfeld, P. F., Berelson, B. & Gaudet, H. (1944). *The People's Choice: How the Voter Makes Up His Mind in a Presidential Campaign*. New York: Columbia University Press.

Lewin, K. (1958). Group decision and social change. In E. E. Maccoby, T. M. Newcomb & E. L. Hartley (eds.), *Readings in Social Psychology* (pp. 197–211). New York: Holt, Reinhart & Winston.

Marsella, A. J. (2004). Reflections on international terrorism: Issues, concepts and directions. In F. M. Moghaddam & A. J. Marsella (eds.), *Understanding Terrorism: Psychological Roots, Consequences and Interventions* (pp. 11–47). Washington, D.C.: American Psycholgical Association.

Maslow, A. H. (1943). A theory of human motivation. *Psychological Review*, 50, 370–396.

McCauley, C. (2004). Psychological issues in understanding terrorism and the response to terrorism. In C. E. Stout (ed.), *Psychology of Terrorism: Coping with the Continued Threat*. Westport, CT: Praeger Publishers.

McGuire, W. J. (1961). The effectiveness of supportive and refutational defenses in immunizing and restoring beliefs against persuasion. *Sociometry*, 24, 184–197.

McGuire, W. J. (1964). Inducing resistance to persuasion: Some contemporary approaches. In L. Berkowitz (ed.), *Advances in Experimental Social Psychology* (vol. 1, pp. 191–229). New York: Academic Press.

Miller, G. M. (2007). Confronting terrorisms: Group motivation and successful state policies. *Terrorism and Political Violence*, 19, 331–350.

Moghadam, A. (2003). Palestinian suicide terrorism in the Second Intifada: motivations and organizational aspects. *Studies in Conflict and Terrorism*, 26, 65–92.

Moghaddam, F. M. (2005). The staircase to terrorism: A psychological exploration. *American Psychologist*, 60(2), 161–169.

Moos, R. H. & Schaefer, J. A. (1986). Life transitions and crises: A conceptual overview. In R. H. Moos (ed.), *Coping with Life Crises: An Integrated Approach* (pp. 3–28). New York: Plenum Press.

Moreland, R. L. & Levine, J. M. (1982). Socialization in small groups: Temporal changes in individual-group relations. In L. Berkowitz (ed.), *Advances in Experimental Social Psychology* (vol. 15, pp. 137–193). New York: Academic Press.

Neria, Y., Roe, D., Beit-Hallahmi, B., Mneimneh, H., Balaban, A. & Marshall, R. (2005). The Al Qaeda 9/11 instructions: a study in the construction of religious martyrdom. *Religion*, 35(1), 1–11.

Newman, E. (2006). Exploring the 'root causes' of terrorism. *Studies in Conflict & Terrorism*, 29(8), 749–772.

Ohnuki-Tierney, E. (2006). *Kamikaze Diaries: Reflections of Japanese Student Soldiers*. Chicago: University of Chicago Press.

Pape, R. A. (2005). *Dying to Win: The Strategic Logic of Suicide Terrorism*. New York: Random House.

Pedahzur, A. (2005). *Suicide Terrorism*. Cambridge: Polity Press.

Petty, R. E. & Cacioppo, J. T. (1986). The Elaboration Likelihood Model of persuasion. In L. Berkowitz (ed.), *Advances in Experimental Social Psychology* (vol. 19, pp. 123–205). New York: Academic Press.

Pillar, P. R. (2003). *Terrorism and U.S. Foreign Policy*. Washington, D.C.: The Brookings Institution.

Post, J. M., Sprinzak, E. & Denny, L. M. (2003). The terrorists in their own words: Interviews with 35 incarcerated Middle Eastern terrorists. *Terrorism and Political Violence*, 15, 171–184.

Pyszczynski, T., Abdolahi, A., Solomon, S., Greenberg, J., Cohen, F. & Weise, D. (2006). Mortality salience, martyrdom, and military might: The great Satan versus the axis of evil. *Personality and Social Psychology Bulletin*, 32, 525–537.

Reinares, F. (2001). *Patriotas de la muerte: Quines militan en ETA y por que. (Patriots of Death: Who Fights in ETA and Why)*. Madrid, Spain: Taurus.

Ricolfi, L. (2005). Palestinians, 1981–2003. In D. Gambetta (ed.), *Making Sense of Suicide Missions* (pp. 77–129). New York: Oxford University Press.

Ross, J. I. (1993). Structural causes of oppositional political terrorism: Towards a causal model. *Journal of Peace Research*, 30(3), 317–329.

Sageman, M. (2004). *Understanding Terror Networks*. Philadelphia: University of Pennsylvania Press.

Saggar, S. (2009). Boomerangs and slingshots: Radical Islamism and counter-terrorism strategy. *Journal of Ethnic and Migration Studies*, 35, 381–402.

Schelling, T. C. (1960/2007). *The Strategy of Conflict*. Cambridge, MA: Harvard University Press.

Schmid, A. P. & Jongman, A. J. (1988). *Political Terrorism: A New Guide to Actors, Authors, Concepts, Databases, Theories and Literature*. New York: Transaction.

Schorn, D. (2007). Terrorists take recruitment efforts online. *60 Minutes*. Available at http://www.cbsnews.com/stories/2007/03/02/60minutes/main2531546.shtml (accessed 15 December 2010).

Shah, J. Y., Friedman, R. & Kruglanski, A. W. (2002). Forgetting all else: On the antecedents and consequences of goal shielding. *Journal of Personality and Social Psychology*, 83, 1261–1280.

Sharvit , K., Kruglanski, A. W., Wang, M., Chen, X., Minacapelli, L., Ganor, B., & Azani, E (2010). *The Effects Of Israeli Coercive and Conciliatory Policies on Palestinian Terrorist Activity: 2000–2006*. Manuscript submitted for publication.

Sharvit , K., Kruglanski, A. W., Wang, M., Sheveland, A., Ganor, B. & Azani, E. (2010). *Terrorism and Public Opinion in Israel and Palestine*. Unpublished manuscript. University of Maryland.

Silke, A. (2003). Becoming a terrorist. In A. Silke (ed.), *Terrorists, Victims and Society: Psychological Perspectives on Terrorism and its Consequences* (pp. 29–54). Chichester: John Wiley & Sons.

Spekhard, A. & Akhmedova, K. (2005). Talking to terrorists. *Journal of Psychohistory*, 33, 125–156.

Sprinzak, E. (2001). The lone gunmen: The global war on terrorism faces a new brand of enemy. *Foreign Policy*, 127, 72–73.

Stern, J. (2003). *Terror in the Name of God. Why Religious Militants Kill*. New York: Harper Collins.

Taarnby, M. (2005). Recruitment of Islamist terrorists in Europe: Trends and perspectives: Research report funded by the Danish Ministry of Justice.

Taylor, S. E. (1983). Adjustment to threatening events: A theory of cognitive adaptation. *American Psychologist*, 38, 1161–1173.

Victoroff, J. (2005). The mind of the terrorist: A review and critique of psychological approaches. *Journal of Conflict Resolution*, 49, 3–42.

Weimann, G. (2006). *Terror on the Internet*. Washington, DC: United States Institute of Peace Press.

Weinerg, L. & Eubank, W. L. (1987). Italian women terrorists. *Terrorism: An International Journal*, 9, 241–262.

PART IV

TOWARDS APPLYING SOCIAL PSYCHOLOGY

13

Applying Social Psychology to Understanding Social Problems

Robert A. C. Ruiter, Karlijn Massar,
Mark van Vugt and Gerjo Kok

●●●

This book presents many examples of the use of social-psychological theories and concepts for understanding and predicting human behaviour in the context of intergroup relations and social unrest. Social psychology is, however, not only a basic social science that studies the nature and determinants of human social behaviour; it is also an applied discipline of relevance for all kinds of societal problems and issues. Applying social-psychology theory helps in making sense of everyday human behaviour and provides tools to change behaviour in preferred directions. In this chapter, we describe several protocols for a systematic and planned approach towards applying social psychology to understanding and reducing social problems. In previous chapters, various types of social prejudice were discussed, such as sexism, ageism and racism. Here we will discuss a form of prejudice that is based on stigmatization by illness. This is widely researched within social psychology and includes topics such as stigmatization related to mental illness (e.g. Wirth & Bodenhausen, 2009), obesity (e.g. Puhl & Latner, 2007), and drug abuse (e.g. Adlaf et al., 2009).

Throughout this chapter, we use HIV-related stigma as a practical case to illustrate the steps and tasks in applying social psychology.

HIV-related stigmatization

Although the annual number of new HIV infections has been declining since the late 1990s, the number of new infections is still high (UNAIDS, 2010). In sub-Saharan Africa, where the majority of new HIV infections continue to occur, an estimated 1.8 million people became infected in 2009. Worldwide, it is estimated that 2.6 million people became newly infected with HIV in 2009 (UNAIDS, 2010). Furthermore, the significant reduction in mortality due to the worldwide implementation of antiretroviral therapy means that the number of people living with HIV worldwide has increased steadily in recent years. Between 1999 and 2009, a 27 per cent increase in the number of people living with HIV/AIDS has been reported, with an estimated 33.3 million people living with HIV/AIDS at the end of 2009 compared with 26.2 million in 1999 (UNAIDS, 2010).

Worldwide, people living with HIV/AIDS experience strong stigma and discrimination (UNAIDS, 2010). Stigmatization is the process through which a person is devalued and discredited because of his (believed) membership with a group that is associated with a specific attribute or characteristic (referred to as stigma) that is deeply discrediting and calls into question the full humanity of the individual group member (Bos, Schaalma & Pryor, 2008; Crocker, Major & Steele, 1998; Dijker & Koomen, 2003).

HIV-related stigma has enormous negative effects on social relationships, access to resources, social support provision and the psychological well-being of people with HIV/AIDS. In addition, HIV-related stigma hampers effective HIV-prevention and treatment efforts, including the use of condoms, voluntary HIV counselling and testing uptake, and uptake of prevention of mother-to-child transmission programmes (Stutterheim et al., 2009; Vermeer et al., 2009). Increasingly, programmes have been implemented to combat stigmatization of, and discrimination against, people living with HIV as part of a rights-based approach to HIV (e.g. law reform, know your rights/legal literacy). However, countries rarely include programmes at the individual and interpersonal level to reduce stigma and discrimination in their national strategies. Relying on the work of our colleagues Arjan Bos, Herman Schaalma,[1] Sarah Stutterheim and John Prior (Bos et al., 2008; Bos, Dijker & Koomen, 2007; Stutterheim et al., 2009), we use research on the psychosocial correlates of HIV-related stigmatization and possible intervention strategies to reduce HIV-related stigmatization to illustrate the application of social psychology in solving social problems.

Theory-driven versus problem-driven social psychology

Within applied social psychology basically two activities can be distinguished: theory-driven and problem-driven applied social psychology (Kok et al.,1996). Theory-driven applied social psychology refers to testing a theory in an applied setting primarily to get insight into the validity of the theory. Problem-driven applied social psychology refers to scientific activities that focus at changing or reducing a practical problem. In problem-driven applied social psychology, although theories are used, the primary focus is on problem-solving and the criteria for success are formulated in terms of problem reduction, with contributions to theory being a useful but unnecessary side-effect. Problem-driven applied psychologists start with a thorough analysis of the practical problem in question, and they consider multiple theoretical perspectives to find answers to this problem. In theory-driven applied social psychology, practical settings are merely used for theory-testing, and as such it is useful in linking important theoretical developments to human behaviour outside the laboratory. Problem-driven applied social psychology is an important activity because it is an ultimate test for the usefulness of social psychology as a discipline and a profession.

Overview

In this chapter, the focus will be on problem-driven applied social psychology. Social psychological theories can be applied to various kinds of societal problems, including those that have been discussed in previous chapters, such as various forms of prejudice, inequality, destructive group identification and terrorism. A difficulty that applied social psychologists may encounter is that of delineating tasks for the development of behaviour-change programmes that are based on theory, empirical findings from the literature, and data collected from the at-risk population. Existing literature, appropriate theories and additional research data are basic tools for the design of any evidence-based behavioural intervention, but often it is unclear how and where these tools should be used in problem analysis and solving. We discuss below different protocols for a systematic, theory- and evidence-based approach from problem definition to problem solution.

Following a general overview of the different stages in doing applied social psychology, from problem definition to problem solution, we start by illustrating the disadvantages of a mono-theory approach over a multi-theory approach in explaining and predicting real-life human behaviour. A systematic working tool, called PATH (Buunk & Van Vugt, 2008), is provided that can help in applying social-psychology theory to practical cases to better understand human behaviour and thus identify possible target points for intervention programmes. Next, we make the switch from behaviour explanation to behaviour change. Behaviour change is a planned activity. A difficulty that planners may encounter is that of delineating tasks for the development and implementation of behaviour-change programmes that are based on theory, empirical findings from the literature, and data collected from the at-risk population, programme users and implementation setting. Intervention Mapping (Bartholomew et al., 2011) provides programme planners with a framework for effective and evidence-based decision-making in each step in intervention planning, implementation and evaluation. In the final part of the chapter, we present the general principles and six steps of Intervention Mapping and illustrate its use in the systematic development of behaviour-change interventions.

Defining applied social psychology: from problem definition to problem solving

The objective of this chapter is to describe how social psychology can be systematically applied to solve social problems that exist in the real world. The problem-driven approach to social psychology should be a systematic and planned activity. A non-systematic approach fails to build on existing knowledge and may omit the involvement of important stakeholders and their opinions, beliefs and expertise in defining and solving the targeted problem. In different domains of applied science such planning models have been developed (Delhomme et al., 2009; Green & Kreuter, 2005; McKenzie-Mohr, 2000; Steg & Vlek, 2009). For example, a planning model best known and most frequently used in health education and health promotion is Green and Kreuter's PRECEDE/PROCEED model (Green & Kreuter, 2005). According to this model, predicting and changing human behaviour is a planned activity that includes four major phases: diagnosis, development, implementation and evaluation.

Problem diagnosis

In the *diagnosis* phase, before beginning to actually plan an intervention, the planner conducts a needs assessment. This assessment encompasses two components: (1) an epidemiological, behavioural and social analysis of the at-risk group or community and its problems; and (2) an assessment of the strengths and capacity of the community and its target members as a part of intervention planning. The product of this step is a description of the problem and its impact on quality of life, followed by a theory- and evidence-based analysis of the proximal behavioural and environmental causes of the problem, and the personal and situational factors that contribute to these causes. In addition, the community's experience with potential solutions is assessed and important stakeholders are identified (Bartholomew et al., 2011). Below we describe the first three steps of a protocol called PATH to illustrate how social-psychology theory and research can be applied in a needs-assessment procedure.

Intervention development

In the *development phase*, intervention planners define objectives for their interventions on the basis of the needs assessment. They specify the changes they want to accomplish in individual behaviour and environmental conditions, and identify the personal and situational factors that must be changed to initiate and sustain the process of behavioural and environmental change. Planners acknowledge that behaviour is a function of individuals and their environments, including families, social networks, organizations and public policy frameworks, and that interventions may target not only members of the at-risk population but also decision-makers in the environment (Bartholomew et al., 2011). Subsequently, planners identify theory-based strategies to accomplish these objectives, and combine these strategies into an intervention programme. Intervention planners guide the production process, and conduct small-scale pilots of programme components. Again, they collaborate with target groups, decision-makers and stakeholders to identify the optimal intervention for a particular problem, target population and intervention context. The complexity of intervention development has been somewhat overlooked in social-psychology training. However, only a systematic approach towards intervention development can help to assure evidence-based practice in solving social problems. Below we present a protocol for systematic intervention development, called Intervention Mapping, to describe in more detail the steps of formulating objectives, selecting behavioural change methods and developing intervention materials.

Programme implementation

In the *implementation phase*, intervention planners design a strategy to facilitate the implementation of the behaviour-change intervention. They design theory-based strategies to facilitate programme adoption by key stakeholders, to support appropriate implementation by programme users, and to encourage programme institutionalization by considering opportunities for incorporating the programme into organizational routines. Thus interventions are required, not only to change individual behaviour, but also to facilitate programme implementation. Indeed, the same steps as for intervention development are repeated to anticipate programme diffusion targeting programme implementers.

Programme evaluation

In the *evaluation phase*, planners evaluate the impact of their intervention on psychosocial correlates of behaviour, on behavioural and environmental conditions, on health, and on quality-of-life outcomes, preferably using an experimental study design (Whittingham et al., 2008). In addition, both qualitative and quantitative methods can be used to study the rate of programme dissemination, adoption and implementation, and the reactions of programme users and participants to the programme. The effect and process evaluations result in feedback and improvement of the programme (Green & Kreuter, 2005). To learn more about programme evaluation we refer the reader to the excellent available literature (Moerbeek, Van Breukelen & Berger, 2003; Patton, 2008; Rossi, Lipsey & Freeman, 2004; Wholey, Hatry & Newcomer, 2004).

Explaining human behaviour: the need for a multi-theoretical framework

Although a theory-driven approach has its merits over a problem-driven approach, usually the former is driven by only one theory. Here, we illustrate the disadvantages of such a single-theoretical approach over a multi-theoretical approach in explaining real-life human behaviour. Consider the case of stigmatization of people living with HIV. Weiner's (1986) attribution theory of motivation and emotion could be used here to understand the conditions under which people are willing to help people with HIV.[2] According to this theory, people make attributions with respect to events happening to themselves, and also with respect to events happening to others (Weiner, 1986). These attributions first cause an emotional response (or attitude), which in turn predicts the behavioural response. According to Weiner's (1986) theory, attributions linked to uncontrollable and/or external causes usually result in positive emotions, whereas attributions linked to controllable and/or internal causes usually lead to negative emotions. Applied to people living with HIV, this implies that an observer will make external/uncontrollable or internal/controllable causal attributions to the causes of the disease. Subsequently, these attributions determine a positive emotion or negative emotion towards the sick person, which may finally result in a positive or negative response to the person, respectively. For example, people may think that the person has contracted HIV because of promiscuous sexual behaviour, and they may consider this cause as being controllable and internal. According to the theory, these attributions will initiate feelings of contempt or even anger rather than sympathy, resulting in a low willingness to provide assistance. However, people might also think that the person contracted HIV through contamination in a hospital, for example during a blood transfusion. In this case, they may make uncontrollable and external attributions, which, in turn, may evoke pity and a willingness to help (Weiner, Perry & Magnusson, 1988).

This case is an interesting example of applying a single theory to a practical problem. The question is, however, whether or not this theoretical approach is useful for solving the problem of stigmatization of people with HIV. Taking Weiner's theory as a point of departure, a logical step to reduce stigmatization would be motivating people to consider the cause of HIV-infection as uncontrollable and external. Communicating such a message, however, may imply a serious problem because it is in contradiction with current AIDS-prevention programmes emphasizing that HIV infection can be prevented by taking self-responsibility. In other words, current HIV-prevention programmes emphasize that causes of HIV infection are controllable and internal. So, although application of Weiner's theory provides a better understanding of the process of stigmatization of persons with HIV, it does not provide a feasible solution to reduce the problem. This example shows that applying theories to practical problems may be counterproductive when researchers use a mono-theoretical perspective as a starting point, instead of the problem in question. It also illustrates that gaining a full understanding of all the facets of the problem is an essential first step in applying social-psychological theories to solve practical problems. In the next section we discuss the PATH model (Buunk & Van Vugt, 2008), a stepwise methodology for applying social psychology to practical social issues with the goal of intervention development. As we shall see, this method emphasizes a thorough problem analysis and offers practical tools to help social psychologists select appropriate theories and empirical support.

PATH: a protocol for applying social psychology

Social problems often seem overwhelmingly complex and it may not always be easy to see how social psychology can contribute to their solution. Furthermore, all social problems are in a way unique, and even if there is applied research available within a certain area, this may not mean that these findings generalize to another domain. The challenge is to redefine social problems in terms that allow the psychologist to find various appropriate theories to help them change or reduce the problem. The PATH model – an acronym of the four steps of the model: problem, analysis, test and help – helps social psychologists with this challenge, and offers tools for applying social psychology to practical problems (Buunk & Van Vugt, 2008). What is important to remember is that the PATH model is not meant to be used in a rigorous way. Instead, going from problem to intervention is often an iterative process, in which one frequently moves back and forth between the different steps to adjust one's work if necessary.

Step 1: Problem

In the first step of the PATH model, the problem is identified and a problem definition is developed. Buunk and Van Vugt (2008) suggest that to reach a solid problem definition, data about the problem and its background need to be gathered from multiple sources. The primary aim of this kind of preliminary research is to better understand all the facets of the problem, but it also functions to estimate the feasibility of possible interventions. Exploratory research can be done by studying the available (scientific) literature, but conducting structured interviews or observations can also be valuable sources of information. Moreover, epidemiological facts and figures can help the social psychologist determine the scope of the problem.

Answers to a series of questions will help in reaching a solid problem definition. First of all, a description of what the problem exactly is needs to be provided: *What is the central problem that needs to be understood and addressed?* Let's go back to our case – the stigmatization of persons with HIV. A social psychologist has been asked to come up with an intervention to reduce stigmatization. First, the psychologist determines how big the problem is and he discovers that being infected with HIV has an enormous impact on people's personal well-being – including being the victim of verbal abuse and physical harassment and being denied employment and health care – as well as people's social life, by being excluded from the community and even the personal family (UNAIDS, 2010). A second question that needs to be answered is the why question: *why is a particular issue perceived as a problem in the first place?* A social psychologist needs to ask the relevant parties what the consequences of the problem are for each of them, and to what extent each of these consequences is perceived to be a problem. Moreover, in answering this question it might be helpful to ask since when the problem exists, and whether its severity has increased or decreased over time. Answering the 'why' question will not only help to specify the problem, but can also already suggest directions for intervention programmes. The social psychologist investigating stigmatization of persons with HIV discovers, for instance, that HIV-related stigma hinders effective HIV-prevention activities. Especially in strong stigmatizing social contexts, people infected with HIV may be reluctant to enter antiretroviral treatment programmes because this might mean that their HIV-status becomes public, resulting in the afore-mentioned negative personal and social consequences (Stutterheim et al., 2009). The implication of HIV-related stigma being a barrier to effective treatment programmes is that such treatment programmes should strictly adhere to procedures that guarantee people remain anonymous while being in the programme.

The third question is for whom it is a problem. In answering this question, the social psychologist needs to describe all the parties that are involved, both in terms of who causes the problem, who suffers from the problem, and who is responsible for tackling the problem. These parties often have different perspectives on the problem, which are not always compatible with each other, and this is something that the psychologist needs to be aware of. For example, family members of people living with HIV might also be victims of stigmatization: a phenomenon defined as stigma-by-association (Neuberg et al., 1994). At the same time, having a close and supportive family helps to disclose one's HIV status and thus gain easier access to social resources and treatment opportunities. Next, one should ask the question what causes the problem – and how do these causes affect the problem? Is there a social-psychological dimension to the problem? The social psychologist needs to distinguish between immediate causes and distal causes to establish the process of events, which reveals clues about the causal model underlying the problem. In answering this question, a preliminary causal process model can be developed. Note, however, that in this phase, one does not need to specify the exact causal chain of events that led to the problem, but having a preliminary model may play a role in choosing appropriate theories to develop the final causal model. A preliminary model on stigmatization of persons with HIV could focus on the social cognitive determinants of people's emotional and behavioural responses to persons with HIV, conditions in the social environment that promote or inhibit HIV-status disclosure, and the success or failure of past intervention programmes to reduce HIV-related stigmatization.

Of course, one needs to specify what actors or groups a possible intervention will need to target. The social psychologist needs to identify who should be convinced of the problem, and whose cooperation is necessary to help solve the problem. Selecting a target group clarifies the problem further, and makes it more specific, which in turn may make it easier to come up with strategies to help find a solution. In our example, the social psychologist could target the general audience, community members and health care workers, or even HIV-positive people themselves. Moreover, from the problem analysis that has been developed in this phase, it should have become clear whether the problem is concrete, social-psychological, applied, and, most importantly, solvable. Can a social-psychological intervention be helpful to tackle the problem at hand?

Step 2: Analysis

Based on a first preliminary analysis of the problem, the social psychologist can formulate a problem definition. This definition functions as the starting point for the next step in the model: the analysis phase. In the analysis phase, scientifically valid explanations for the problem are determined, again by following a number of steps. The first of these steps consists of specifying the outcome variable, that is, the variable that needs to be changed. There are a few requirements for an outcome variable, in order to make it a useful target of influence. First, the outcome variable must be relevant to the problem and it must follow logically from the problem definition. Furthermore, the outcome variable needs to be described in specific, concrete terms. Outcome variables that are defined too broadly make it difficult to develop an intervention programme that deals effectively with the problem. The outcome variable must also be continuous, so that it can be described in quantitative terms. A quantitative – measurable – outcome variable makes it easier to generate explanations for the problem, and also makes it possible to evaluate the success of an intervention programme. Most social-psychological outcome variables will pertain to behaviours, attitudes, cognitions or affect, and will be stated in terms of the desired end state (e.g. more positive attitudes towards persons living with HIV).

Divergent phase

After the outcome variable has been specified, the social psychologist can start to generate explanations. The aim of the divergent phase is to generate as many explanations as possible, using several methods, and to identify the relevant causes of the problem. The social psychologist has a number of methods to his disposal to help him or her generate a list of explanations, among which are a number of association or brainstorm techniques. One association technique is to start with the problem and generate explanations by asking oneself why the problem is a problem (problem association). One could also generate explanations by taking a conceptually similar phenomenon as a starting point, which has the advantage of translating the problem into more abstract, scientific terms (concept association). And, finally, one could take the perspective of various actors involved in the problem to generate explanations (perspective-taking). In addition to association techniques, the social psychologist could conduct structured interviews and observations to identify explanations for the outcome of interest.

Next, the social psychologist uses the brainstorm for accessing the social-psychological literature to sustain the provisional explanations with a theoretical and empirical evidence base. As mentioned above, social-psychological theories specify the causes underlying social behaviours ranging from aggression to altruism. Buunk and Van Vugt (2008; but see also Kok et al., 1996) describe three strategies to approach the social-psychological literature and to generate evidence-based explanations. First, there is the *topical or issue-related strategy*. This approach refers to a search for theories or insights that are specifically tailored to the problem in question, i.e. to find out what has already been written on the problem at hand. For example, to determine the explanations for HIV-related stigmatization one could search in a straightforward way for social-psychological studies that have been conducted to identify determinants of HIV-related stigmatization and come up with quite a number of studies that have applied different theories to understand the problem at hand.

Second, there is the *conceptual strategy*, which is a search based on the translation of specific problem-related concepts into more general explaining principles. For example, during the brainstorm, the social psychologist has identified several reasons why people might stigmatize people with HIV, and came up with emotions that are evoked by thinking about HIV-positive people, such as anger and pity. In the conceptual strategy, the social psychologist uses these concepts as search words, and looks for research on the role of pity and anger in the stigmatization of minority groups. This will reveal research by Bos and colleagues (2001, 2007), who have identified anger as being positively influenced by perceptions that people with HIV are personally responsible for their disease, thereby increasing stigmatization. Pity, on the other hand, was identified as a positive emotion that might decrease stigmatization and was positively influenced to the extent that HIV/AIDS was considered less severe; people were not held personally responsible for contracting HIV/AIDS, and HIV/AIDS was less associated with norm-violating behaviour (Bos, Dijker & Koomen, 2007; Bos, Kok & Dijker, 2001; Dijker & Koomen, 2003). The issue-related and conceptual strategies are considered 'bottom-up' strategies, in that one moves from the problem to the explanation.

When it is difficult to use the issue-related and conceptual strategies, such as when a problem is relatively new (e.g. in the case of attitudes towards a new disease), it could be useful to employ a *general theory strategy*. This third strategy is a 'top-down' method, moving from a general theory of human behaviour that might at first not appear to be directly relevant to the problem or potential explanations (for theories, see Bartholomew et al., 2011; DiClemente, Crosby & Kegler, 2009; Glanz, Rimer & Viswanath, 2008). We provided above an example (and limitation) of a top-down approach, by applying Weiner's attribution theory to explain people's willingness to help people living with HIV/AIDS. In practice, the social psychologist should preferably merge the three strategies to access the social-psychological literature when solving a practical problem, resulting in a more comprehensive understanding of the problem.

Convergent phase

Whereas the aim of the divergent phase was to produce as many explanations as possible, in the convergent phase the aim is to reduce these explanations drastically, so only the most plausible ones remain. In reducing explanations, social psychologists should first get rid of redundant and overlapping explanations, by combining them. Also, irrelevant explanations need to be removed, although care must be taken not to remove explanations that indirectly influence the outcome variable. The validity of the remaining explanations must then be examined: under which conditions is the theory applicable? To find out about a theory's boundaries, often it is necessary to investigate how experiments were conducted. Thus, the social psychologist that wants to investigate a certain theory should have a basic knowledge of the research literature on that theory. As a final way to reduce the number of explanations, their plausibility must be assessed. The plausibility of a theory can be established by carrying out real or thought experiments. Would there be a change in the outcome variable in either situation if the particular condition that might cause the problem is either present or absent?

For example, our social psychologist examining the causes of HIV-related stigmatization comes up with the following theoretical and empirical explanations: people stigmatize persons with HIV because they hold them personally responsible for having contracted it; consider the consequences of HIV/AIDS as being serious; perceive the risk of being infected themselves as high; and associate HIV/AIDS with norm-violating behaviour. This analysis of the correlates of HIV-related stigmatization is largely based on studies conducted in Western countries. Although research in developing countries suggests that similar social cognitive factors determine

HIV-related stigma, it is most likely that the relative importance of these determinants may vary for each context (Stutterheim et al., in press). For example, the successful introduction of antiretroviral therapy in large parts of the Western world has gradually changed the perception of AIDS as a deadly disease into a chronic illness, gendering a less prominent role for perceived severity in decision-making processes towards persons with HIV.

At the end of this second step,' the social psychologist has identified and selected a set of explanations for the problem. The current book, with its multi-theoretical approach, provides assistance in this second step of the model – after all, in the previous chapters, first a problem was described, after which the authors reviewed possible theoretical explanations for these problems. The next step consists of developing a process model – the test phase of the PATH model.

Step 3: Test

Using relevant social-psychological theories that were generated via the issue-related, conceptual and general theory strategies, in this phase a process model is developed and tested. Formulating a process model provides a structured account of the problem and its underlying causes, and can also give clues as to where interventions must be targeted. A process model is a pictorial representation of the explanatory variables, and their relationships with each other and with the focal problem. Each variable is represented as a box, and these are connected with arrows. The valence of the arrows indicates whether there is a positive or a negative relationship between the two variables. Taking the outcome variable – often depicted in a box on the right side of the process model – as the starting point, the social psychologist works his way back to the causal variables (on the left). To be able to determine where an intervention must be targeted, it is important that the variables in the process model are described as much as possible in concrete, continuous and quantitative terms. More abstract and general terms should be translated into (several) concrete and specific variables. Moreover, these variables should be described in social-psychological terms – that is, in terms of behaviours, attitudes, cognitions or affect. For example, to be able to develop an effective intervention to reduce HIV-related stigmatization, a social psychologist should specify what a reduction of HIV-related stigmatization entails in terms of specific behaviours, e.g. objective treatment of HIV-infected persons in job interviews, establishing an anonymous procedure in voluntary counselling and testing programmes, providing social support by close family members.

The variables in the process model can influence each other and the outcome variables in several ways. First, the relationship can be direct, with a change in one variable directly causing a change in another variable. Relationships between variables can also be indirect. In this case, a change in one variable affects another variable via a third variable (mediation). For example, the belief that people are personally to be blamed for HIV-infection renders the attitude towards HIV-positive people (mediator) less positive, which in turn will lower the intention to help. Third, there are reinforcing or undermining effects between variables. This is the case when one variable strengthens or weakens the relationship between two other variables (moderation). For example, being conscious of the fact that often one is not fully up-to-date with the sexual history of one's partner (moderator) may weaken the influence of perceived personal responsibility on the attitude towards people living with HIV. A process model should not contain too many variables – often no more than ten are needed to make the process model workable. Also, there should not be too many steps between the outcome variable and the most distal variables, and Buunk and Van Vugt (2008) recommend a maximum of four steps (or levels) to make the model manageable. Finally, it is important that the process model not only has a theoretical basis, but a solid empirical basis as well. Determining the strength of the relationships between variables will, after all, also provide indications for the development of an intervention, since those variables with the strongest influence on the outcome variable would be the most useful ones for an intervention. For an illustration of a process model summarizing the explanations for HIV-related stigma provided above, see Figure 13.1.

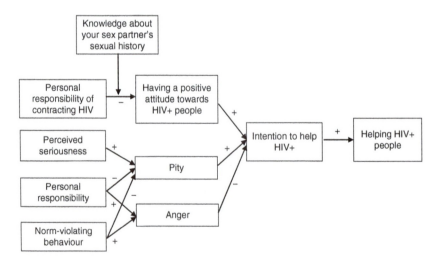

Figure 13.1 Process model of explanation of HIV-related stigma.

Step 4: Help

Once the factors causing the outcome variable have been defined and mapped in the process model, the intervention can be developed. The social psychologist therefore chooses the variables that are modifiable and that have the greatest effect on the outcome variable. A convenient way to make choices is to list all the variables from the process model, and to put them into a balance table. However, not all factors are equally modifiable. In particular, personality traits, deeply held religious or political values, and stable environmental conditions are hard to change (Bartholomew et al., 2011; Buunk & Van Vugt, 2008).

After identifying target variables for the planned behavioural-change programme, the intervention materials need to be developed. It is important to realize that identification of the factors that can be targeted in an intervention to make it maximally effective is really all that social cognitive models of human behaviour can offer. These models have little to say about the theoretical methods and practical strategies or techniques that can be used to bring about desired changes in the identified factors (Fishbein & Ajzen, 2010). Indeed, changing needs understanding, but understanding the determinants of behaviour is not sufficient to design effective behaviour-change programmes. Again, similar to a multi-theoretical and systematic approach to identifying modifiable factors (i.e. determinants) that predict behaviour, the development of behaviour-change programmes is best served by a comprehensive framework that provides the tools and planning process to systematically apply behavioural and social-sciences theories to intervention design. Intervention Mapping provides this systematic approach to programme development.

Intervention Mapping is a planning protocol for the systematic development, implementation and evaluation of evidence-based behaviour-change programmes. It elaborates on the programme development, implementation and evaluation phases in Green and Kreuter's (2005) PRECEDE/PROCEED model for planning behaviour-change interventions (as described earlier in this chapter). Applying Intervention Mapping may improve interventions by providing more detail and guidance for the planning process and the logic of change. Intervention Mapping helps to clarify the programme theory and components to those who search to improve the quality of interventions. It also enables them to ask relevant questions about interventions one is interested in, so adoption decisions are based on adequate insights about an intervention. Below, the general principles and six steps of Intervention Mapping are briefly outlined. For a more detailed application of Intervention Mapping we refer the reader to case-study descriptions that have been published (e.g. Kok et al., 2006; Van Stralen et al., 2008).

Intervention Mapping

Intervention Mapping (IM) is a planning process based on the systematic use of evidence from empirical research and theories (Bartholomew et al., 2011; Kok et al. 1996). IM is not a new theory or model. It is an additional tool for the planning and development of behaviour-change programmes. It maps the path from recognition of a need or problem to the identification of a solution. Although IM is presented as a series of steps, Bartholomew et al. (2011) see the planning process as iterative rather than linear. Programme planners move back and forth between tasks and steps. The process is also cumulative: each step is based on previous steps, and inattention to a particular step may lead to mistakes and inadequate decisions.

Although IM is tailored to the development of health-promotion interventions, the general guidelines for intervention development provided by IM are transferable to a wide range of other domains that are concerned with changing personal, social and economic barriers to performing desirable behaviours, such as energy conservation and traffic safety. IM has been introduced to guide the use of evidence from empirical research and theories and protect against Type III error – failing to find intervention effectiveness because the programme is poorly designed or implemented (cf. Bartholomew et al., 2011).

An IM approach is characterized by four perspectives that are applied during the entire planning process and in all steps. First, from a participation perspective, it is acknowledged that the target population (and programme implementers) should be involved in all aspects of decision-making. This results in empowerment, which can be defined as having the knowledge, skills-set and attitude needed to cope with the changing world and the circumstances in which one lives (Wendel et al., 2009). Second, IM stimulates an eclectic use of theories. Theories are by definition abstractions of reality, and real-life problems should be approached from multiple theories, for example by following the PATH model described above (Buunk & Van Vugt, 2008). Third, from the systems perspective, interventions are seen as events occurring in systems (Hawe, Shiell & Riley, 2009). Other factors within a system can reinforce or dampen the influence of an intervention on the target behaviour or environmental change. Fourth, from an ecological perspective, the relevance of social and physical environmental conditions that influence individual behaviours is recognized. These social and physical environmental conditions may have a much stronger impact on the target behaviour than individual-related factors (Kok et al., 2008). Importantly, at all levels, environmental conditions are determined by decision-makers, or environmental agents (Kok et al., 2008). Examples of possibly relevant environmental agents in the domain of HIV/AIDS stigmatization are politicians, health-care workers and schoolteachers. These environmental agents have reasons for their behaviour, which are not necessarily the same as the reasons planners have for their intervention.

Step 1: Needs assessment

The first step in IM is problem diagnosis. Planners need to have insight into the problem at hand, its behavioural and environmental factors, and the personal and situational determinants of these factors. It is important that this information is supported by existing scientific knowledge, as well as information collected from the target population within the intervention context and from programme implementers and stakeholders. The PATH model should be used here. On the basis of these analyses, planners should be able to define and select the goals for behaviour change.

Step 2: Programme objectives

In the second step of IM, the problem-increasing behaviours and environmental conditions are translated to their problem-reducing behavioural and environmental counterparts. Planners ask the *who*, *what* and *why* question for individuals and environmental agents: *who* is going to do *what* behaviour and *why* would they do that?

At the individual level, the *who* may be community members of people living with HIV/AIDS; at the organizational level health-care workers and health management involved in voluntary counselling and testing programmes; and, at the societal level, politicians. The *what* may be establishing interpersonal contact with HIV-infected persons at the individual level, installing standard treatment procedures to guarantee confidential treatment of HIV-infected people at the organizational level, and developing laws to prevent discrimination at the social level (Bos, Schaalma & Pryor, 2008). There should be consensus among experts about the relationship between reducing HIV-stigmatization and the recommended changes in individual behaviours and environmental conditions.

Next, the desired stigma-reducing behaviours are translated into specific performance objectives: *what* is it exactly that planners want people *to do*? For example, the performance objectives for establishing interpersonal contact at the individual level may include that community members express willingness to meet persons with HIV, treat people with HIV in a respectful manner, and provide social support by participating in joint activities. At the environmental level, performance objectives are formulated to answer this question. In health-care organization, the managers (agents) could identify successful confidentiality procedures (environmental condition) implemented in similar organizations and adapt these procedures for internal use.

After the *what* question is answered, the *why* question follows. The *why* question asks for determinants of the specific performance objectives of individuals and environmental agents. Most interventions are directed at reasons for deliberate behaviour, but not all behaviour is deliberate. Some behaviour is impulsive (Hofmann, Friese & Wiers, 2008) and some behaviour is habitual or automatic (Orbell & Verplanken, 2010). When behaviour is deliberate, there is consensus among experts that people will change their behaviour under the following conditions (Fishbein et al., 2001):

- A strong positive intention, following from: (1) advantages outweigh disadvantages of the recommended action (attitude); (2) perceived social norms/support; (3) behaviour is consistent with self-image/self-evaluation; (4) positive emotional/affective reaction; (5) perceived capability/self-efficacy
- No environmental constraints
- Necessary skills

To create immediate targets for behaviour-change programmes (i.e. the programme objectives), the *who, what* and *why* are combined in separate matrices for each target group with the performance objectives corresponding to rows (on the left side; see Table 13.1) and the determinants corresponding to columns (on top). The end products of step two are matrices for each target population, listing performance objectives, determinants and programme objectives (for an example, see Table 13.1). For example, to establish interpersonal contact between the stigmatized and those that stigmatize, one of the performance objectives for those that stigmatize is to express willingness to meet people living with HIV. Two of the determinants of this performance objective is the perceived contagiousness of HIV and the extent to which persons with HIV are held personally responsible for contracting the disease. In the cell where this performance objective is crossed with the determinant contagiousness, a programme objective is that the target group member acknowledge that the risk of getting infected by HIV by mere contact is non-existent.

Table 13.1   Matrix with examples of performance objectives, determinants and change objectives

Performance objectives	Personal and situational determinants		
Community members:	Risk perceptron	Attributions of personal responsibility	Social norms
Express willingness to get in contact with people with HIV/AIDS	Acknowledge the risk of getting infected by mere contact as non-existent		Community leaders express a positive attitude towards people with HIV/AIDS
Do not blame people with HIV/AIDS		Recognize that not all factors of HIV transmission are under personal control	
Etc.	Etc.		

In the cell corresponding to the determinant personal responsibility, a programme objective is that the target group members realize that in their private sexual life they might not always be sure about the safe-sex history of their partner.

Step 3: Theoretical methods and practical strategies

Intervention Mapping (IM) step three is the selection of theoretical methods and practical applications. A theoretical method is a technique derived from theory and research to realize a proximal programme objective, an application is the translation of that method to the specific intervention context. For instance, a theoretical method for self-efficacy improvement to approach HIV patients in an unbiased manner could be modelling, and an application could be a role play. An important task in this step is to identify the conditions or parameters that limit the effectiveness of theoretical models (Schaalma & Kok, 2009). Modelling, for instance, is only effective when the model is reinforced (rewarded), and when observers pay attention, have sufficient self-efficacy and skills, identify with the model, and observe a coping model instead of a mastery model (Bartholomew et al., 2011). Other theoretical methods have other conditions that need to be met. For example, providing people with stereotype-inconsistent information requires many different examples, but these examples should not be too discrepant from the original stereotype. Successful interventions must also change the environmental cues that sustain or illicit targeted behaviours, for example by mitigating negative social norms towards persons with HIV. Bringing people into personal contact with members of stigmatized groups might be of help here but is considered only to be effective when there is no status difference and both groups have intensive contact and share common goals (Pettigrew & Tropp, 2006).

Step 4: Programme development

Intervention Mapping (IM) step four is the actual design of the programme, organizing the strategies into a deliverable programme, taking into account target groups and settings, and producing and pre-testing the materials. Programme planners have to integrate separate strategies into one coherent programme; they have to make decisions on the programme structure, its theme, the sequence of strategies and communication vehicles. In programme design, the Internet has had a huge impact on the possibilities for behaviour-change programmes. The Internet provides means for tailored communication on a mass scale, sometimes using so-called computational artifacts: animated virtual persons designed to build and maintain social-emotional relationships with their users. In the health promotion field, Internet interventions and computer tailoring have been shown to be effective in reaching and changing the behaviour of large numbers of people (Kroeze, Werkman & Brug, 2006; Noar, Black & Pierce, 2009; Ruiter et al., 2006). A review of interventions to reduce HIV-stigma suggests that the provision of information, together with skills-building, is more effective than only the provision of information, and that personal contact with persons with HIV is one of the most promising approaches to reduce stigma – on condition that it goes together with information about the disease (Bos, Schaalma & Pryor, 2008).

In designing the actual programme, planners usually have to collaborate with creative resources. Planners' major task is to convey their intervention plans to creative people, and to guard whether or not final programme products adequately incorporate theoretical underpinnings. Individual components of the intervention programme should be pilot tested on their effectiveness before final production and implementation, which can be done relatively easily using experimental research designs (Whittingham et al., 2008). The end product of step four is the intervention programme ready for implementation.

Step 5: Implementation plan

A solid diffusion process is vital to ensure programme success. So, in Intervention Mapping (IM) step five, programme planners develop a plan for the systematic implementation of the programme. Research shows that the number of implementers usually decreases drastically in the course of the implementation process. Assessing the implementation of their sex-education programme, Paulussen et al. (1995) found, for example, that while around 70 per cent of potential implementers were aware of the programme, 50 per cent adopted the programme (intention), only 30 per cent implemented the programme (actual use), and a scant 10 per cent eventually institutionalized the programme (continued use). Thus, the actual effect of the intervention is merely 10 per cent of the potential effect. The first thing to do in step five, but preferably already at the start of intervention development, is the development of a linkage system that guarantees a continued interaction and information exchange between programme developers and programme users. For example, to reduce HIV-related stigma in health-care settings involvement of staff members is necessary, but often difficult to realize because professionals do not recognize the problem, or else perceive a lack of time to get involved (Stutterheim et al., 2009). Subsequently, planners should develop a plan for how they can systematically promote the adoption and implementation of the programme by the intended programme users. In practice, IM step five is a rerun through the IM protocol, but now aimed at identifying objectives, methods and strategies to promote the adoption and implementation of the actual intervention programme by the programme users. It may be clear that the anticipation of implementation is a relevant process from the very beginning of the planning process, not only at the end. Similarly, thinking about implementation might result in revising previous decisions with regard to selected behaviour-change methods and selected programme objectives. The end product of step five is an implementation plan with performance objectives, determinants, and programme objectives for programme adopters and implementers.

Step 6: Evaluation plan

Finally, Intervention Mapping (IM) step six focuses on anticipating process and effect evaluation. Again, this process is relevant from the start of intervention development, not only at the end. The list of programme objectives guides the evaluation of programme effects. For instance, the programme objective *community members acknowledge the risk of getting infected by mere contact as non-existent* should also be operationalized as a measure of that objective, that can be used in pre- and post-intervention tests with experimental and control-group subjects (for example, *If you share your table with a person with HIV, to what extent do you feel confident that your risk of getting infected with HIV is non-existent?*). Adequate evaluation research is based on (quasi-) experimental designs and provides planners with information on successes and failures as well as information on where in the planning process the failures were located, thereby indicating where improvement of the programme is needed. The end product of step 6 is an evaluation plan.

Using PATH and Intervention Mapping

The key words in PATH and Intervention Mapping are planning, research and theory. PATH provides a method for accessing scientific literature to answer practical questions with empirical data and theory. IM provides a vocabulary for intervention planning, procedures for planning activities, and technical assistance with identifying theory-based determinants and methods for change. Earlier in this chapter we restricted the application of the PATH model to the diagnosis phase of planned behaviour change by describing its use in coming to an evidence-based problem definition. However, the same strategy of asking questions, brainstorming provisional answers, and accessing the literature to find empirical and theoretical support should be applied in the other stages of intervention development, including the search for behaviour-change methods and the development of an implementation plan. More specifically, combining PATH and IM ensures that theoretical models and empirical evidence guide planners in two areas: (1) the identification of behavioural and environmental determinants related to a target problem; and (2) the selection of the most appropriate theoretical methods and practical applications to address the identified determinants. Although IM in particular is a complex and time-consuming process, the benefits of its consistent application may outweigh its costs by ensuring more effectiveness and efficient learning through its evaluation processes.

Conclusion

In this chapter we have argued that social psychology should not only be considered as a basic social science that studies the nature and determinants of human social behaviour, but that it is also an applied discipline. Using the example of stigmatization of people living with HIV, we have emphasized the importance of using a multi-theoretical, problem-driven perspective in applying social psychology to practical problems, and we have introduced two protocols that assist social psychologists with this task. These protocols, the PATH model and Intervention Mapping (IM), provide a systematic, theory- and evidence-based approach to get from problem definition to problem solution. Both stress the importance of careful problem analysis and intervention planning based on theory and empirical data, and their iterative nature allows users to move back and forth between the different steps to adjust their work if necessary.

Social psychologists, because they have a profound knowledge of individual and interpersonal processes of human behaviour, can make important contributions to solving all kinds of societal problems. Therefore, we feel that applied social psychology should be a central component in the training of future social psychologists – we hope this chapter has contributed to that objective.

Suggested reading

For more details on the PATH model, read Buunk and Van Vugt (2008). The Bartholomew et al. (2011) handbook offers a comprehensive introduction to Intervention Mapping, including examples and applications.

References

Adlaf, E. M., Hamilton, H. A., Wu, F. & Noh, S. (2009). Adolescent stigma towards drug addiction: Effects of age and drug use behaviour. *Addictive Behaviors*, 34, 360–364.

Bartholomew, L. K., Parcel, G. S., Kok, G., Gottlieb, N. H. & Fernández, M. E. (2011). *Planning Health Promotion Programs: An Intervention Mapping Approach* (3rd edn). San Francisco: Jossey-Bass.

Bos, A. E. R., Dijker, A. J. M. & Koomen, W. (2007). Sex differences in emotional and behavioral responses to HIV + individuals' expression of distress. *Psychology & Health*, 22, 493–511.

Bos, A. E. R., Kok, G. & Dijker, A. J. (2001). Public reactions to people with HIV/AIDS in The Netherlands. *AIDS Education and Prevention*, 13, 219–28.

Bos, A. E. R., Schaalma, H. P. & Pryor, J. B. (2008). Reducing AIDS-related stigma in developing countries: the importance of theory- and evidence-based interventions. *Psychology Health Medicine*, 13, 450–460.

Buunk, A. P. & Van Vugt, M. (2008). *Applying Social Psychology: From Problems to Solutions*. Los Angeles, CA: Sage.

Crocker, J., Major, B. & Steele, C. (1998). Social stigma. In D. T. Gilbert, S. T. Fiske & G. Lindzey (eds.) *The Handbook of Social Psychology* (vol. 2, pp. 504–553). Boston, MA: McGraw-Hill.

Delhomme, P., De Dobbeleer, W., Forward, S. & Simões, A. (eds.). (2009). *CAST: Manual for Designing, Implementing, and Evaluating Road Safety Communication Campaigns*. Brussels: Belgian Road Safety Institute.

DiClemente, R. J., Crosby, R. A. & Kegler, M. (eds.). (2009). *Emerging Theories in Health Promotion Practice and Research* (second edn). San Francisco, CA: Jossey-Bass.

Dijker, A. J. & Koomen, W. (2003). Extending Weiner's attribution-emotion model of stigmatization of ill persons. *Basic and Applied Social Psychology*, 25, 51–68.

Fishbein, M., & Ajzen, I. (2010). *Predicting and Changing Behavior: The Reasoned Action Approach*. New York: Psychology Press.

Fishbein, M., Triandis, H. C., Kanfer, F. H., Becker, M. H., Middlestadt, S. E, Eichler, E., Baum, A., & Revenson, T.A (2001). Factors influencing behavior and behavior change. In A. Baum, T. R. Revenson & J. E. Singer (eds.), *Handbook of Health Psychology* (pp. 3–17). Hillsdale, NJ: Lawrence Erlbaum.

Glanz, K., Rimer, B. K. & Viswanath, K. (eds.). (2008). *Health Behavior and Health Education: Theory, Research, and Practice* (3rd edn). San Francisco, CA: Jossey-Bass.

Green, L. W. & Kreuter, M. W. (2005). *Health Program Planning: An Educational and Ecological Approach*. New York: McGraw Hill.

Hawe, P., Shiell, A. & Riley, T. (2009). Theorising interventions as events in systems. *American Journal of Community Psychology*, 43, 267–276.

Hofmann, W., Friese, M. & Wiers, R. (2008). Impulsive versus reflective influences on health behavior: A theoretical framework and empirical review. *Health Psychology Review*, 2, 111–137.

Kok, G., Gottlieb, N. H., Commers, M. & Smerecnik, C. (2008). The ecological approach in health promotion programs: A decade later. *American Journal of Health Promotion*, 22, 437–442.

Kok, G., Harterink, P., Vriens, P., de Zwart, O. & Hospers, H. J. (2006). The gay cruise: Developing a theory- and evidence-based internet HIV-prevention intervention. *Sexuality Research and Social Policy*, 3, 52–67.

Kok, G., Schaalma, H., De Vries, H., Parcel, G. & Paulussen, T. (1996). Social psychology and health education. In W. Stroebe & M. Hewstone (eds.), *European Review of Social Psychology* (vol. 7, pp. 241–282). Chichester: John Wiley & Sons Ltd.

Kroeze, W., Werkman, A. & Brug, J. (2006). A systematic review of randomized trials on the effectiveness of computer-tailored education on physical activity and dietary behaviors. *Annals of Behavioral Medicine*, 31, 205–223.

McKenzie-Mohr, D. (2000). Fostering sustainable behavior through community-based social marketing. *American Psychologist*, 55, 531–537.

Moerbeek, M., Van Breukelen, G. J. P. & Berger, M. P. F. (2003). A comparison between traditional methods and multilevel regression for the analysis of multicenter intervention studies. *Journal of Clinical Epidemiology*, 56, 341–350.

Neuberg, S. L., Smith, D. M., Hoffman, J. C. & Russell, F. J. (1994). When we observe stigmatized and 'normal' individuals interacting: Stigma by association. *Personality and Social Psychology Bulletin*, 20, 196–209.

Noar, S. M., Black, H. G. & Pierce, L. B. (2009). Efficacy of computer technology-based HIV prevention interventions: A meta-analysis. *AIDS*, 23, 107–115.

Orbell, S. & Verplanken, B. (2010). The automatic component of habit in health behavior: habit as cue-contingent automaticity. *Health Psychology*, 29, 374–383.

Oskamp, S. & Schultz, P. W. (1998). *Applied Social Psychology* (2nd edn). Upper Saddle River, NJ: Prentice-Hall.

Patton, M. Q. (2008). *Utilization-focused Evaluation* (4th edn). Los Angeles, CA: Sage.

Paulussen, T. G. W., Kok, G., Schaalma, H. P. & Parcel, G. S. (1995). Diffusion of AIDS curricula among Dutch secondary school teachers. *Health Education Quarterly*, 22, 227–243.

Pettigrew, T. F. & Tropp, L. R. (2006). A meta-analytic test of intergroup contact theory. *Journal of Personality and Social Psychology*, 90, 751–783.

Puhl, R. M. & Latner, J. D. (2007). Stigma, obesity, and the health of the nation's children. *Psychological Bulletin*, 133, 557–580.

Reece, M., Tanner, A., Karpiak, S. & Coffey, K. (2007). The impact of HIV-related stigma on HIV care and prevention providers. *Journal of HIVAIDS Social Services*, 6, 55–73.

Rossi, P. H., Lipsey, M. W. & Freeman, H. E. (2004). *Evaluation: A Systematic Approach*. Newbury Park, CA: Sage.

Ruiter, R. A. C., Kessels, L. T. E., Jansma, B. M. & Brug, J. (2006). Increased attention for computer-tailored health communications: An event-related potential study. *Health Psychology*, 25, 300–306.

Schaalma, H. & Kok, G. (2009). Decoding health education interventions: The times are a-changin'. *Psychology & Health*, 24, 5–9.

Steg, L. & Vlek, C. (2009). Encouraging pro-environmental behaviour: An integrative review and research agenda. *Journal of Environmental Psychology*, 29, 309–317.

Stutterheim, S. E., Bos, A. E. R., Shiripinda, I., de Bruin, M., Pryor, J. B. & Schaalma, H. P. (in press). HIV-related stigma in African and Afro-Caribbean communities in the Netherlands: manifestations, consequences, and coping. *Psychology and Health*.

Stutterheim, S. E., Pryor, J. B., Bos, A. E. R., Hoogendijk, R., Muris, P. & Schaalma, H. P. (2009). HIV-related stigma and psychological distress: The harmful effects of specific stigma manifestations in various social settings. *AIDS*, 23, 2353–2357.

UNAIDS. (2010). *Global Report: UNAIDS Report on the Global AIDS Epidemic 2010*. Geneva.

Van Stralen, M. M., Kok, G., de Vries, H., Mudde, A. N., Bolman, C. & Lechner, L. (2008). The Active plus protocol: Systematic development of two theory and evidence-based tailored physical activity interventions for the over-fifties. *BMC Public Health*, 8, 399.

Vermeer, W., Bos, A. E. R., Mbwambo, J., Kaaya, S. & Schaalma, H. P. (2009). Social and cognitive variables predicting voluntary HIV counseling and testing among Tanzanian medical students. *Patient Education and Counseling*, 75, 135–140.

Weiner, B. (1986). *An Attributional Theory of Motivation and Emotion*. New York: Springer-Verlag.

Weiner, B., Perry, R. P. & Magnusson, J. (1988). *An Attributional Analysis of Reactions to Stigmas*, 55, 738–748.

Wendel, M. L., Burdine, J. N., McLeroy, K. R., Alaniz, A., Norton, B. & Felix, M. R. J. (2009). Community capacity: Theory and application. In R. J. DiClemente, R. A. Crosby & M. C. Kegler (eds.), *Emerging Theories in Health Promotion Practice and Research* (pp. 277–302). San Francisco: Jossey-Bass.

Whittingham, J. R., Ruiter, R. A. C., Castermans, D., Huiberts, A. & Kok, G. (2008). Designing effective health education materials: Experimental pre-testing of a theory-based brochure to increase knowledge. *Health Education Research*, 23, 414–426.

Wholey, J. S., Hatry, H. P. & Newcomer, K. E. (2004). *Handbook of Practical Program Evaluation* (2nd edn). San Francisco, CA: Jossey-Bass.

Wirth, J. H. & Bodenhausen, G. V. (2009). The role of gender in mental-illness stigma: A national experiment. *Psychological Science*, 20, 169–173.

Notes

1. This chapter is written in memory of Herman Schaalma, 1960-2009, whose academic writing and teaching focused on applying psychology to understanding and predicting health and prosocial behaviour.
2. The example of using Weiner's attribution theory to explain stigmatization of PLWHA is directly taken from a chapter on social psychology and health education of which Gerjo Kok was the lead author (Kok et al., 1996, pp. 249–249; see also Dijker & Koomen, 2003).

Index